FIZZ
POP
FSHHH

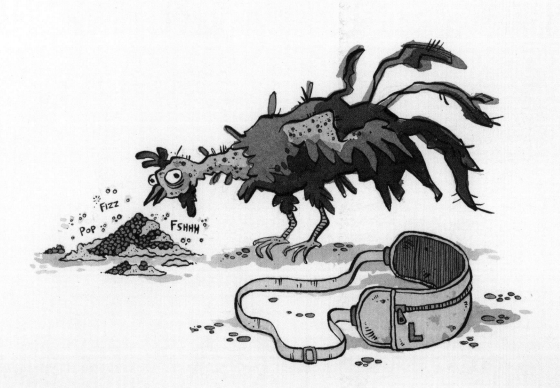

PUBLISHED BY TOP SHELF PRODUCTIONS P.O. BOX 1282 MARIETTA, GA ~~3061~~ 30061-1282, EDITOR IN ~~CHEI~~ CHIEF CHRIS STAROS. TOP SHELF IS AN IMPRINT OF IDW PUBLISHING, A DIVISION OF IDEA AND DESIGN WORKS, LLC. VISIT OUR ONLINE CATALOG www.topshelfcomics.com

ISBN: 978-1-60309-466-5

23 22 21 20 4 3 2 1

PRINTED IN LATVIA

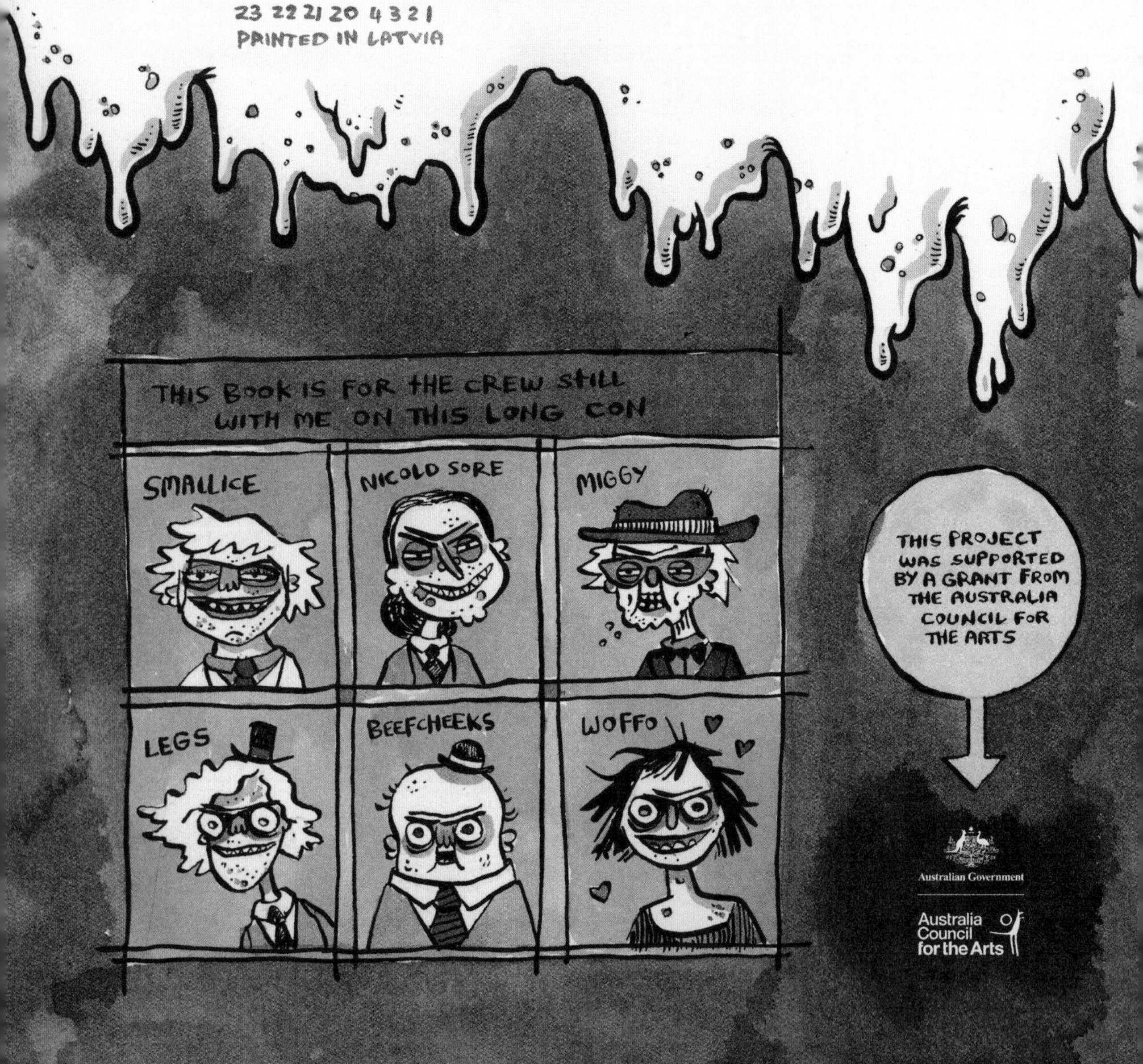
THIS BOOK IS FOR THE CREW STILL WITH ME ON THIS LONG CON
SMALLICE
NICOLD SORE
MIGGY
LEGS
BEEFCHEEKS
WOFFO
THIS PROJECT WAS SUPPORTED BY A GRANT FROM THE AUSTRALIA COUNCIL FOR THE ARTS
Australian Government
Australia Council for the Arts

the GROT

BOOK ONE IN
THE STORY OF THE
SWAMP CITY
GRIFTERS

WRITTEN AND DRAWN BY

PAT GRANT

WITH COLOURING BY

FIONN MCCABE

PROLOGUE

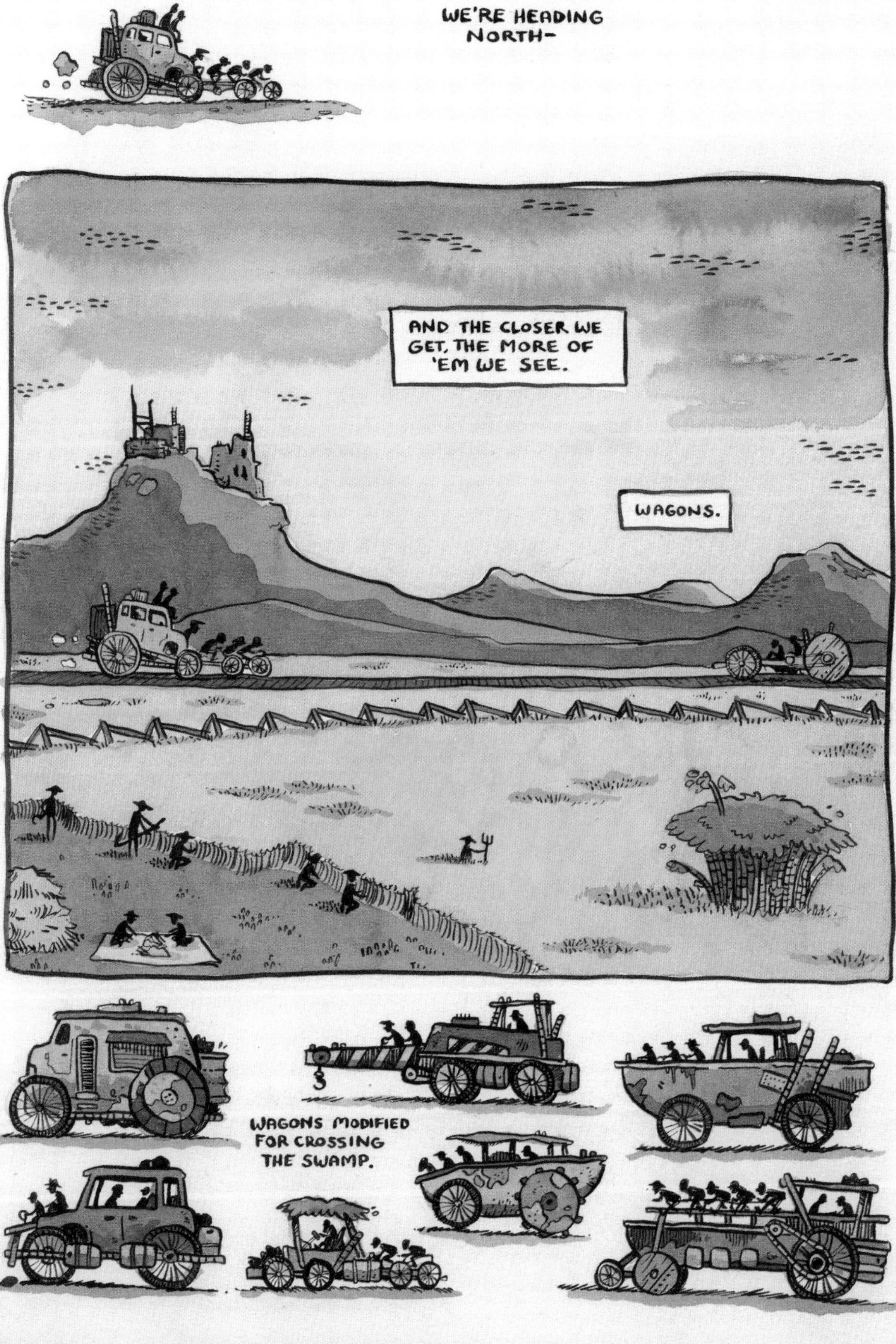
WE'RE HEADING NORTH-
AND THE CLOSER WE GET, THE MORE OF 'EM WE SEE.
WAGONS.
WAGONS MODIFIED FOR CROSSING THE SWAMP.

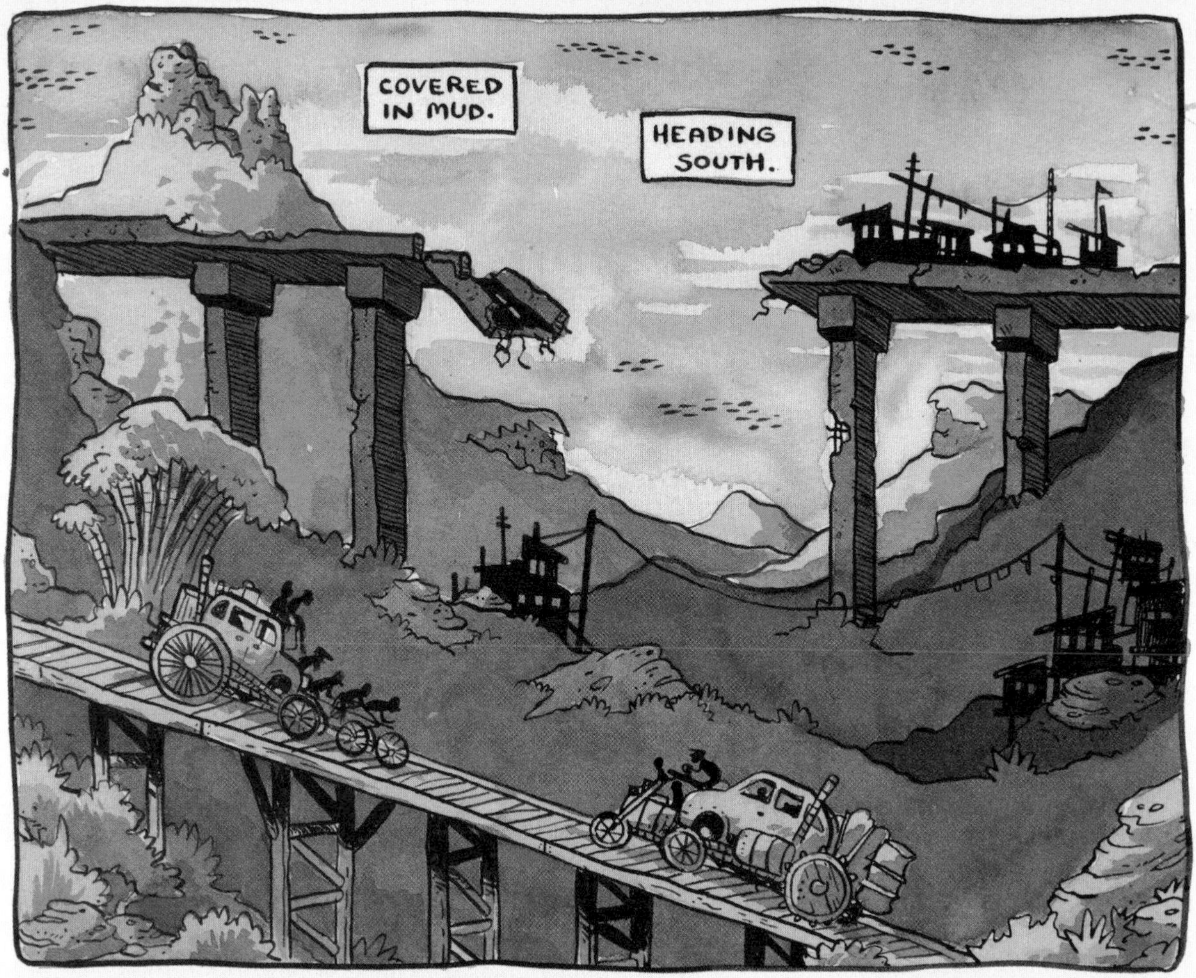
COVERED IN MUD.
HEADING SOUTH.

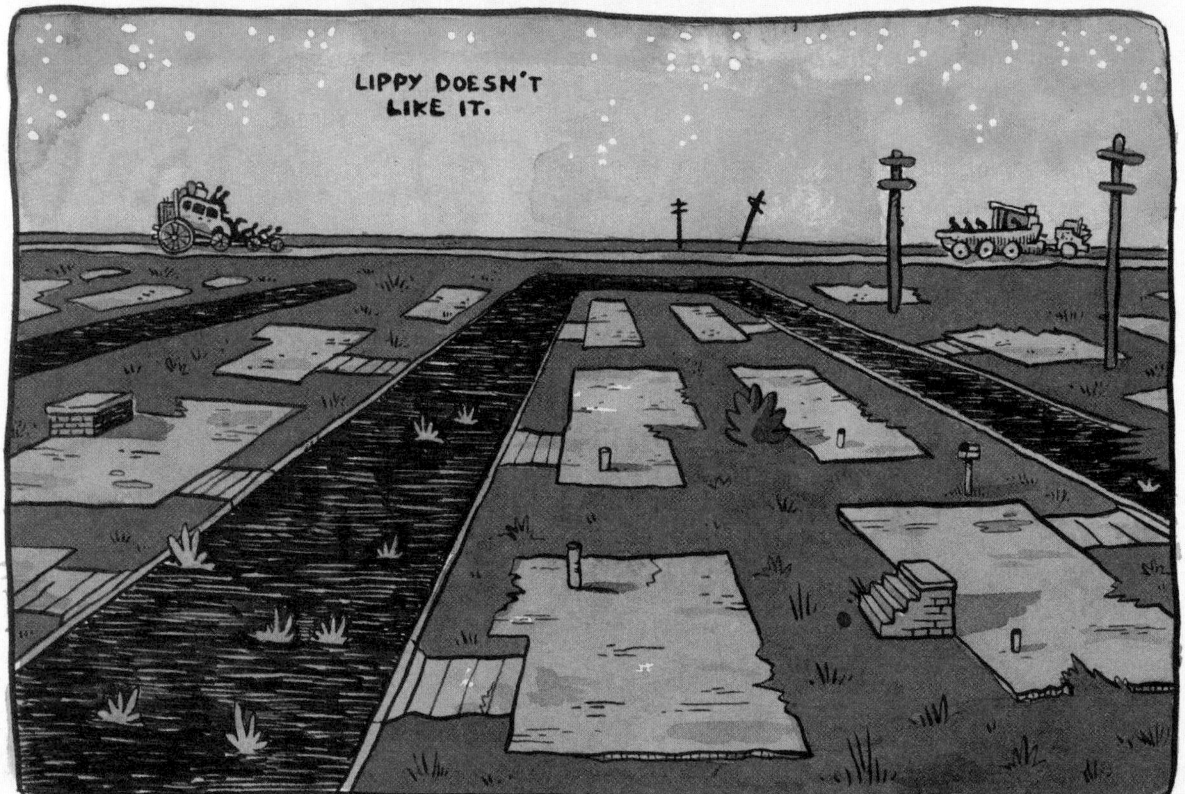
LIPPY DOESN'T LIKE IT.

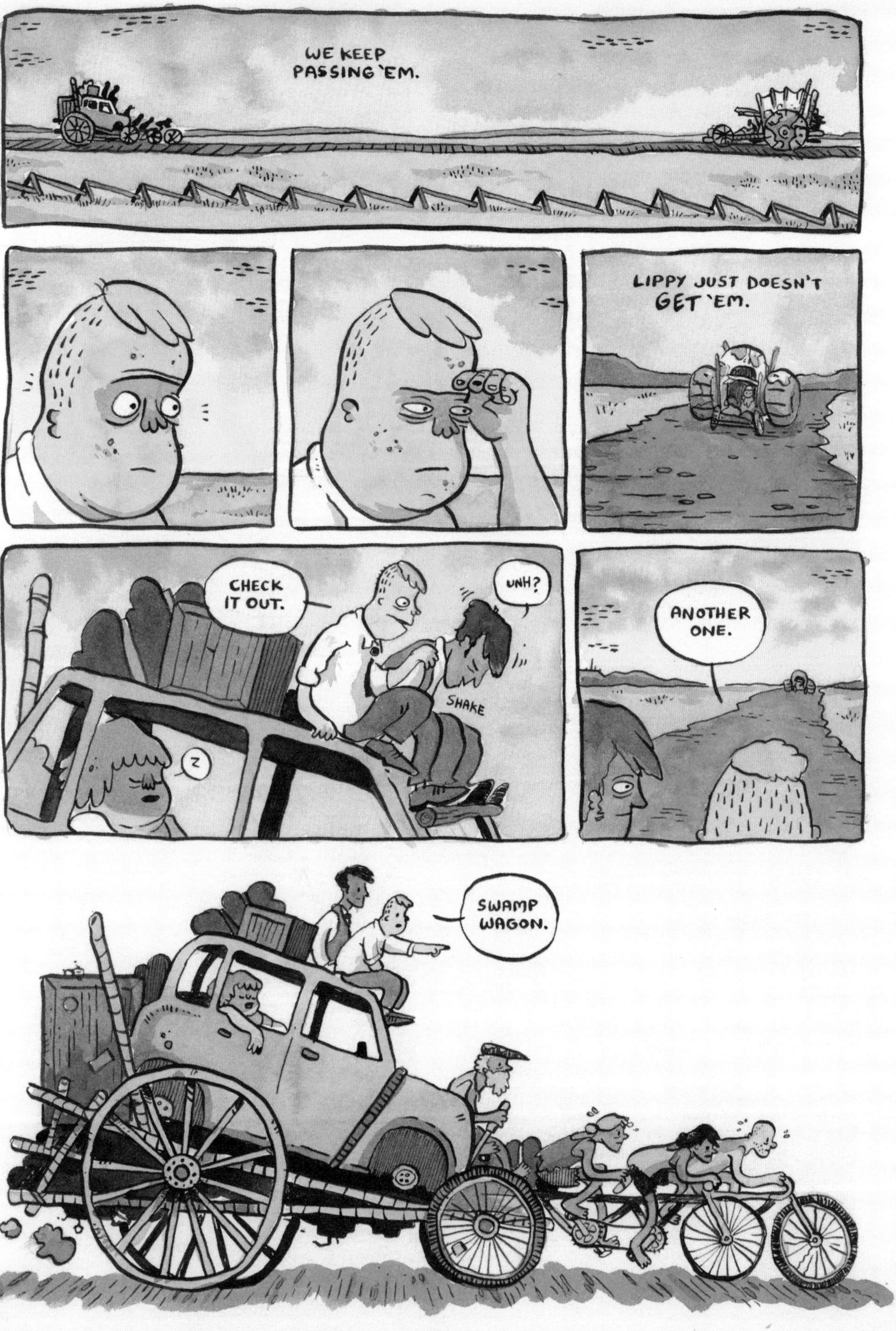
WE KEEP PASSING 'EM.
LIPPY JUST DOESN'T GET 'EM.
CHECK IT OUT.
UNH?
SHAKE
Z
ANOTHER ONE.
SWAMP WAGON.

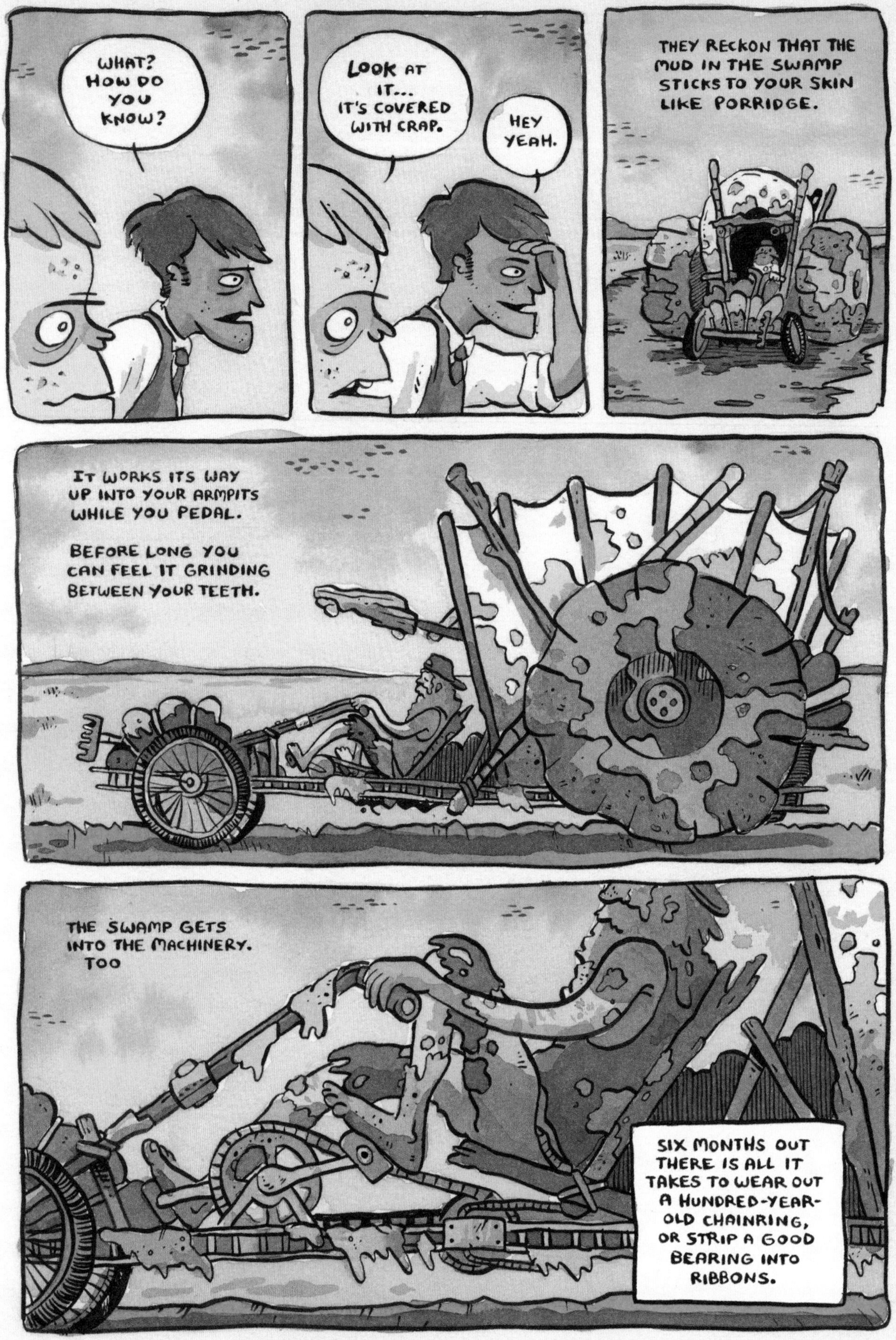

WHAT? HOW DO YOU KNOW?
LOOK AT IT... IT'S COVERED WITH CRAP.
HEY YEAH.
THEY RECKON THAT THE MUD IN THE SWAMP STICKS TO YOUR SKIN LIKE PORRIDGE.
IT WORKS ITS WAY UP INTO YOUR ARMPITS WHILE YOU PEDAL.
BEFORE LONG YOU CAN FEEL IT GRINDING BETWEEN YOUR TEETH.
THE SWAMP GETS INTO THE MACHINERY. TOO
SIX MONTHS OUT THERE IS ALL IT TAKES TO WEAR OUT A HUNDRED-YEAR-OLD CHAINRING, OR STRIP A GOOD BEARING INTO RIBBONS.

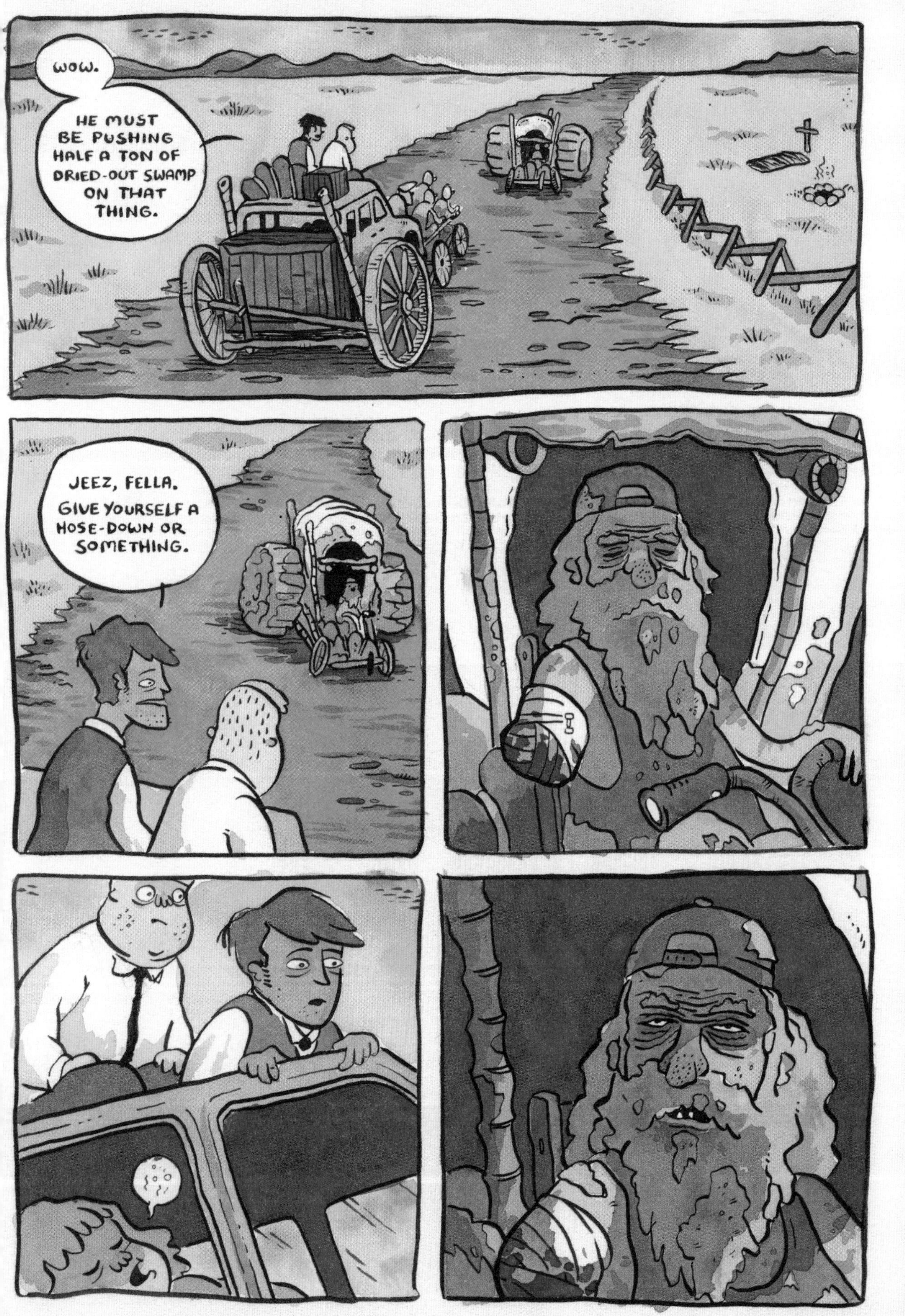
WOW.
HE MUST BE PUSHING HALF A TON OF DRIED-OUT SWAMP ON THAT THING.
JEEZ, FELLA. GIVE YOURSELF A HOSE-DOWN OR SOMETHING.

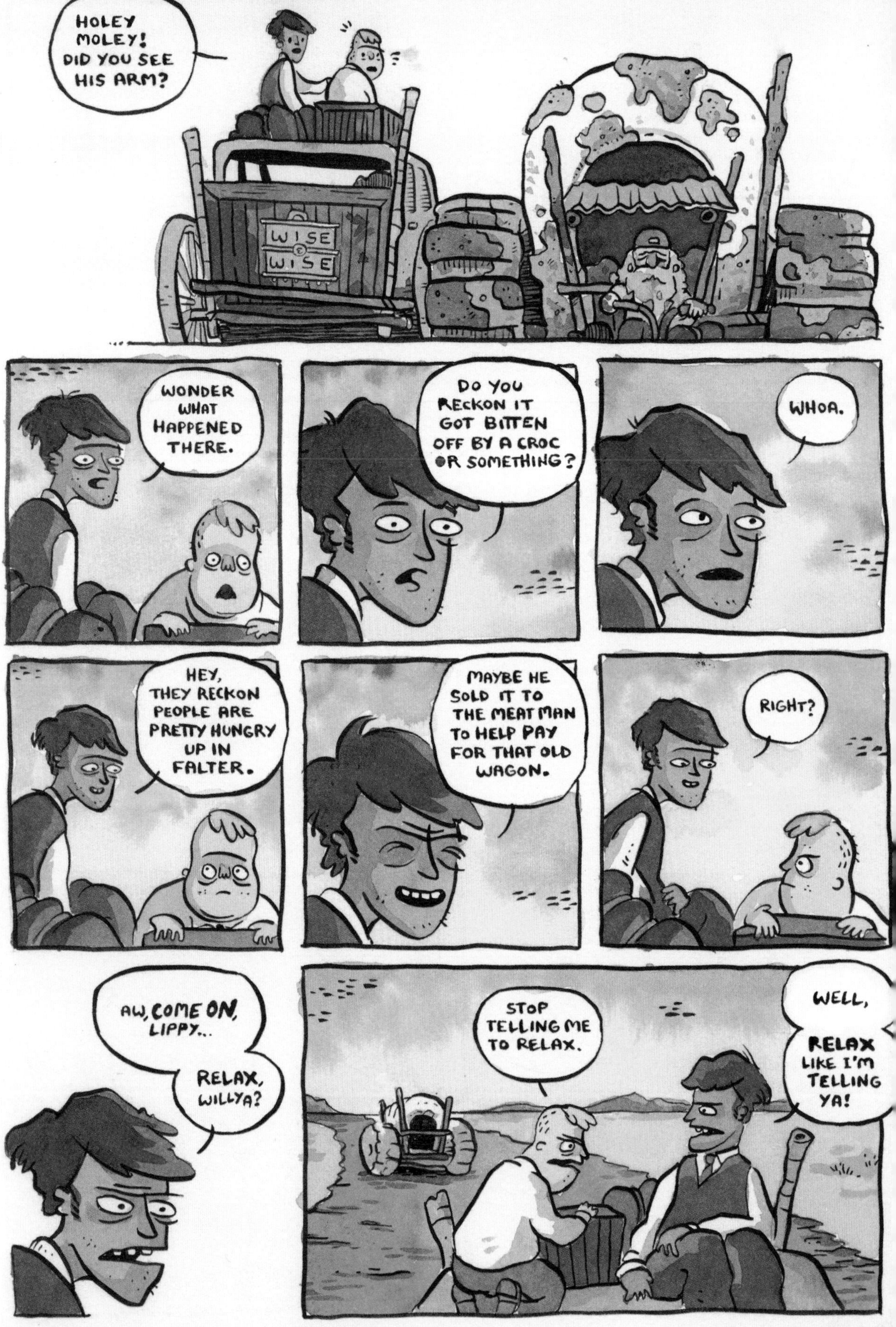
HOLEY MOLEY! DID YOU SEE HIS ARM?
WISE & WISE
WONDER WHAT HAPPENED THERE.
DO YOU RECKON IT GOT BITTEN OFF BY A CROC OR SOMETHING?
WHOA.
HEY, THEY RECKON PEOPLE ARE PRETTY HUNGRY UP IN FALTER.
MAYBE HE SOLD IT TO THE MEAT MAN TO HELP PAY FOR THAT OLD WAGON.
RIGHT?
AW, COME ON, LIPPY...
RELAX, WILLYA?
STOP TELLING ME TO RELAX.
WELL, RELAX LIKE I'M TELLING YA!

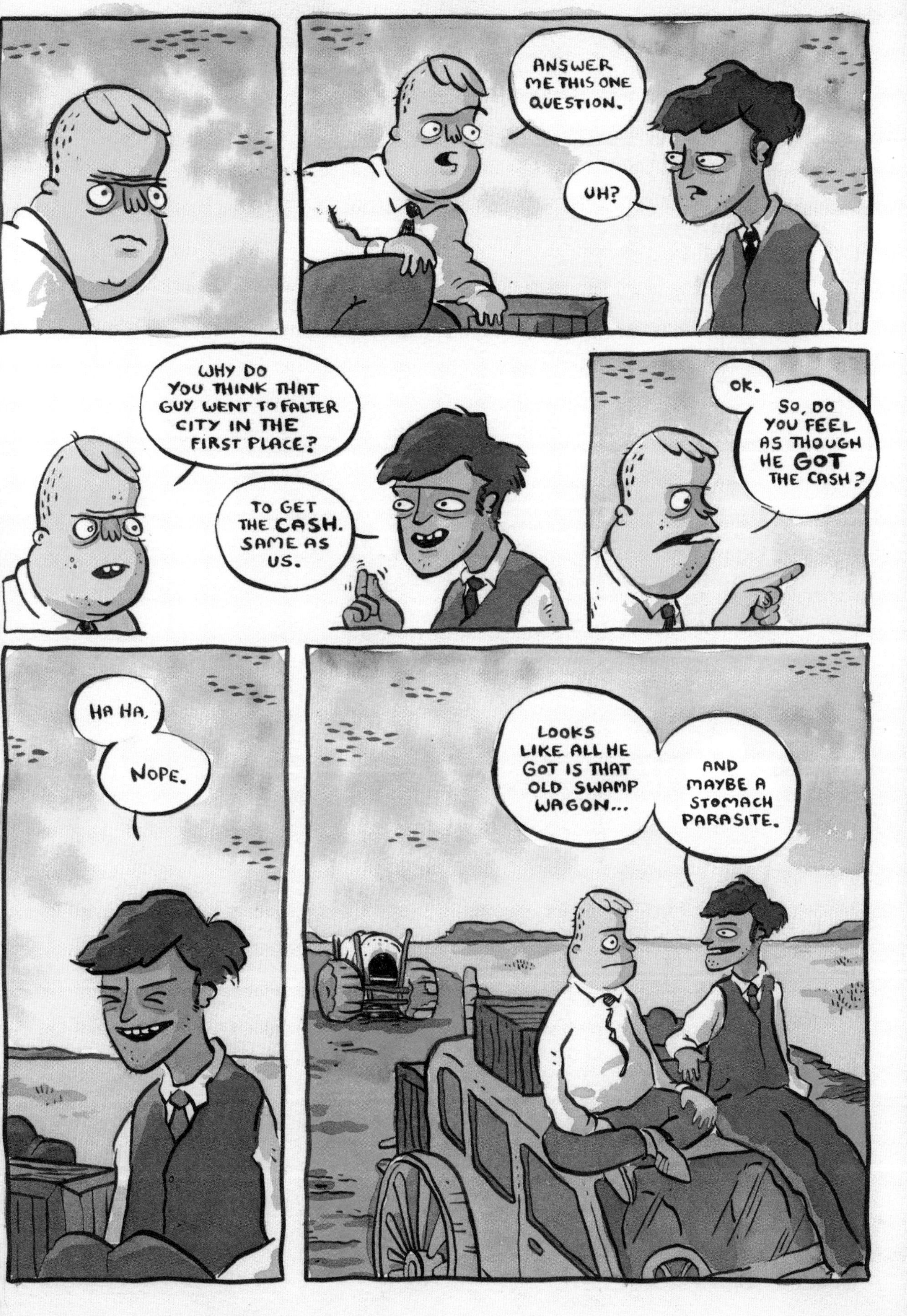

ANSWER ME THIS ONE QUESTION.
UH?
WHY DO YOU THINK THAT GUY WENT TO FALTER CITY IN THE FIRST PLACE?
TO GET THE CASH. SAME AS US.
OK.
SO, DO YOU FEEL AS THOUGH HE GOT THE CASH?
HA HA,
NOPE.
LOOKS LIKE ALL HE GOT IS THAT OLD SWAMP WAGON...
AND MAYBE A STOMACH PARASITE.

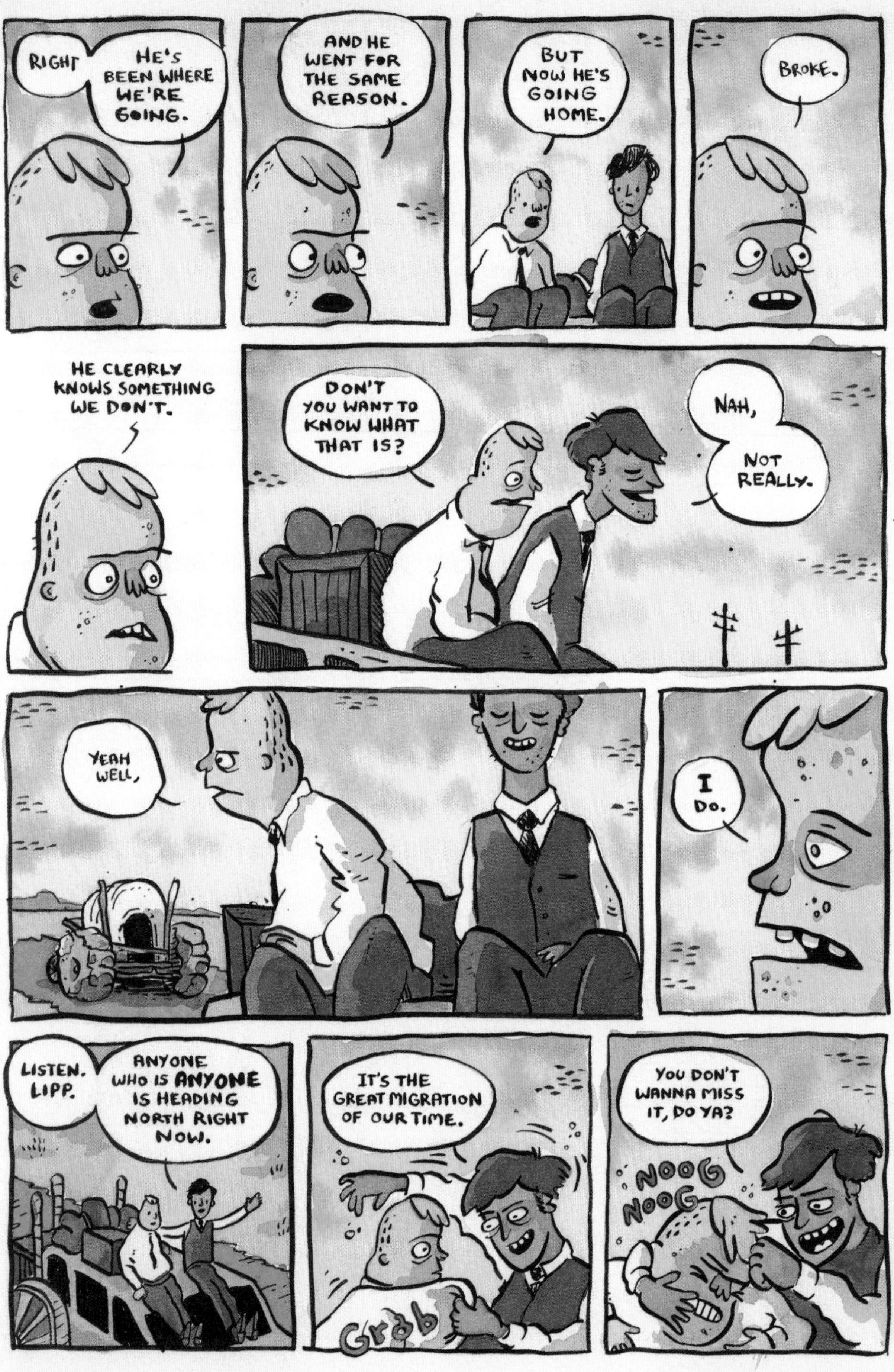
RIGHT
HE'S BEEN WHERE WE'RE GOING.
AND HE WENT FOR THE SAME REASON.
BUT NOW HE'S GOING HOME.
BROKE.
HE CLEARLY KNOWS SOMETHING WE DON'T.
DON'T YOU WANT TO KNOW WHAT THAT IS?
NAH,
NOT REALLY.
YEAH WELL,
I DO.
LISTEN. LIPP.
ANYONE WHO IS ANYONE IS HEADING NORTH RIGHT NOW.
IT'S THE GREAT MIGRATION OF OUR TIME.
Grab
YOU DON'T WANNA MISS IT, DO YA?
NOOG NOOG

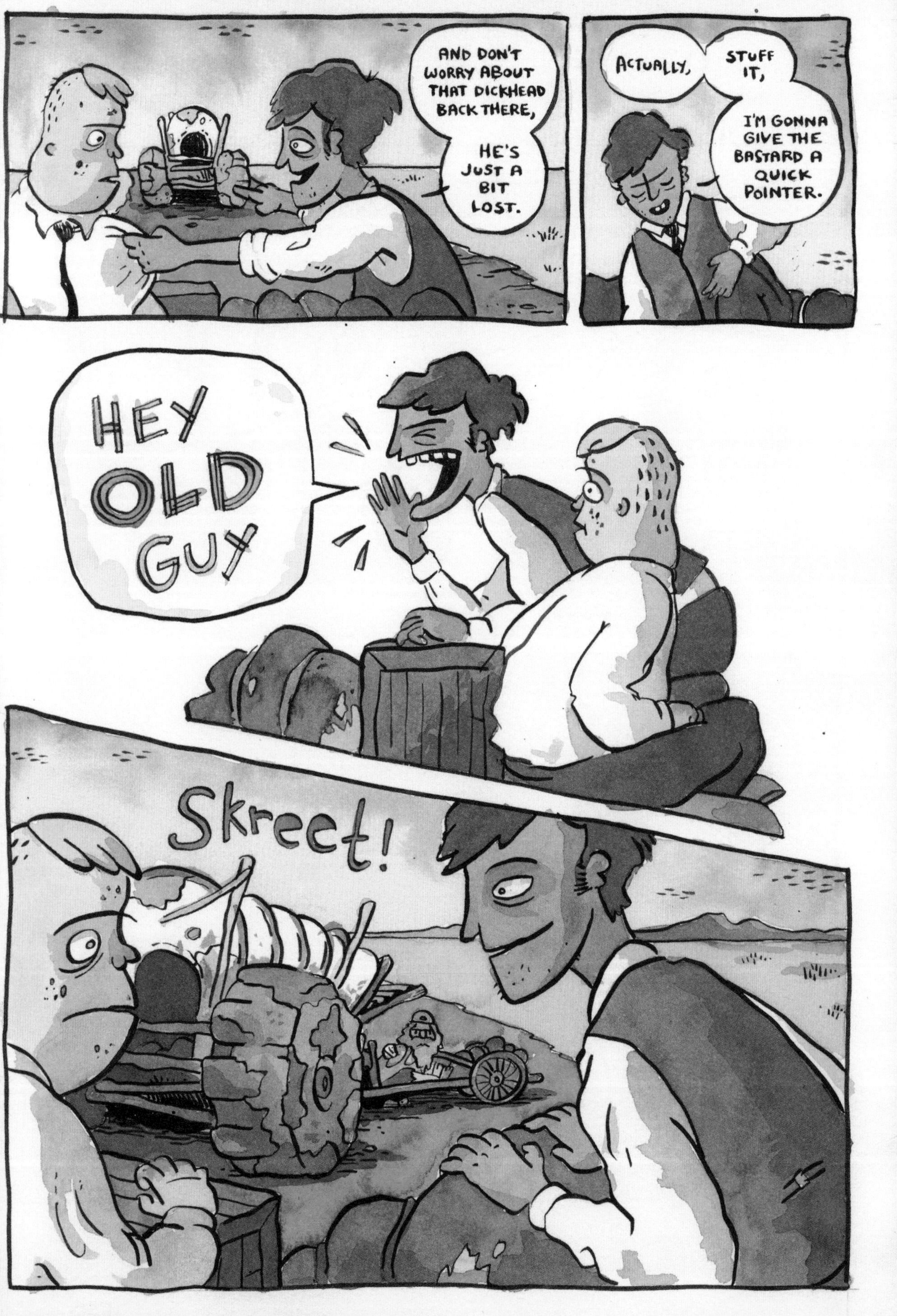
AND DON'T WORRY ABOUT THAT DICKHEAD BACK THERE,
HE'S JUST A BIT LOST.
ACTUALLY,
STUFF IT,
I'M GONNA GIVE THE BASTARD A QUICK POINTER.
HEY OLD GUY
Skreet!

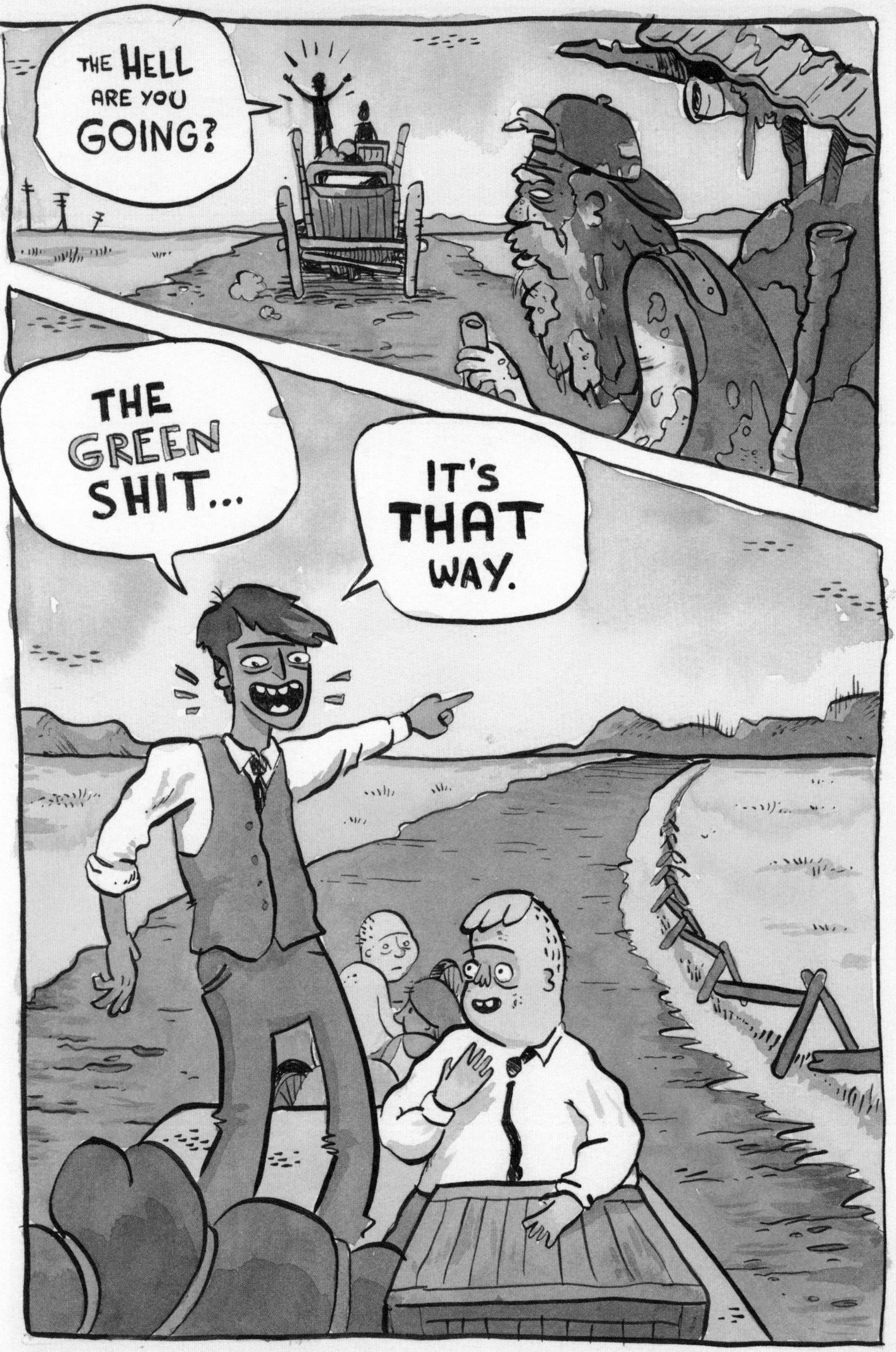
THE HELL ARE YOU GOING?
THE GREEN SHIT...
IT'S THAT WAY.

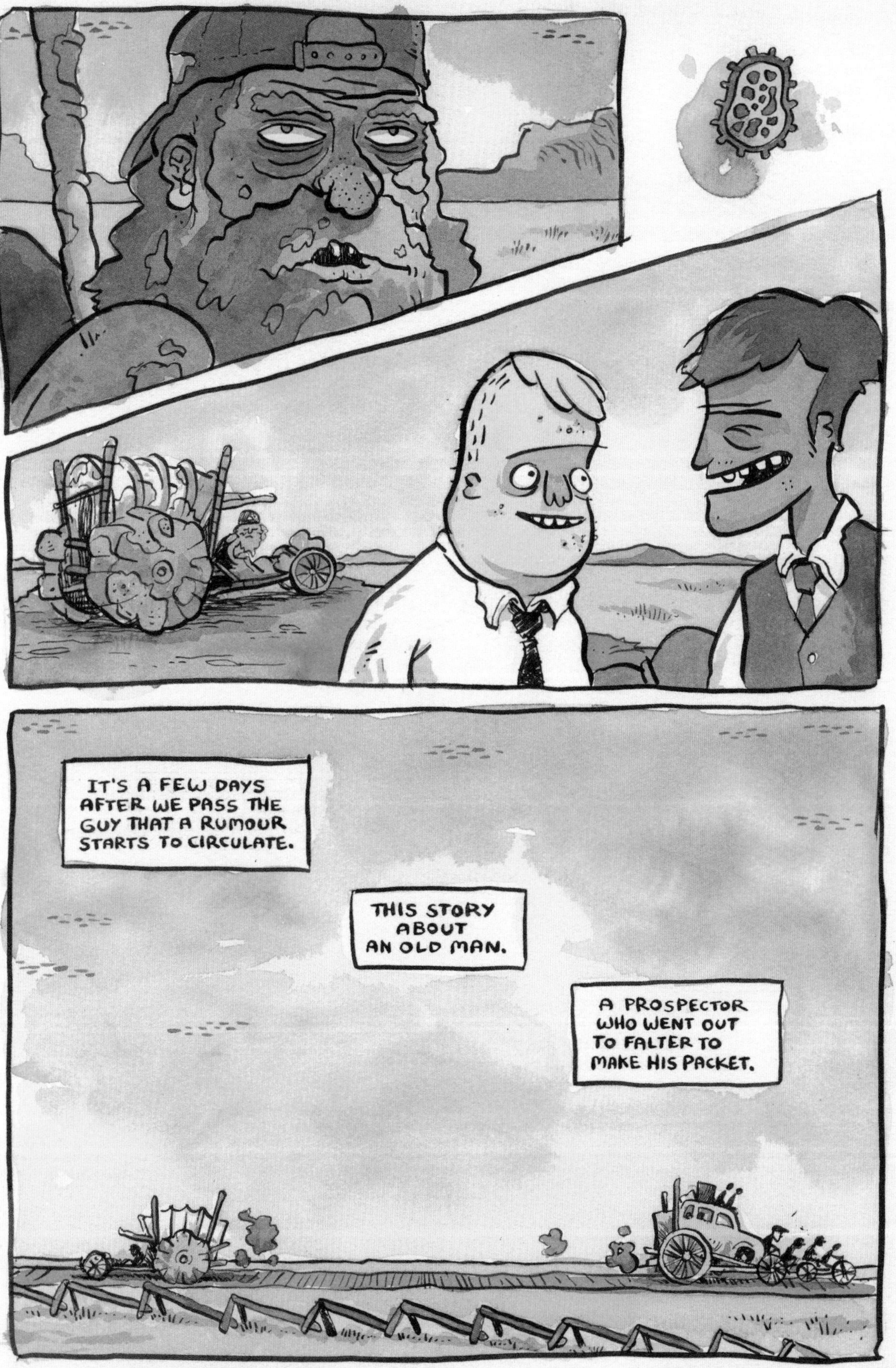
IT'S A FEW DAYS AFTER WE PASS THE GUY THAT A RUMOUR STARTS TO CIRCULATE.
THIS STORY ABOUT AN OLD MAN.
A PROSPECTOR WHO WENT OUT TO FALTER TO MAKE HIS PACKET.

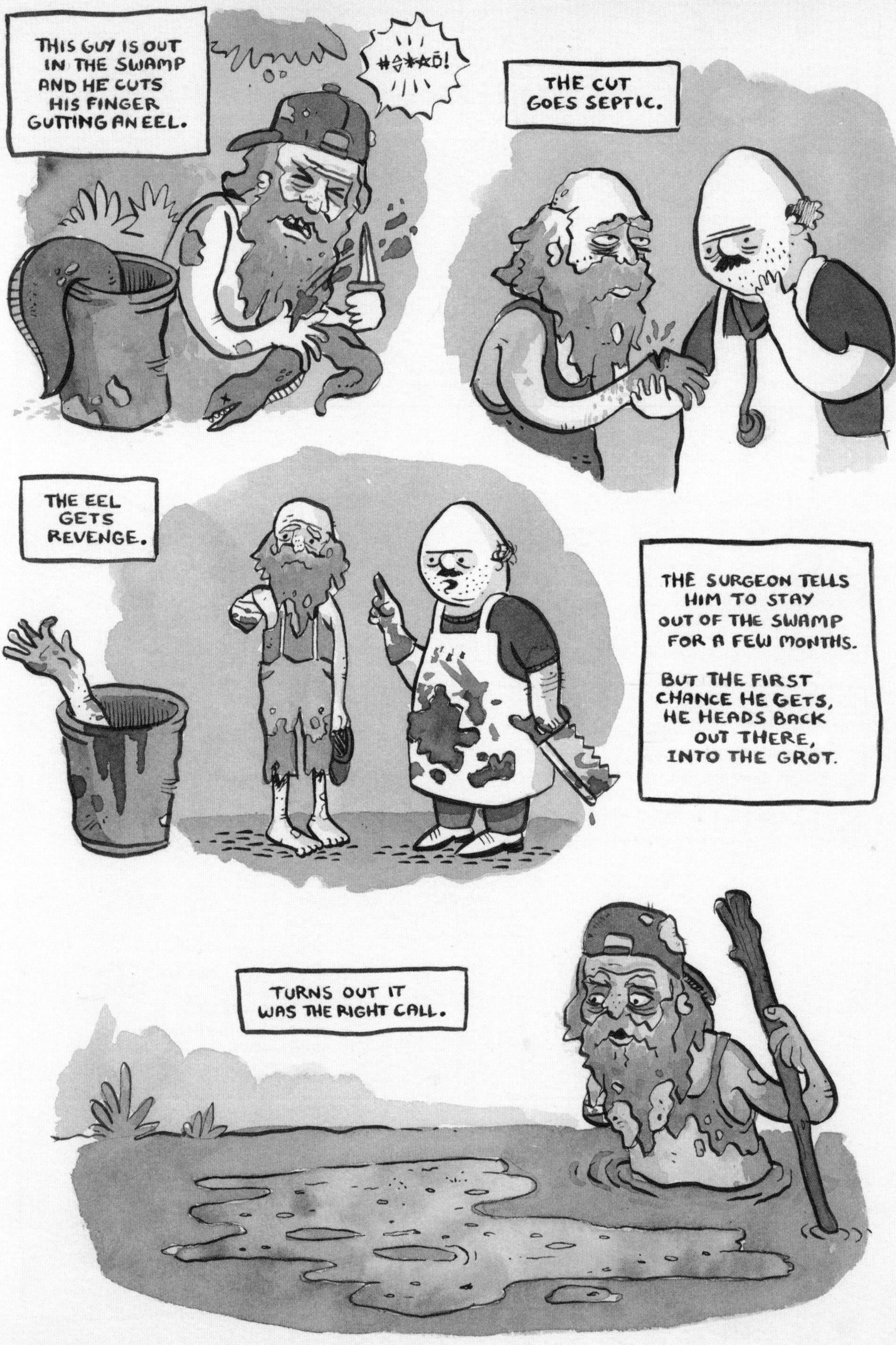
THIS GUY IS OUT IN THE SWAMP AND HE CUTS HIS FINGER GUTTING AN EEL.
THE CUT GOES SEPTIC.
THE EEL GETS REVENGE.
THE SURGEON TELLS HIM TO STAY OUT OF THE SWAMP FOR A FEW MONTHS.
BUT THE FIRST CHANCE HE GETS, HE HEADS BACK OUT THERE, INTO THE GROT.
TURNS OUT IT WAS THE RIGHT CALL.

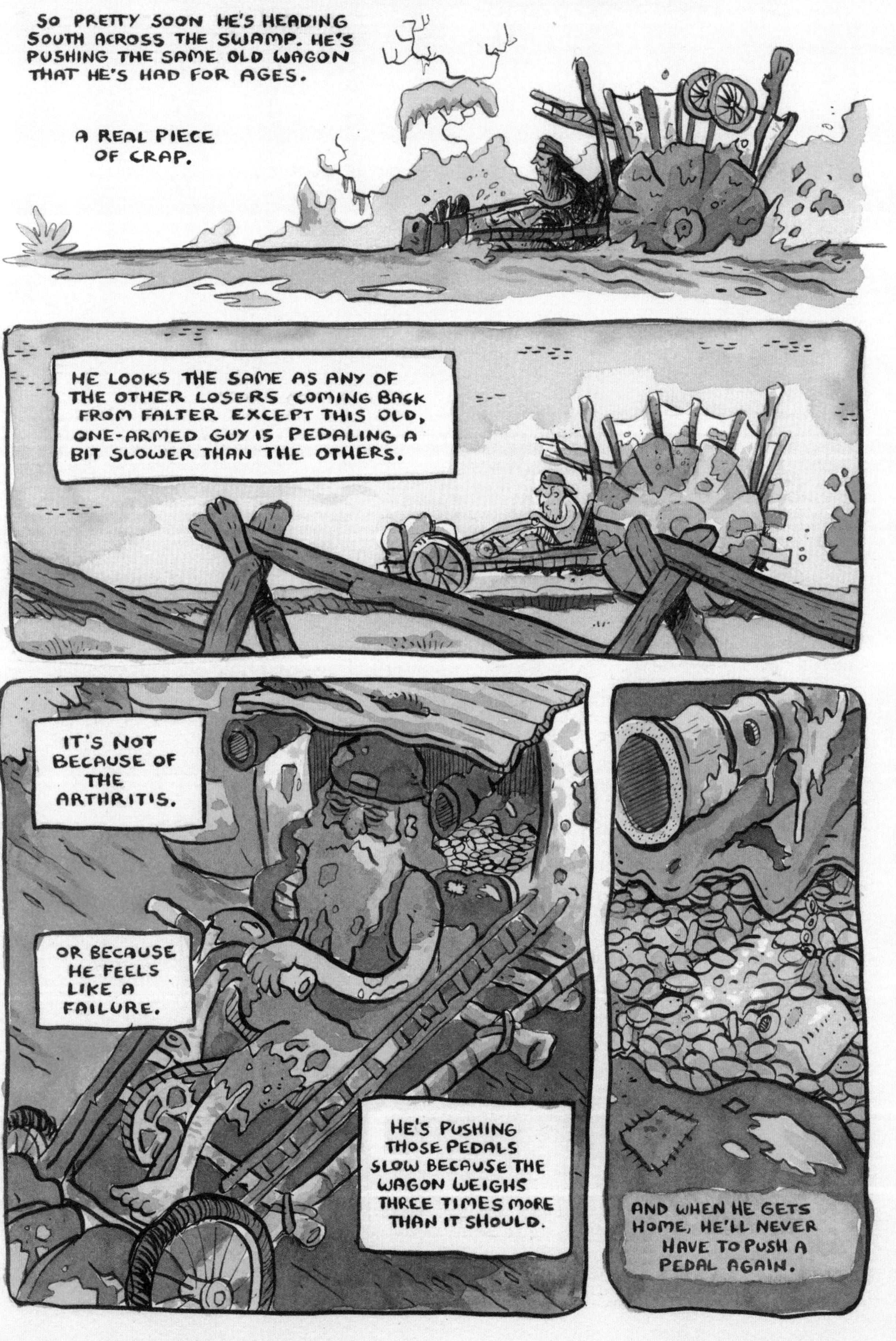
SO PRETTY SOON HE'S HEADING SOUTH ACROSS THE SWAMP. HE'S PUSHING THE SAME OLD WAGON THAT HE'S HAD FOR AGES.
A REAL PIECE OF CRAP.
HE LOOKS THE SAME AS ANY OF THE OTHER LOSERS COMING BACK FROM FALTER EXCEPT THIS OLD, ONE-ARMED GUY IS PEDALING A BIT SLOWER THAN THE OTHERS.
IT'S NOT BECAUSE OF THE ARTHRITIS.
OR BECAUSE HE FEELS LIKE A FAILURE.
HE'S PUSHING THOSE PEDALS SLOW BECAUSE THE WAGON WEIGHS THREE TIMES MORE THAN IT SHOULD.
AND WHEN HE GETS HOME, HE'LL NEVER HAVE TO PUSH A PEDAL AGAIN.

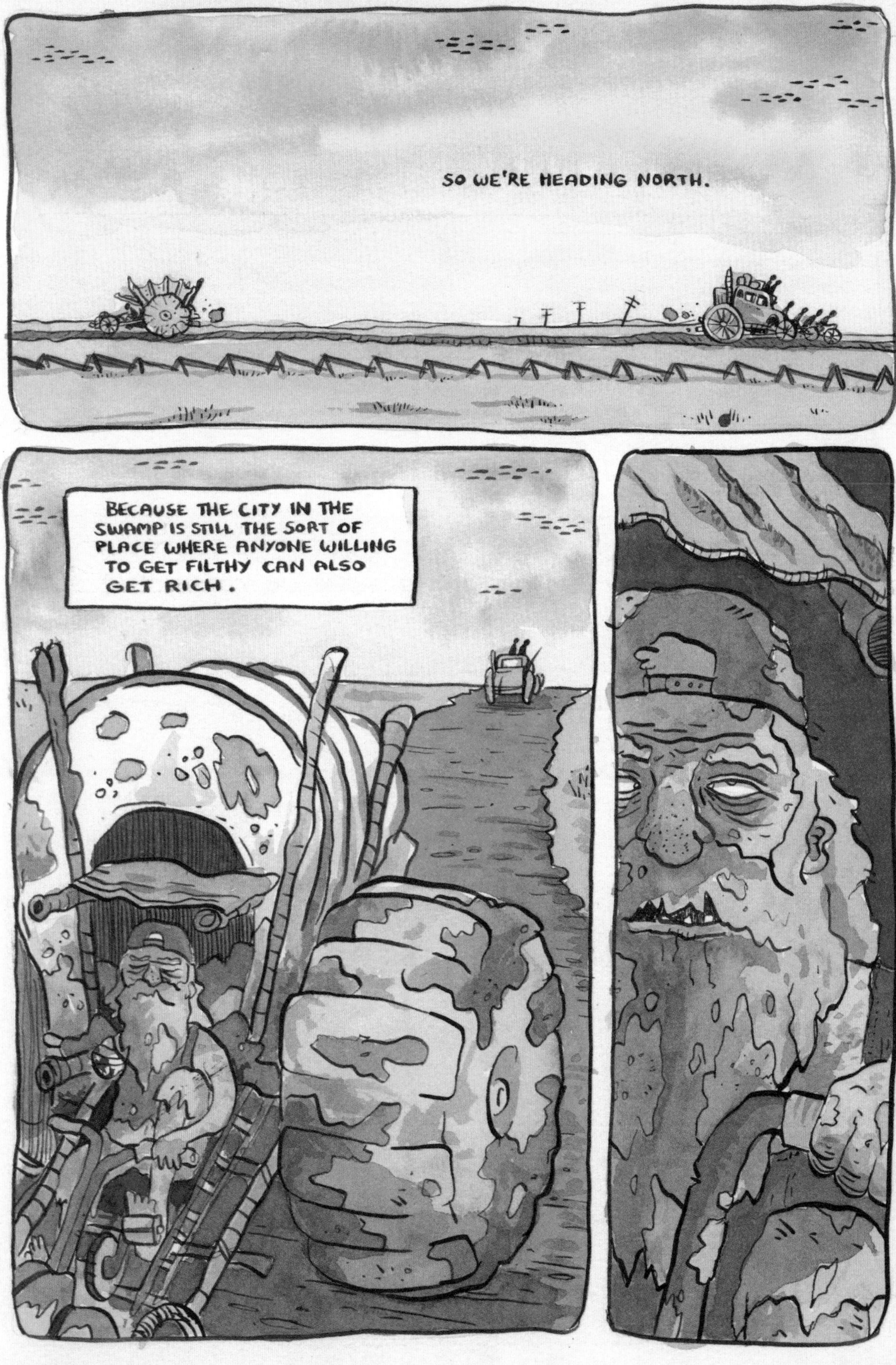
SO WE'RE HEADING NORTH.
BECAUSE THE CITY IN THE SWAMP IS STILL THE SORT OF PLACE WHERE ANYONE WILLING TO GET FILTHY CAN ALSO GET RICH.

PART ONE

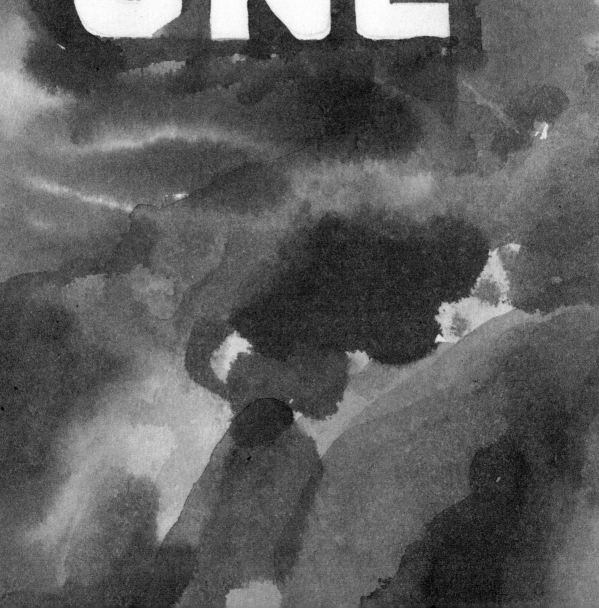

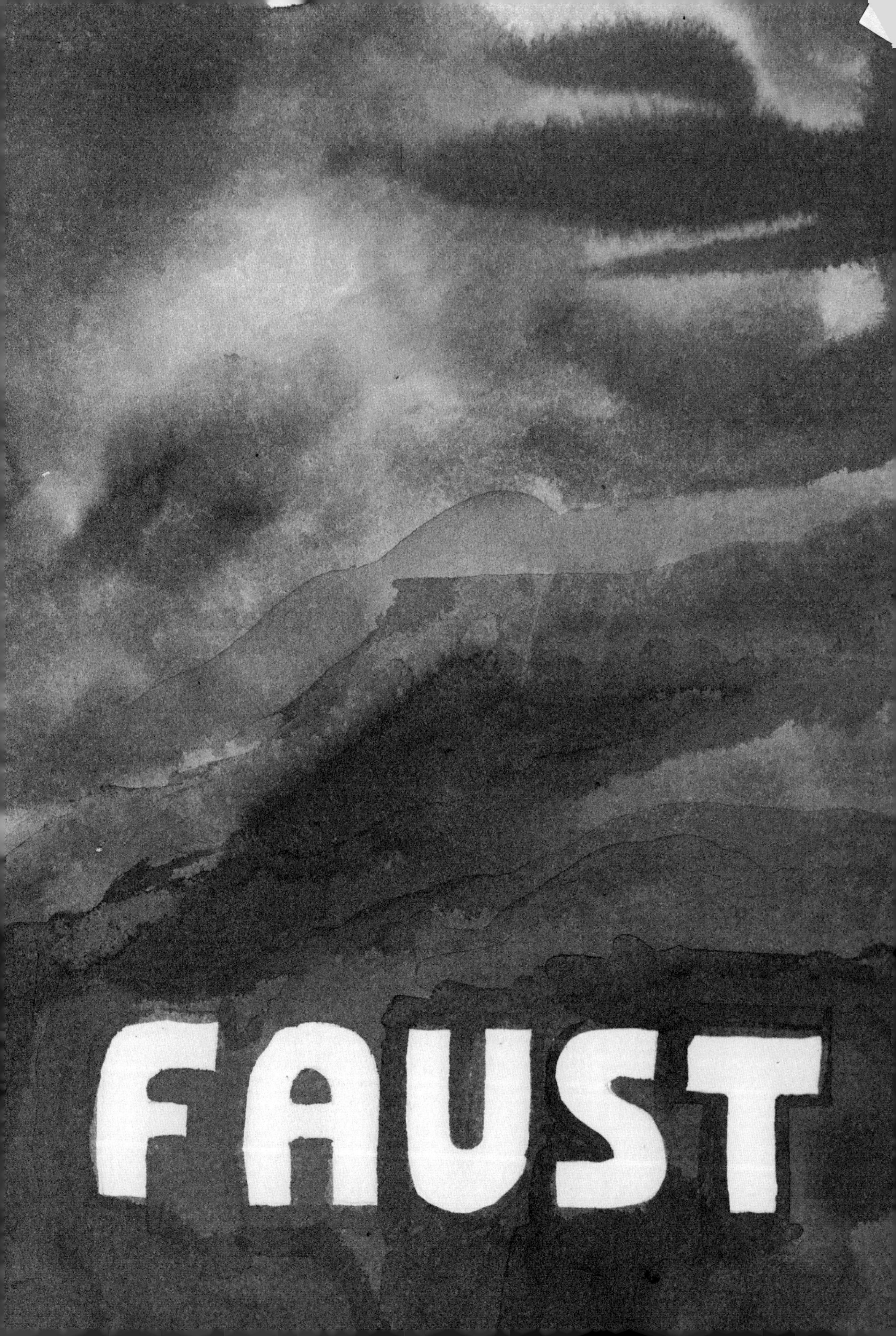
FAUST

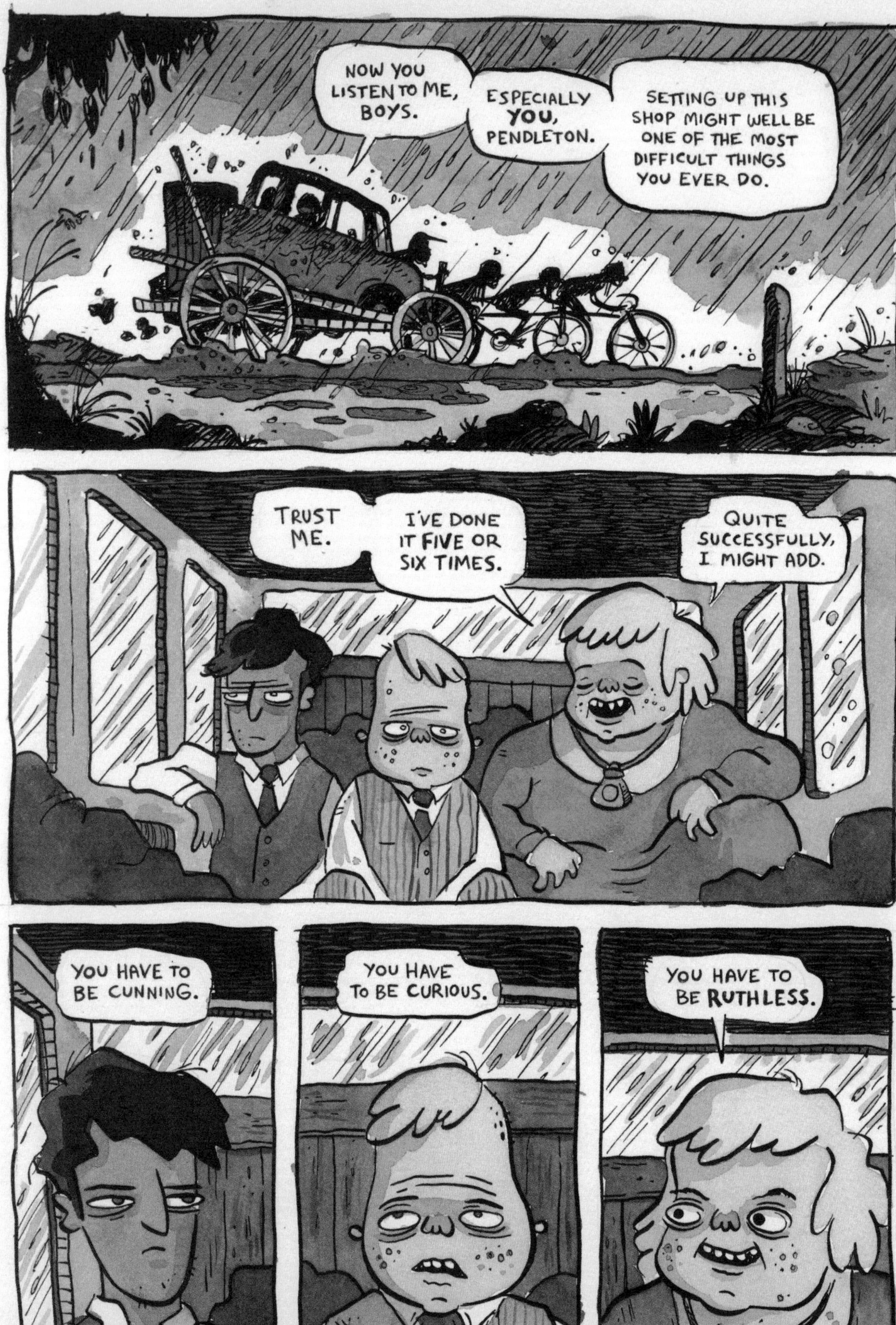
NOW YOU LISTEN TO ME, BOYS.
ESPECIALLY YOU, PENDLETON.
SETTING UP THIS SHOP MIGHT WELL BE ONE OF THE MOST DIFFICULT THINGS YOU EVER DO.
TRUST ME.
I'VE DONE IT FIVE OR SIX TIMES.
QUITE SUCCESSFULLY, I MIGHT ADD.
YOU HAVE TO BE CUNNING.
YOU HAVE TO BE CURIOUS.
YOU HAVE TO BE RUTHLESS.

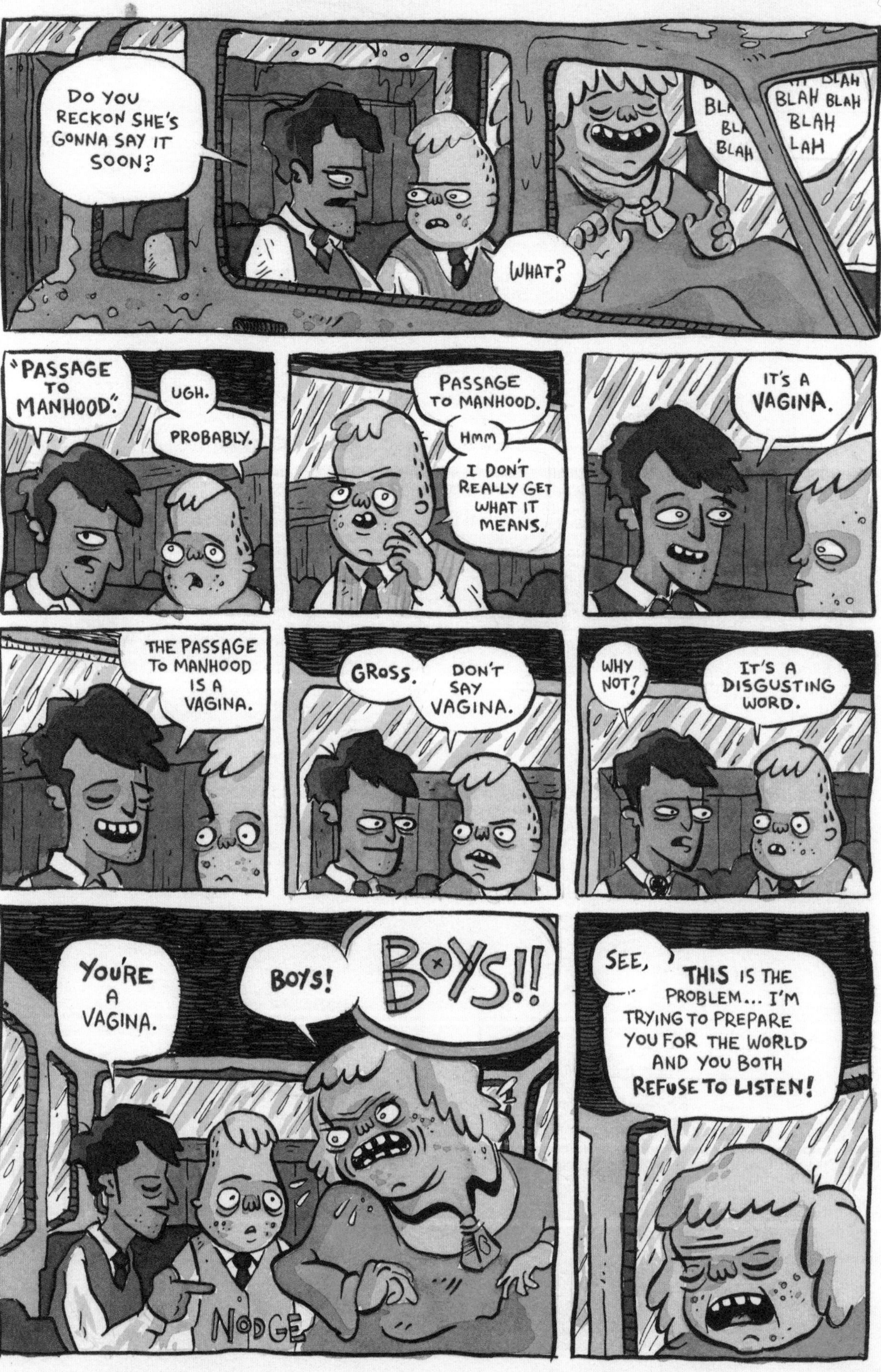
DO YOU RECKON SHE'S GONNA SAY IT SOON?
BLAH BLAH BLAH BLAH
BLAH BLAH BLAH BLAH
WHAT?
"PASSAGE TO MANHOOD".
UGH.
PROBABLY.
PASSAGE TO MANHOOD.
HMM
I DON'T REALLY GET WHAT IT MEANS.
IT'S A VAGINA.
THE PASSAGE TO MANHOOD IS A VAGINA.
GROSS.
DON'T SAY VAGINA.
WHY NOT?
IT'S A DISGUSTING WORD.
YOU'RE A VAGINA.
BOYS!
BOYS!!
NODGE
SEE, THIS IS THE PROBLEM... I'M TRYING TO PREPARE YOU FOR THE WORLD AND YOU BOTH REFUSE TO LISTEN!

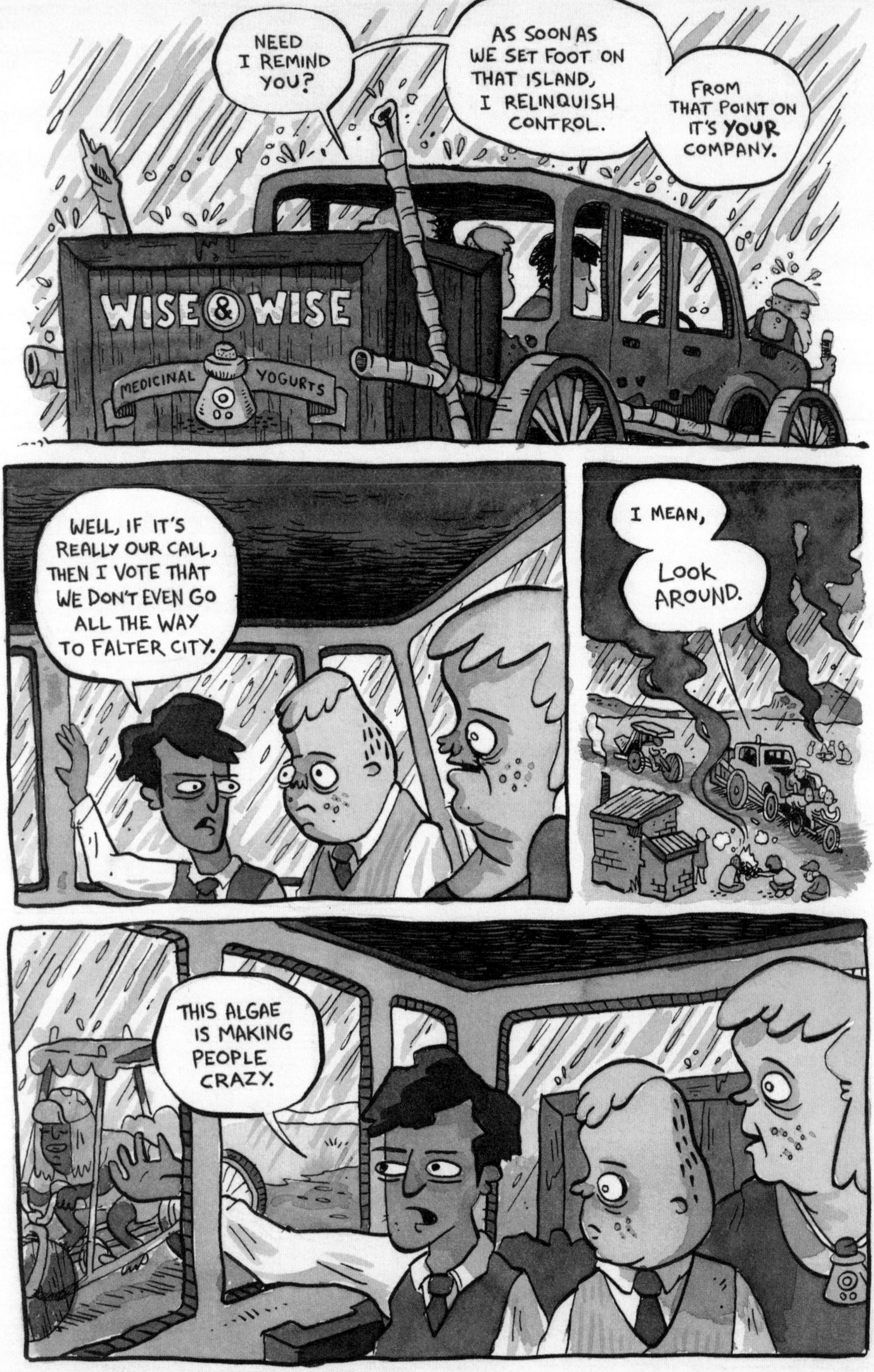
NEED I REMIND YOU?
AS SOON AS WE SET FOOT ON THAT ISLAND, I RELINQUISH CONTROL.
FROM THAT POINT ON IT'S **YOUR** COMPANY.
WISE & WISE
MEDICINAL YOGURTS
WELL, IF IT'S REALLY OUR CALL, THEN I VOTE THAT WE DON'T EVEN GO ALL THE WAY TO FALTER CITY.
I MEAN,
LOOK AROUND.
THIS ALGAE IS MAKING PEOPLE CRAZY.

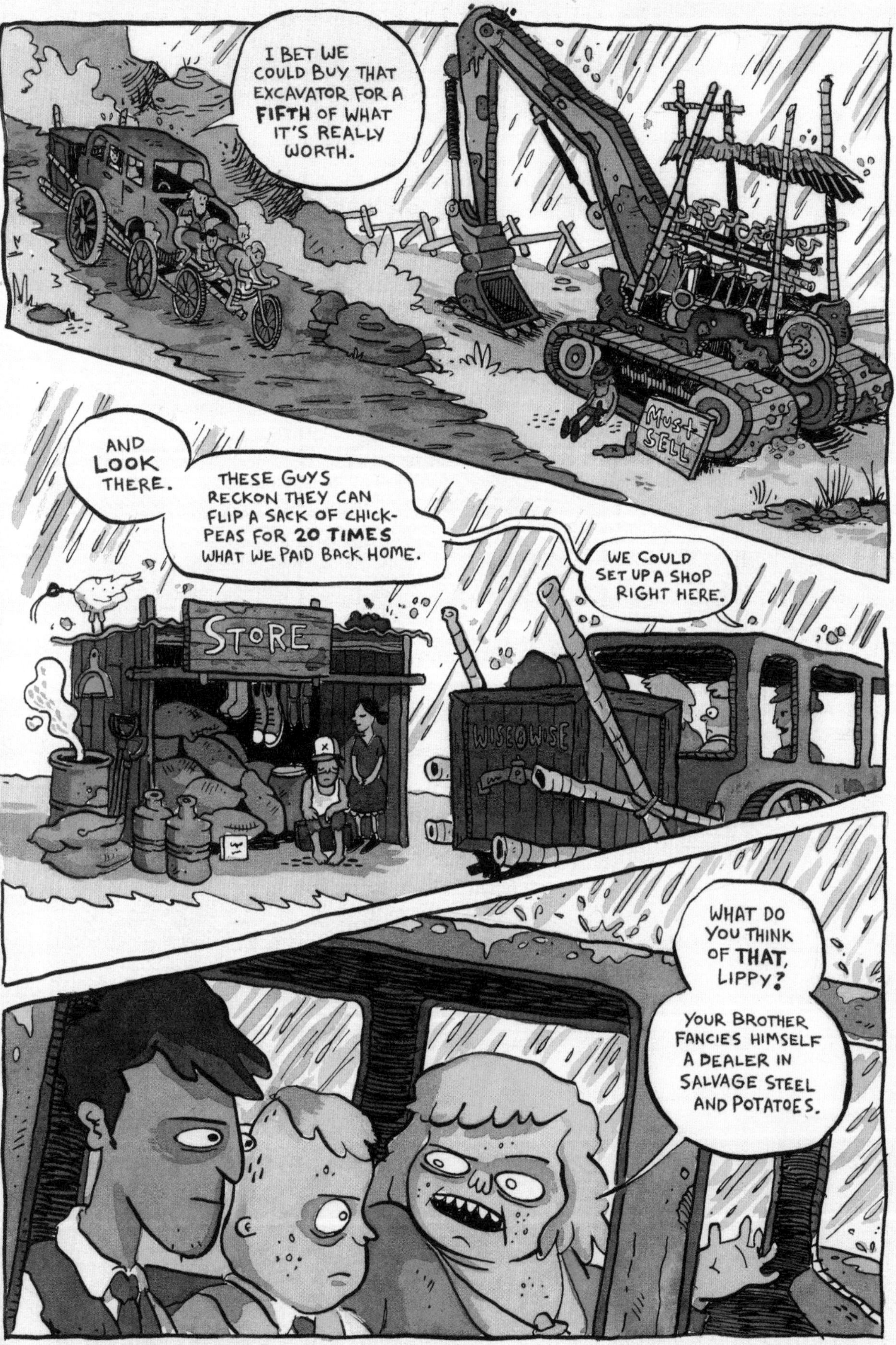
I BET WE COULD BUY THAT EXCAVATOR FOR A FIFTH OF WHAT IT'S REALLY WORTH.
MUST SELL
AND LOOK THERE.
THESE GUYS RECKON THEY CAN FLIP A SACK OF CHICK-PEAS FOR 20 TIMES WHAT WE PAID BACK HOME.
WE COULD SET UP A SHOP RIGHT HERE.
STORE
WISEOWISE
WHAT DO YOU THINK OF THAT, LIPPY?
YOUR BROTHER FANCIES HIMSELF A DEALER IN SALVAGE STEEL AND POTATOES.

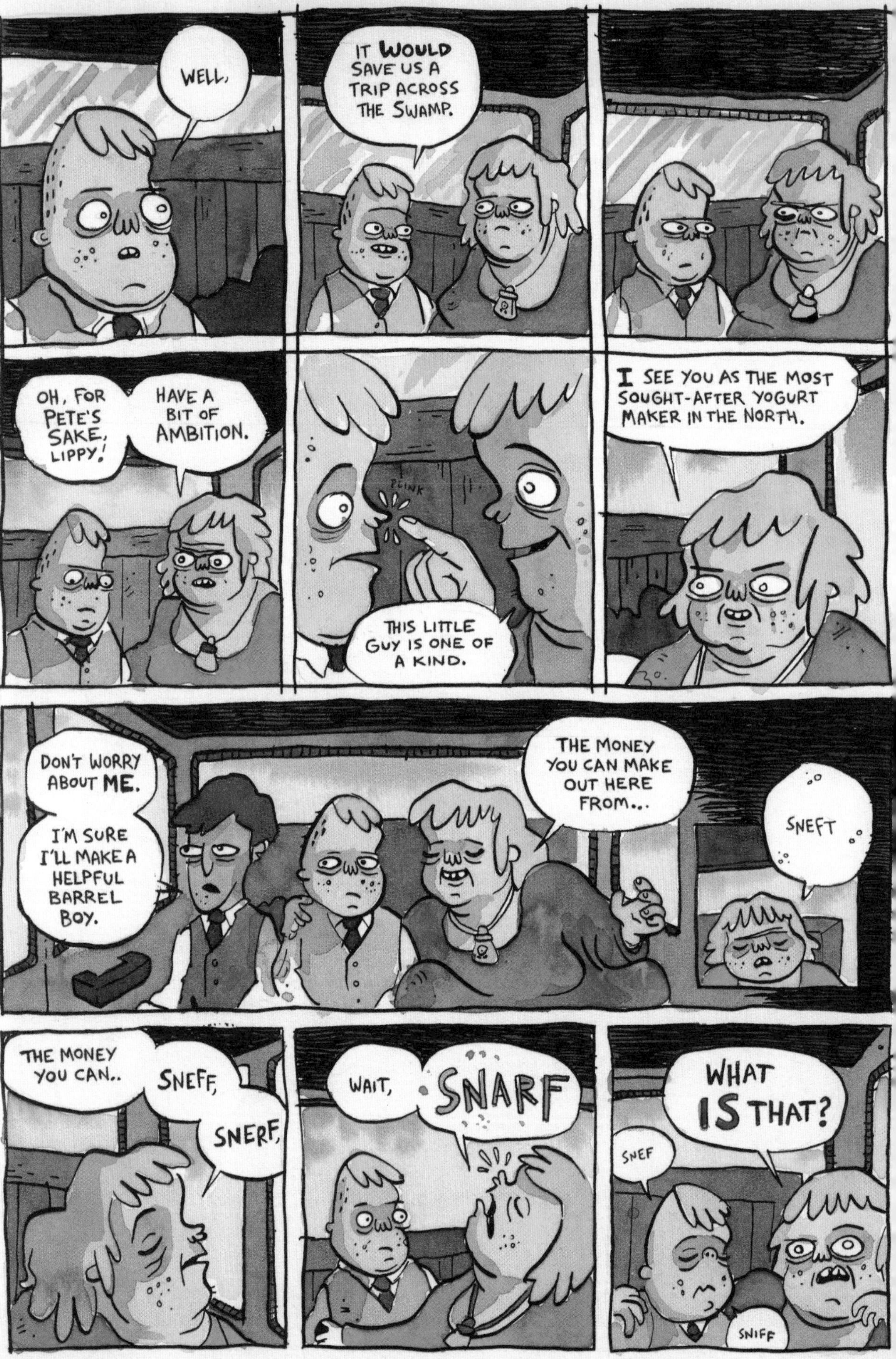
WELL,
IT WOULD SAVE US A TRIP ACROSS THE SWAMP.
OH, FOR PETE'S SAKE, LIPPY!
HAVE A BIT OF AMBITION.
PLINK
THIS LITTLE GUY IS ONE OF A KIND.
I SEE YOU AS THE MOST SOUGHT-AFTER YOGURT MAKER IN THE NORTH.
DON'T WORRY ABOUT ME.
I'M SURE I'LL MAKE A HELPFUL BARREL BOY.
THE MONEY YOU CAN MAKE OUT HERE FROM...
SNEFT
THE MONEY YOU CAN..
SNEFF,
SNERF,
WAIT,
SNARF
WHAT IS THAT?
SNEF
SNIFF

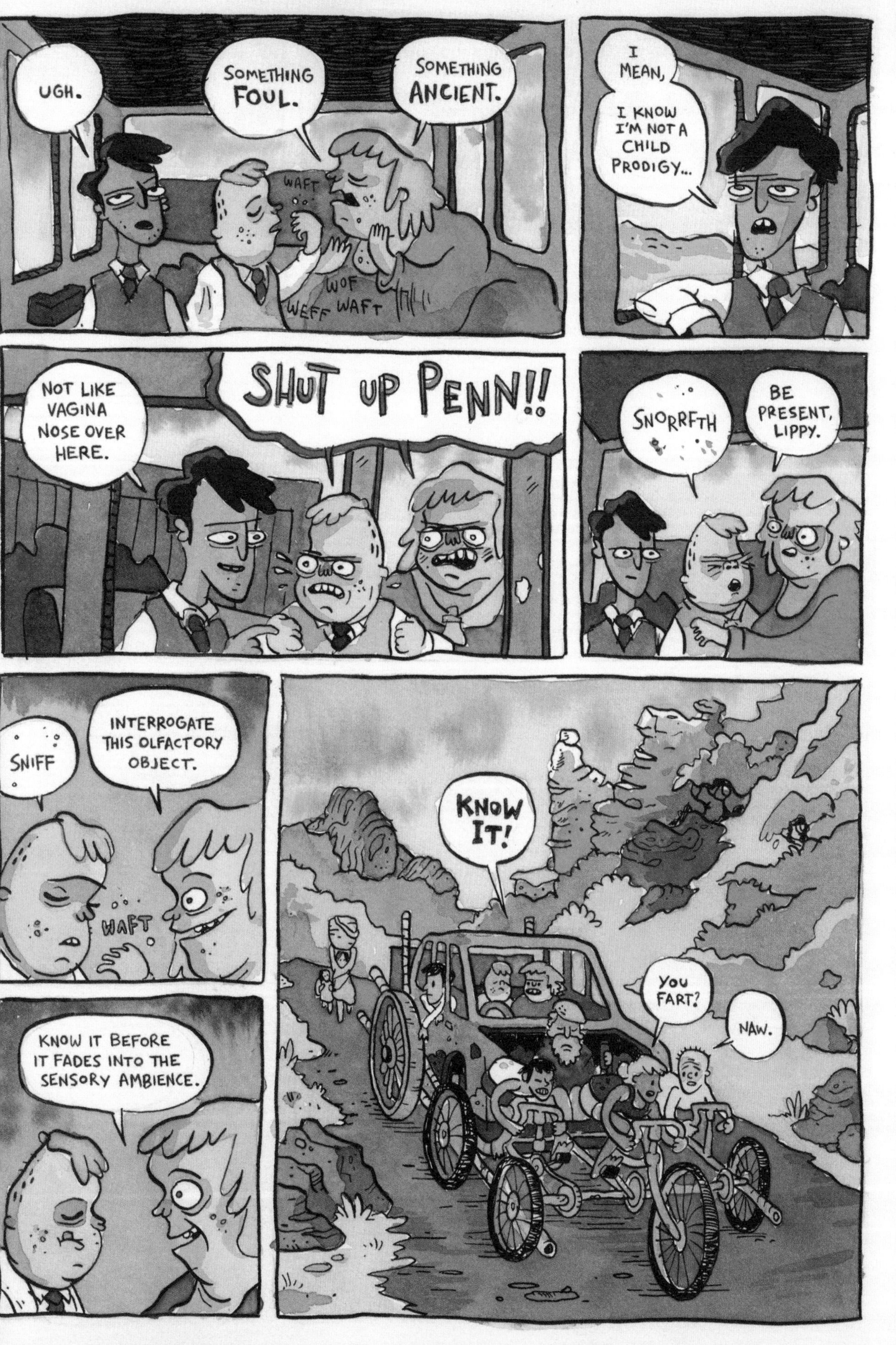
UGH.
SOMETHING FOUL.
SOMETHING ANCIENT.
WAFT
WOF
WEFF WAFT
I MEAN,
I KNOW I'M NOT A CHILD PRODIGY...
NOT LIKE VAGINA NOSE OVER HERE.
SHUT UP PENN!!
SNORRFTH
BE PRESENT, LIPPY.
SNIFF
INTERROGATE THIS OLFACTORY OBJECT.
WAFT
KNOW IT BEFORE IT FADES INTO THE SENSORY AMBIENCE.
KNOW IT!
YOU FART?
NAW.

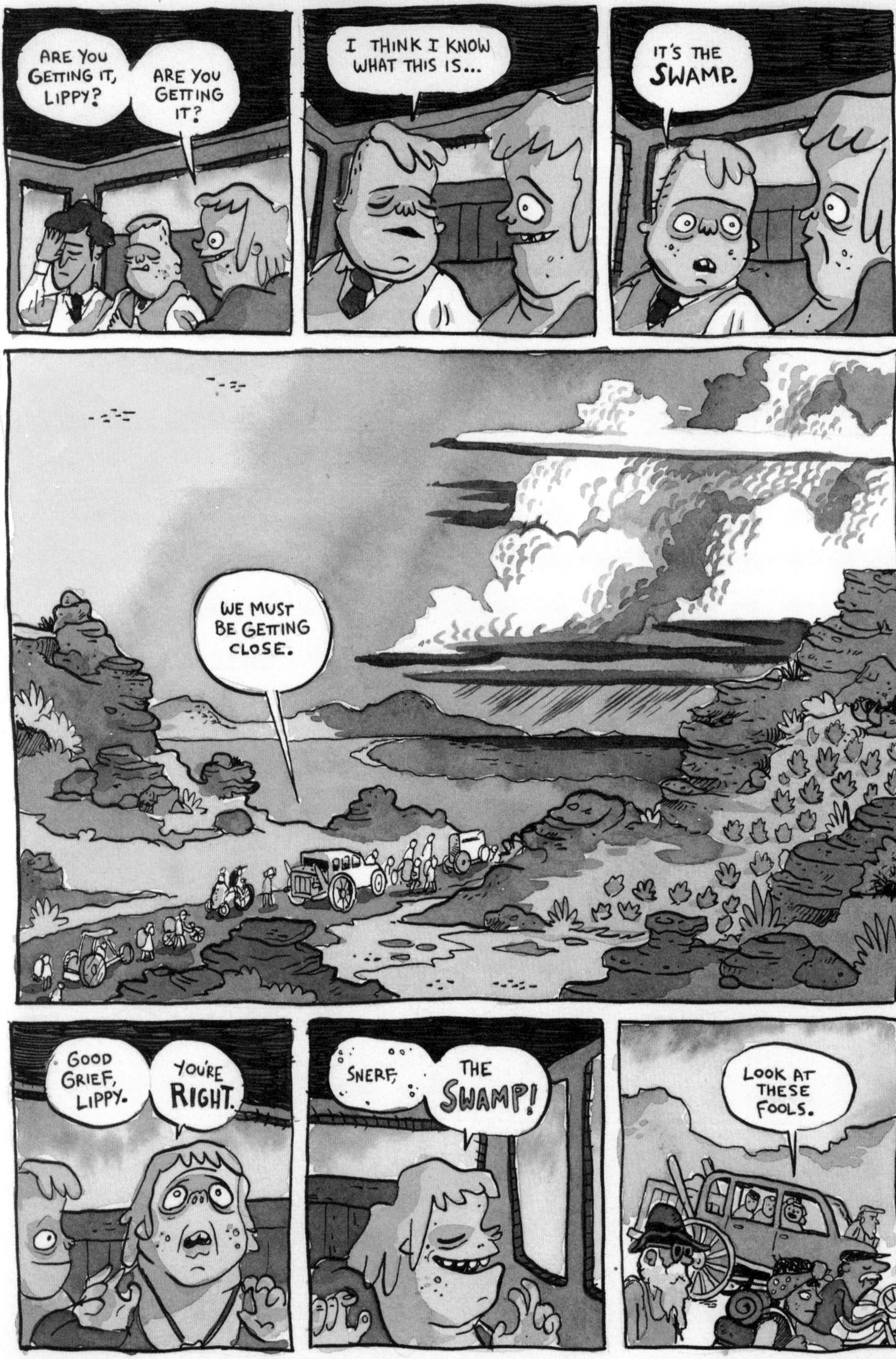
ARE YOU GETTING IT, LIPPY?
ARE YOU GETTING IT?
I THINK I KNOW WHAT THIS IS...
IT'S THE SWAMP.
WE MUST BE GETTING CLOSE.
GOOD GRIEF, LIPPY.
YOU'RE RIGHT.
SNERF,
THE SWAMP!
LOOK AT THESE FOOLS.

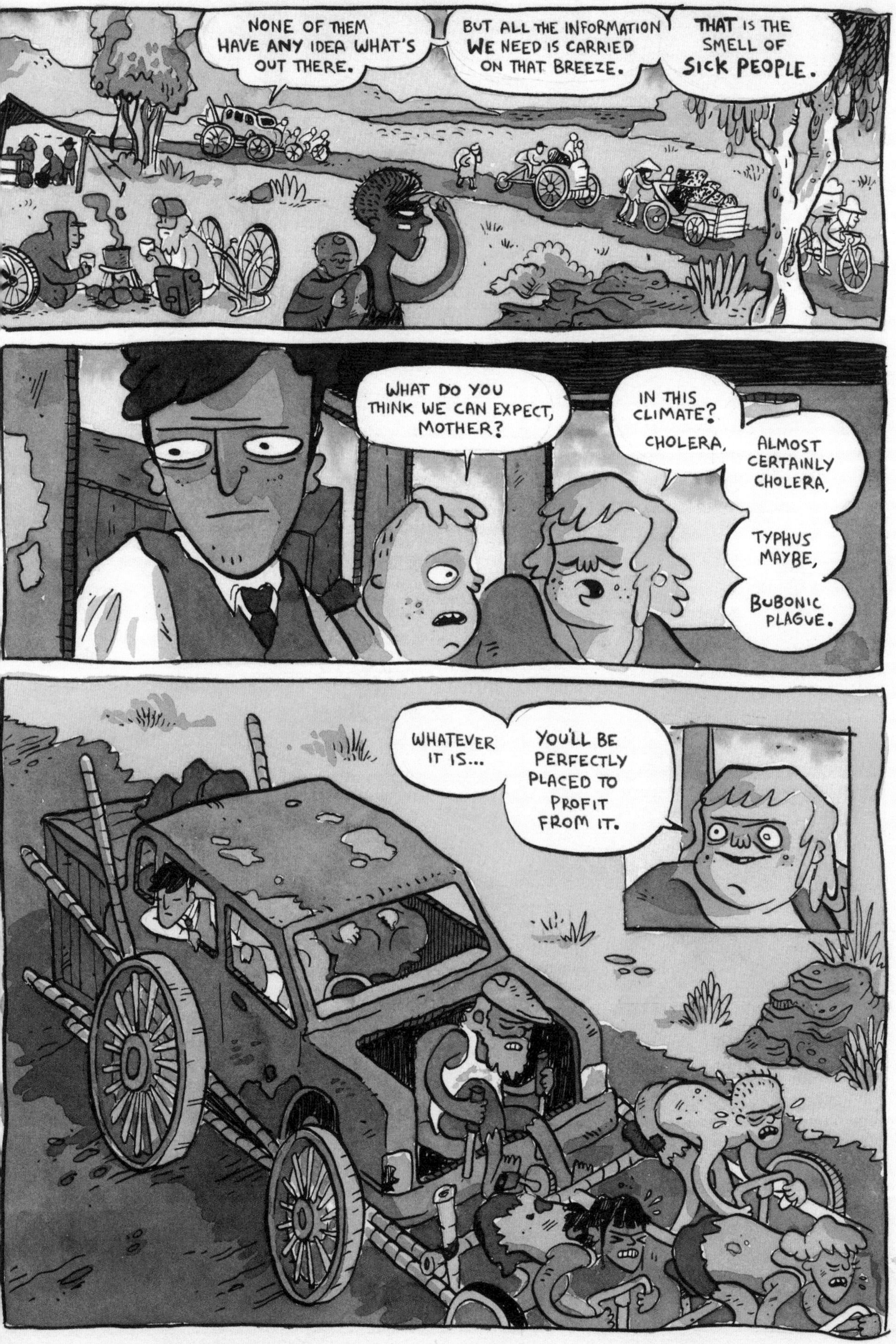
NONE OF THEM HAVE ANY IDEA WHAT'S OUT THERE.
BUT ALL THE INFORMATION WE NEED IS CARRIED ON THAT BREEZE.
THAT IS THE SMELL OF SICK PEOPLE.
WHAT DO YOU THINK WE CAN EXPECT, MOTHER?
IN THIS CLIMATE?
CHOLERA,
ALMOST CERTAINLY CHOLERA,
TYPHUS MAYBE,
BUBONIC PLAGUE.
WHATEVER IT IS...
YOU'LL BE PERFECTLY PLACED TO PROFIT FROM IT.

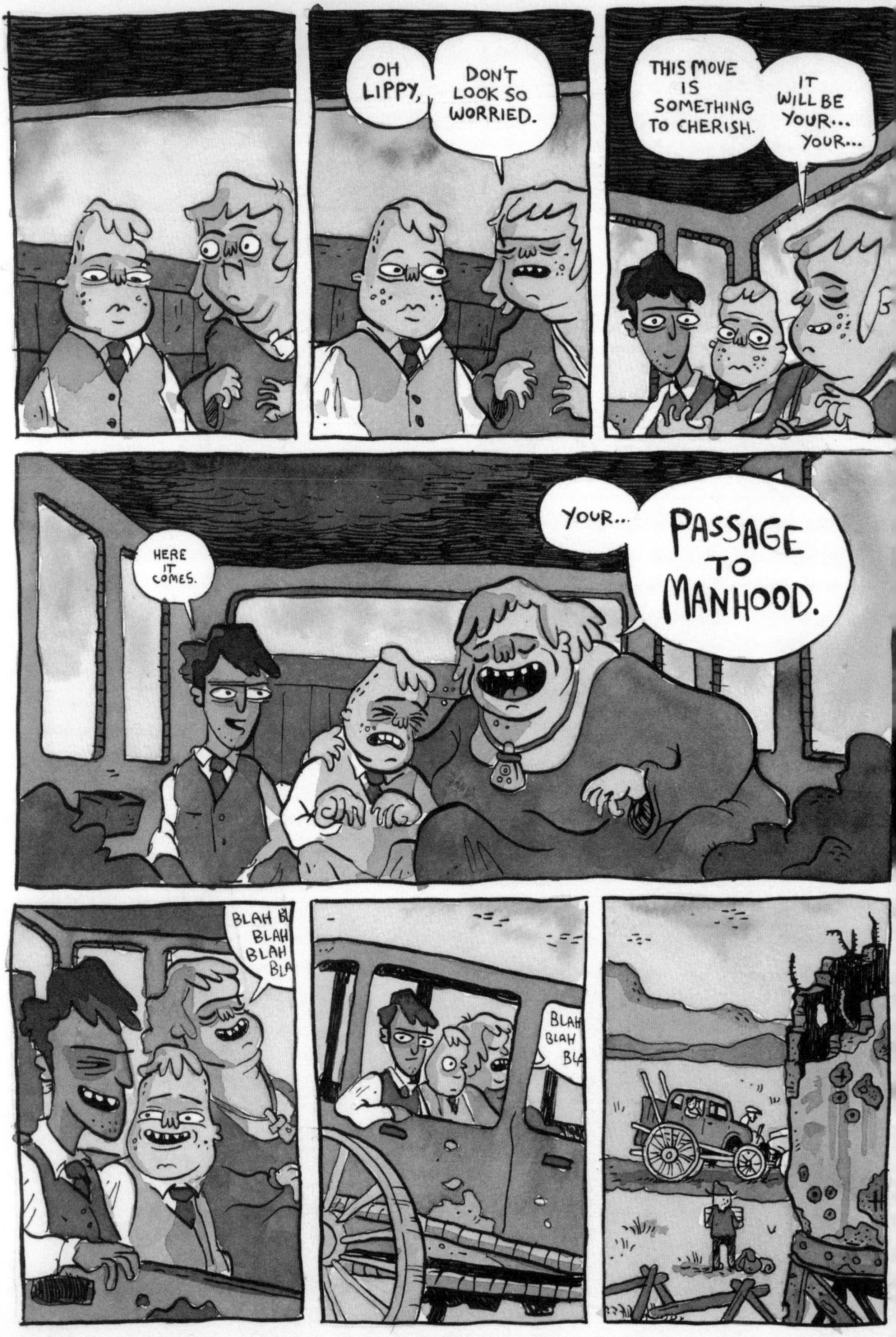
OH LIPPY,
DON'T LOOK SO WORRIED.
THIS MOVE IS SOMETHING TO CHERISH.
IT WILL BE YOUR... YOUR...
HERE IT COMES.
YOUR...
PASSAGE TO MANHOOD.
BLAH BLAH BLAH BLAH
BLAH BLAH

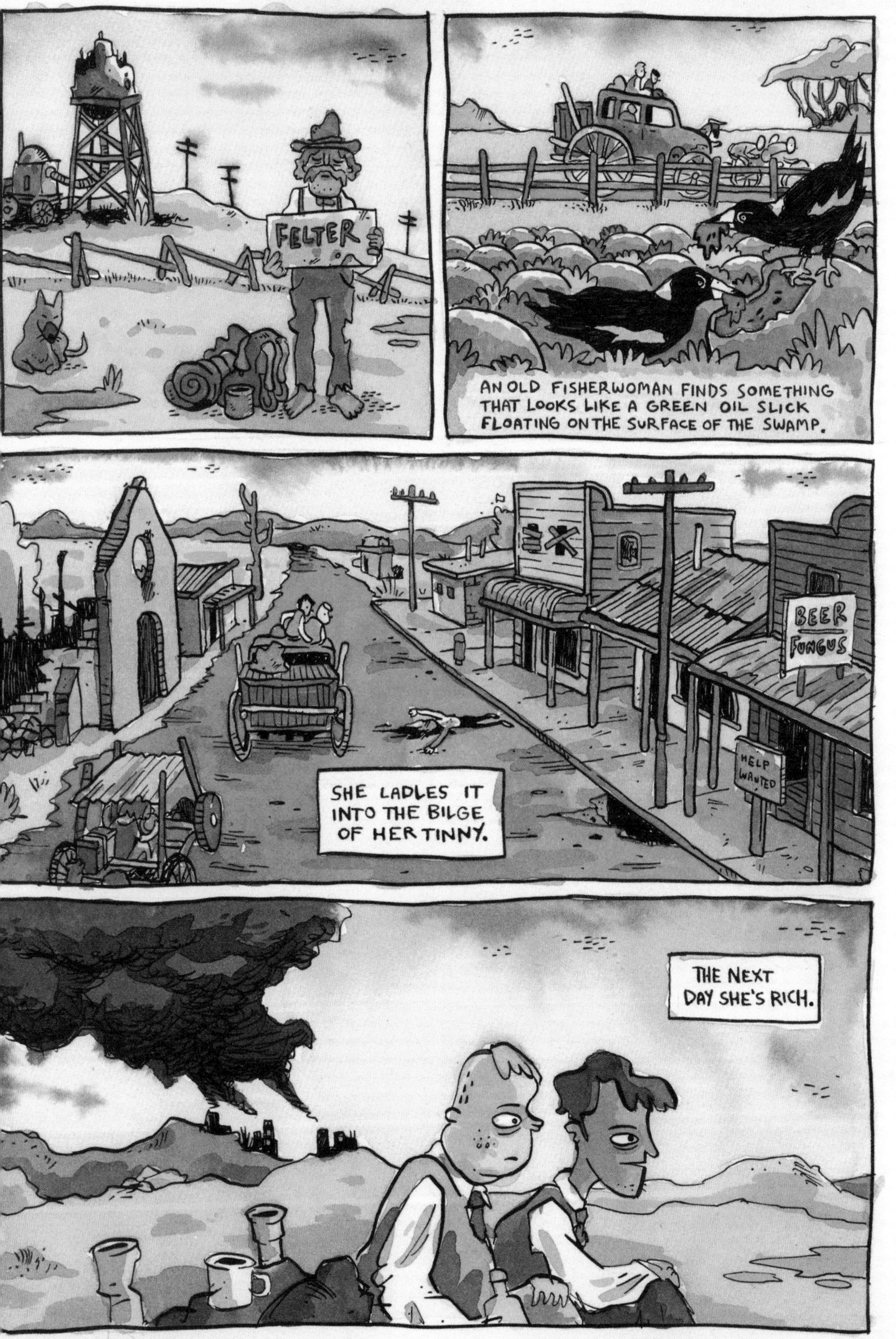
FELTER
AN OLD FISHERWOMAN FINDS SOMETHING THAT LOOKS LIKE A GREEN OIL SLICK FLOATING ON THE SURFACE OF THE SWAMP.
BEER
FUNGUS
HELP WANTED
SHE LADLES IT INTO THE BILGE OF HER TINNY.
THE NEXT DAY SHE'S RICH.

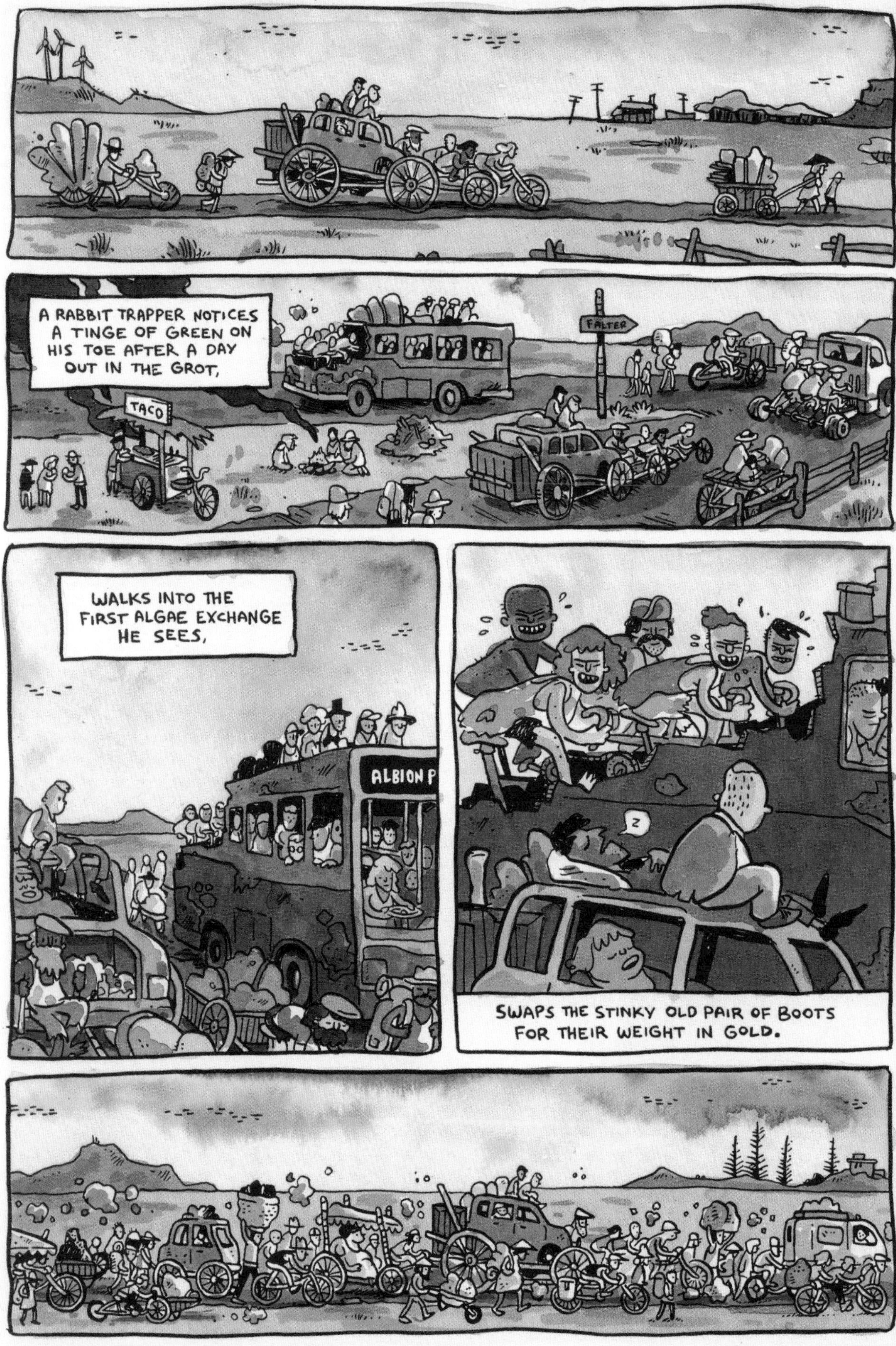
A RABBIT TRAPPER NOTICES A TINGE OF GREEN ON HIS TOE AFTER A DAY OUT IN THE GROT,
FALTER
TACO
WALKS INTO THE FIRST ALGAE EXCHANGE HE SEES,
ALBION P
Z
SWAPS THE STINKY OLD PAIR OF BOOTS FOR THEIR WEIGHT IN GOLD.

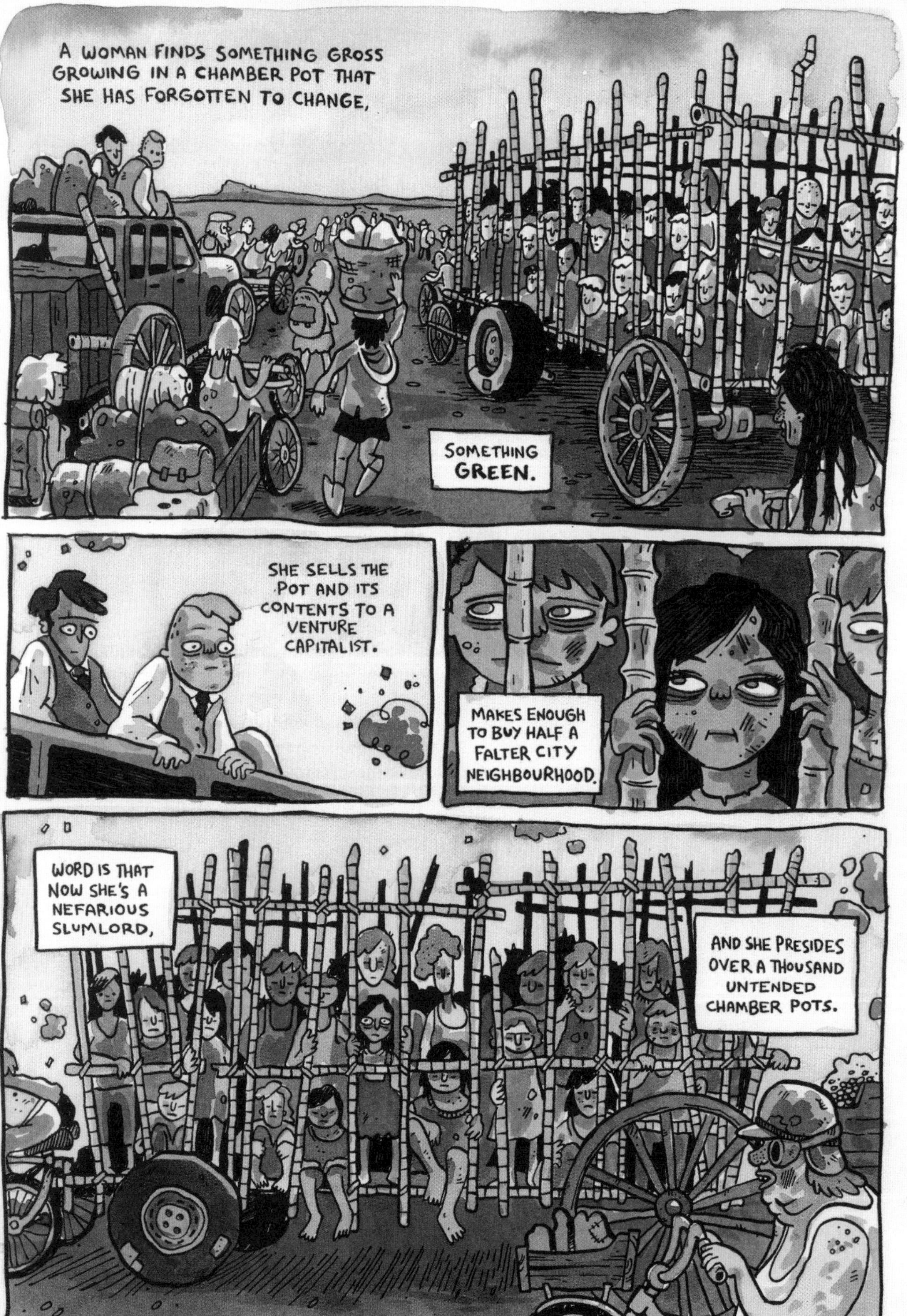
A WOMAN FINDS SOMETHING GROSS GROWING IN A CHAMBER POT THAT SHE HAS FORGOTTEN TO CHANGE,
SOMETHING GREEN.
SHE SELLS THE POT AND ITS CONTENTS TO A VENTURE CAPITALIST.
MAKES ENOUGH TO BUY HALF A FALTER CITY NEIGHBOURHOOD.
WORD IS THAT NOW SHE'S A NEFARIOUS SLUMLORD,
AND SHE PRESIDES OVER A THOUSAND UNTENDED CHAMBER POTS.

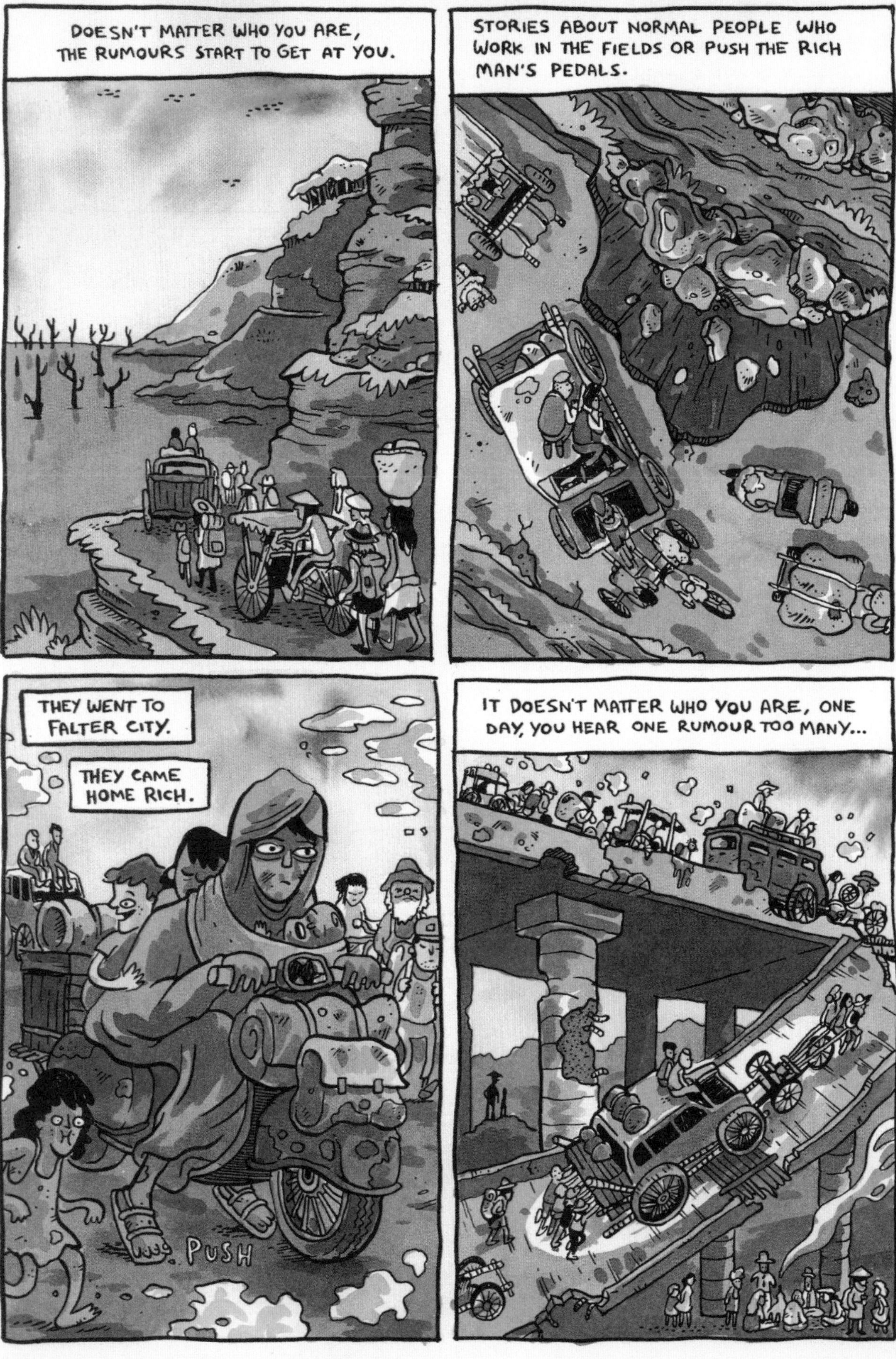
DOESN'T MATTER WHO YOU ARE, THE RUMOURS START TO GET AT YOU.
STORIES ABOUT NORMAL PEOPLE WHO WORK IN THE FIELDS OR PUSH THE RICH MAN'S PEDALS.
THEY WENT TO FALTER CITY.
THEY CAME HOME RICH.
PUSH
IT DOESN'T MATTER WHO YOU ARE, ONE DAY, YOU HEAR ONE RUMOUR TOO MANY...

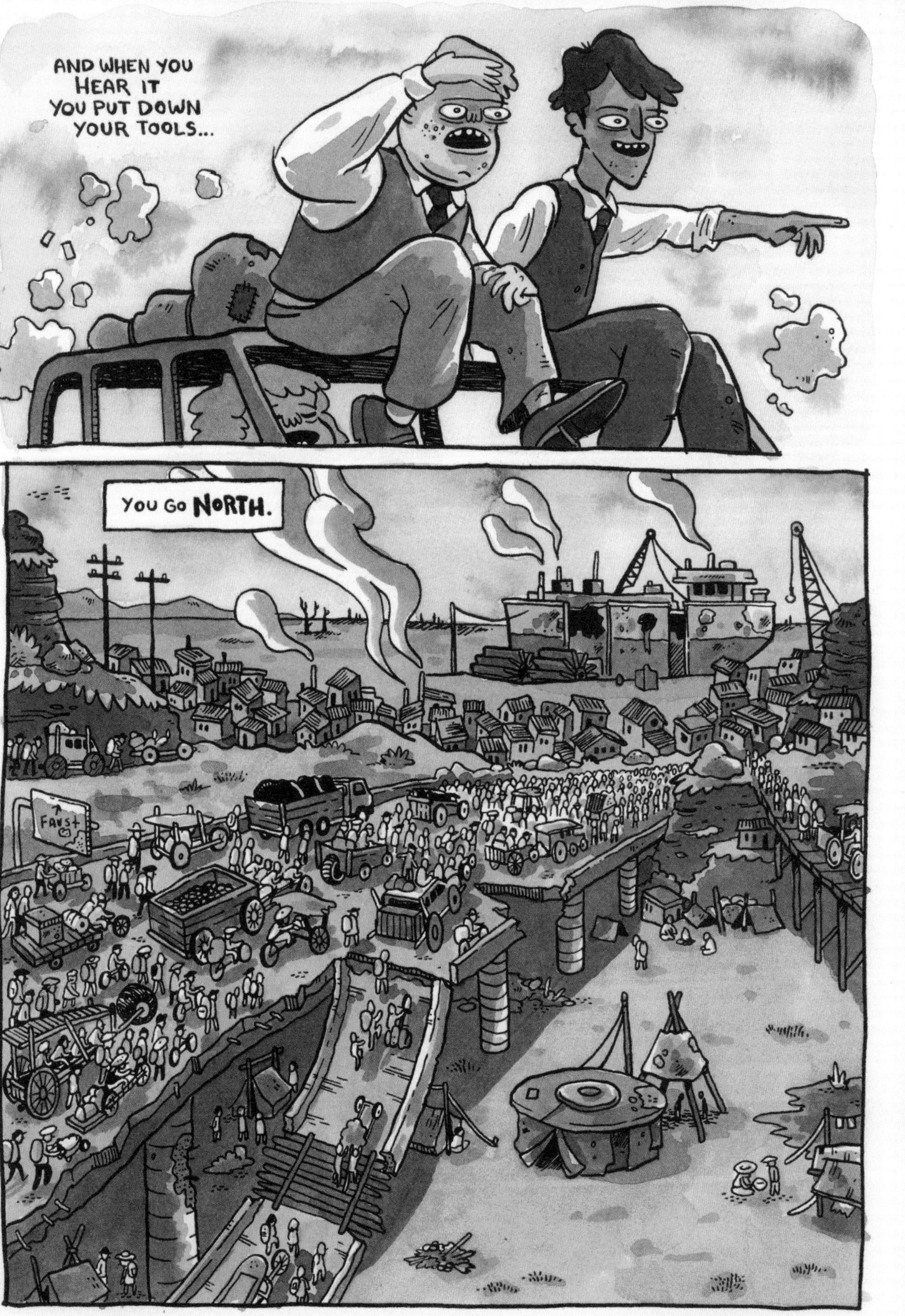
AND WHEN YOU HEAR IT YOU PUT DOWN YOUR TOOLS...
YOU GO NORTH.
FAUST

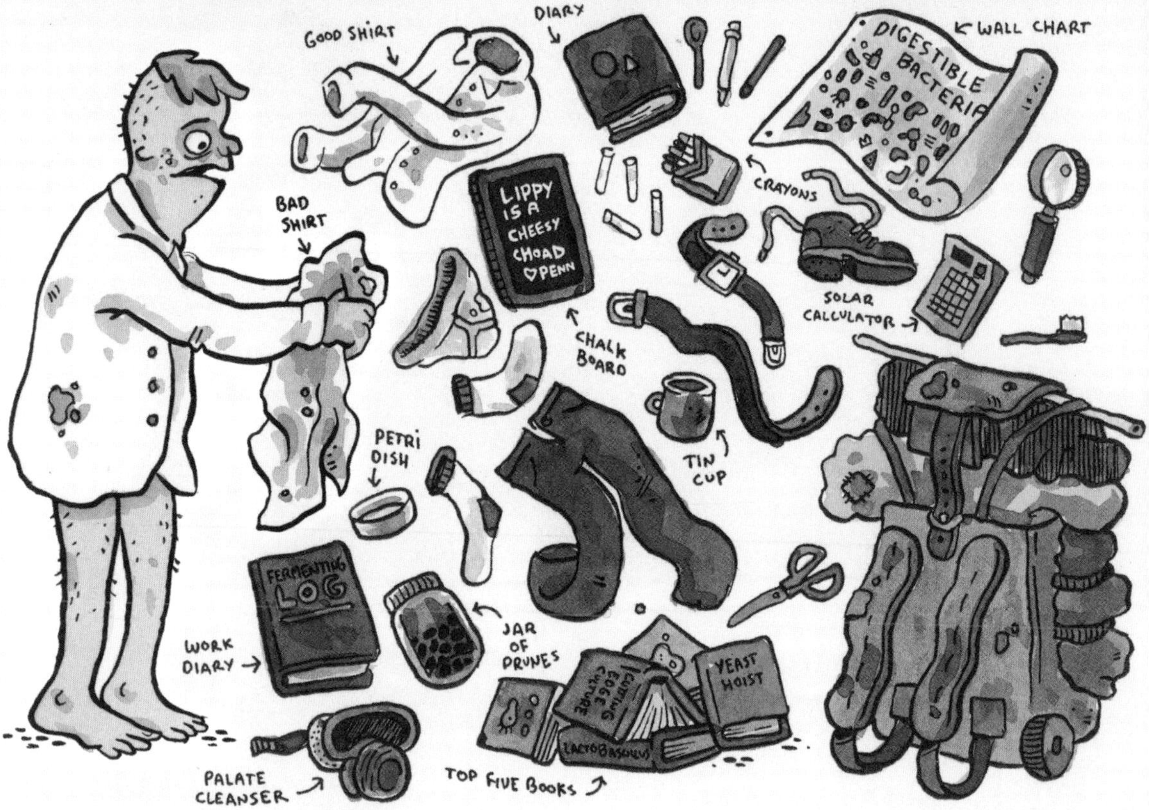
GOOD SHIRT
DIARY
WALL CHART
DIGESTIBLE BACTERIA
BAD SHIRT
LIPPY IS A CHEESY CHOAD ♥PENN
CRAYONS
SOLAR CALCULATOR
CHALK BOARD
TIN CUP
PETRI DISH
FERMENTING LOG
WORK DIARY
JAR OF PRUNES
YEAST HOIST
PALATE CLEANSER
TOP FIVE BOOKS

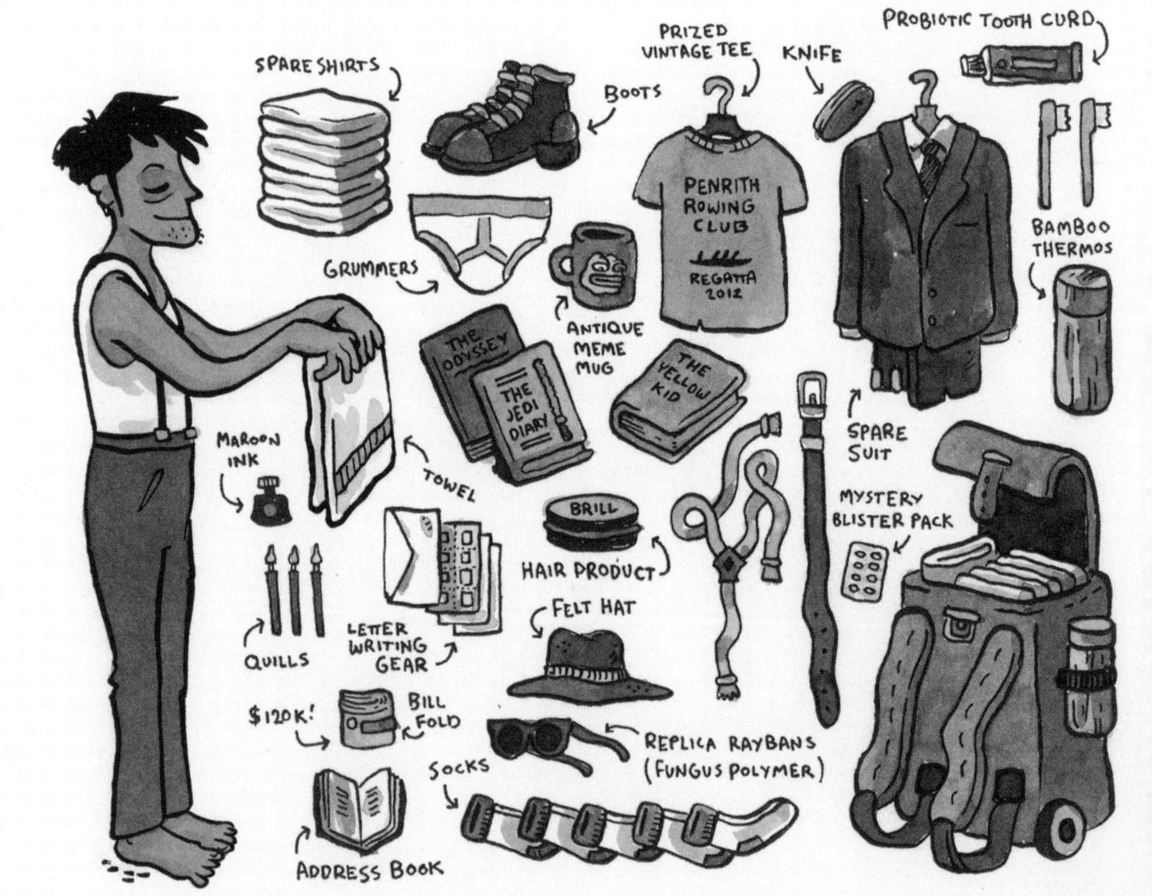
SPARE SHIRTS
BOOTS
PRIZED VINTAGE TEE
KNIFE
PROBIOTIC TOOTH CURD
PENRITH ROWING CLUB
REGATTA 2012
BAMBOO THERMOS
GRUMMERS
ANTIQUE MEME MUG
THE ODYSSEY
THE JEDI DIARY
THE YELLOW KID
SPARE SUIT
MAROON INK
TOWEL
BRILL
HAIR PRODUCT
MYSTERY BLISTER PACK
QUILLS
LETTER WRITING GEAR
FELT HAT
$120K!
BILL FOLD
REPLICA RAYBANS (FUNGUS POLYMER)
SOCKS
ADDRESS BOOK

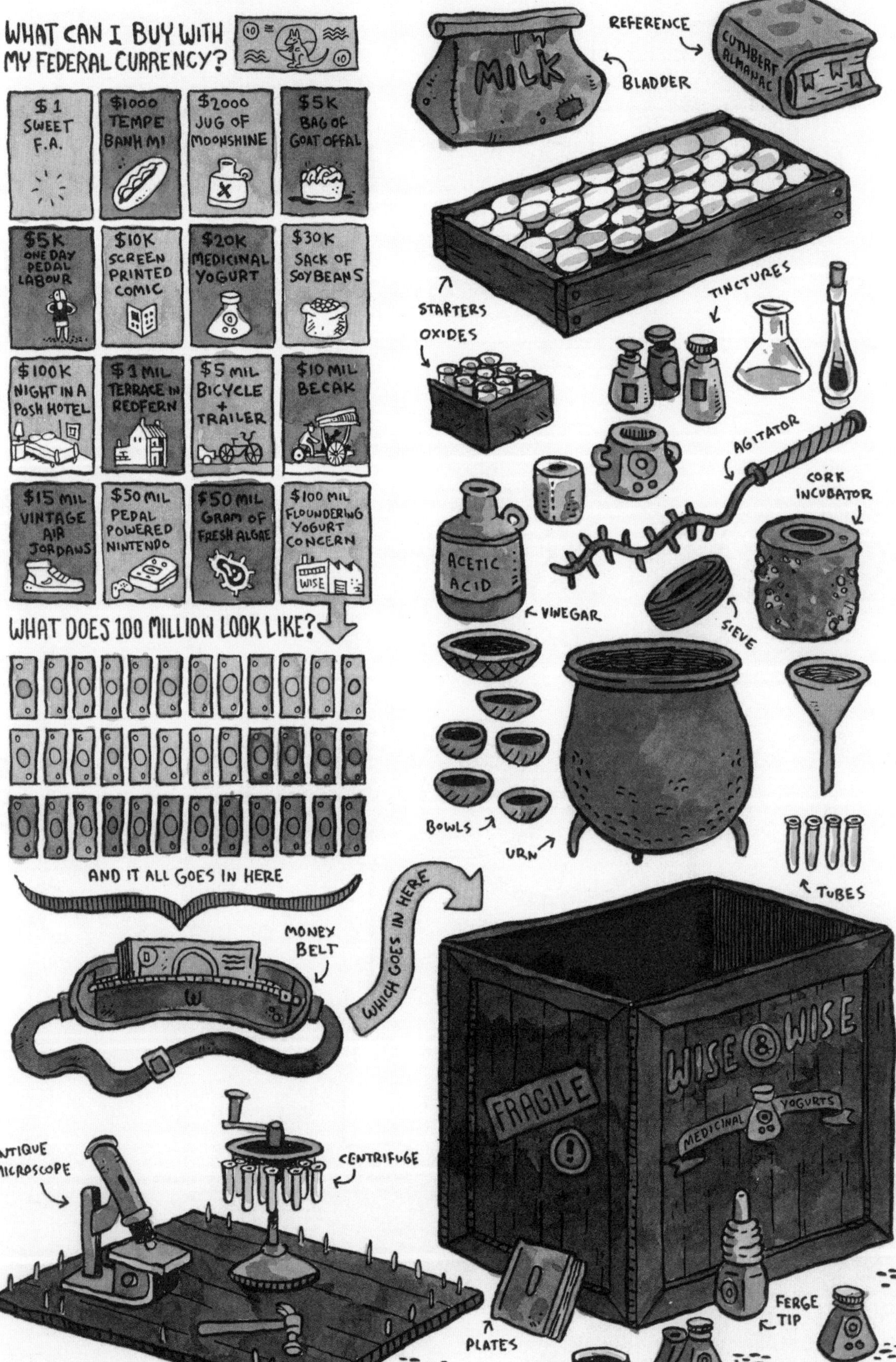
WHAT CAN I BUY WITH MY FEDERAL CURRENCY?
$1 SWEET F.A.
$1000 TEMPE BANH MI
$2000 JUG OF MOONSHINE
$5K BAG OF GOAT OFFAL
$5K ONE DAY PEDAL LABOUR
$10K SCREEN PRINTED COMIC
$20K MEDICINAL YOGURT
$30K SACK OF SOYBEANS
$100K NIGHT IN A POSH HOTEL
$1 MIL TERRACE IN REDFERN
$5 MIL BICYCLE + TRAILER
$10 MIL BECAK
$15 MIL VINTAGE AIR JORDANS
$50 MIL PEDAL POWERED NINTENDO
$50 MIL GRAM OF FRESH ALGAE
$100 MIL FLOUNDERING YOGURT CONCERN
WISE
WHAT DOES 100 MILLION LOOK LIKE?
AND IT ALL GOES IN HERE
MONEY BELT
WHICH GOES IN HERE
MILK
BLADDER
REFERENCE
CUTHBERT ALMANAC
STARTERS
TINCTURES
OXIDES
AGITATOR
CORK INCUBATOR
ACETIC ACID
VINEGAR
SIEVE
BOWLS
URN
TUBES
WISE & WISE
MEDICINAL YOGURTS
FRAGILE
ANTIQUE MICROSCOPE
CENTRIFUGE
PLATES
FERGE TIP

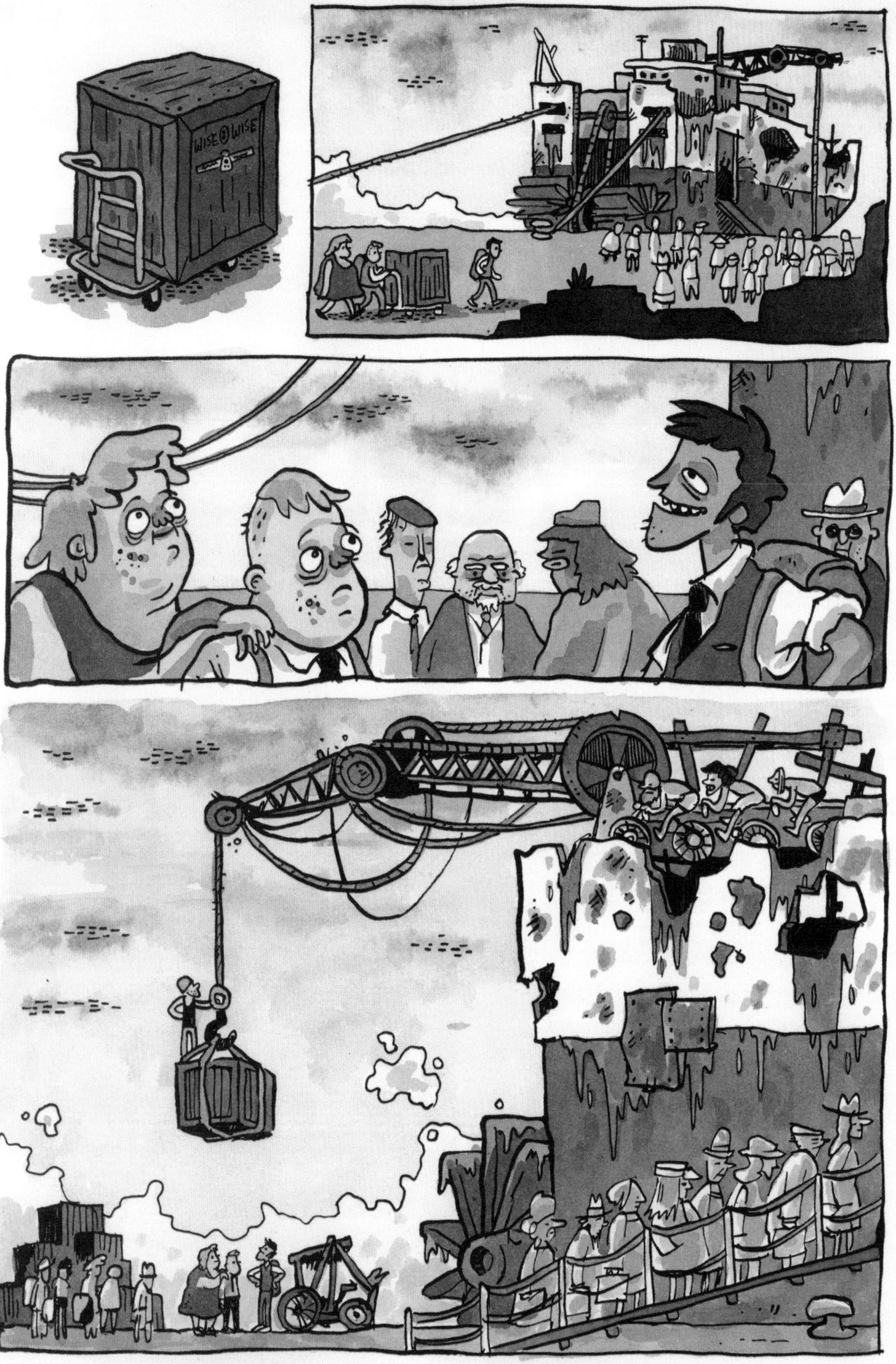
WISE & WISE

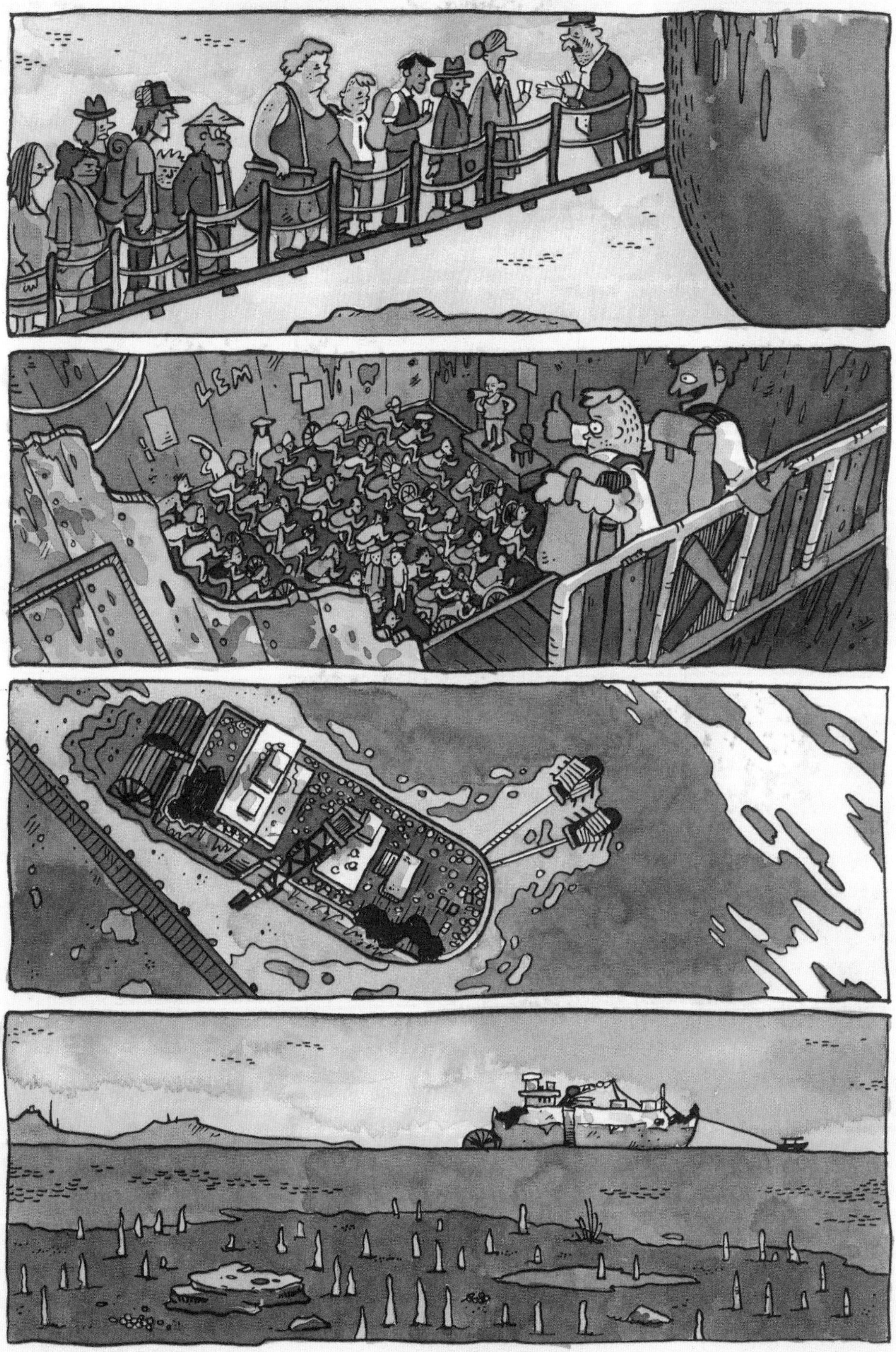
LEM

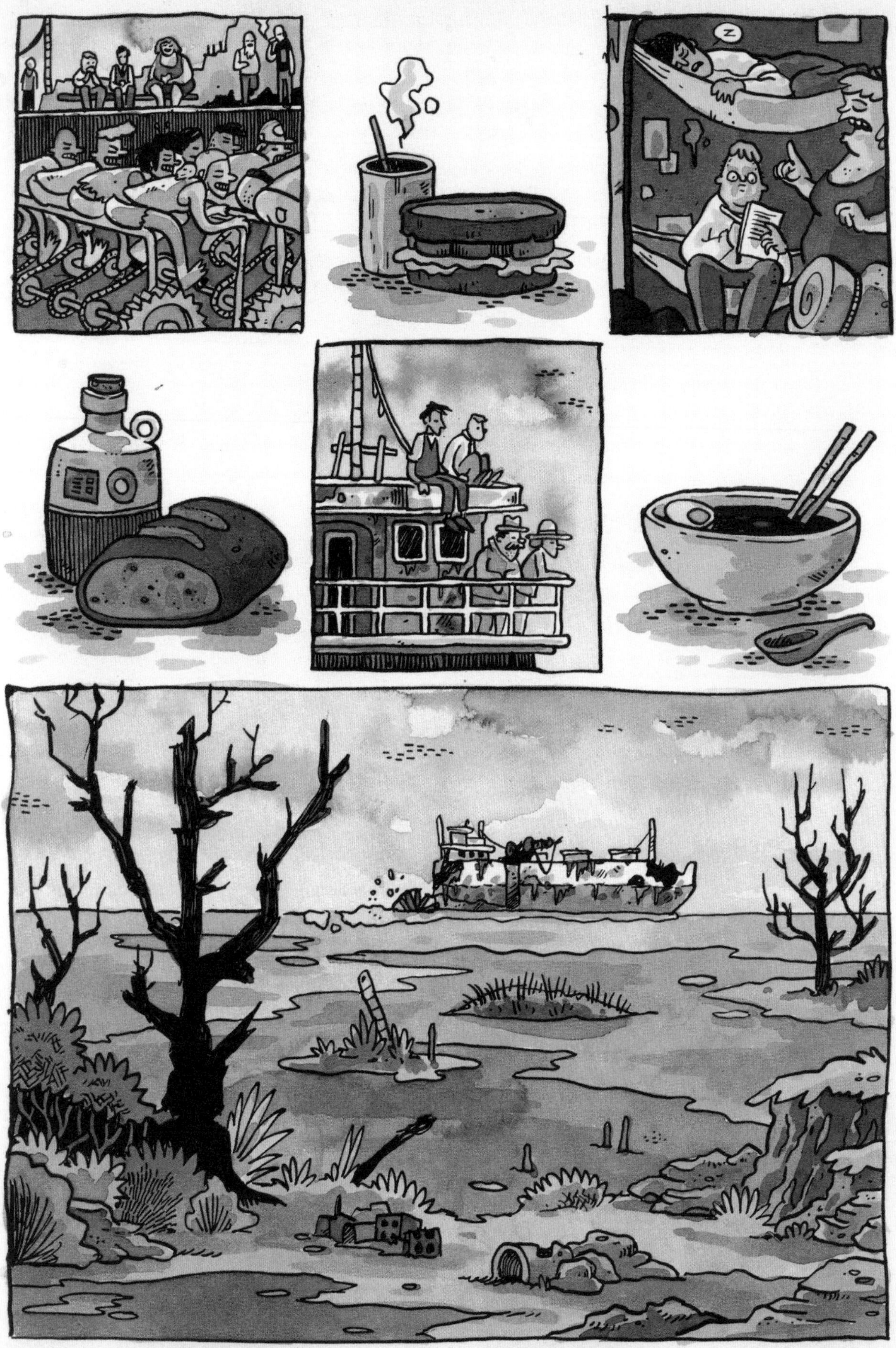
Z

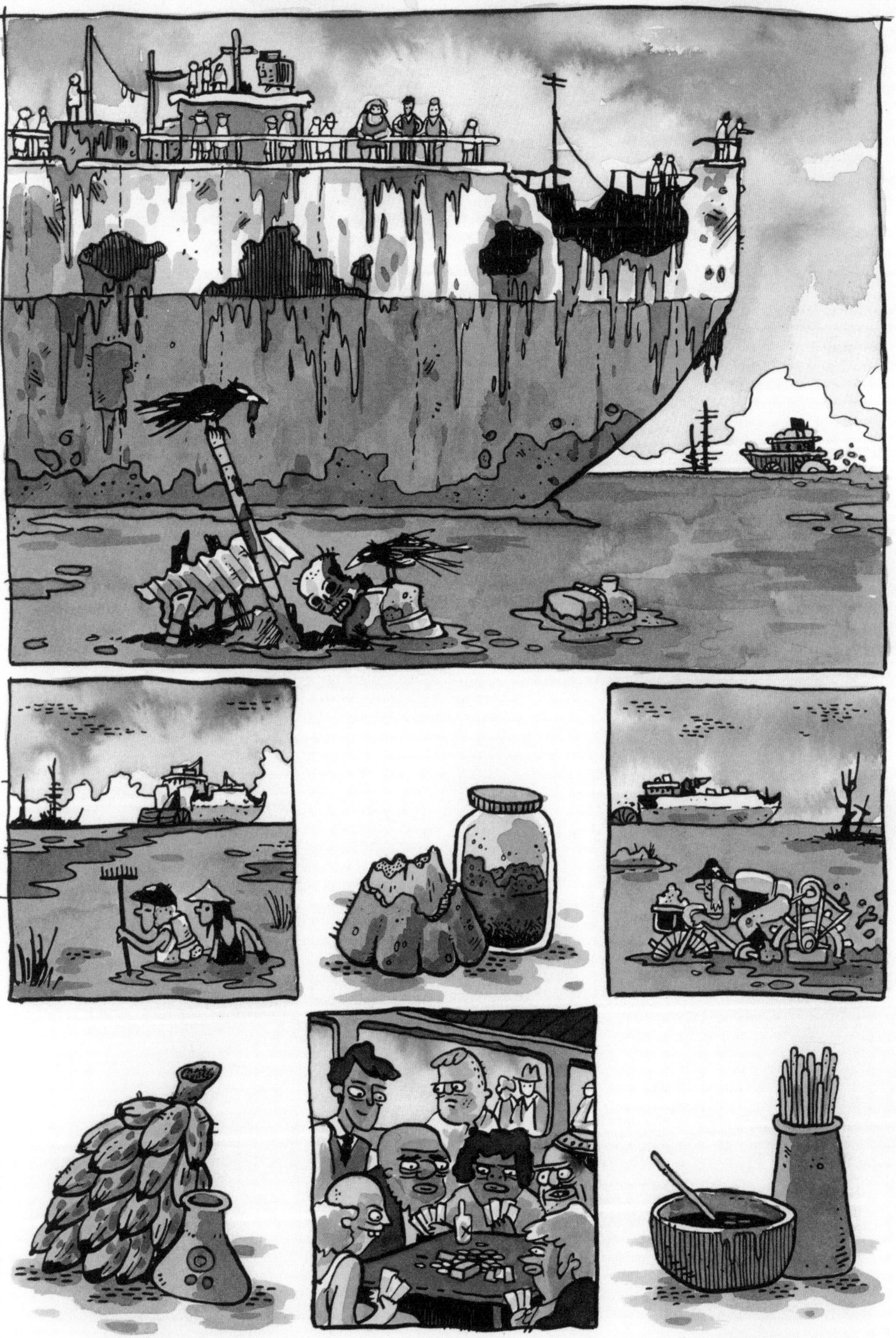

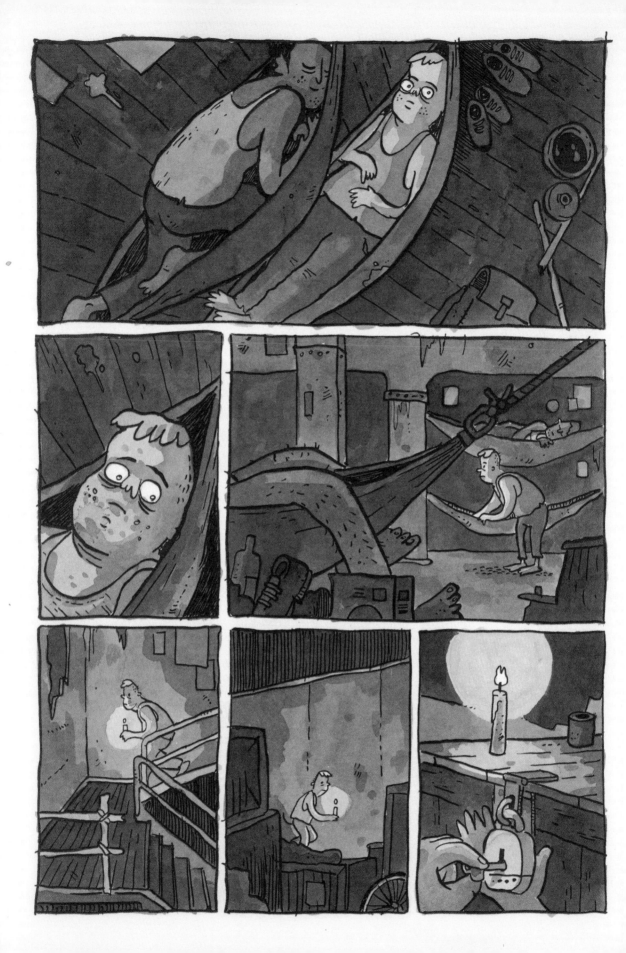

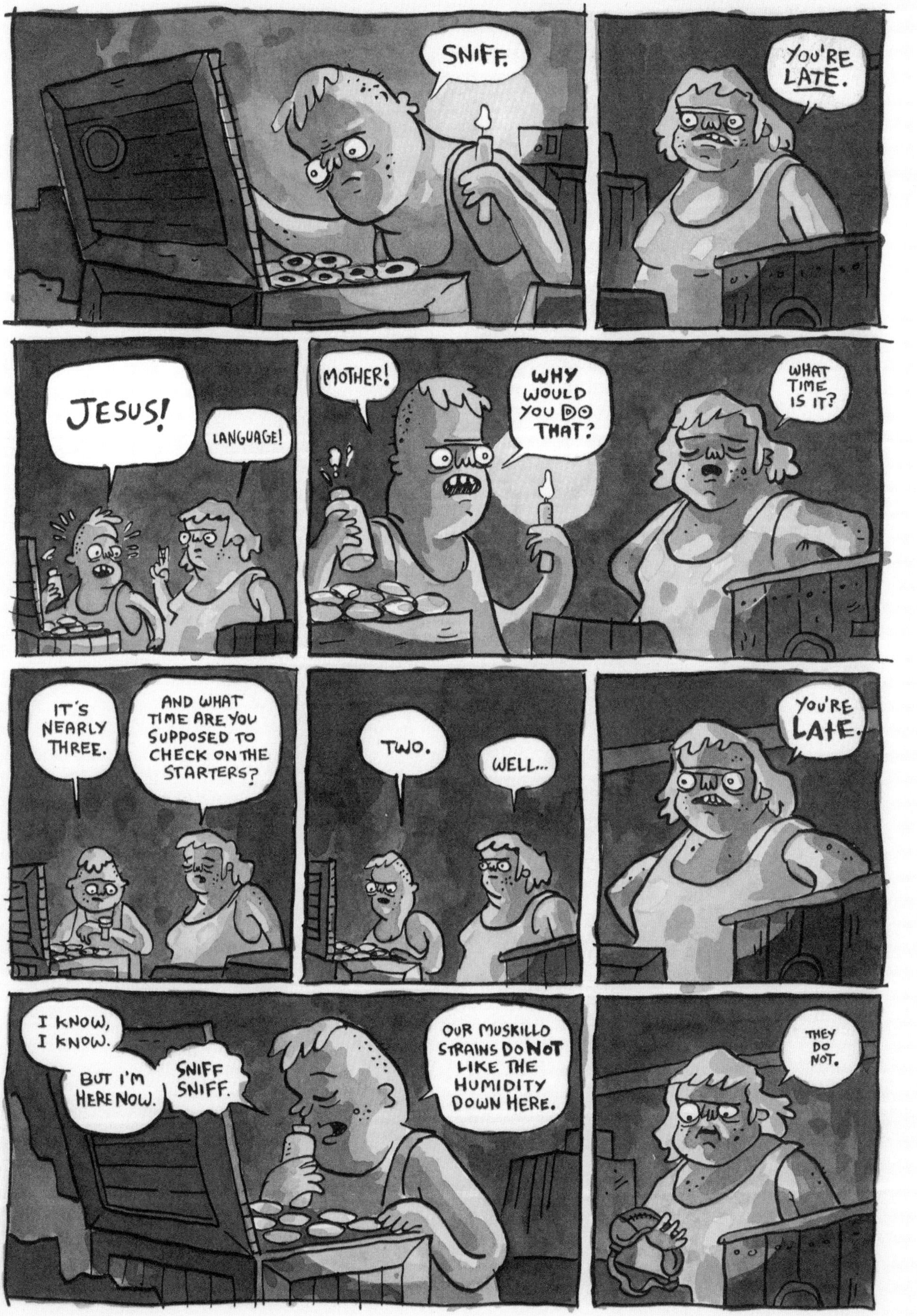

SNIFF.
YOU'RE LATE.
JESUS!
LANGUAGE!
MOTHER!
WHY WOULD YOU DO THAT?
WHAT TIME IS IT?
IT'S NEARLY THREE.
AND WHAT TIME ARE YOU SUPPOSED TO CHECK ON THE STARTERS?
TWO.
WELL...
YOU'RE LATE.
I KNOW, I KNOW.
BUT I'M HERE NOW.
SNIFF SNIFF.
OUR MUSKILLO STRAINS DO NOT LIKE THE HUMIDITY DOWN HERE.
THEY DO NOT.

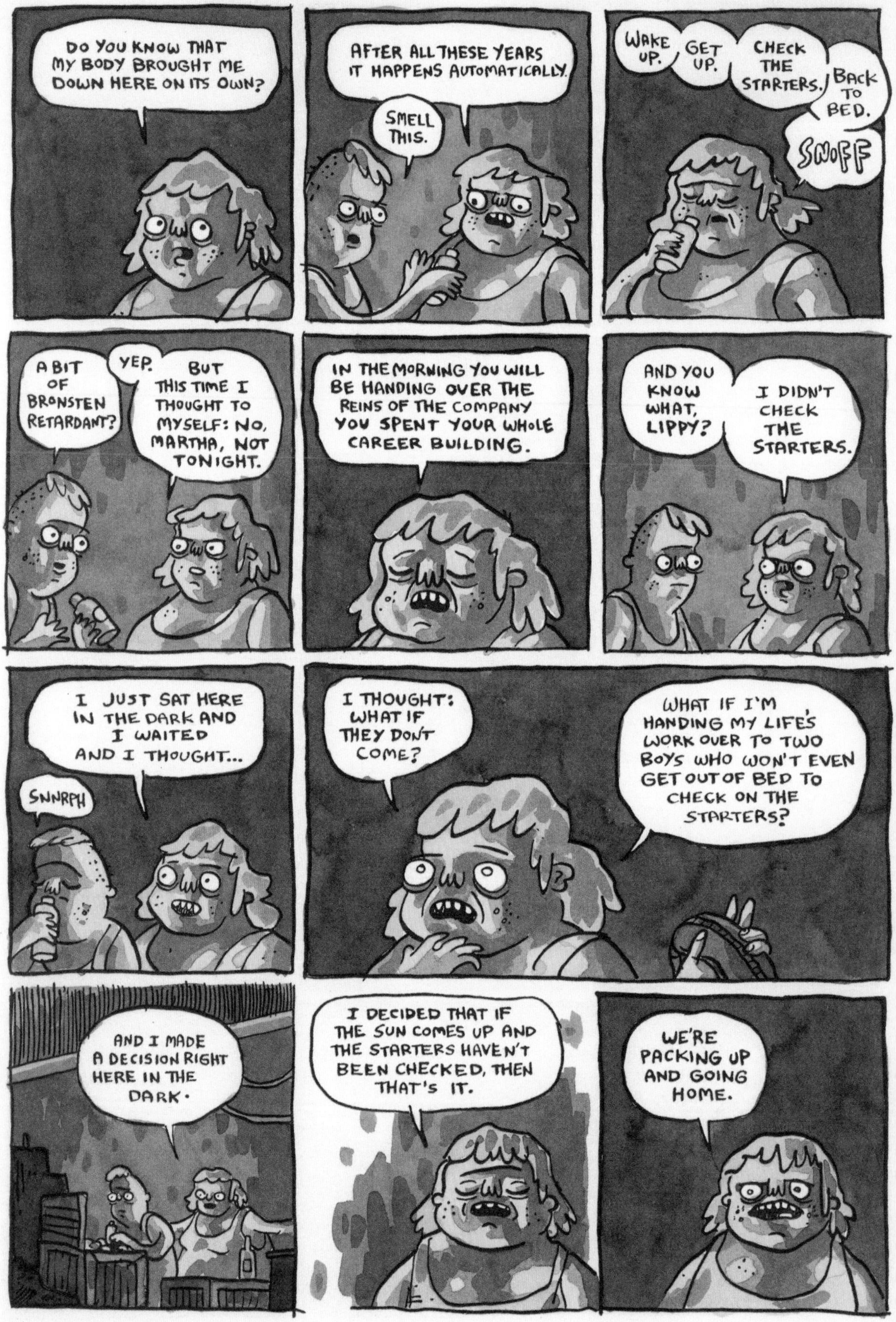
DO YOU KNOW THAT MY BODY BROUGHT ME DOWN HERE ON ITS OWN?
AFTER ALL THESE YEARS IT HAPPENS AUTOMATICALLY.
SMELL THIS.
WAKE UP.
GET UP.
CHECK THE STARTERS.
BACK TO BED.
SNOFF
A BIT OF BRONSTEN RETARDANT?
YEP.
BUT THIS TIME I THOUGHT TO MYSELF: NO, MARTHA, NOT TONIGHT.
IN THE MORNING YOU WILL BE HANDING OVER THE REINS OF THE COMPANY YOU SPENT YOUR WHOLE CAREER BUILDING.
AND YOU KNOW WHAT, LIPPY?
I DIDN'T CHECK THE STARTERS.
I JUST SAT HERE IN THE DARK AND I WAITED AND I THOUGHT...
SNNRPH
I THOUGHT: WHAT IF THEY DON'T COME?
WHAT IF I'M HANDING MY LIFE'S WORK OVER TO TWO BOYS WHO WON'T EVEN GET OUT OF BED TO CHECK ON THE STARTERS?
AND I MADE A DECISION RIGHT HERE IN THE DARK.
I DECIDED THAT IF THE SUN COMES UP AND THE STARTERS HAVEN'T BEEN CHECKED, THEN THAT'S IT.
WE'RE PACKING UP AND GOING HOME.

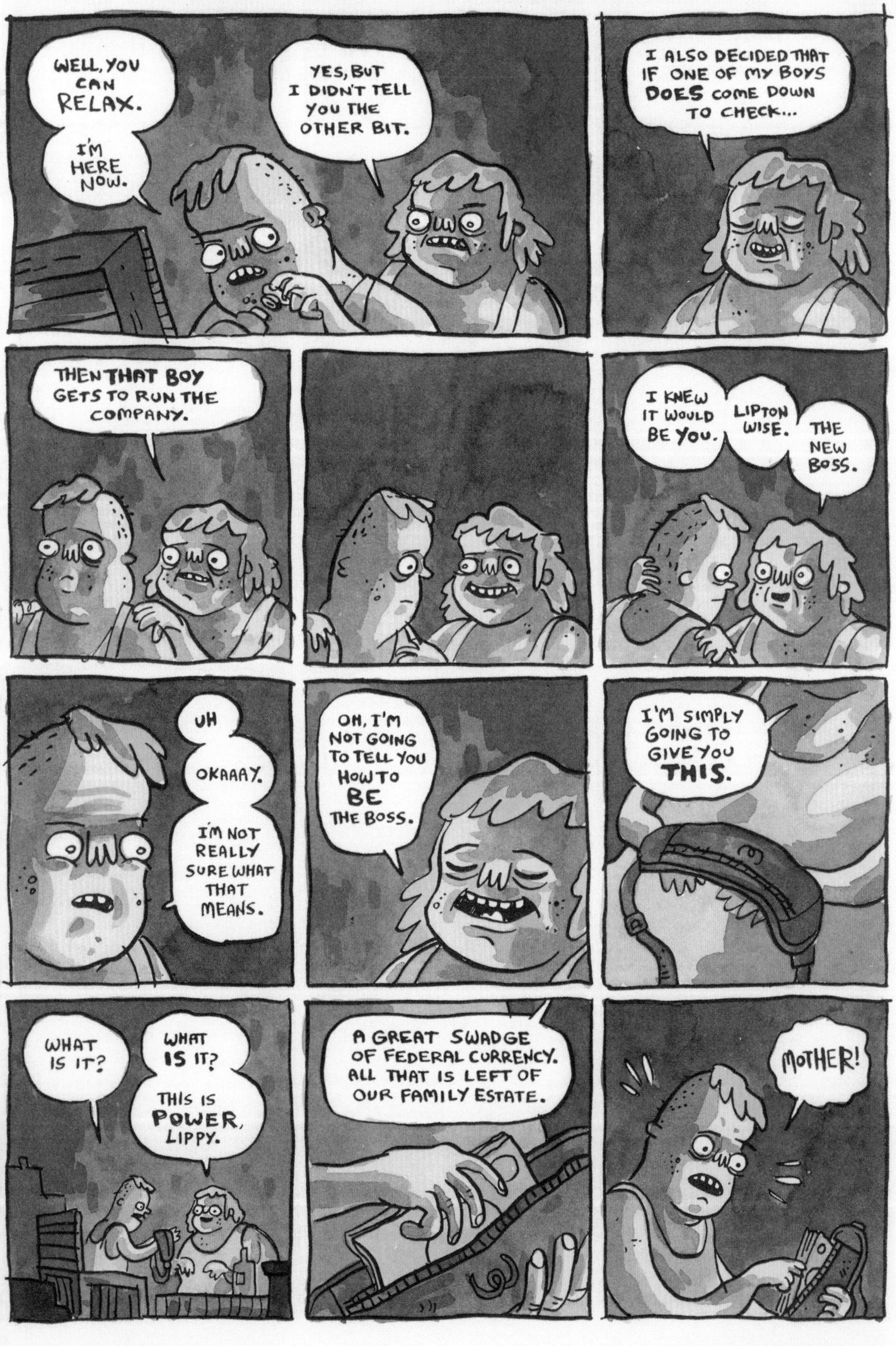
WELL, YOU CAN RELAX.
I'M HERE NOW.
YES, BUT I DIDN'T TELL YOU THE OTHER BIT.
I ALSO DECIDED THAT IF ONE OF MY BOYS DOES COME DOWN TO CHECK...
THEN THAT BOY GETS TO RUN THE COMPANY.
I KNEW IT WOULD BE YOU.
LIPTON WISE.
THE NEW BOSS.
UH
OKAAAY.
I'M NOT REALLY SURE WHAT THAT MEANS.
OH, I'M NOT GOING TO TELL YOU HOW TO BE THE BOSS.
I'M SIMPLY GOING TO GIVE YOU THIS.
WHAT IS IT?
WHAT IS IT?
THIS IS POWER, LIPPY.
A GREAT SWADGE OF FEDERAL CURRENCY. ALL THAT IS LEFT OF OUR FAMILY ESTATE.
MOTHER!

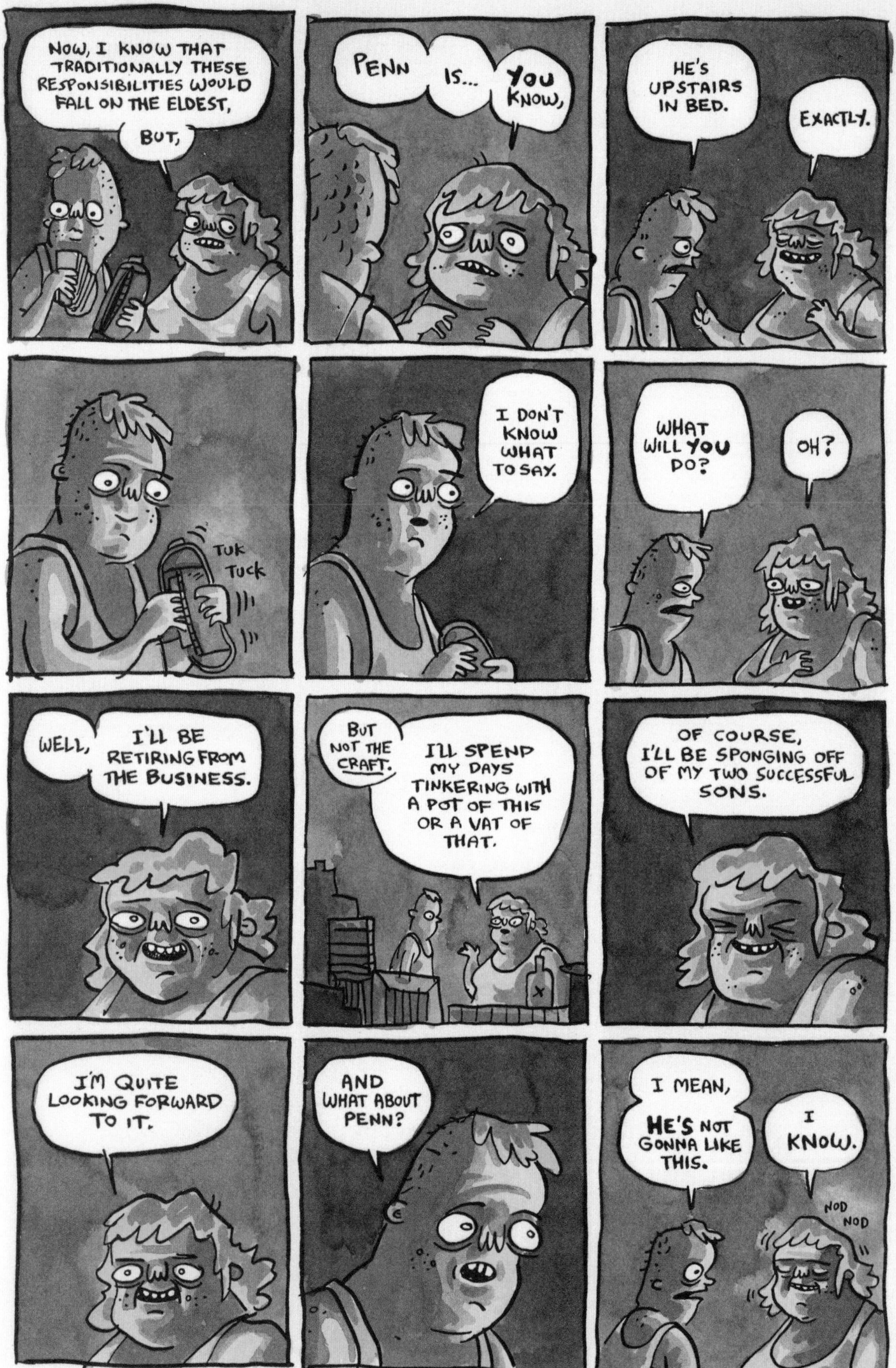
NOW, I KNOW THAT TRADITIONALLY THESE RESPONSIBILITIES WOULD FALL ON THE ELDEST,
BUT,
PENN
IS...
YOU KNOW,
HE'S UPSTAIRS IN BED.
EXACTLY.
TUK
TUCK
I DON'T KNOW WHAT TO SAY.
WHAT WILL YOU DO?
OH?
WELL,
I'LL BE RETIRING FROM THE BUSINESS.
BUT NOT THE CRAFT.
I'LL SPEND MY DAYS TINKERING WITH A POT OF THIS OR A VAT OF THAT.
OF COURSE, I'LL BE SPONGING OFF OF MY TWO SUCCESSFUL SONS.
I'M QUITE LOOKING FORWARD TO IT.
AND WHAT ABOUT PENN?
I MEAN,
HE'S NOT GONNA LIKE THIS.
I KNOW.
NOD
NOD

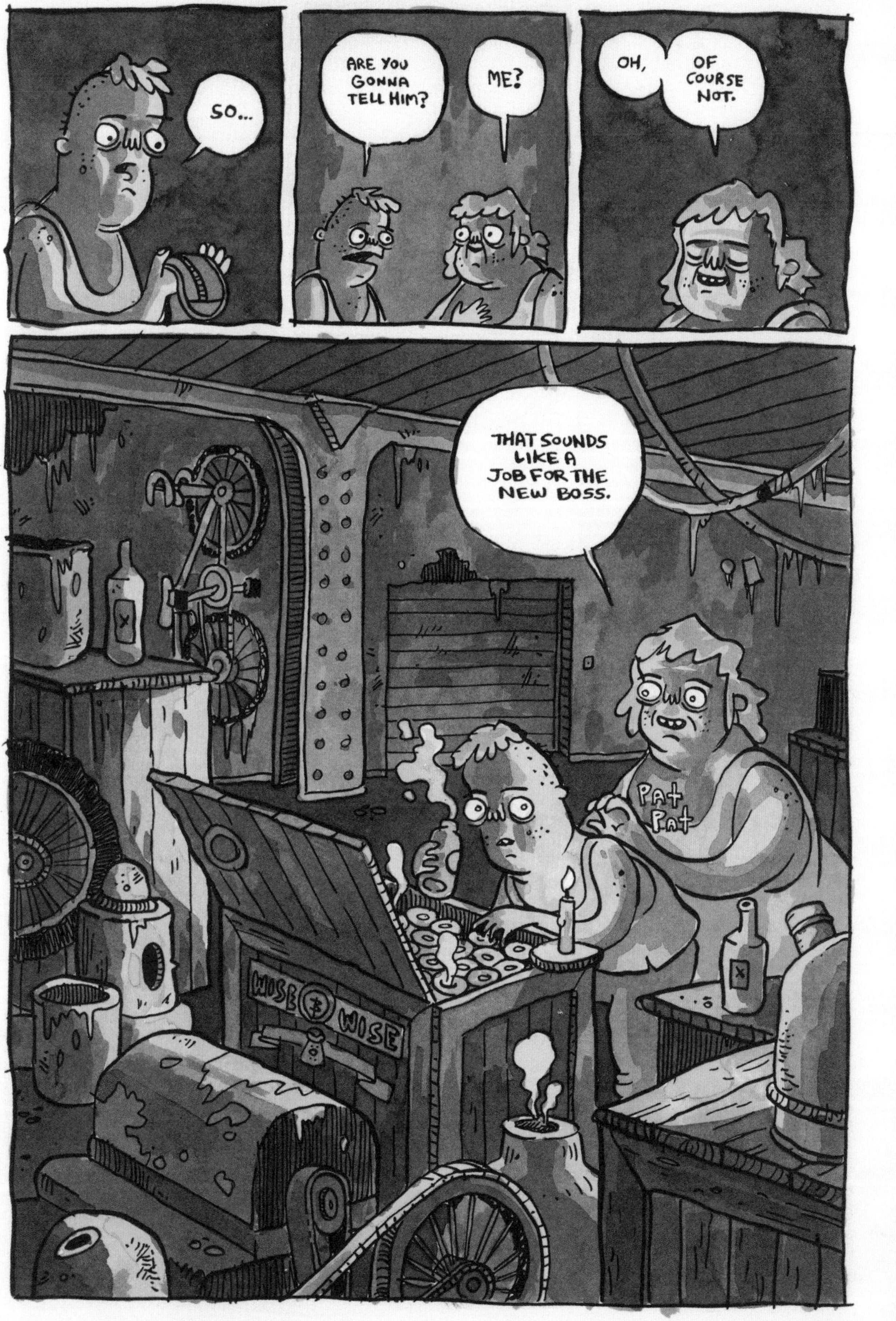
SO...
ARE YOU GONNA TELL HIM?
ME?
OH,
OF COURSE NOT.
THAT SOUNDS LIKE A JOB FOR THE NEW BOSS.
Pat Pat
WISE WISE

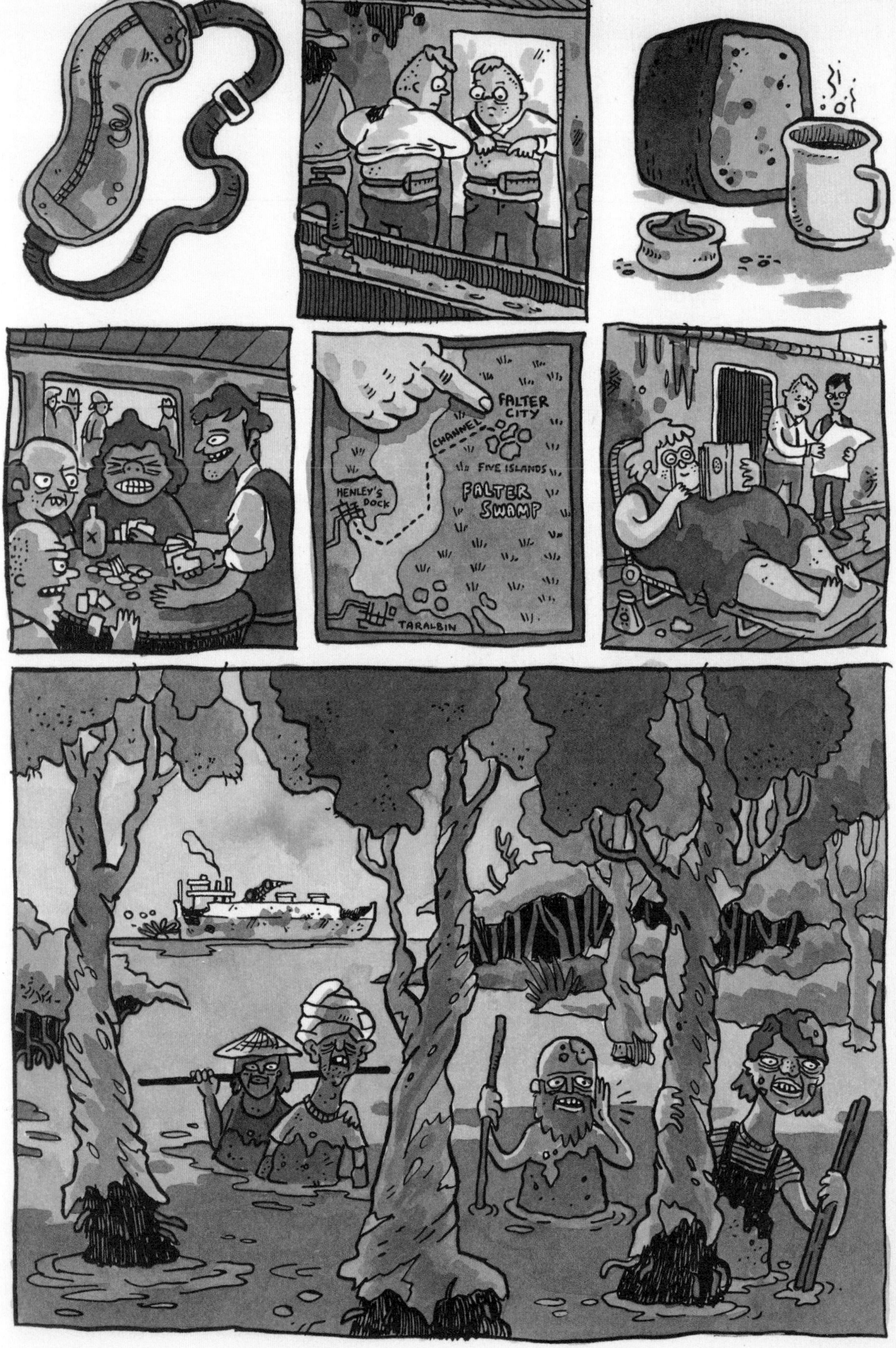
FALTER CITY
CHANNEL
FIVE ISLANDS
FALTER SWAMP
HENLEY'S DOCK
TARALBIN

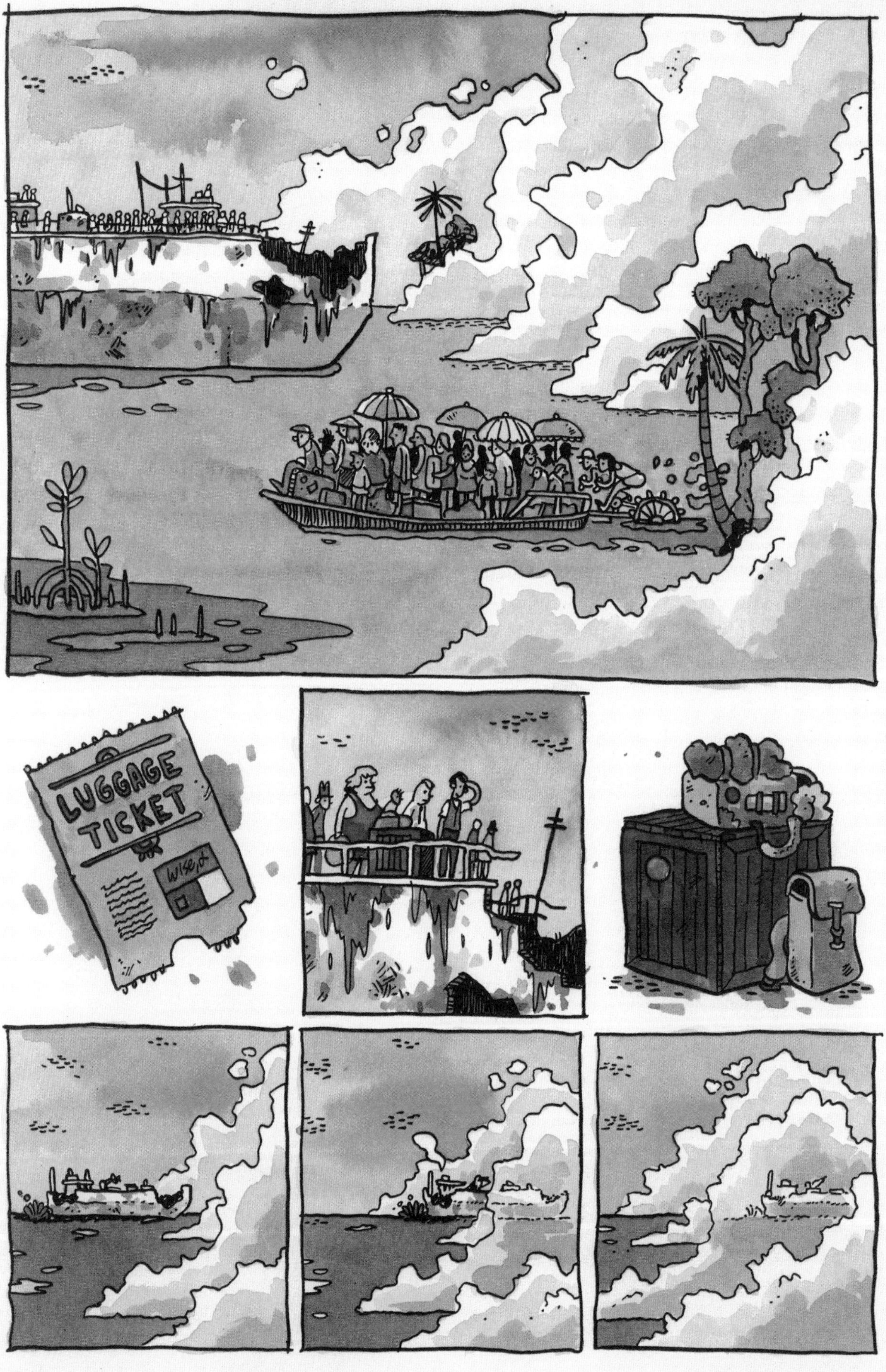
LUGGAGE TICKET
wise

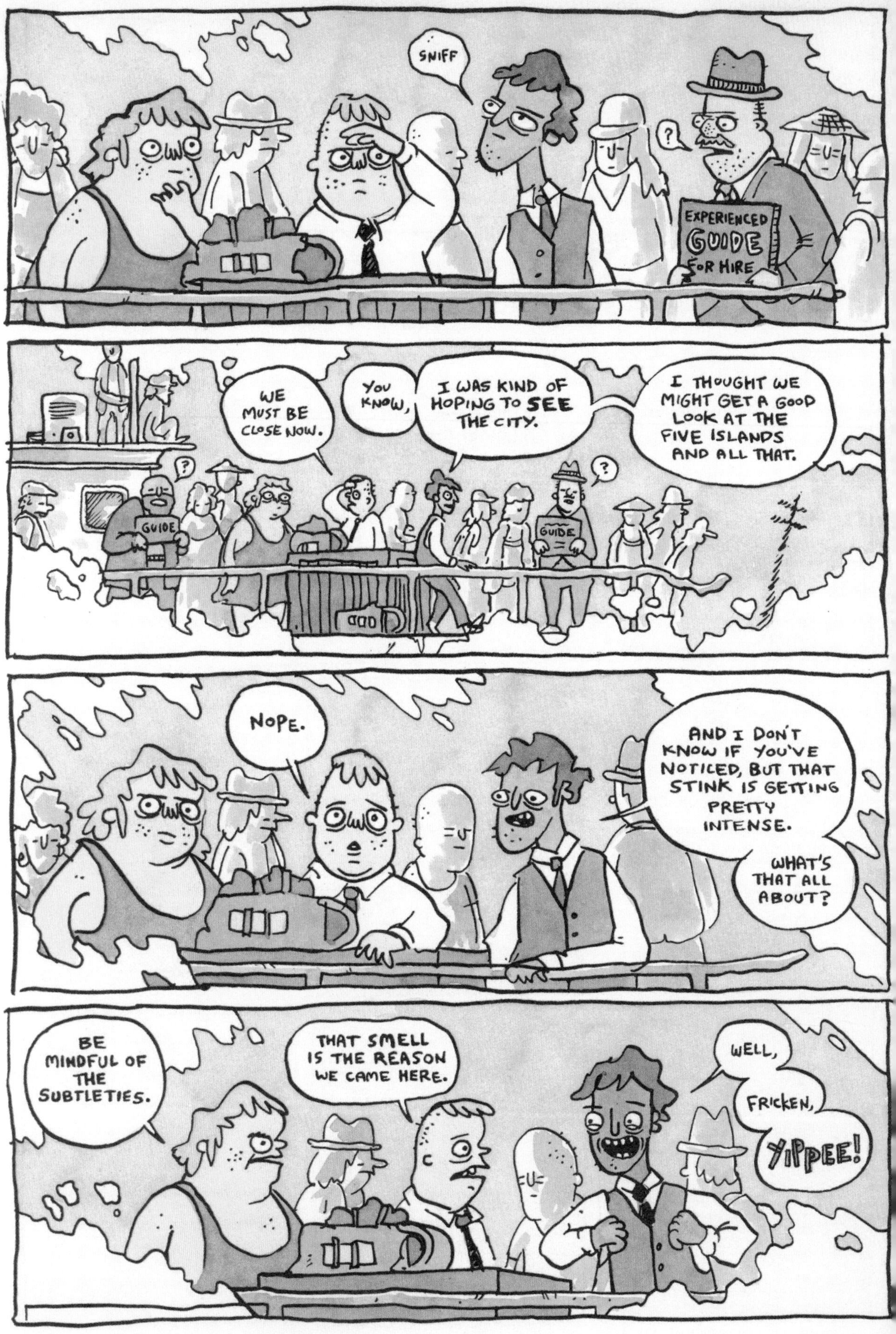
SNIFF
?
EXPERIENCED GUIDE FOR HIRE
WE MUST BE CLOSE NOW.
YOU KNOW,
I WAS KIND OF HOPING TO SEE THE CITY.
I THOUGHT WE MIGHT GET A GOOD LOOK AT THE FIVE ISLANDS AND ALL THAT.
?
?
GUIDE
GUIDE
NOPE.
AND I DON'T KNOW IF YOU'VE NOTICED, BUT THAT STINK IS GETTING PRETTY INTENSE.
WHAT'S THAT ALL ABOUT?
BE MINDFUL OF THE SUBTLETIES.
THAT SMELL IS THE REASON WE CAME HERE.
WELL,
FRICKEN,
YIPPEE!

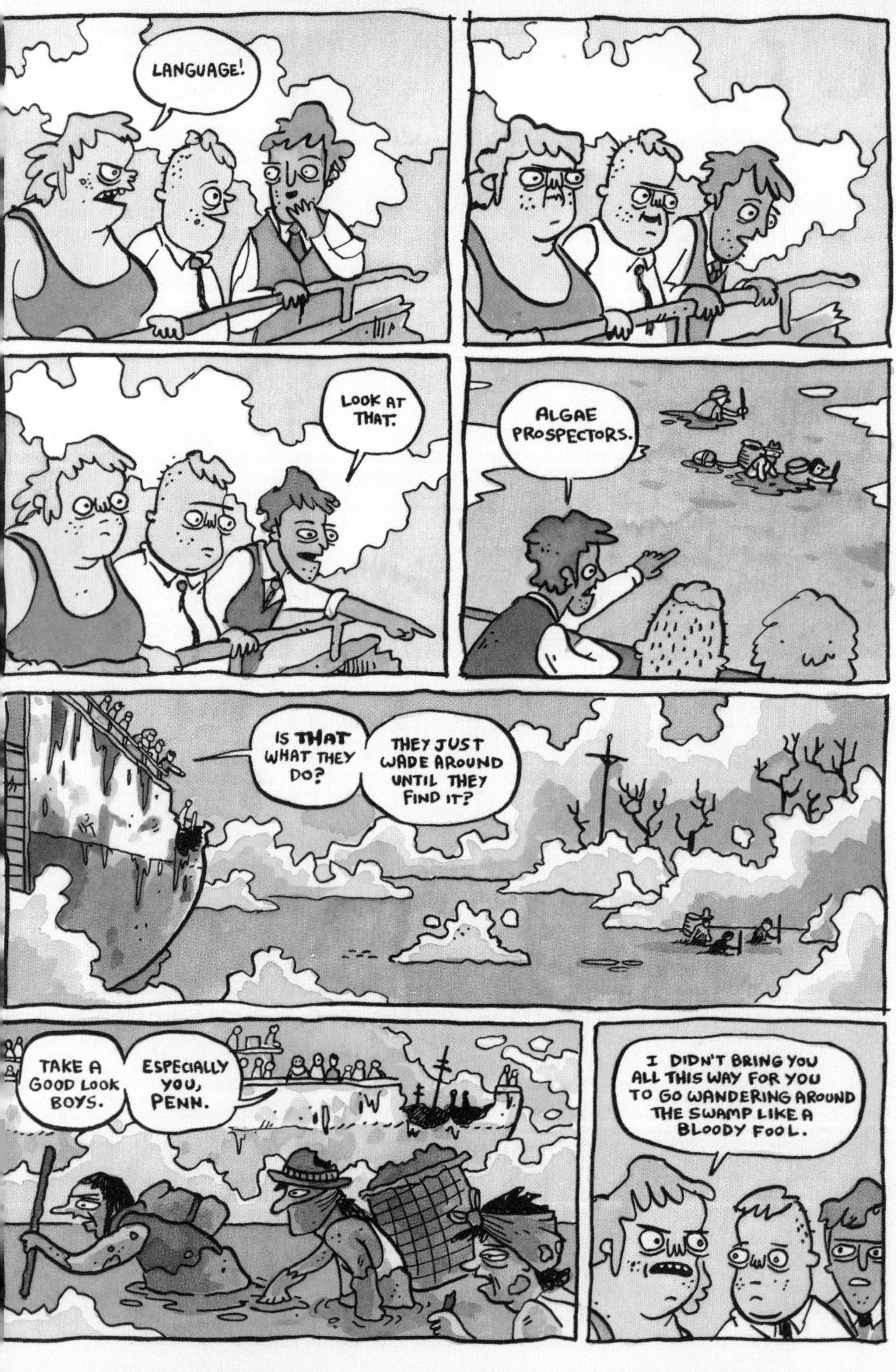
LANGUAGE!
LOOK AT THAT.
ALGAE PROSPECTORS.
IS THAT WHAT THEY DO?
THEY JUST WADE AROUND UNTIL THEY FIND IT?
TAKE A GOOD LOOK BOYS.
ESPECIALLY YOU, PENN.
I DIDN'T BRING YOU ALL THIS WAY FOR YOU TO GO WANDERING AROUND THE SWAMP LIKE A BLOODY FOOL.

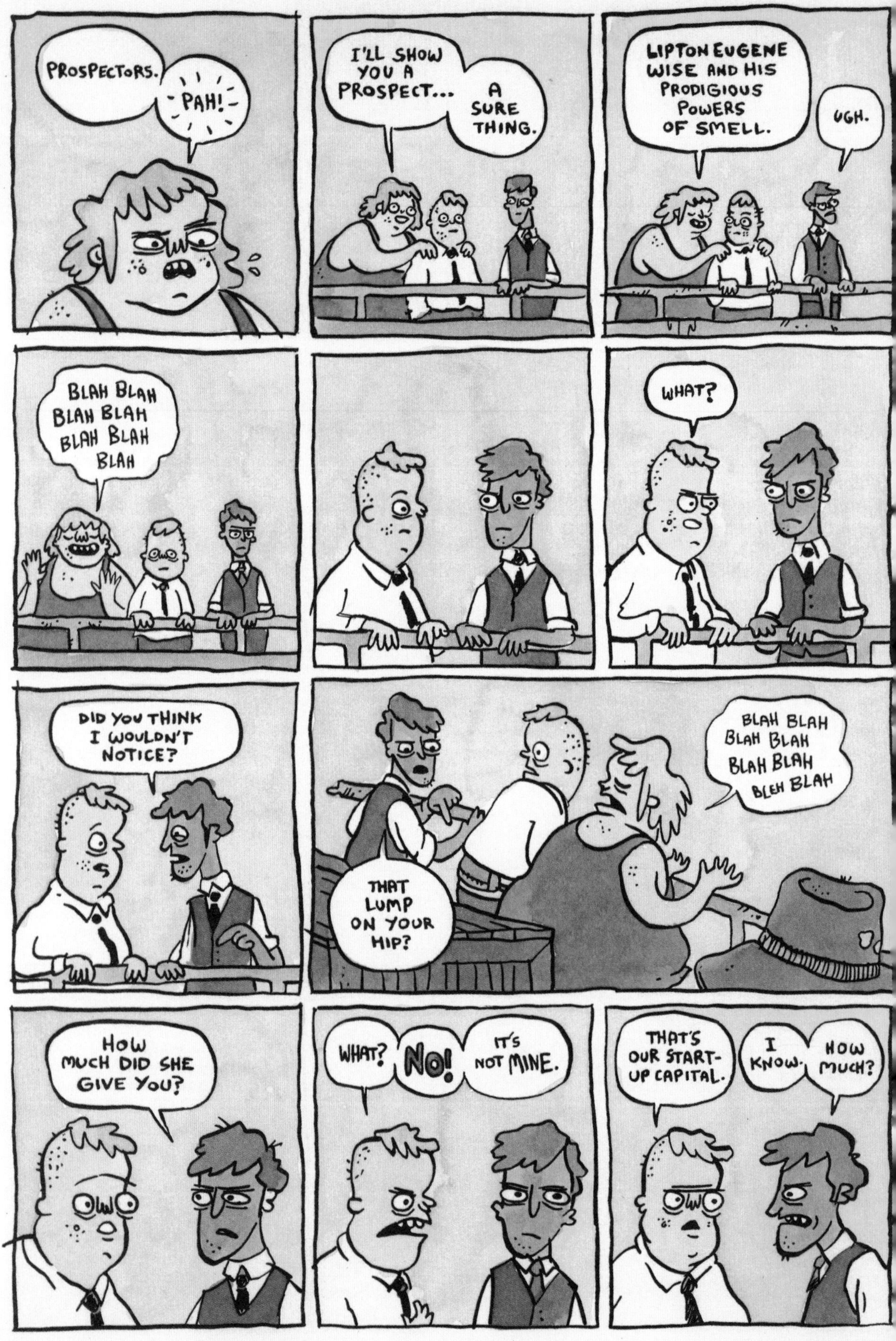
PROSPECTORS.
PAH!
I'LL SHOW YOU A PROSPECT...
A SURE THING.
LIPTON EUGENE WISE AND HIS PRODIGIOUS POWERS OF SMELL.
UGH.
BLAH BLAH BLAH BLAH BLAH BLAH BLAH
WHAT?
DID YOU THINK I WOULDN'T NOTICE?
THAT LUMP ON YOUR HIP?
BLAH BLAH BLAH BLAH BLAH BLAH BLEH BLAH
HOW MUCH DID SHE GIVE YOU?
WHAT?
NO!
IT'S NOT MINE.
THAT'S OUR START-UP CAPITAL.
I KNOW.
HOW MUCH?

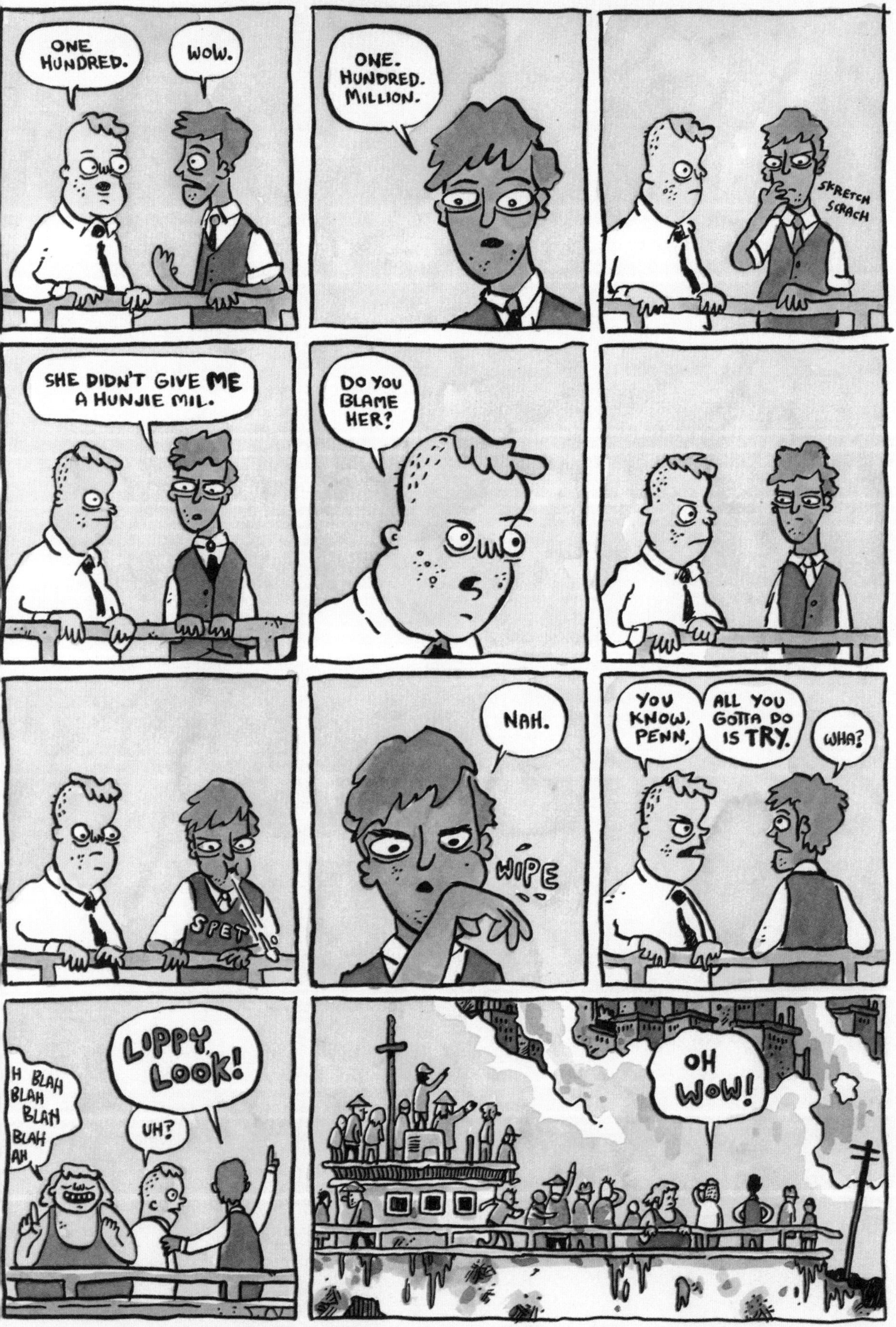

ONE HUNDRED.
WOW.
ONE. HUNDRED. MILLION.
SKRETCH SCRACH
SHE DIDN'T GIVE ME A HUNJIE MIL.
DO YOU BLAME HER?
SPET
NAH.
WIPE
YOU KNOW, PENN,
ALL YOU GOTTA DO IS TRY.
WHA?
H BLAH BLAH BLAH BLAH AH
LIPPY, LOOK!
UH?
OH WOW!

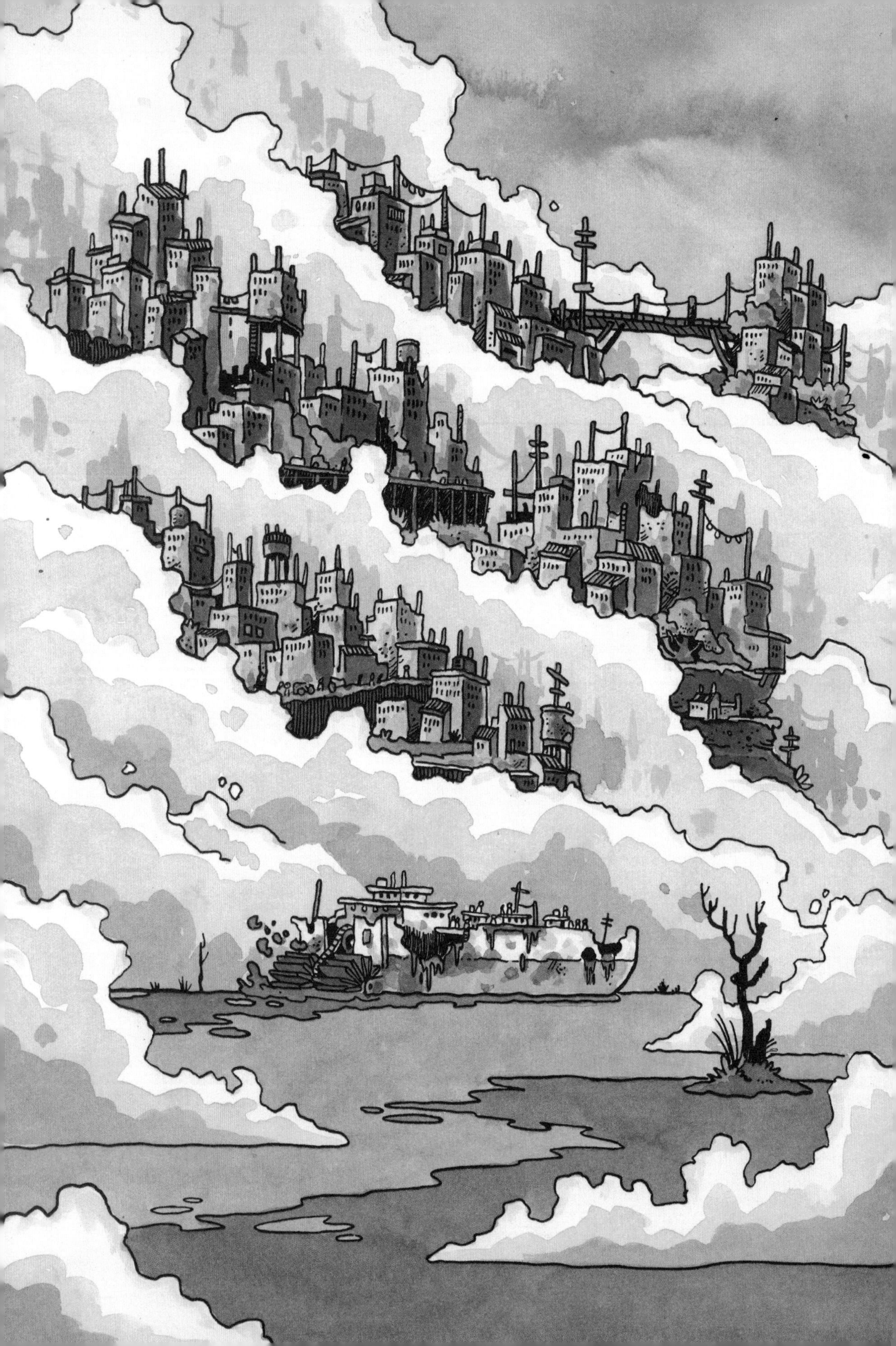

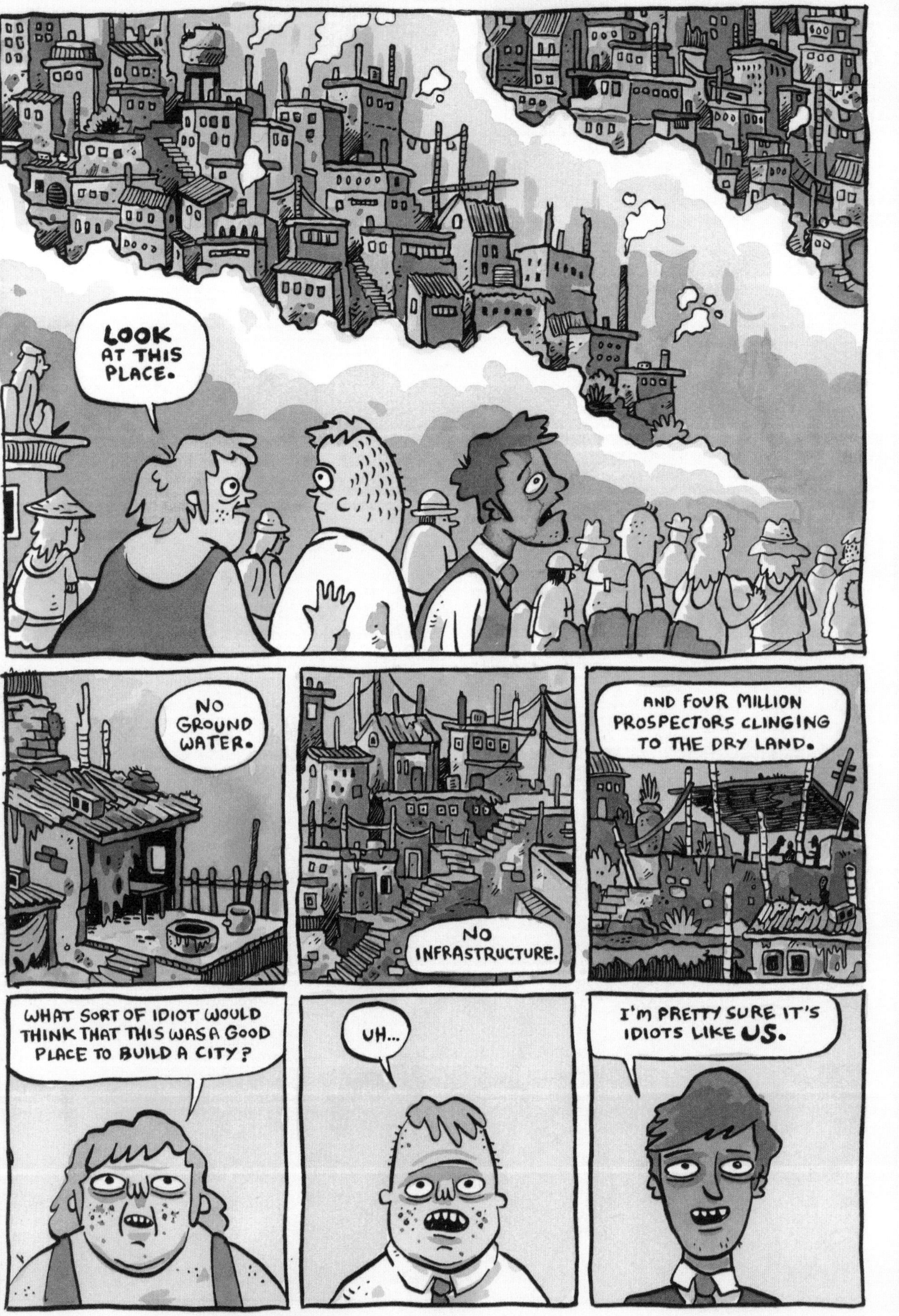
LOOK AT THIS PLACE.
NO GROUND WATER.
NO INFRASTRUCTURE.
AND FOUR MILLION PROSPECTORS CLINGING TO THE DRY LAND.
WHAT SORT OF IDIOT WOULD THINK THAT THIS WAS A GOOD PLACE TO BUILD A CITY?
UH...
I'M PRETTY SURE IT'S IDIOTS LIKE US.

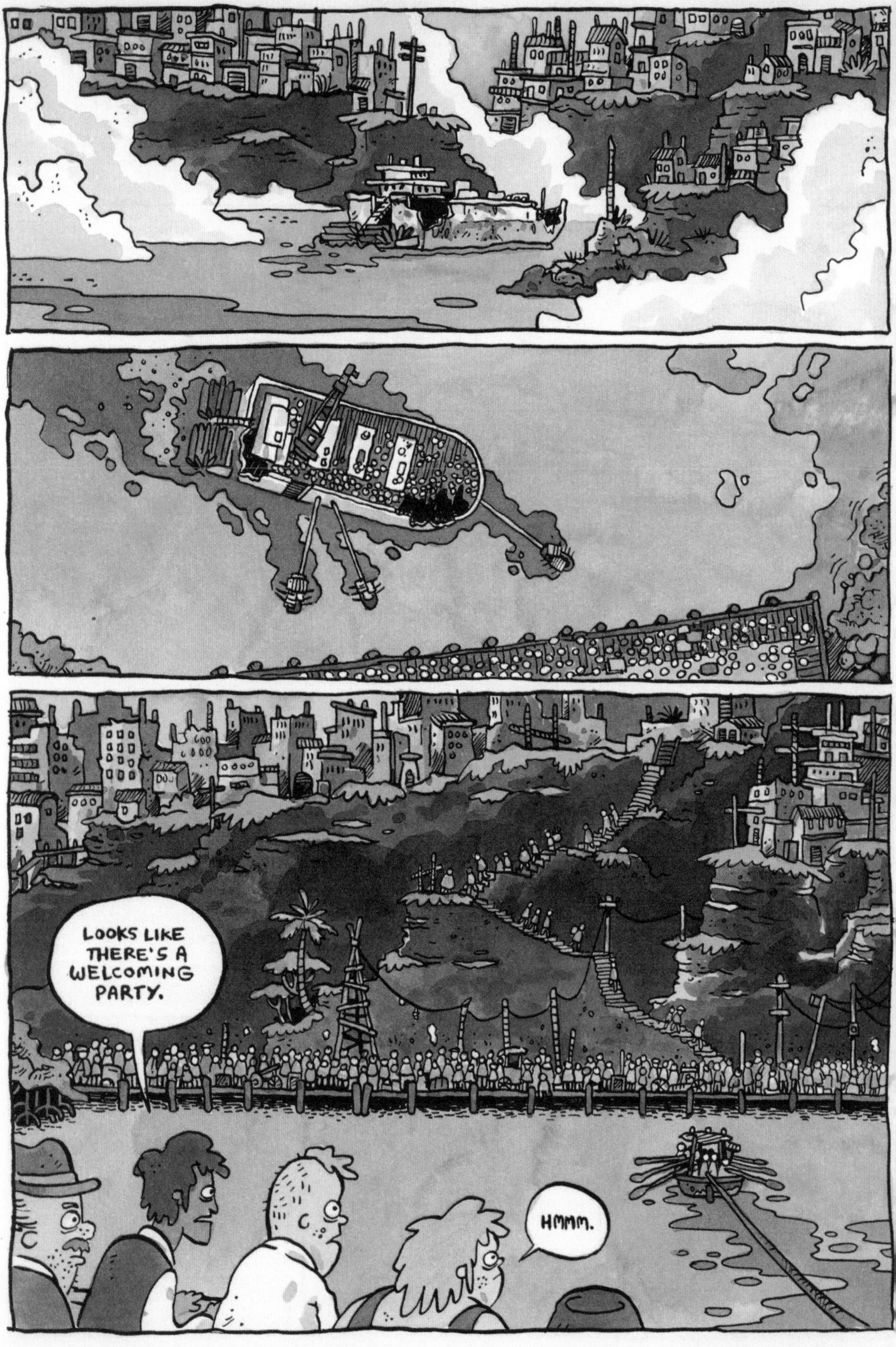
LOOKS LIKE THERE'S A WELCOMING PARTY.
HMMM.

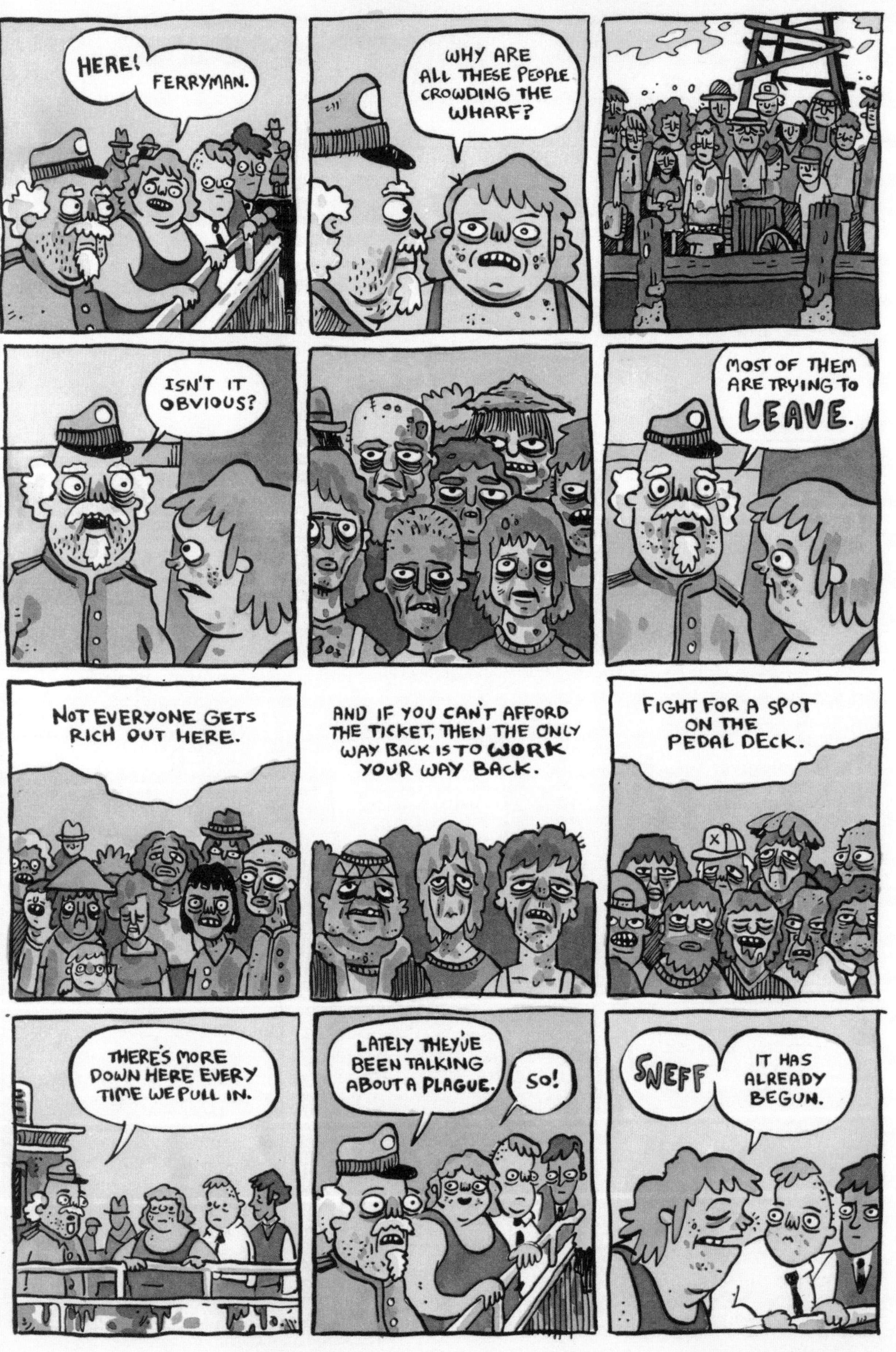

HERE!
FERRYMAN.
WHY ARE ALL THESE PEOPLE CROWDING THE WHARF?
ISN'T IT OBVIOUS?
MOST OF THEM ARE TRYING TO LEAVE.
NOT EVERYONE GETS RICH OUT HERE.
AND IF YOU CAN'T AFFORD THE TICKET, THEN THE ONLY WAY BACK IS TO WORK YOUR WAY BACK.
FIGHT FOR A SPOT ON THE PEDAL DECK.
THERE'S MORE DOWN HERE EVERY TIME WE PULL IN.
LATELY THEY'VE BEEN TALKING ABOUT A PLAGUE.
SO!
SNEFF
IT HAS ALREADY BEGUN.

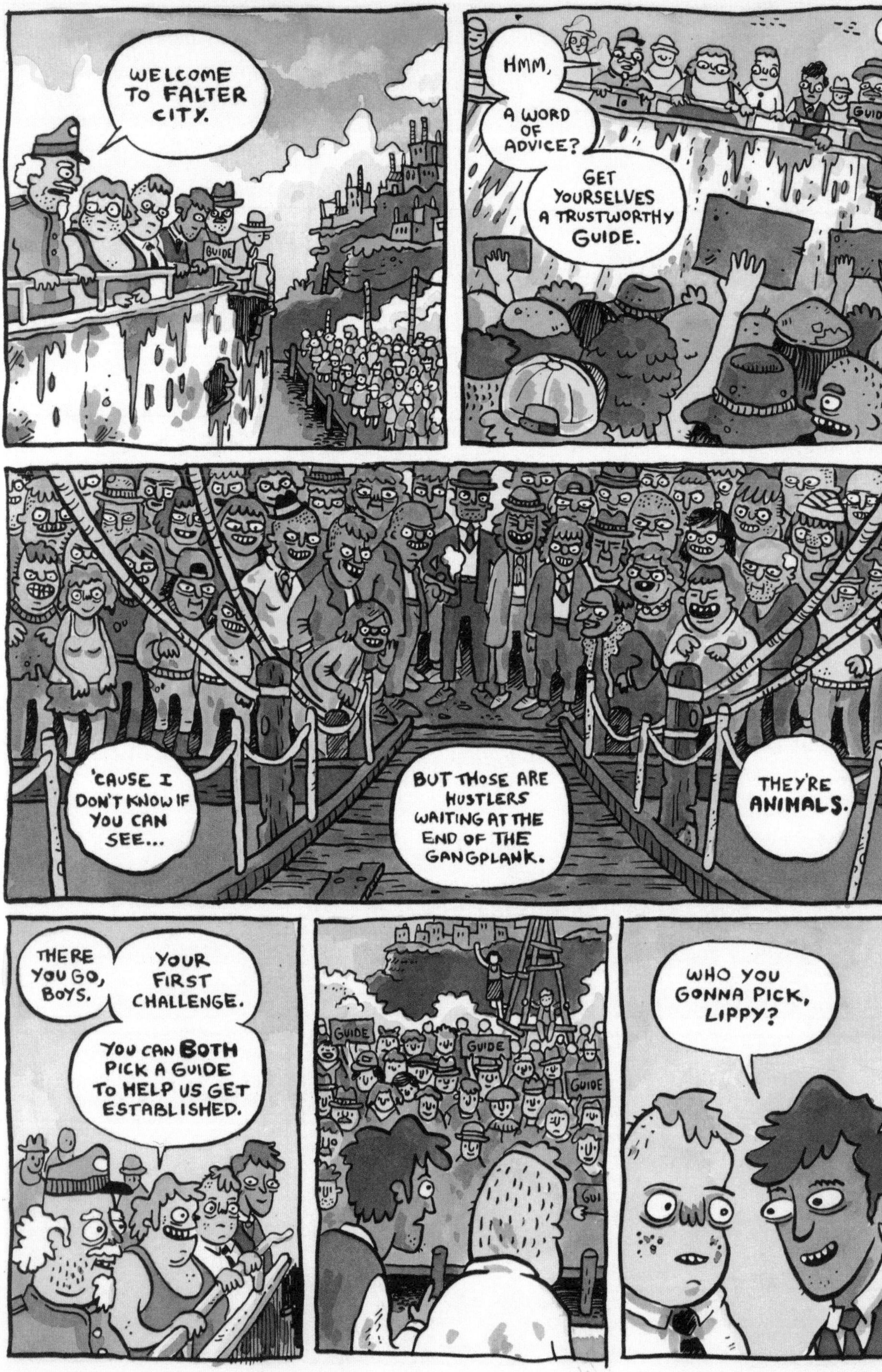
WELCOME TO FALTER CITY.
GUIDE
HMM,
A WORD OF ADVICE?
GET YOURSELVES A TRUSTWORTHY GUIDE.
?
GUIDE
'CAUSE I DON'T KNOW IF YOU CAN SEE...
BUT THOSE ARE HUSTLERS WAITING AT THE END OF THE GANGPLANK.
THEY'RE ANIMALS.
THERE YOU GO, BOYS.
YOUR FIRST CHALLENGE.
YOU CAN BOTH PICK A GUIDE TO HELP US GET ESTABLISHED.
GUIDE
GUIDE
GUIDE
WHO YOU GONNA PICK, LIPPY?

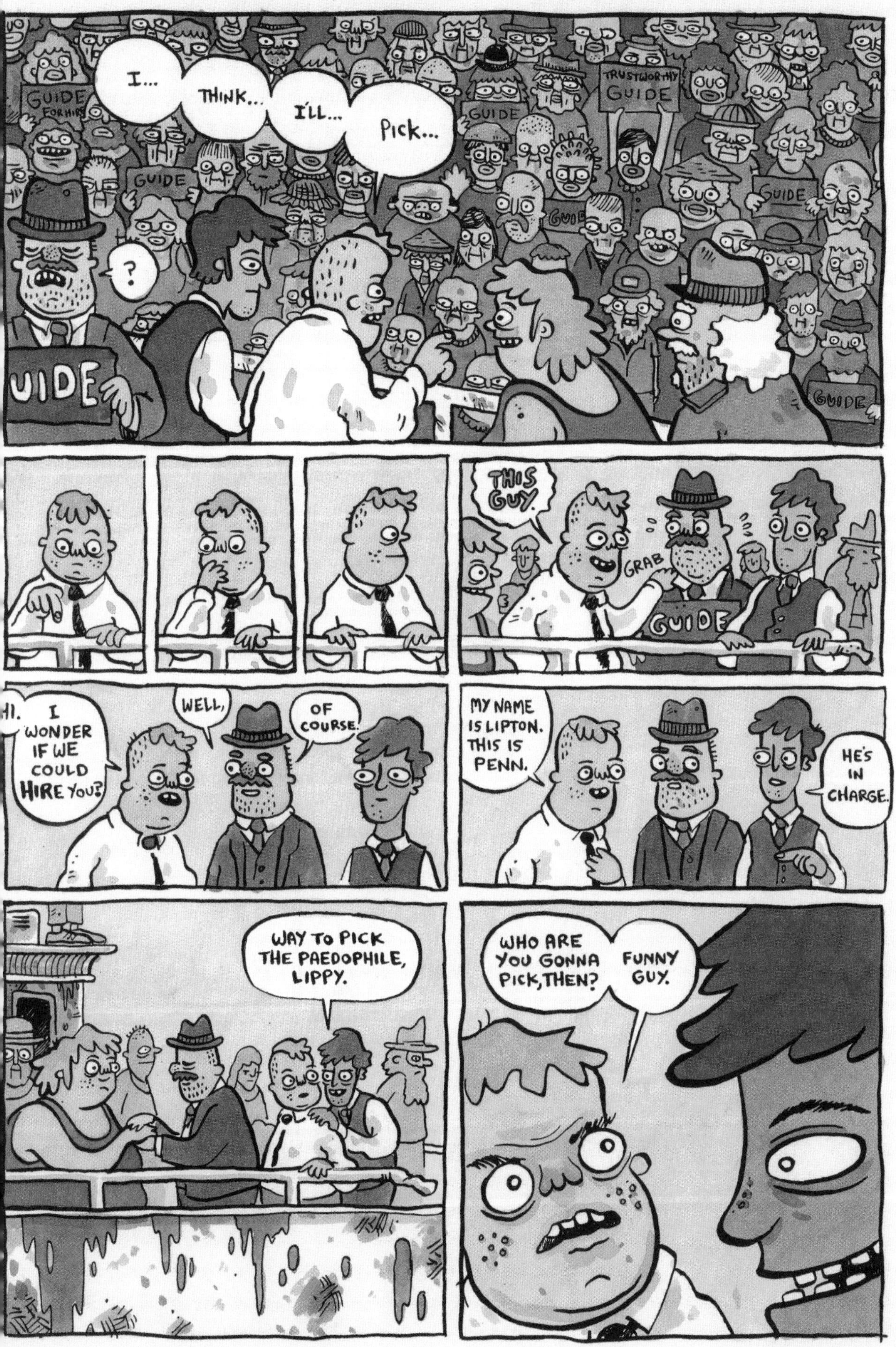

GUIDE FOR HIRE
I... THINK... I'LL... PICK...
GUIDE
TRUSTWORTHY GUIDE
GUIDE
GUIDE
GUIDE
GUIDE
?
UIDE
GUIDE
THIS GUY.
GRAB
GUIDE
HI. I WONDER IF WE COULD HIRE YOU?
WELL,
OF COURSE.
MY NAME IS LIPTON. THIS IS PENN.
HE'S IN CHARGE.
WAY TO PICK THE PAEDOPHILE, LIPPY.
WHO ARE YOU GONNA PICK, THEN?
FUNNY GUY.

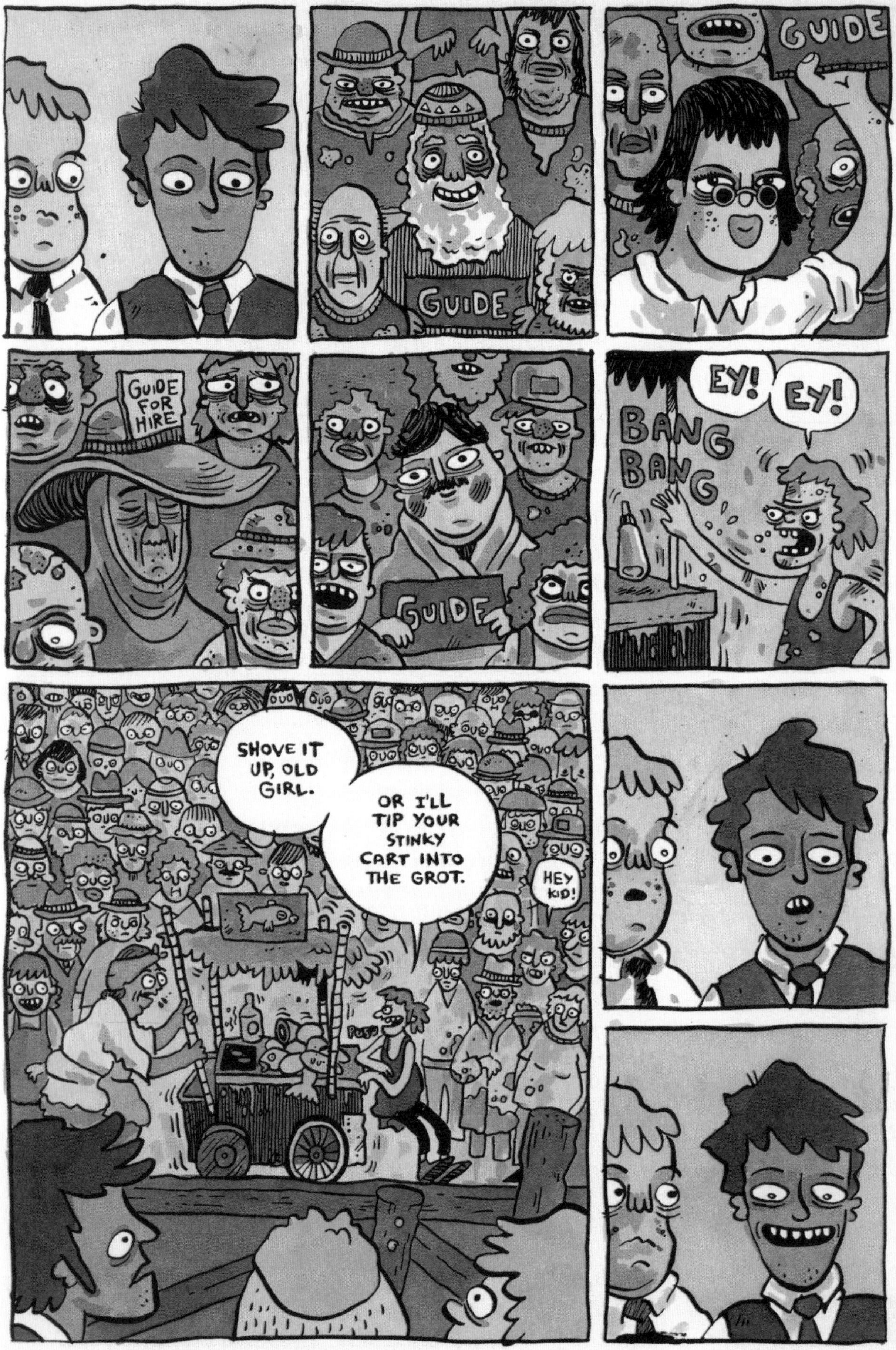
GUIDE
GUIDE
GUIDE FOR HIRE
GUIDE
EY!
EY!
BANG BANG
SHOVE IT UP, OLD GIRL.
OR I'LL TIP YOUR STINKY CART INTO THE GROT.
HEY KID!

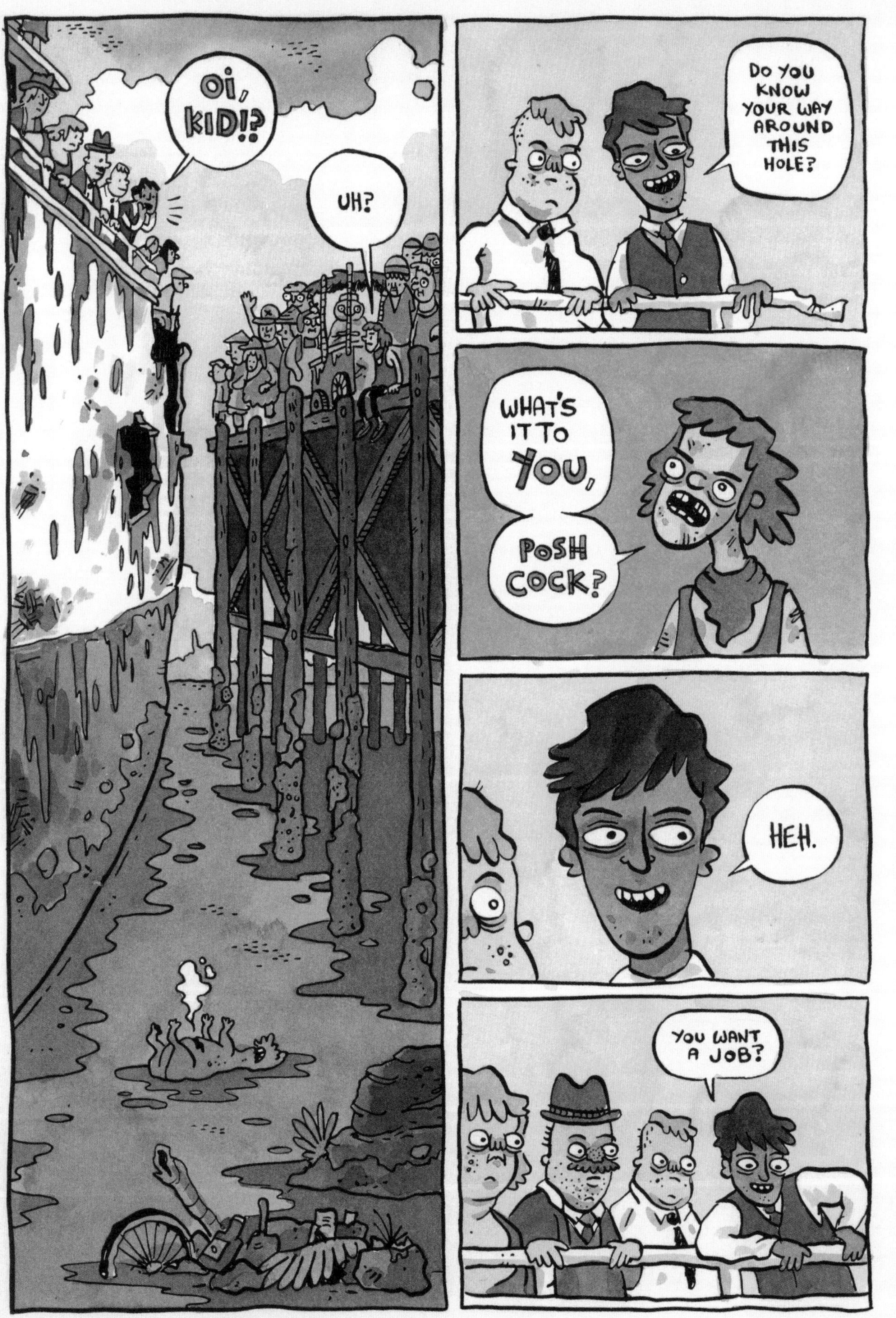
OI, KID!?
UH?
DO YOU KNOW YOUR WAY AROUND THIS HOLE?
WHAT'S IT TO YOU,
POSH COCK?
HEH.
YOU WANT A JOB?

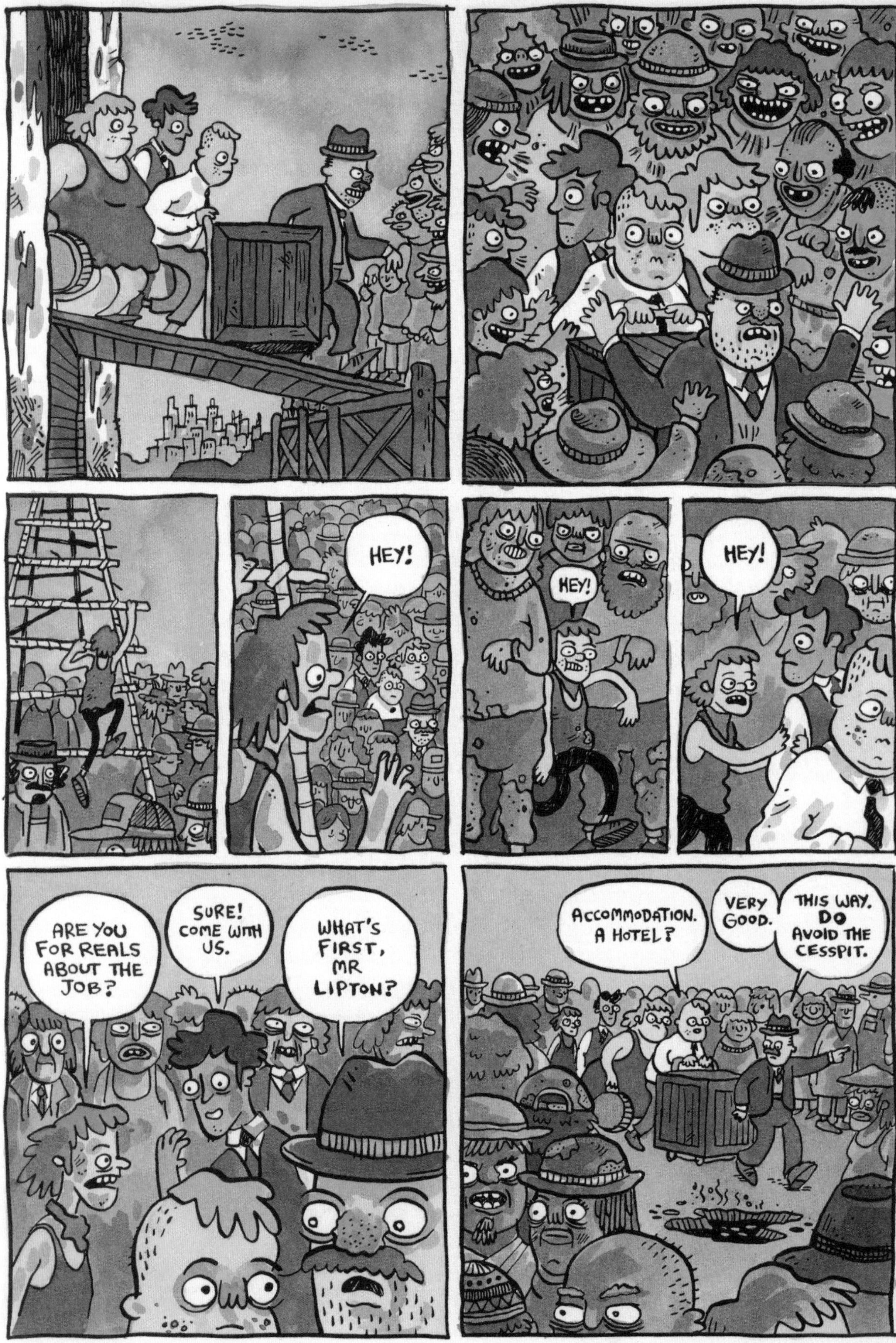
HEY!
HEY!
HEY!
ARE YOU FOR REALS ABOUT THE JOB?
SURE! COME WITH US.
WHAT'S FIRST, MR LIPTON?
ACCOMMODATION. A HOTEL?
VERY GOOD.
THIS WAY. DO AVOID THE CESSPIT.

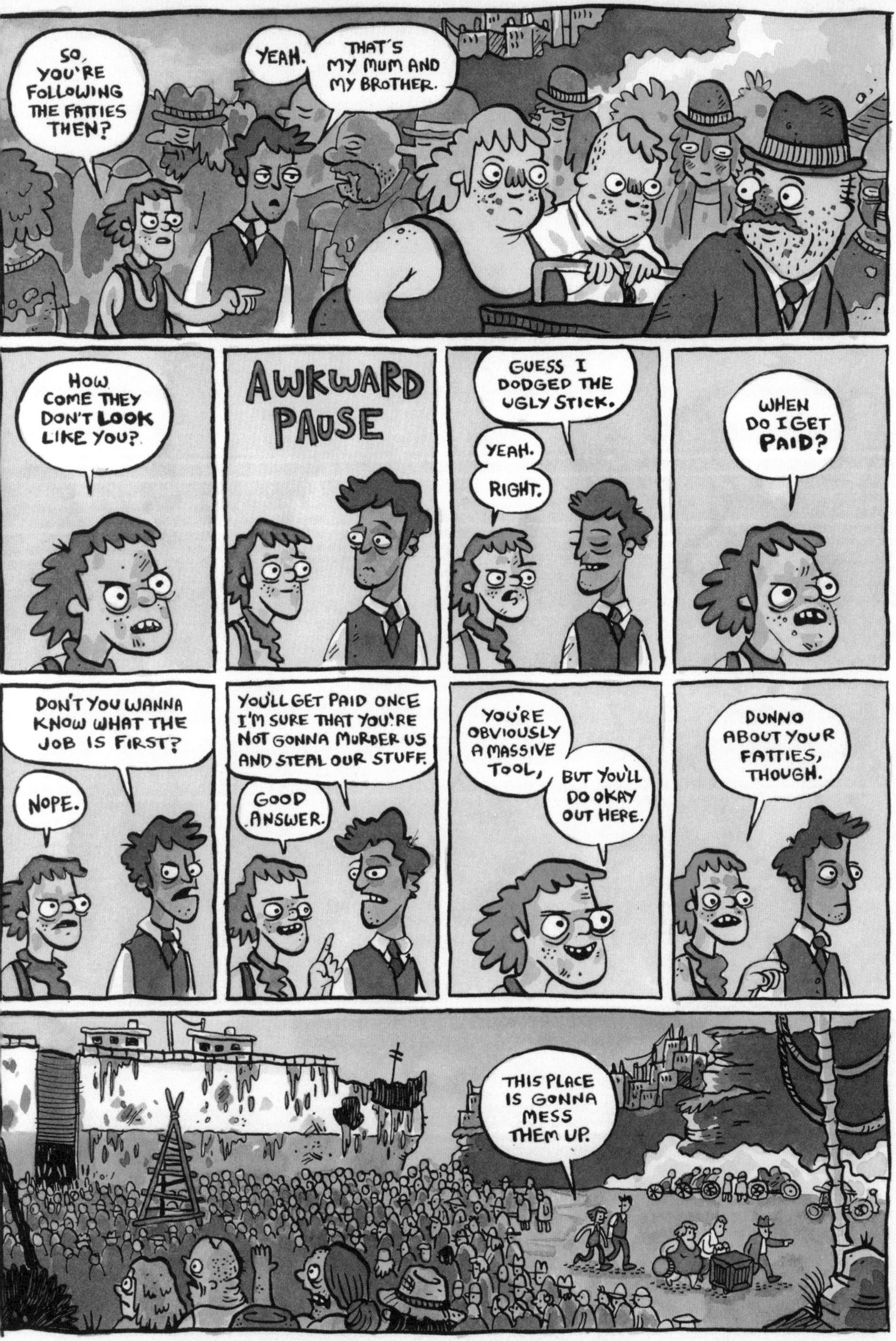
SO, YOU'RE FOLLOWING THE FATTIES THEN?
YEAH.
THAT'S MY MUM AND MY BROTHER.
HOW COME THEY DON'T LOOK LIKE YOU?
AWKWARD PAUSE
GUESS I DODGED THE UGLY STICK.
YEAH.
RIGHT.
WHEN DO I GET PAID?
DON'T YOU WANNA KNOW WHAT THE JOB IS FIRST?
NOPE.
YOU'LL GET PAID ONCE I'M SURE THAT YOU'RE NOT GONNA MURDER US AND STEAL OUR STUFF.
GOOD ANSWER.
YOU'RE OBVIOUSLY A MASSIVE TOOL,
BUT YOU'LL DO OKAY OUT HERE.
DUNNO ABOUT YOUR FATTIES, THOUGH.
THIS PLACE IS GONNA MESS THEM UP.

PART
TWO

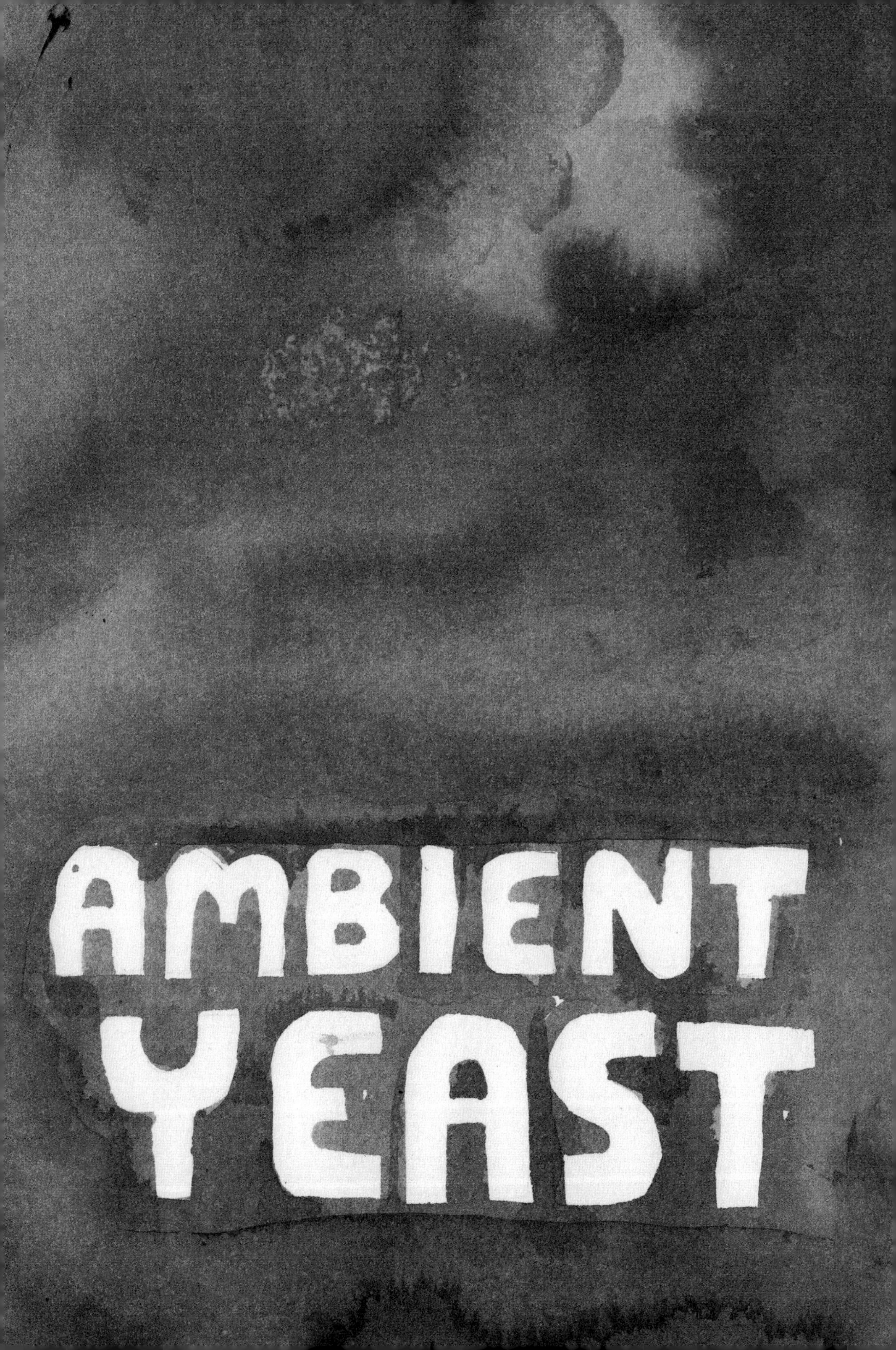
AMBIENT
YEAST

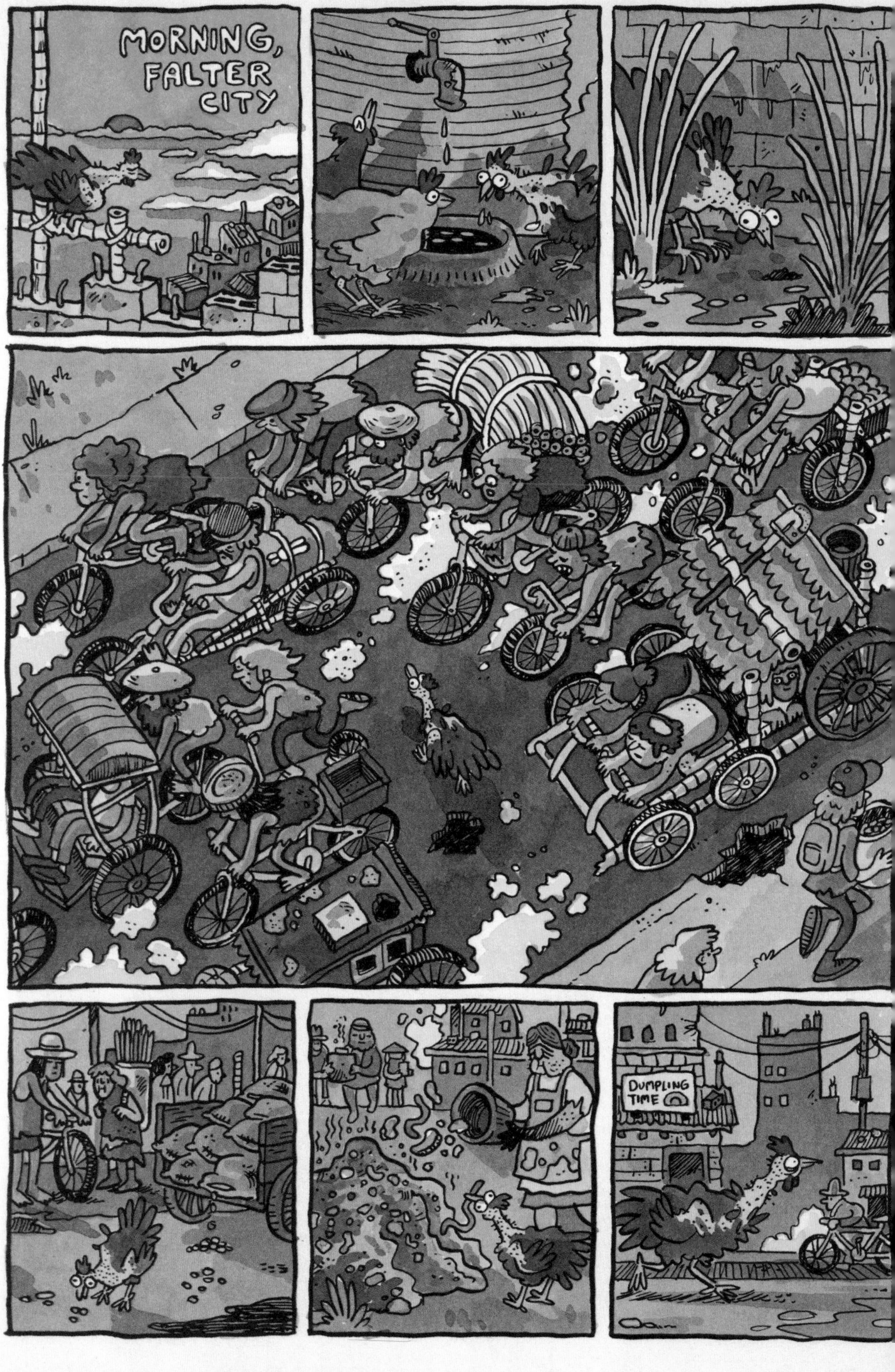
MORNING, FALTER CITY
DUMPLING TIME

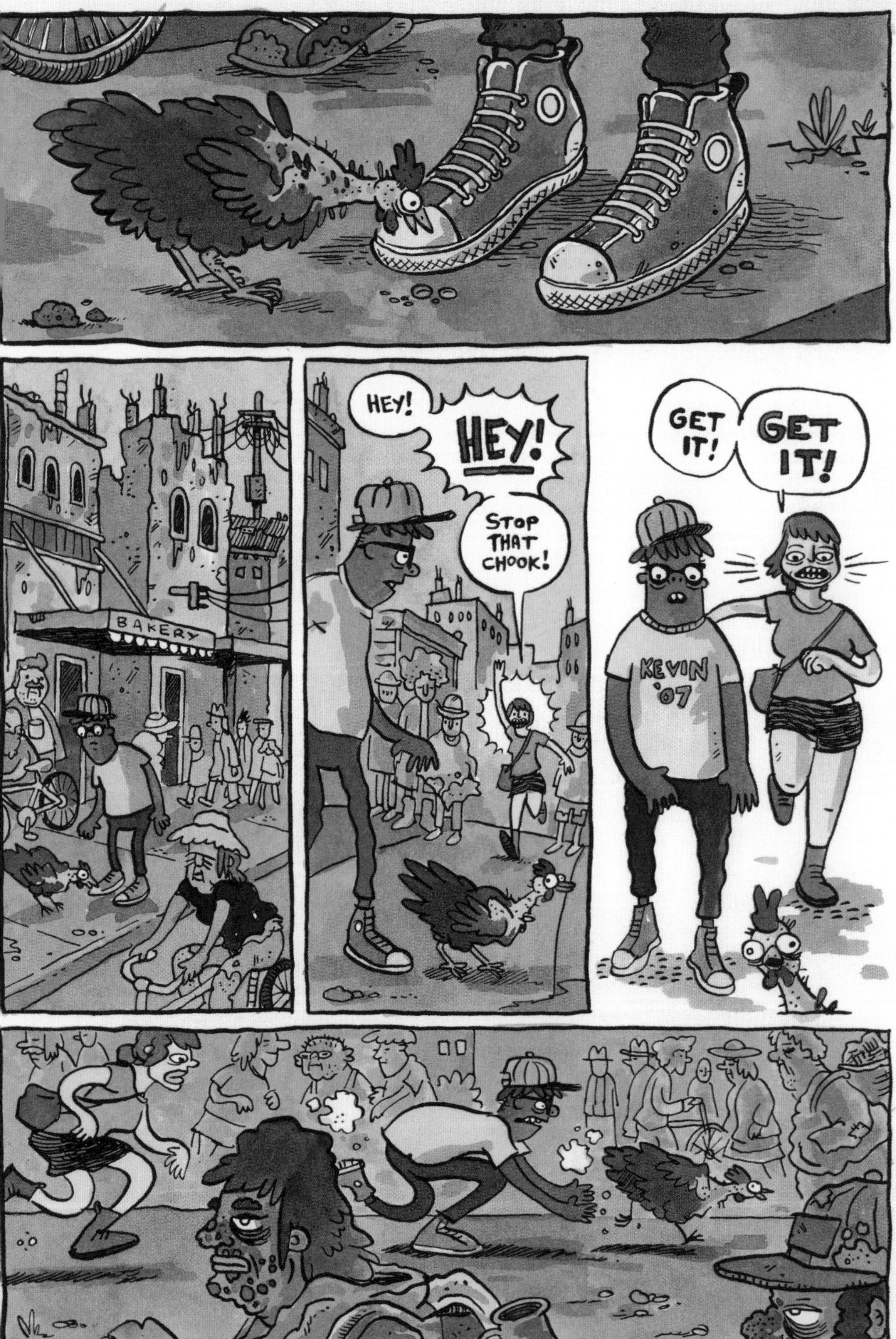
BAKERY
HEY!
HEY!
STOP THAT CHOOK!
GET IT!
GET IT!
KEVIN '07

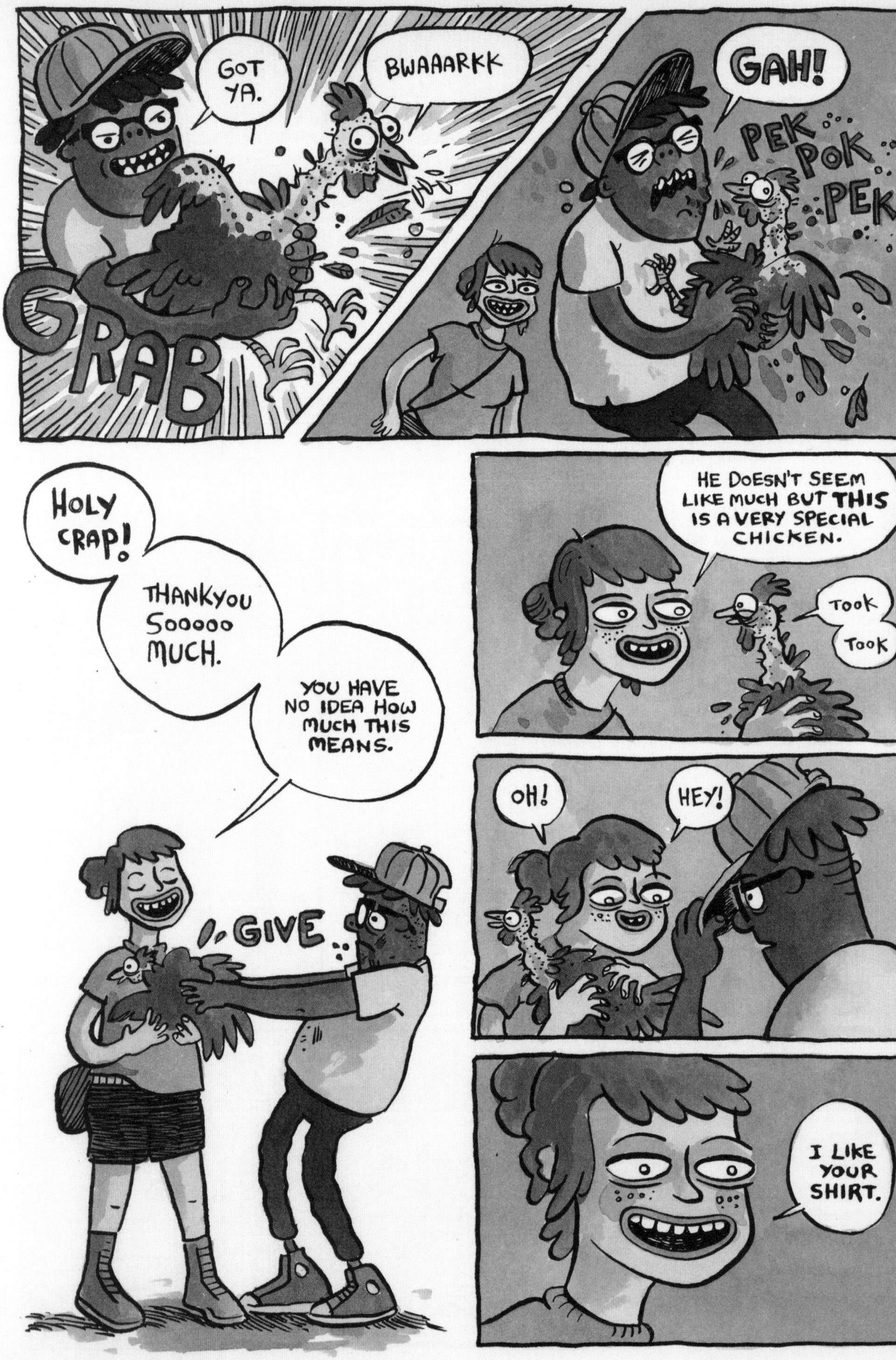
GOT YA.
BWAAARKK
GRAB
GAH!
PEK POK PEK
HOLY CRAP!
THANKYOU SOOOOO MUCH.
YOU HAVE NO IDEA HOW MUCH THIS MEANS.
GIVE
HE DOESN'T SEEM LIKE MUCH BUT THIS IS A VERY SPECIAL CHICKEN.
TOOK
TOOK
OH!
HEY!
I LIKE YOUR SHIRT.

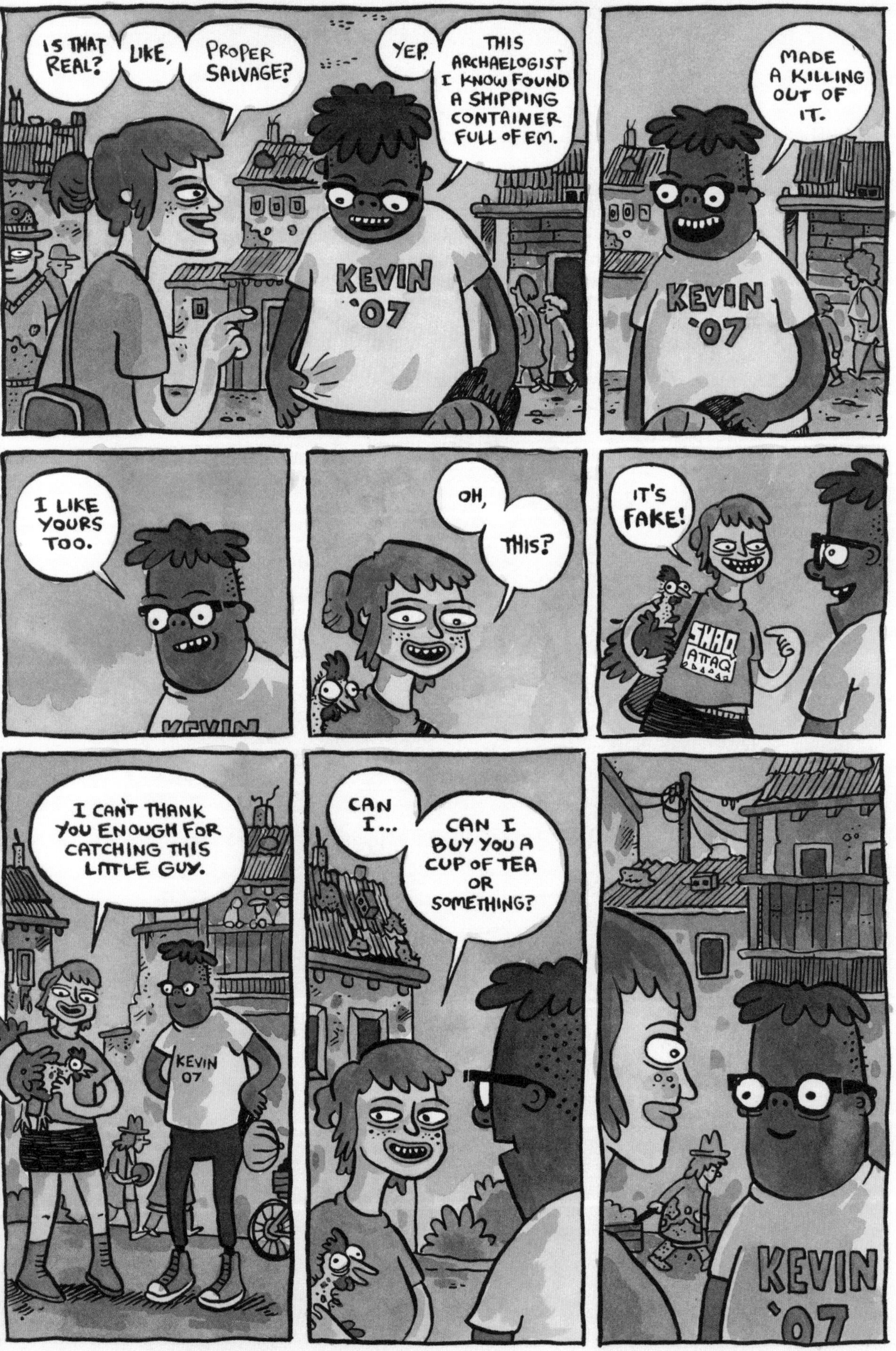
IS THAT REAL?
LIKE,
PROPER SALVAGE?
YEP.
THIS ARCHAELOGIST I KNOW FOUND A SHIPPING CONTAINER FULL OF EM.
KEVIN '07
MADE A KILLING OUT OF IT.
KEVIN '07
I LIKE YOURS TOO.
OH,
THIS?
IT'S FAKE!
SHAQ ATTAQ
I CAN'T THANK YOU ENOUGH FOR CATCHING THIS LITTLE GUY.
KEVIN 07
CAN I...
CAN I BUY YOU A CUP OF TEA OR SOMETHING?
KEVIN '07

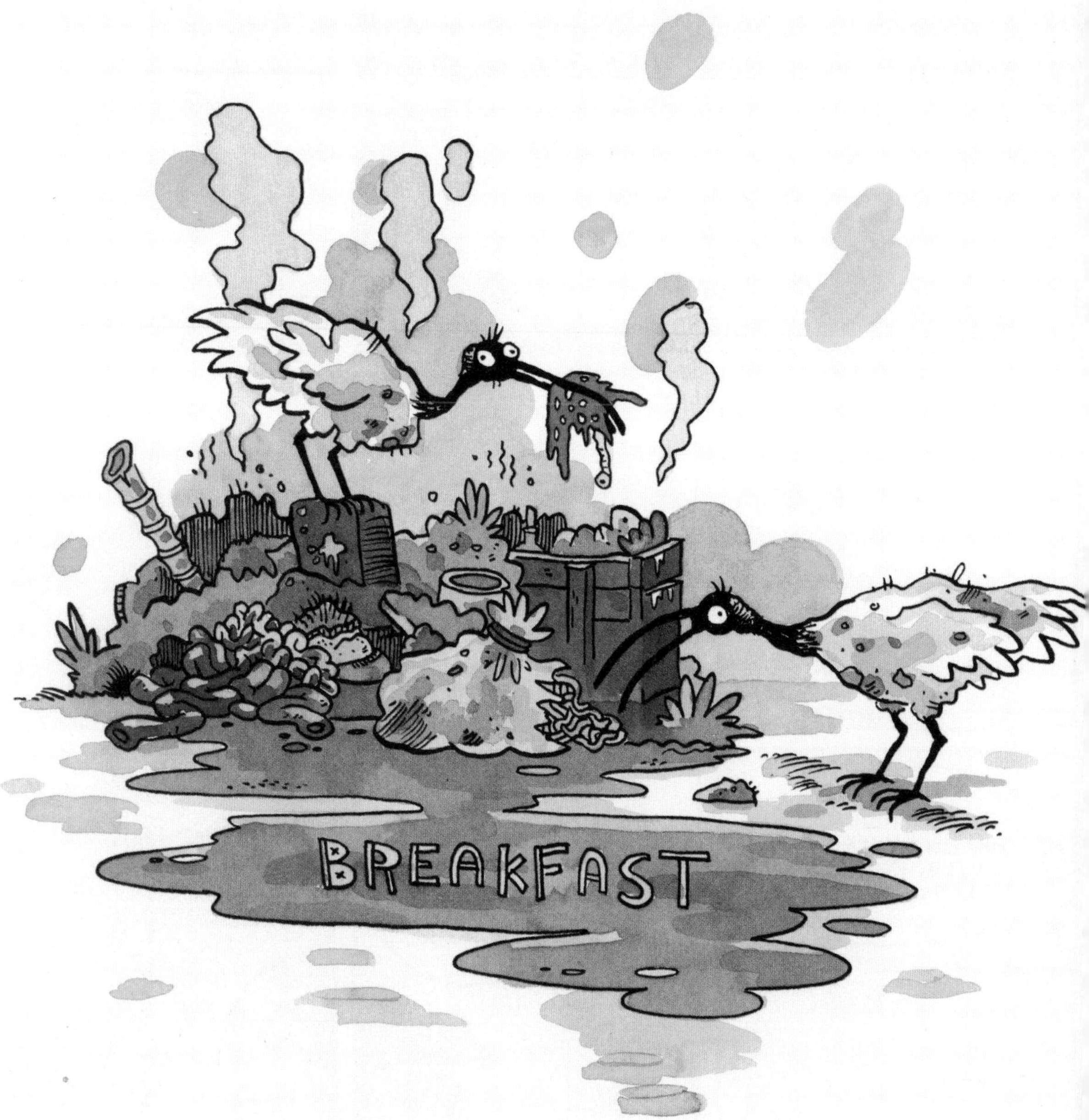
BREAKFAST

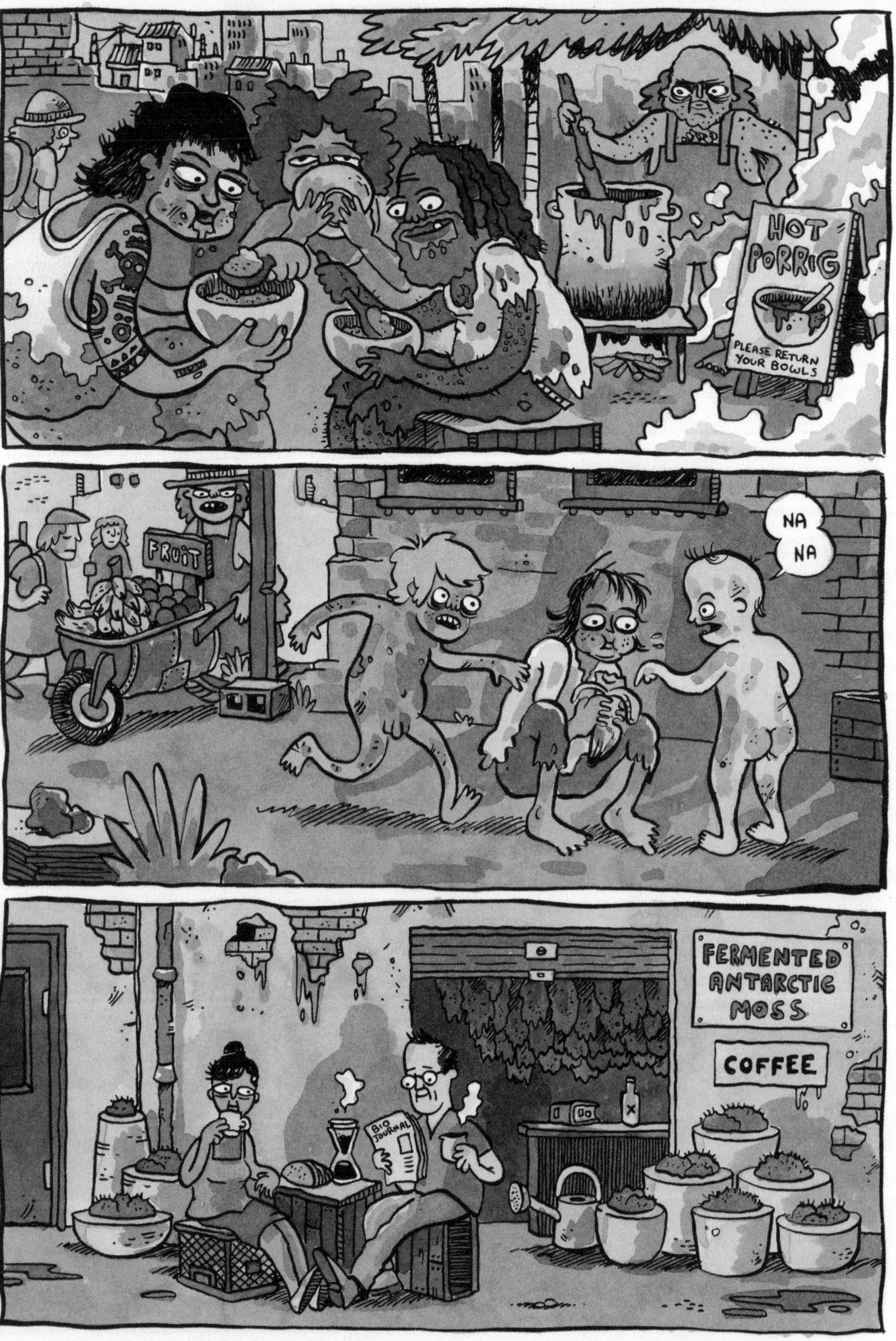
HOT PORRIG
PLEASE RETURN YOUR BOWLS
FRUIT
NA
NA
BIO JOURNAL
FERMENTED ANTARCTIC MOSS
COFFEE

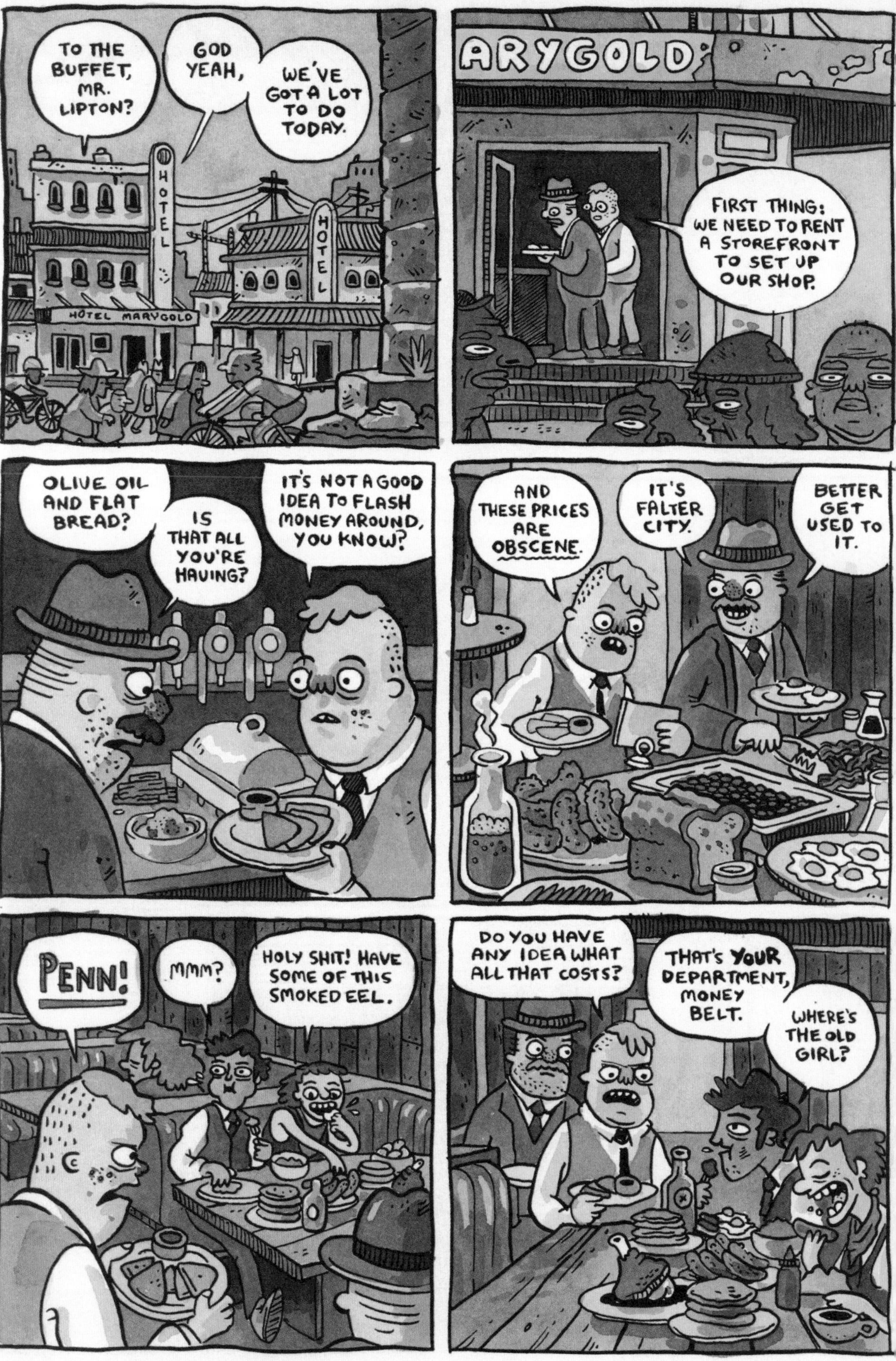
TO THE BUFFET, MR. LIPTON?
GOD YEAH,
WE'VE GOT A LOT TO DO TODAY.
HOTEL
HOTEL
HOTEL MARYGOLD
ARYGOLD
FIRST THING: WE NEED TO RENT A STOREFRONT TO SET UP OUR SHOP.
OLIVE OIL AND FLAT BREAD?
IS THAT ALL YOU'RE HAVING?
IT'S NOT A GOOD IDEA TO FLASH MONEY AROUND, YOU KNOW?
AND THESE PRICES ARE OBSCENE.
IT'S FALTER CITY.
BETTER GET USED TO IT.
PENN!
MMM?
HOLY SHIT! HAVE SOME OF THIS SMOKED EEL.
DO YOU HAVE ANY IDEA WHAT ALL THAT COSTS?
THAT'S YOUR DEPARTMENT, MONEY BELT.
WHERE'S THE OLD GIRL?

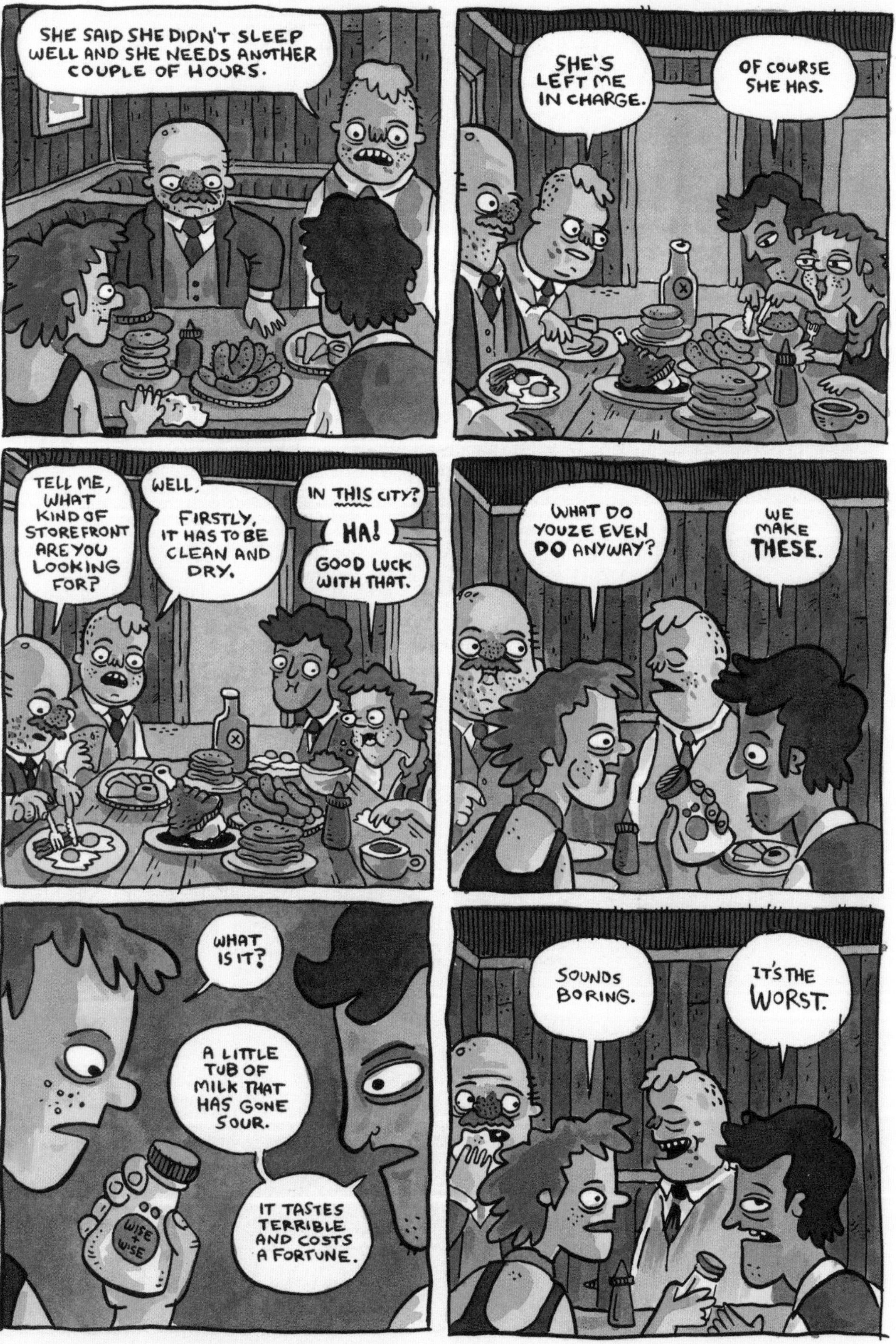
SHE SAID SHE DIDN'T SLEEP WELL AND SHE NEEDS ANOTHER COUPLE OF HOURS.
SHE'S LEFT ME IN CHARGE.
OF COURSE SHE HAS.
TELL ME, WHAT KIND OF STOREFRONT ARE YOU LOOKING FOR?
WELL,
FIRSTLY, IT HAS TO BE CLEAN AND DRY.
IN THIS CITY?
HA!
GOOD LUCK WITH THAT.
WHAT DO YOUZE EVEN DO ANYWAY?
WE MAKE THESE.
WHAT IS IT?
A LITTLE TUB OF MILK THAT HAS GONE SOUR.
IT TASTES TERRIBLE AND COSTS A FORTUNE.
WISE + WISE
SOUNDS BORING.
IT'S THE WORST.

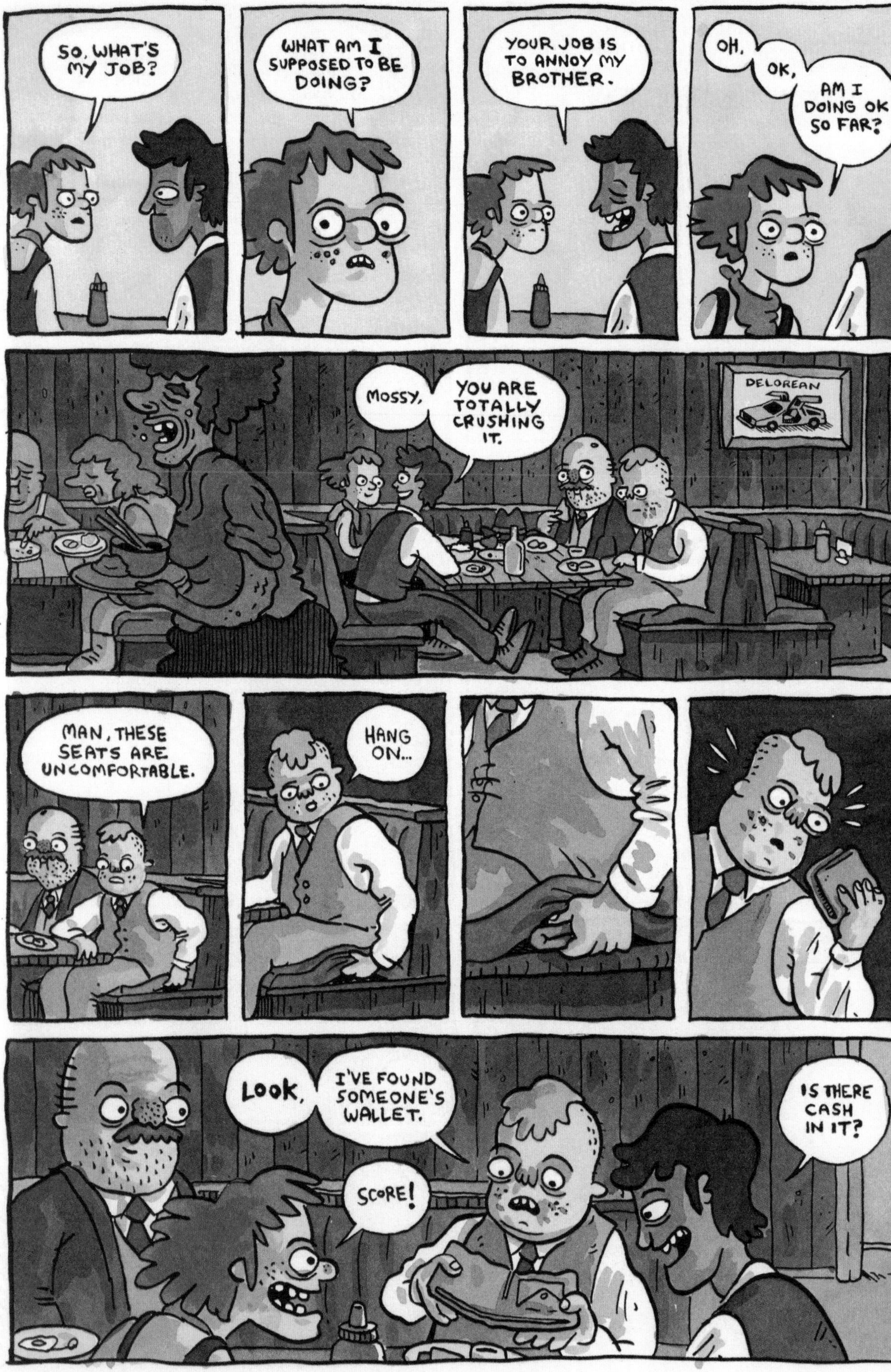
SO, WHAT'S MY JOB?
WHAT AM I SUPPOSED TO BE DOING?
YOUR JOB IS TO ANNOY MY BROTHER.
OH,
OK,
AM I DOING OK SO FAR?
MOSSY,
YOU ARE TOTALLY CRUSHING IT.
DELOREAN
MAN, THESE SEATS ARE UNCOMFORTABLE.
HANG ON...
LOOK,
I'VE FOUND SOMEONE'S WALLET.
SCORE!
IS THERE CASH IN IT?

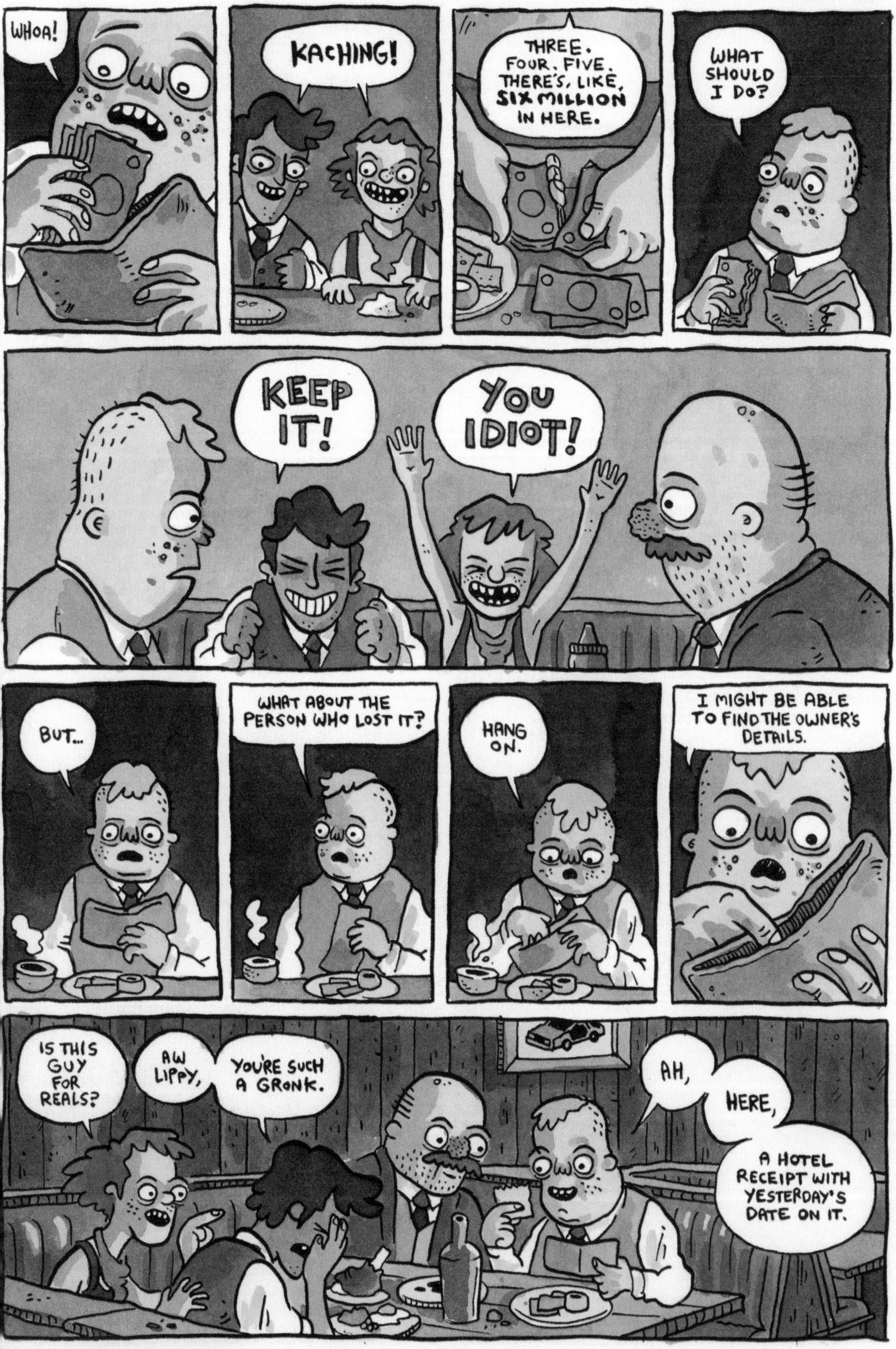
WHOA!
KACHING!
THREE. FOUR. FIVE. THERE'S, LIKE, SIX MILLION IN HERE.
WHAT SHOULD I DO?
KEEP IT!
YOU IDIOT!
BUT...
WHAT ABOUT THE PERSON WHO LOST IT?
HANG ON.
I MIGHT BE ABLE TO FIND THE OWNER'S DETAILS.
IS THIS GUY FOR REALS?
AW LIPPY,
YOU'RE SUCH A GRONK.
AH,
HERE,
A HOTEL RECEIPT WITH YESTERDAY'S DATE ON IT.

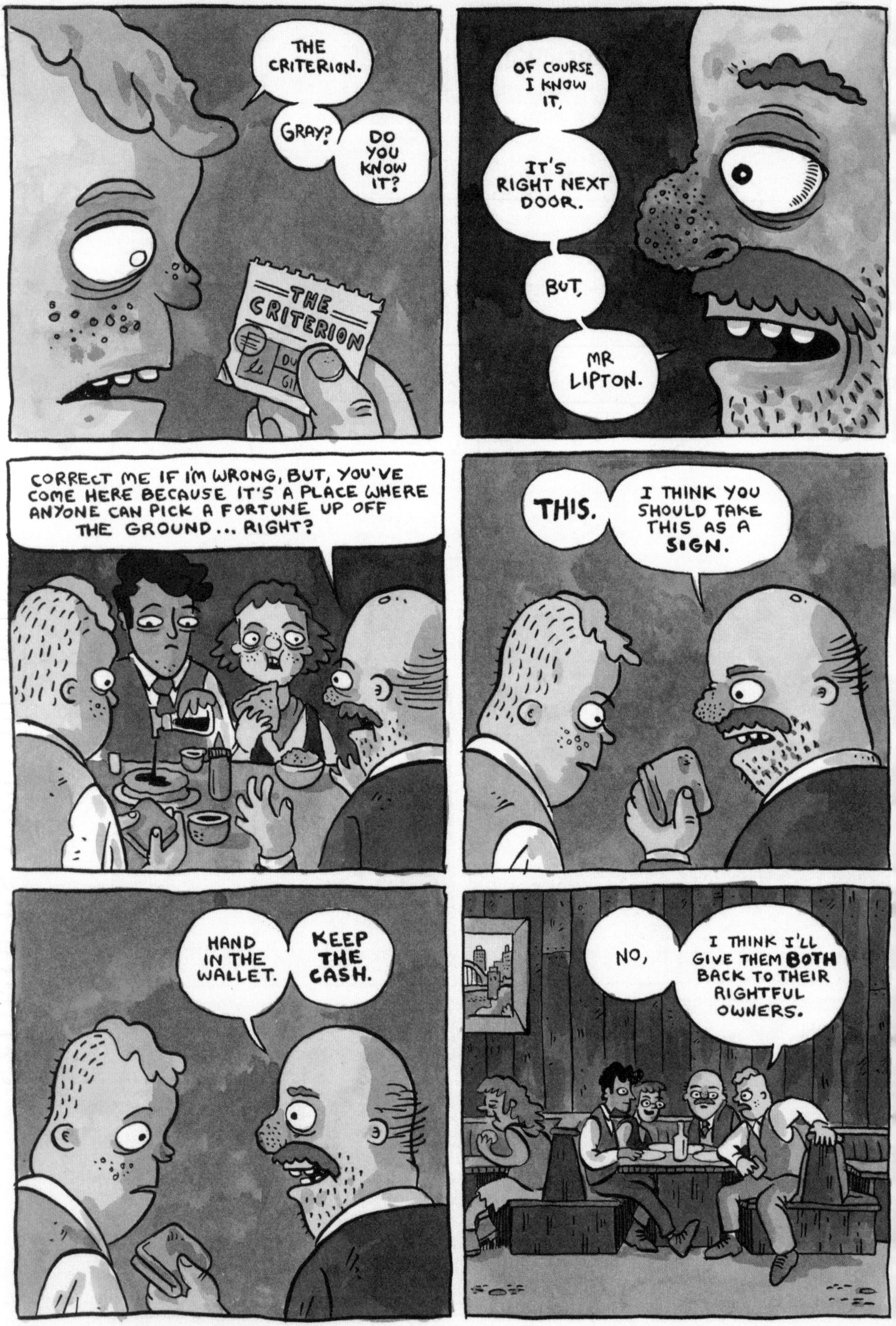
THE CRITERION.
GRAY?
DO YOU KNOW IT?
THE CRITERION
OF COURSE I KNOW IT,
IT'S RIGHT NEXT DOOR.
BUT,
MR LIPTON.
CORRECT ME IF I'M WRONG, BUT, YOU'VE COME HERE BECAUSE IT'S A PLACE WHERE ANYONE CAN PICK A FORTUNE UP OFF THE GROUND... RIGHT?
THIS.
I THINK YOU SHOULD TAKE THIS AS A SIGN.
HAND IN THE WALLET.
KEEP THE CASH.
NO,
I THINK I'LL GIVE THEM BOTH BACK TO THEIR RIGHTFUL OWNERS.

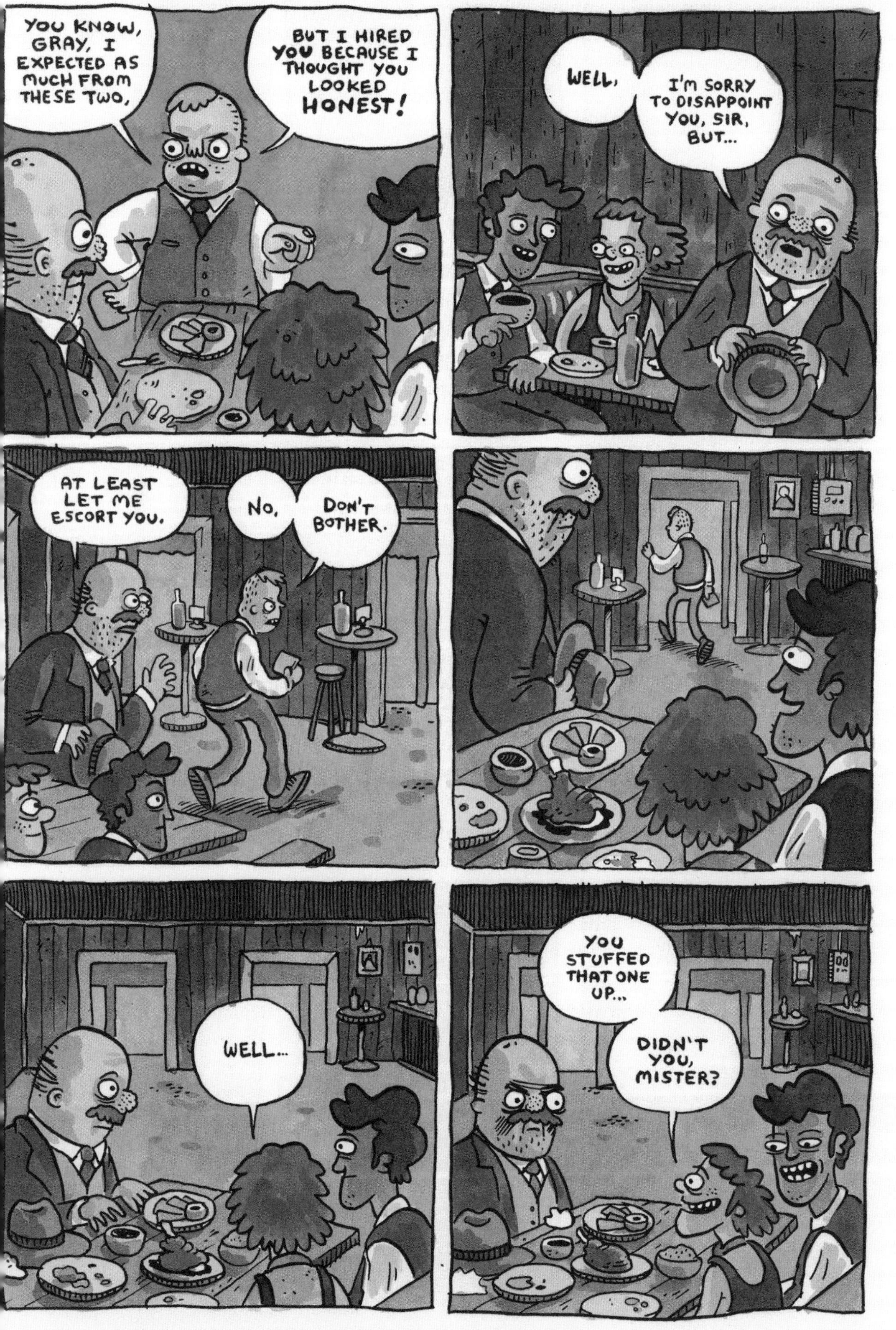
YOU KNOW, GRAY, I EXPECTED AS MUCH FROM THESE TWO,
BUT I HIRED YOU BECAUSE I THOUGHT YOU LOOKED HONEST!
WELL,
I'M SORRY TO DISAPPOINT YOU, SIR, BUT...
AT LEAST LET ME ESCORT YOU.
No,
DON'T BOTHER.
WELL...
YOU STUFFED THAT ONE UP...
DIDN'T YOU, MISTER?

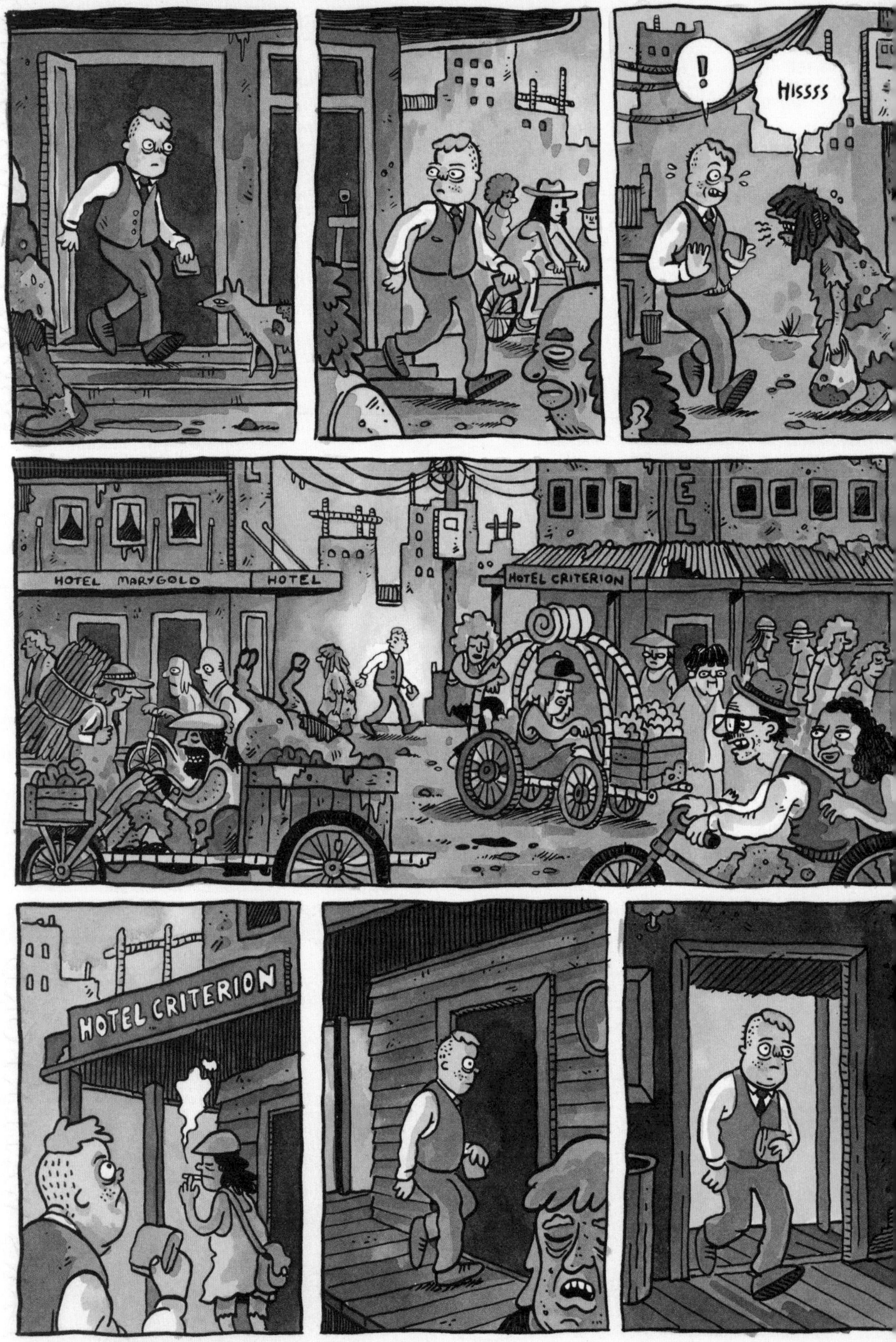

!
HISSSS
HOTEL MARYGOLD
HOTEL
HOTEL CRITERION
HOTEL CRITERION

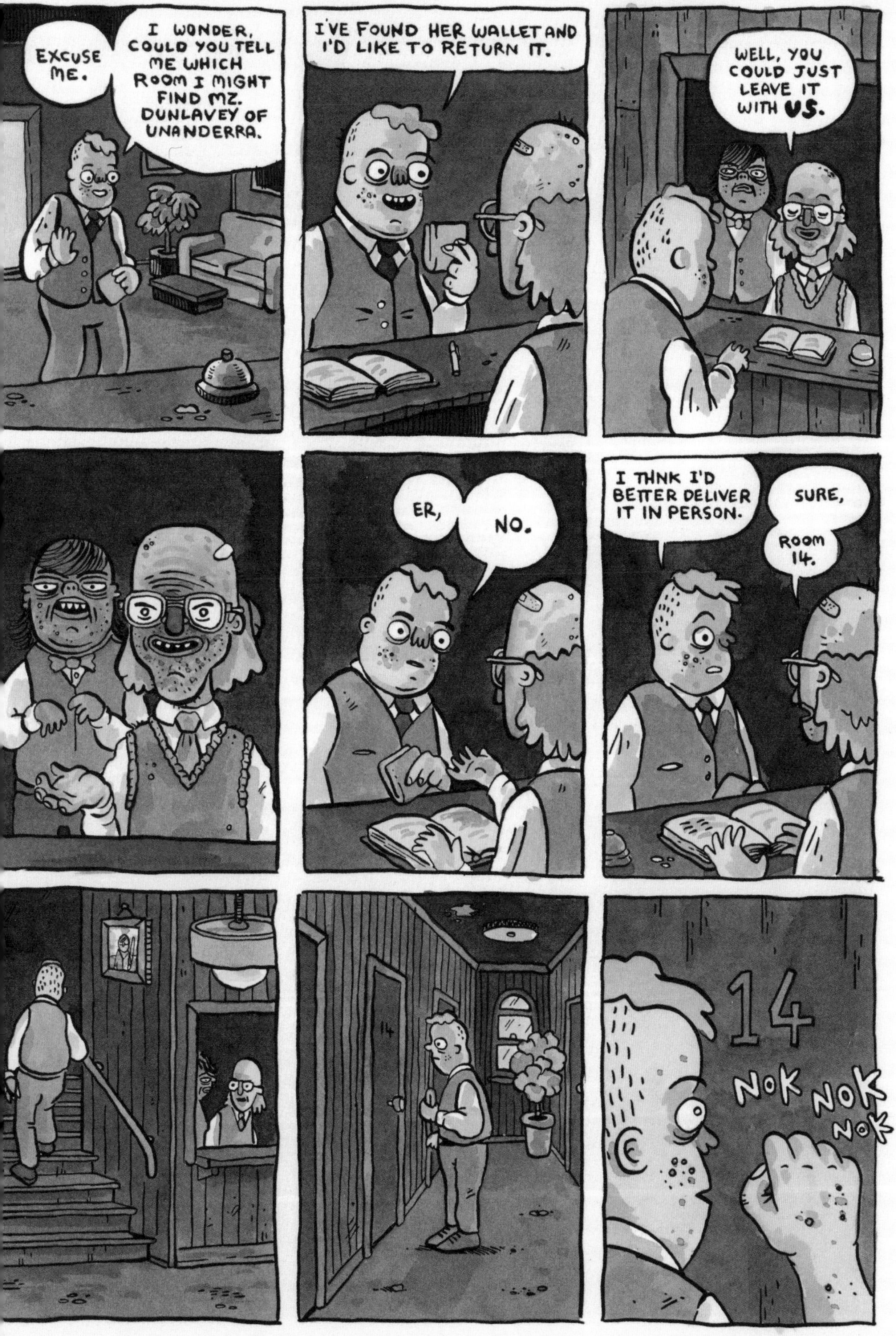
EXCUSE ME.
I WONDER, COULD YOU TELL ME WHICH ROOM I MIGHT FIND MZ. DUNLAVEY OF UNANDERRA.
I'VE FOUND HER WALLET AND I'D LIKE TO RETURN IT.
WELL, YOU COULD JUST LEAVE IT WITH US.
ER,
NO.
I THNK I'D BETTER DELIVER IT IN PERSON.
SURE,
ROOM 14.
14
NOK NOK NOK

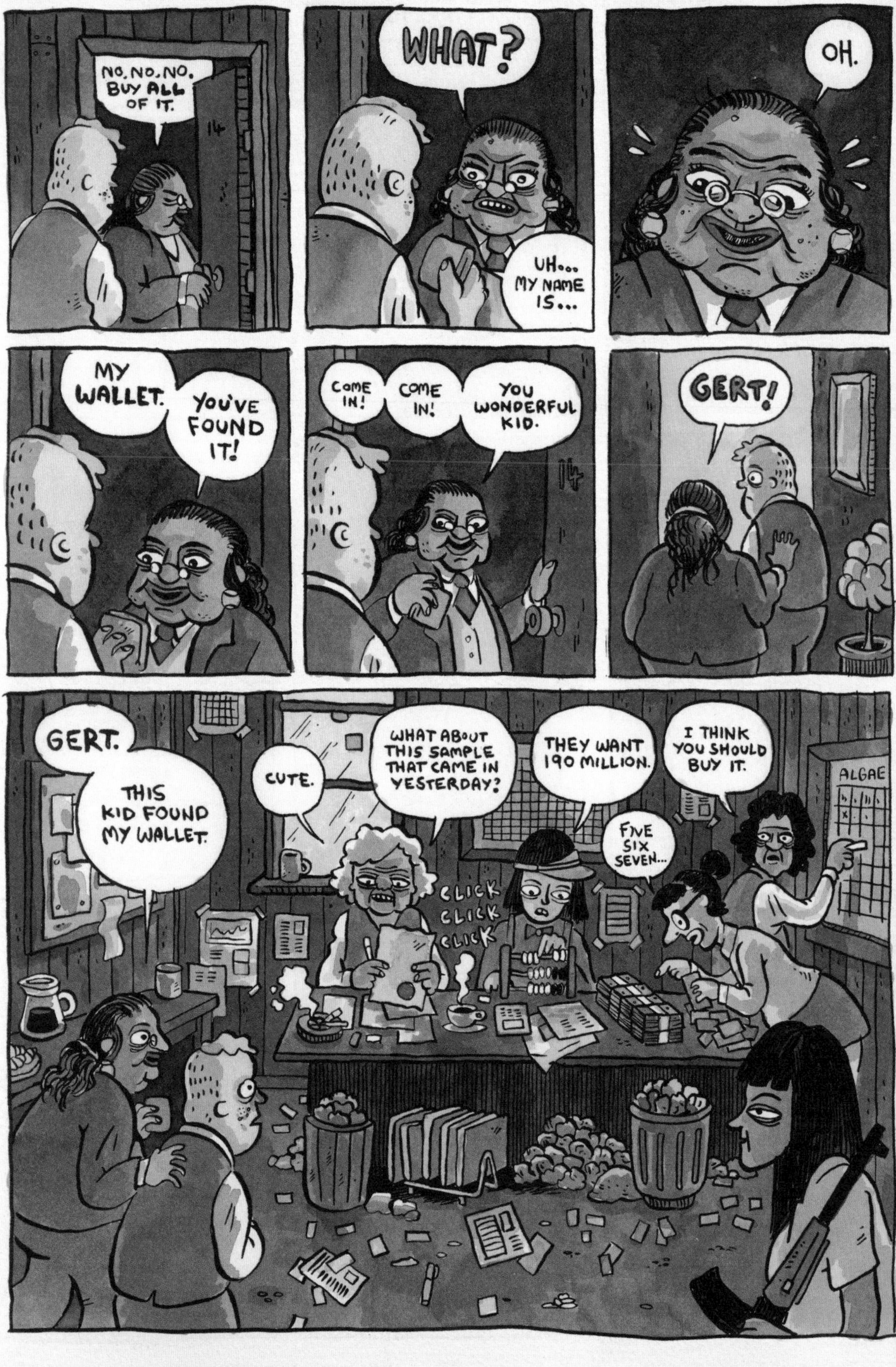
NO, NO, NO. BUY ALL OF IT.
14
WHAT?
UH... MY NAME IS...
OH.
MY WALLET.
YOU'VE FOUND IT!
COME IN!
COME IN!
YOU WONDERFUL KID.
14
GERT!
GERT.
THIS KID FOUND MY WALLET.
CUTE.
WHAT ABOUT THIS SAMPLE THAT CAME IN YESTERDAY?
THEY WANT 190 MILLION.
I THINK YOU SHOULD BUY IT.
FIVE SIX SEVEN...
CLICK CLICK CLICK
ALGAE

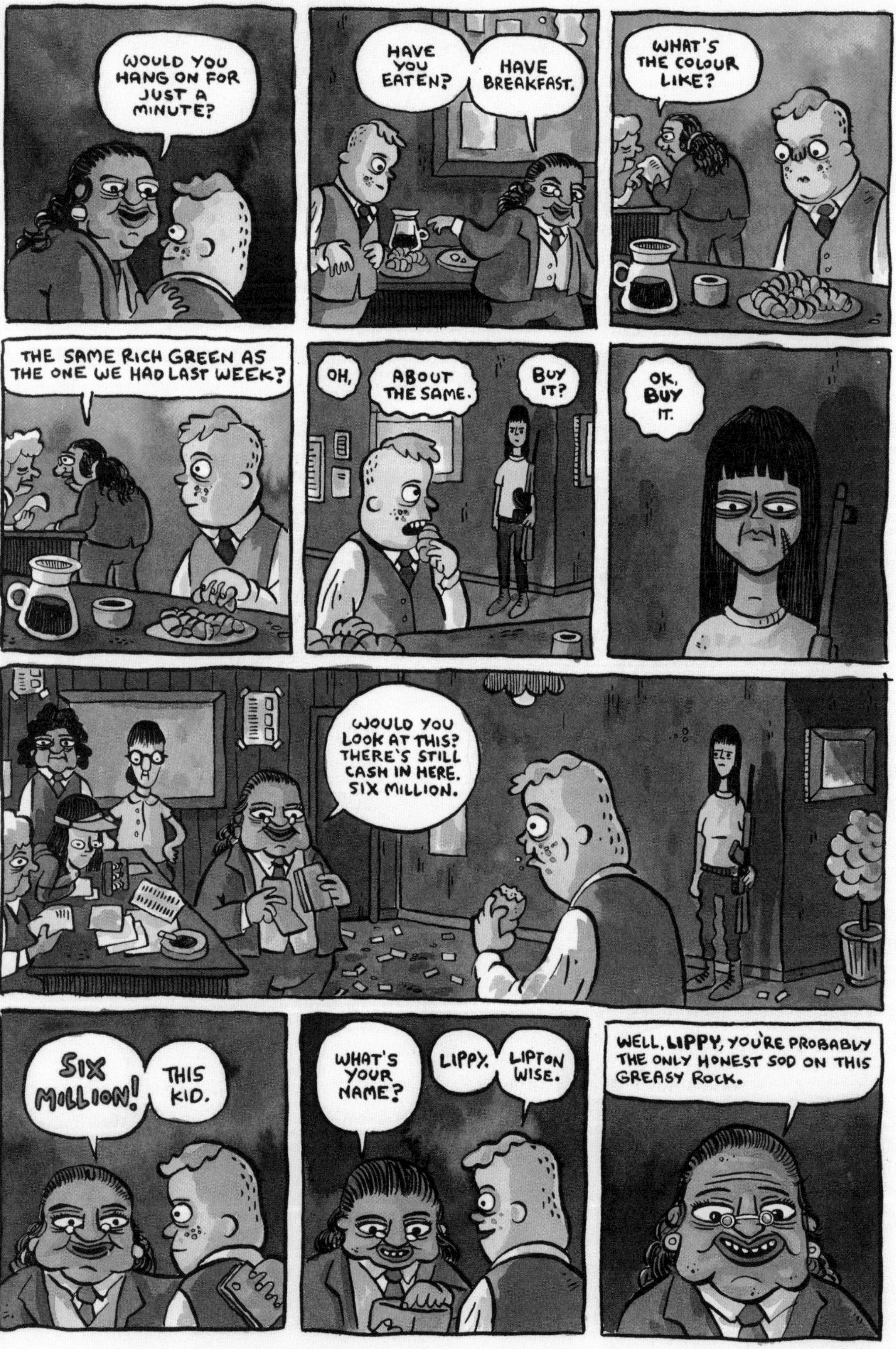
WOULD YOU HANG ON FOR JUST A MINUTE?
HAVE YOU EATEN?
HAVE BREAKFAST.
WHAT'S THE COLOUR LIKE?
THE SAME RICH GREEN AS THE ONE WE HAD LAST WEEK?
OH,
ABOUT THE SAME.
BUY IT?
OK, BUY IT.
WOULD YOU LOOK AT THIS? THERE'S STILL CASH IN HERE. SIX MILLION.
SIX MILLION!
THIS KID.
WHAT'S YOUR NAME?
LIPPY.
LIPTON WISE.
WELL, LIPPY, YOU'RE PROBABLY THE ONLY HONEST SOD ON THIS GREASY ROCK.

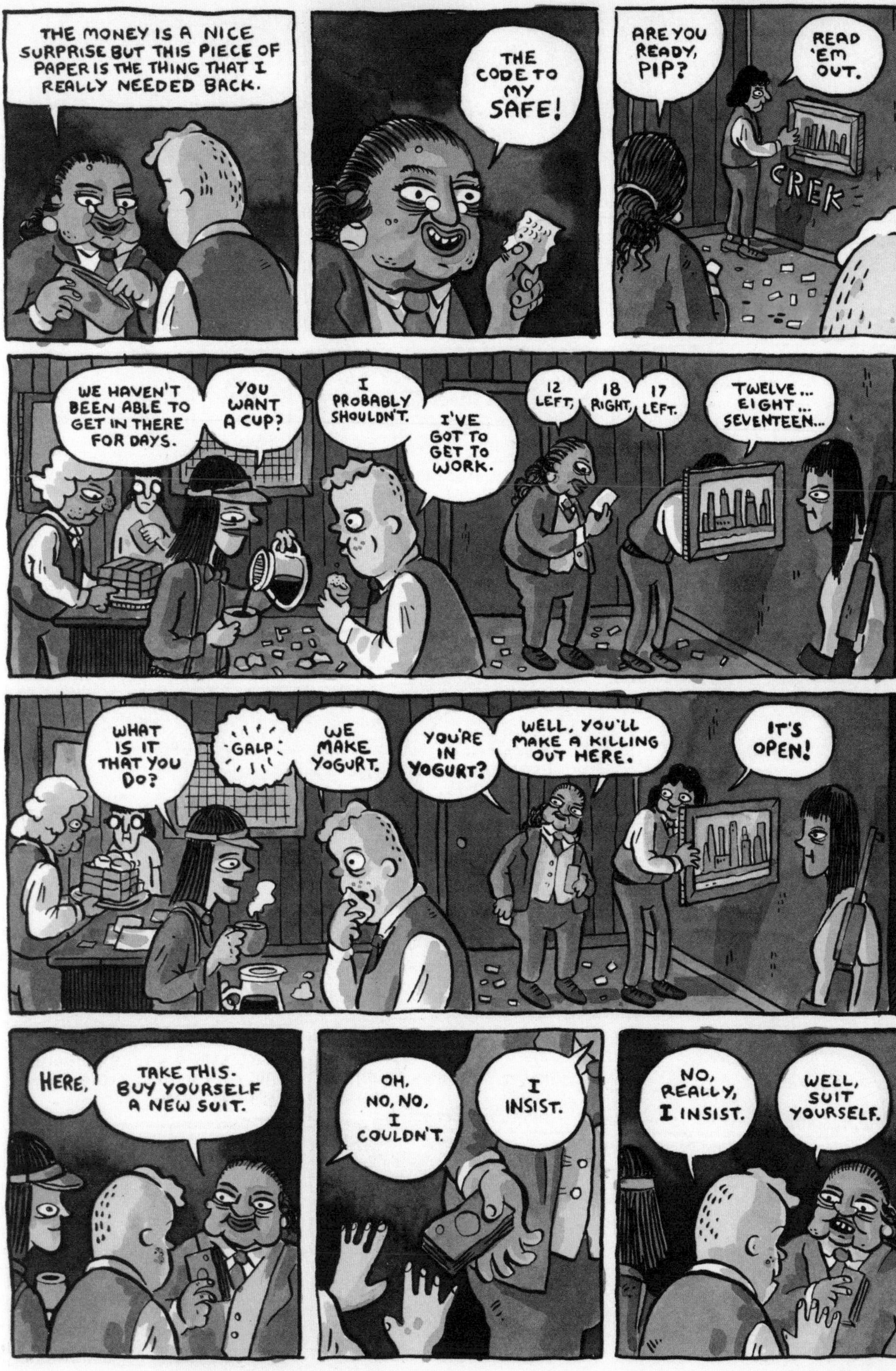
THE MONEY IS A NICE SURPRISE BUT THIS PIECE OF PAPER IS THE THING THAT I REALLY NEEDED BACK.
THE CODE TO MY SAFE!
ARE YOU READY, PIP?
READ 'EM OUT.
CREK
WE HAVEN'T BEEN ABLE TO GET IN THERE FOR DAYS.
YOU WANT A CUP?
I PROBABLY SHOULDN'T.
I'VE GOT TO GET TO WORK.
12 LEFT,
18 RIGHT,
17 LEFT.
TWELVE... EIGHT... SEVENTEEN...
WHAT IS IT THAT YOU DO?
GALP
WE MAKE YOGURT.
YOU'RE IN YOGURT?
WELL, YOU'LL MAKE A KILLING OUT HERE.
IT'S OPEN!
HERE,
TAKE THIS. BUY YOURSELF A NEW SUIT.
OH, NO, NO, I COULDN'T.
I INSIST.
NO, REALLY, I INSIST.
WELL, SUIT YOURSELF.

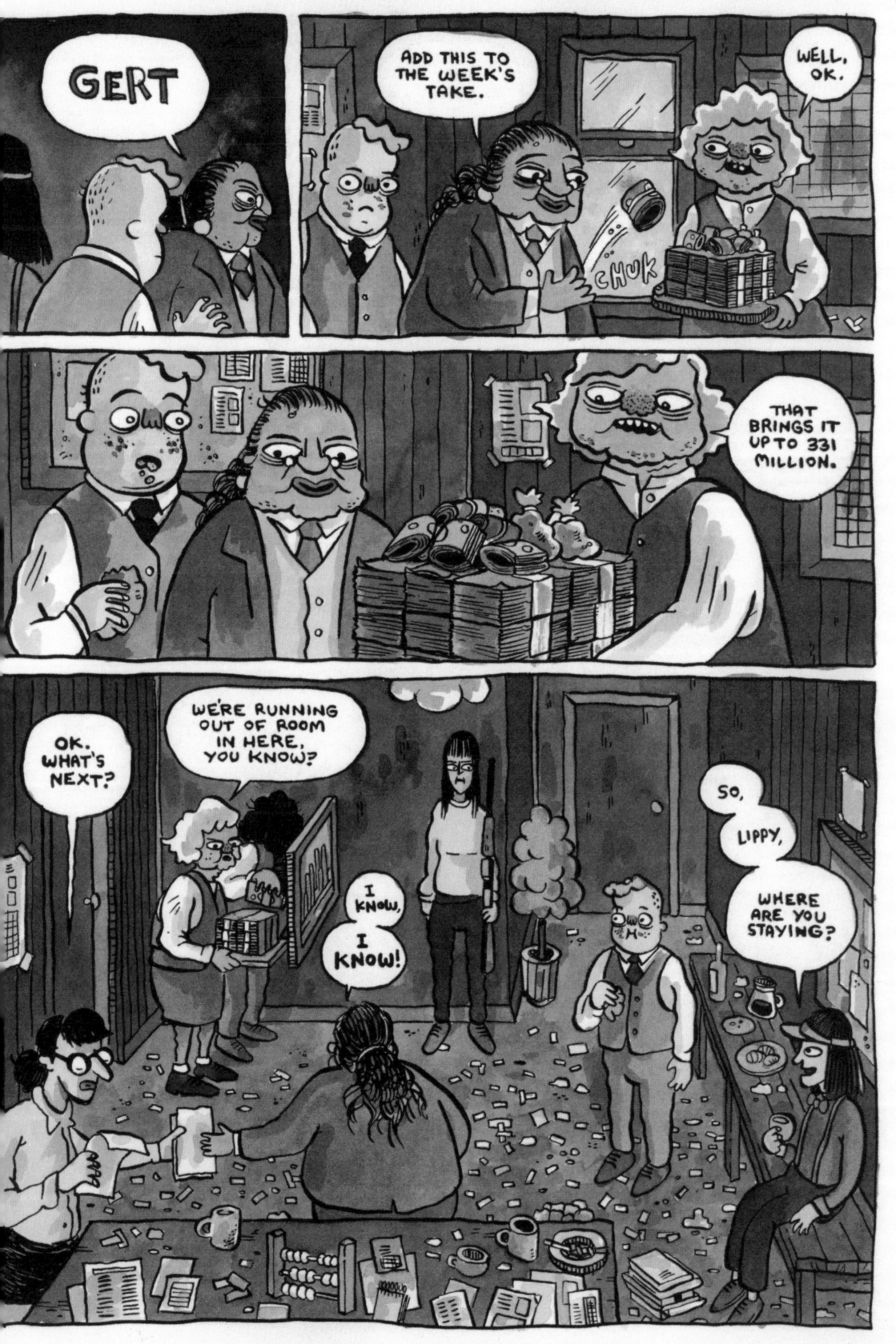
GERT
ADD THIS TO THE WEEK'S TAKE.
CHUK
WELL, OK.
THAT BRINGS IT UP TO 331 MILLION.
OK. WHAT'S NEXT?
WE'RE RUNNING OUT OF ROOM IN HERE, YOU KNOW?
I KNOW,
I KNOW!
SO,
LIPPY,
WHERE ARE YOU STAYING?

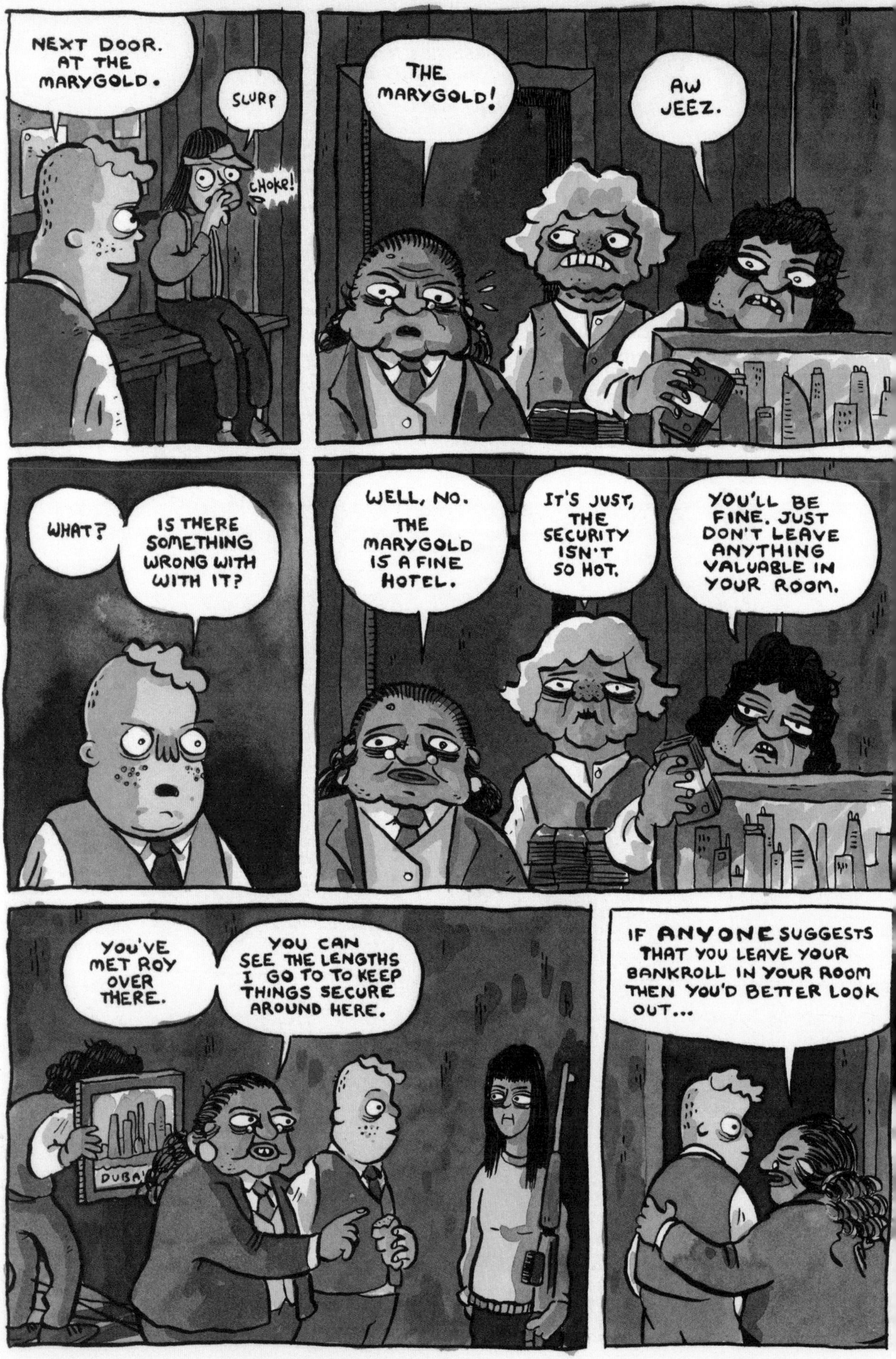
NEXT DOOR. AT THE MARYGOLD.
SLURP
CHOKE!
THE MARYGOLD!
AW JEEZ.
WHAT?
IS THERE SOMETHING WRONG WITH WITH IT?
WELL, NO. THE MARYGOLD IS A FINE HOTEL.
IT'S JUST, THE SECURITY ISN'T SO HOT.
YOU'LL BE FINE. JUST DON'T LEAVE ANYTHING VALUABLE IN YOUR ROOM.
YOU'VE MET ROY OVER THERE.
YOU CAN SEE THE LENGTHS I GO TO TO KEEP THINGS SECURE AROUND HERE.
DUBAI
IF ANYONE SUGGESTS THAT YOU LEAVE YOUR BANKROLL IN YOUR ROOM THEN YOU'D BETTER LOOK OUT...

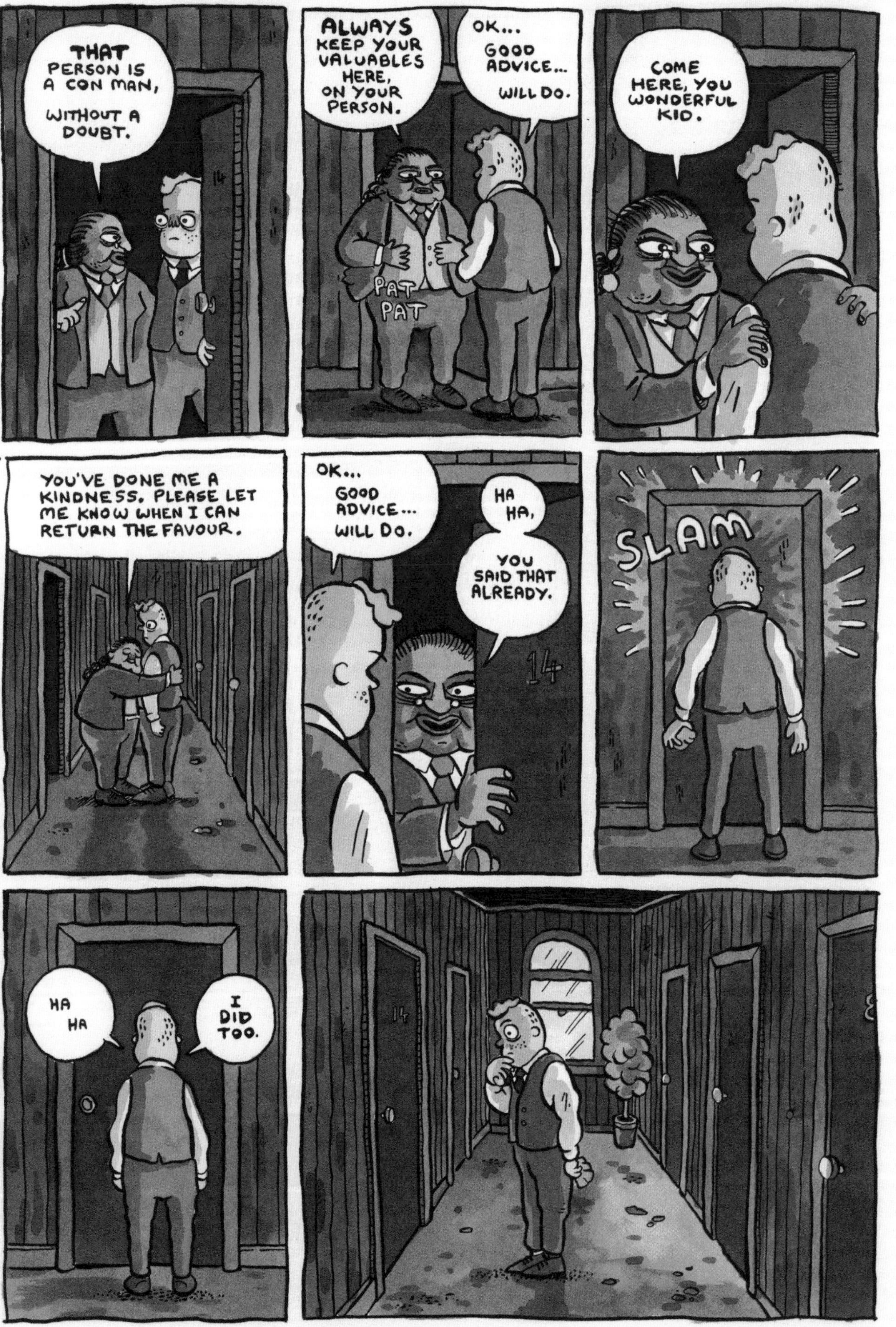
THAT PERSON IS A CON MAN,
WITHOUT A DOUBT.
14
ALWAYS KEEP YOUR VALUABLES HERE, ON YOUR PERSON.
OK... GOOD ADVICE... WILL DO.
PAT PAT
COME HERE, YOU WONDERFUL KID.
YOU'VE DONE ME A KINDNESS. PLEASE LET ME KNOW WHEN I CAN RETURN THE FAVOUR.
OK... GOOD ADVICE... WILL DO.
HA HA,
YOU SAID THAT ALREADY.
14
SLAM
HA HA
I DID TOO.
14

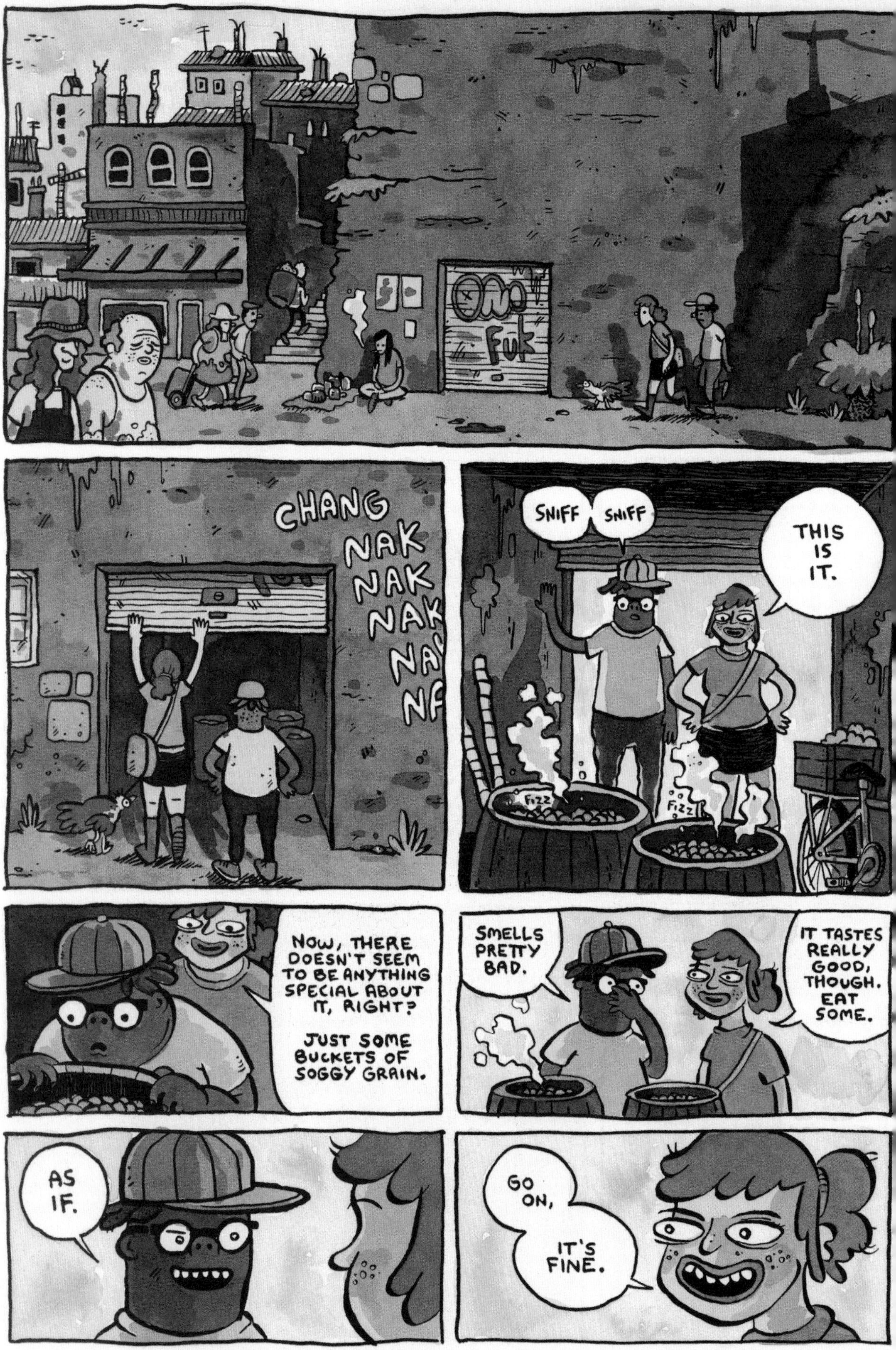
Fuk
CHANG
NAK
NAK
NAK
SNIFF
SNIFF
THIS IS IT.
FIZZ
FIZZ
NOW, THERE DOESN'T SEEM TO BE ANYTHING SPECIAL ABOUT IT, RIGHT?
JUST SOME BUCKETS OF SOGGY GRAIN.
SMELLS PRETTY BAD.
IT TASTES REALLY GOOD, THOUGH. EAT SOME.
AS IF.
GO ON,
IT'S FINE.

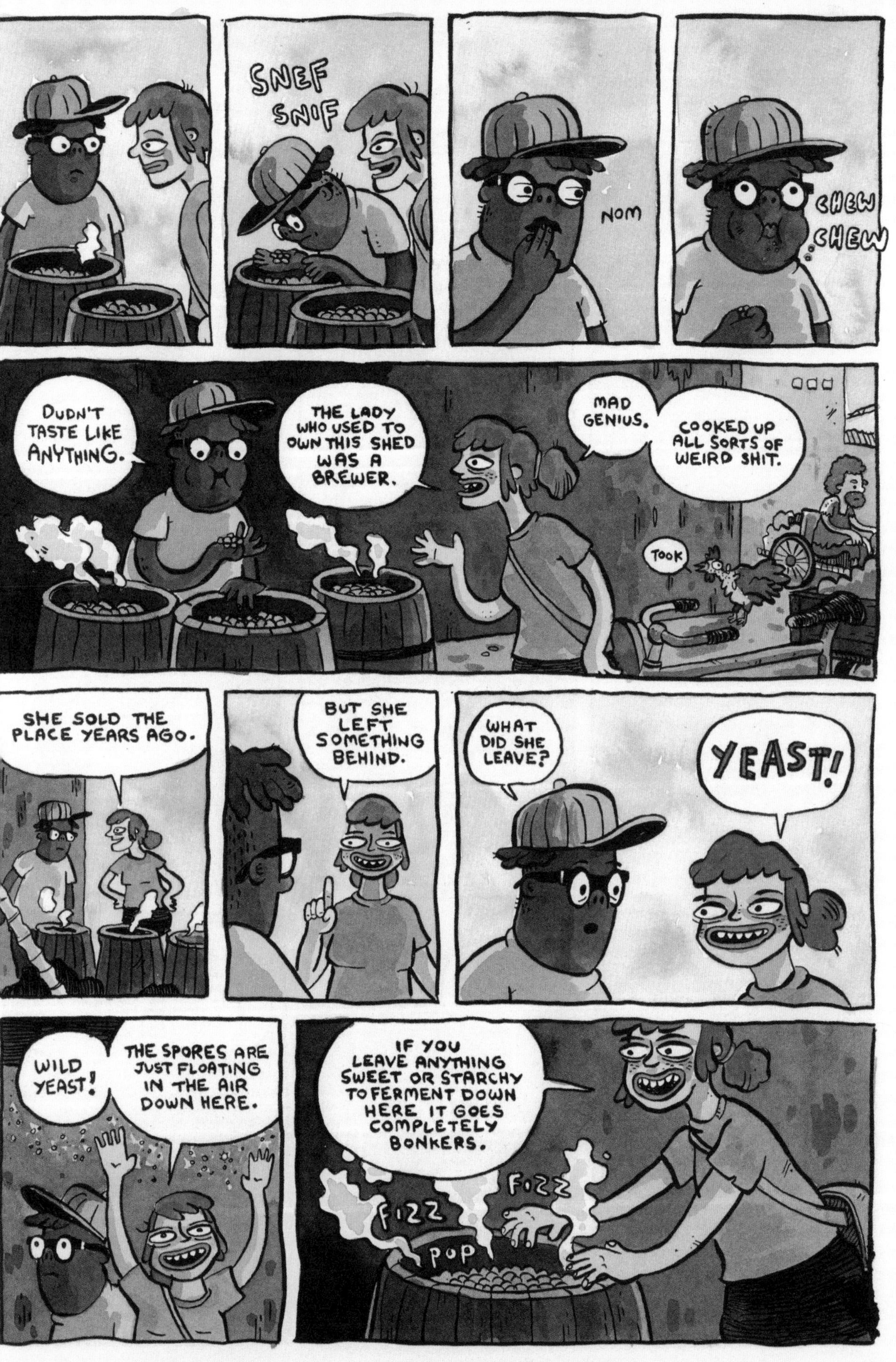
SNEF
SNIF
NOM
CHEW
CHEW
DUDN'T TASTE LIKE ANYTHING.
THE LADY WHO USED TO OWN THIS SHED WAS A BREWER.
MAD GENIUS.
COOKED UP ALL SORTS OF WEIRD SHIT.
TOOK
SHE SOLD THE PLACE YEARS AGO.
BUT SHE LEFT SOMETHING BEHIND.
WHAT DID SHE LEAVE?
YEAST!
WILD YEAST!
THE SPORES ARE JUST FLOATING IN THE AIR DOWN HERE.
IF YOU LEAVE ANYTHING SWEET OR STARCHY TO FERMENT DOWN HERE IT GOES COMPLETELY BONKERS.
FIZZ
FIZZ
POP

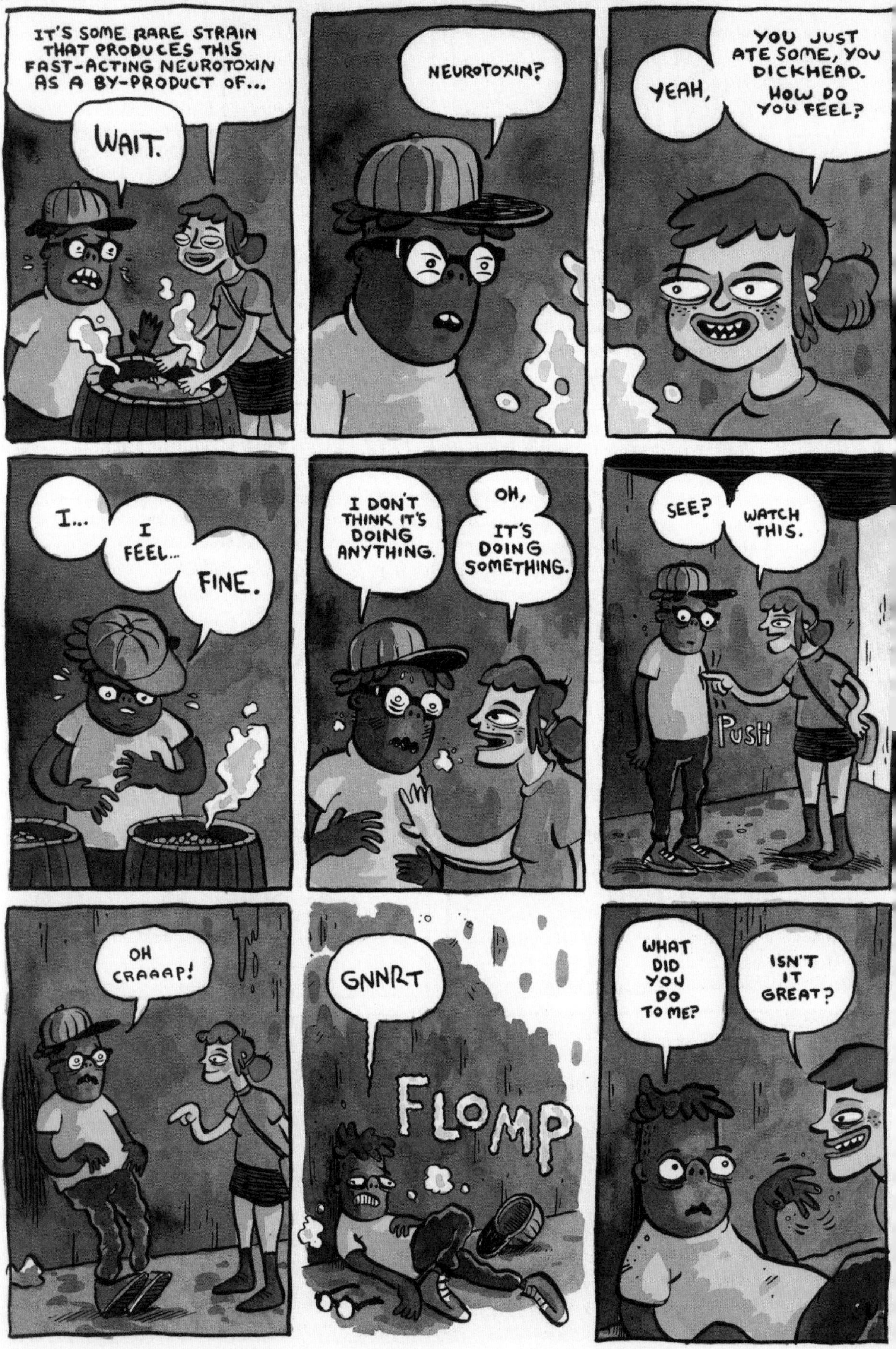
IT'S SOME RARE STRAIN THAT PRODUCES THIS FAST-ACTING NEUROTOXIN AS A BY-PRODUCT OF...
WAIT.
NEUROTOXIN?
YEAH,
YOU JUST ATE SOME, YOU DICKHEAD.
HOW DO YOU FEEL?
I...
I FEEL...
FINE.
I DON'T THINK IT'S DOING ANYTHING.
OH,
IT'S DOING SOMETHING.
SEE?
WATCH THIS.
PUSH
OH CRAAAP!
GNNRT
FLOMP
WHAT DID YOU DO TO ME?
ISN'T IT GREAT?

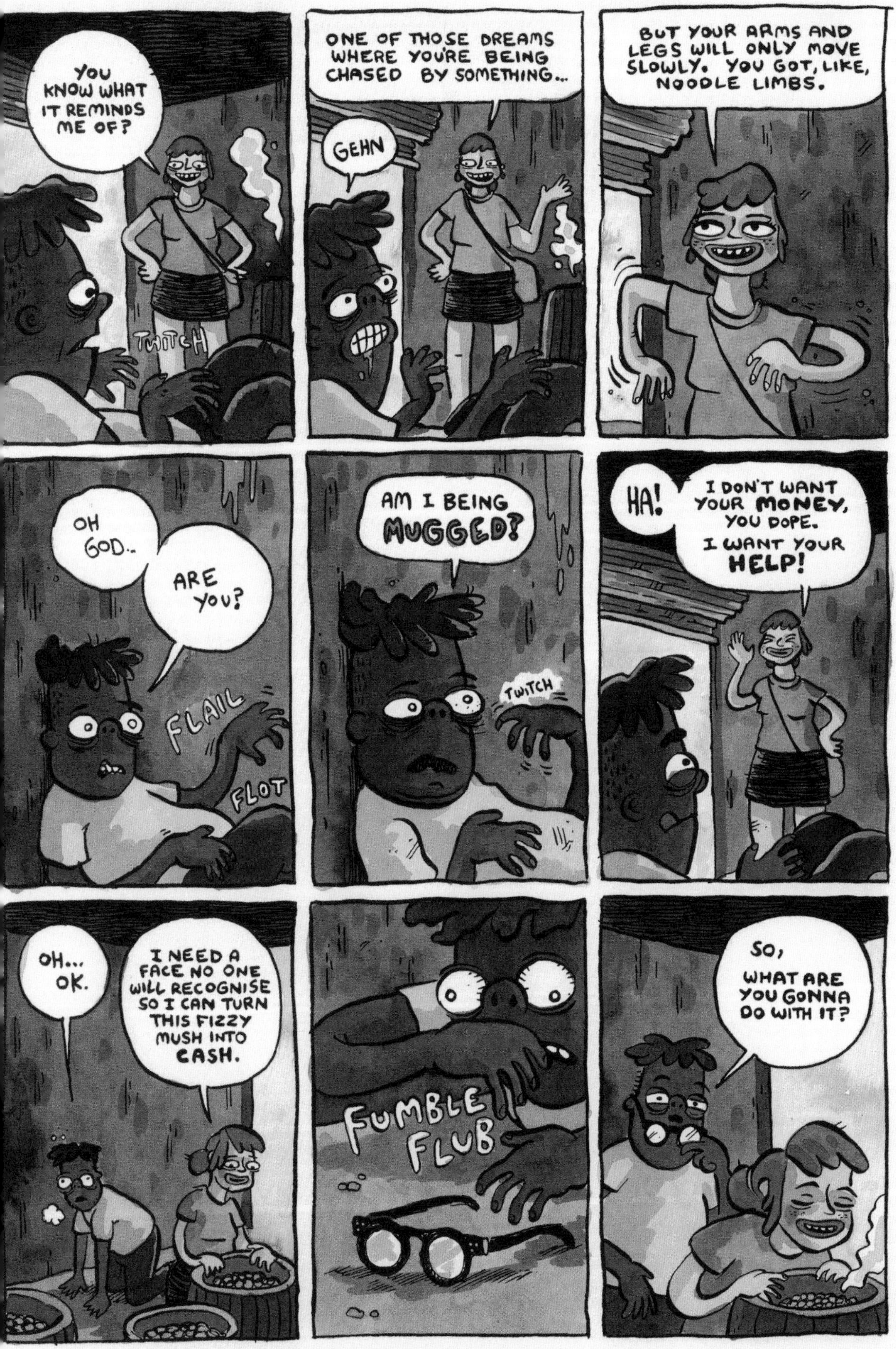
YOU KNOW WHAT IT REMINDS ME OF?
TWITCH
ONE OF THOSE DREAMS WHERE YOU'RE BEING CHASED BY SOMETHING...
GEHN
BUT YOUR ARMS AND LEGS WILL ONLY MOVE SLOWLY. YOU GOT, LIKE, NOODLE LIMBS.
OH GOD..
ARE YOU?
FLAIL
FLOT
AM I BEING MUGGED?
TWITCH
HA!
I DON'T WANT YOUR MONEY, YOU DOPE.
I WANT YOUR HELP!
OH... OK.
I NEED A FACE NO ONE WILL RECOGNISE SO I CAN TURN THIS FIZZY MUSH INTO CASH.
FUMBLE
FLUB
SO, WHAT ARE YOU GONNA DO WITH IT?

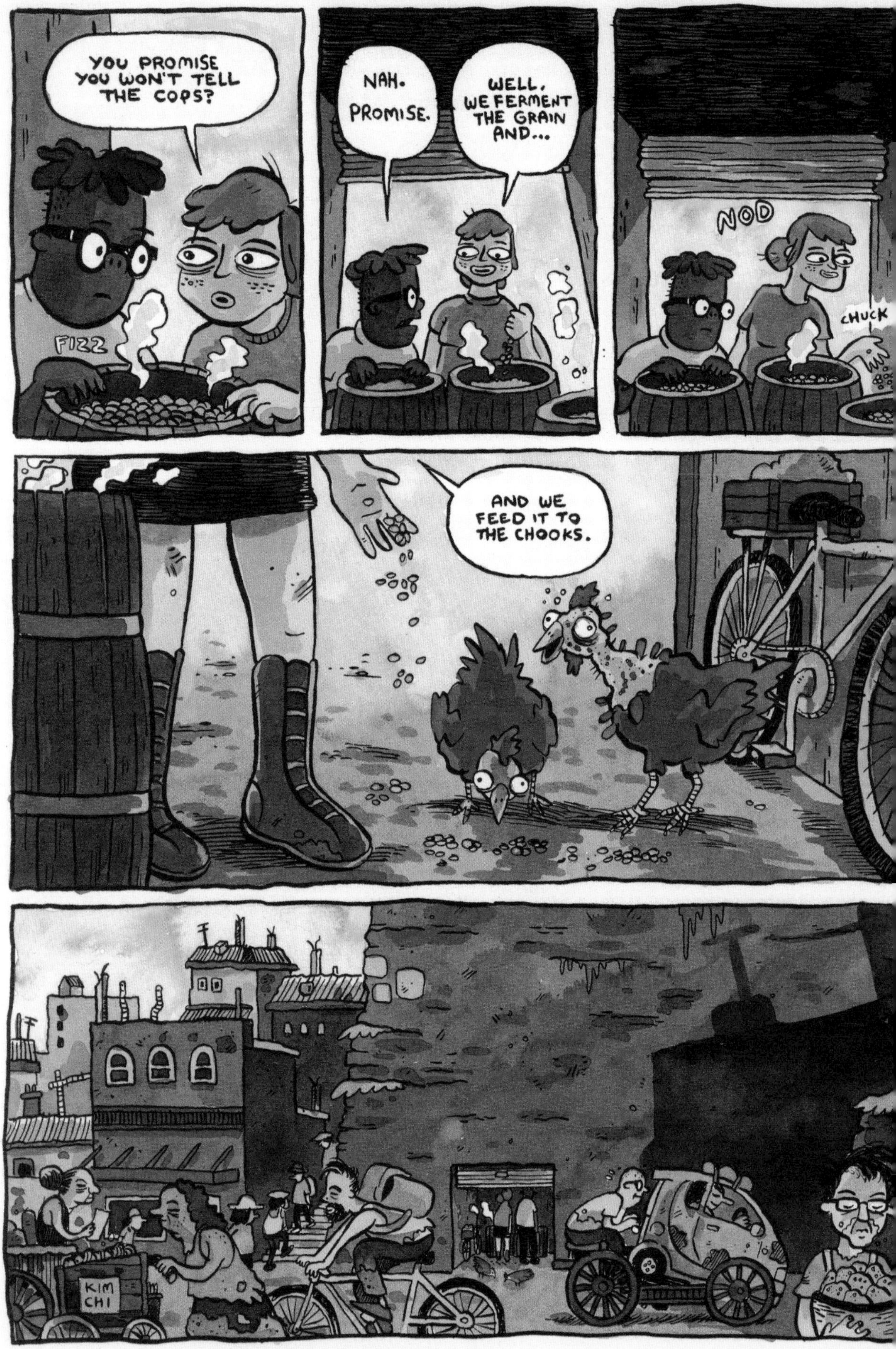
YOU PROMISE YOU WON'T TELL THE COPS?
FIZZ
NAH.
PROMISE.
WELL, WE FERMENT THE GRAIN AND...
NOD
CHUCK
AND WE FEED IT TO THE CHOOKS.
KIM CHI

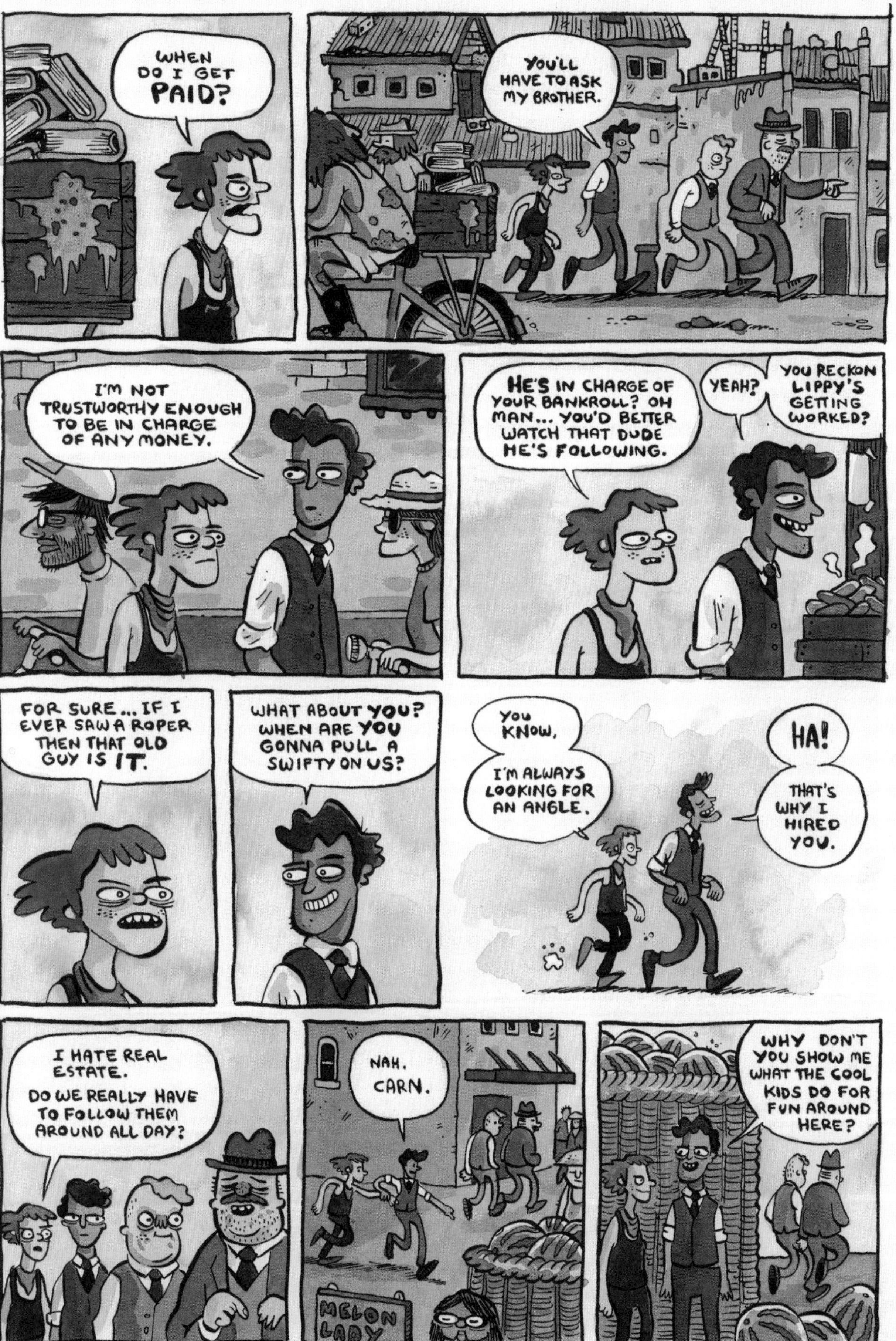
WHEN DO I GET PAID?
YOU'LL HAVE TO ASK MY BROTHER.
I'M NOT TRUSTWORTHY ENOUGH TO BE IN CHARGE OF ANY MONEY.
HE'S IN CHARGE OF YOUR BANKROLL? OH MAN... YOU'D BETTER WATCH THAT DUDE HE'S FOLLOWING.
YEAH?
YOU RECKON LIPPY'S GETTING WORKED?
FOR SURE... IF I EVER SAW A ROPER THEN THAT OLD GUY IS IT.
WHAT ABOUT YOU? WHEN ARE YOU GONNA PULL A SWIFTY ON US?
YOU KNOW.
I'M ALWAYS LOOKING FOR AN ANGLE.
HA!
THAT'S WHY I HIRED YOU.
I HATE REAL ESTATE.
DO WE REALLY HAVE TO FOLLOW THEM AROUND ALL DAY?
NAH. CARN.
MELON LADY
WHY DON'T YOU SHOW ME WHAT THE COOL KIDS DO FOR FUN AROUND HERE?

HERE THEY ARE...THE FIVE ISLANDS.

EACH ISLAND USED TO HAVE AN INDIGENOUS NAME BUT NO ONE REMEMBERS THOSE.

FALTER CITY

FLUBS

USUALLY THEY GO BY THE NAME OF THE FAMILY WHO RUNS THEM.

FAMILY? YOU MEAN FAMILY?

RIGHT.

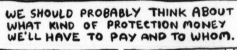

WE SHOULD PROBABLY THINK ABOUT WHAT KIND OF PROTECTION MONEY WE'LL HAVE TO PAY AND TO WHOM.

WE'RE HERE NOW, ON KOHN.

KOHN IS HAVING TROUBLE WITH HER ELDEST CHILDREN.

POE

KOHN

SHANKER

SALAD SPOONS

McGINTY

THINGS ARE STARTING TO GET LOOSE... DANGEROUS...

I'D SUGGEST WE HEAD OVER THE BRIDGE TO SALAD SPOONS.

HEY!

WHAT HAPPENED TO PENN AND THAT SCABBY LITTLE KID?

GUESS WE LOST 'EM.

YEAH, RIGHT.

WE LOST THEM.

SHOULD WE WAIT, OR PUSH ON?

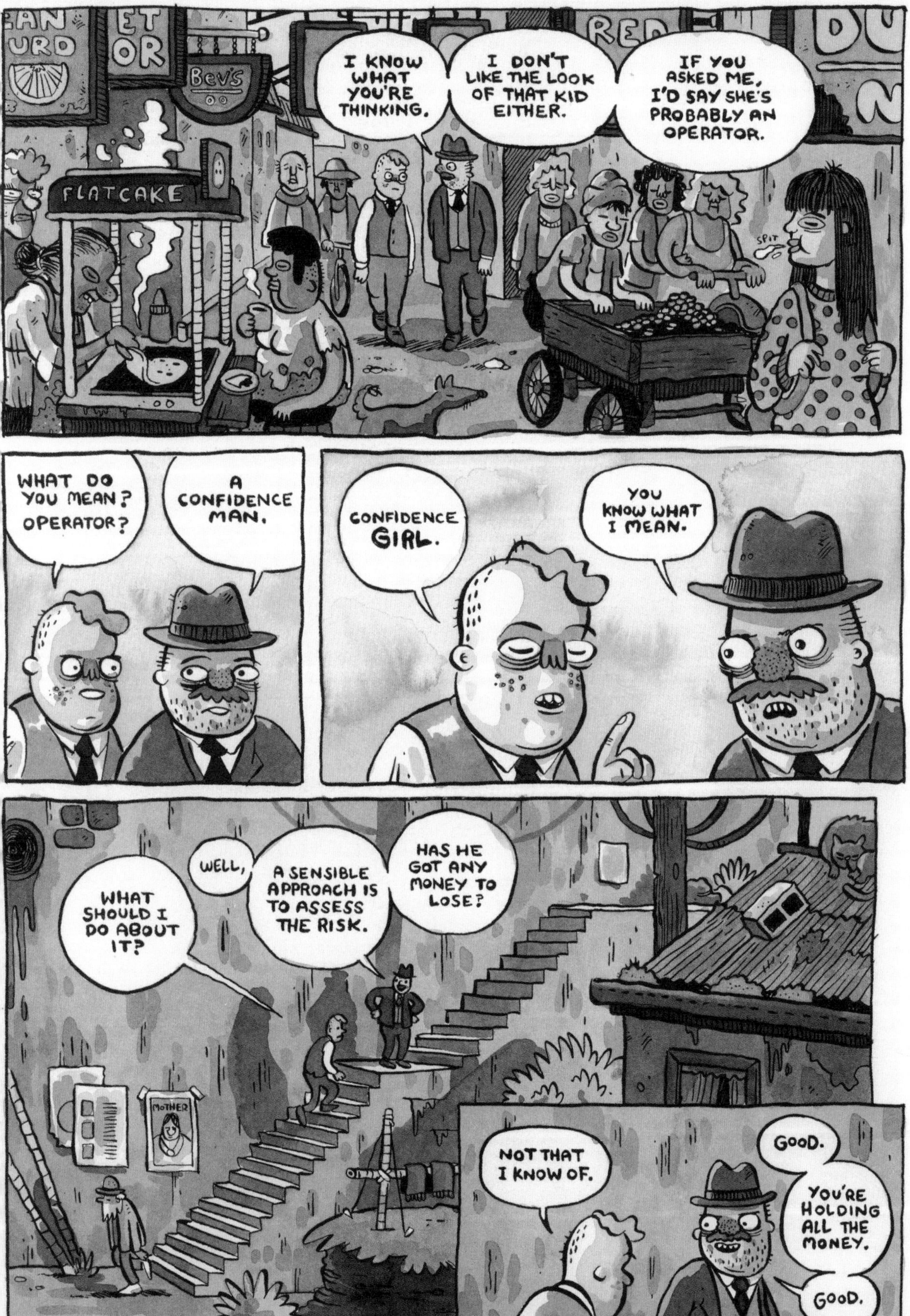
FLATCAKE
BEV'S
RED
I KNOW WHAT YOU'RE THINKING.
I DON'T LIKE THE LOOK OF THAT KID EITHER.
IF YOU ASKED ME, I'D SAY SHE'S PROBABLY AN OPERATOR.
SPIT
WHAT DO YOU MEAN? OPERATOR?
A CONFIDENCE MAN.
CONFIDENCE GIRL.
YOU KNOW WHAT I MEAN.
WHAT SHOULD I DO ABOUT IT?
WELL,
A SENSIBLE APPROACH IS TO ASSESS THE RISK.
HAS HE GOT ANY MONEY TO LOSE?
MOTHER
NOT THAT I KNOW OF.
GOOD.
YOU'RE HOLDING ALL THE MONEY.
GOOD.

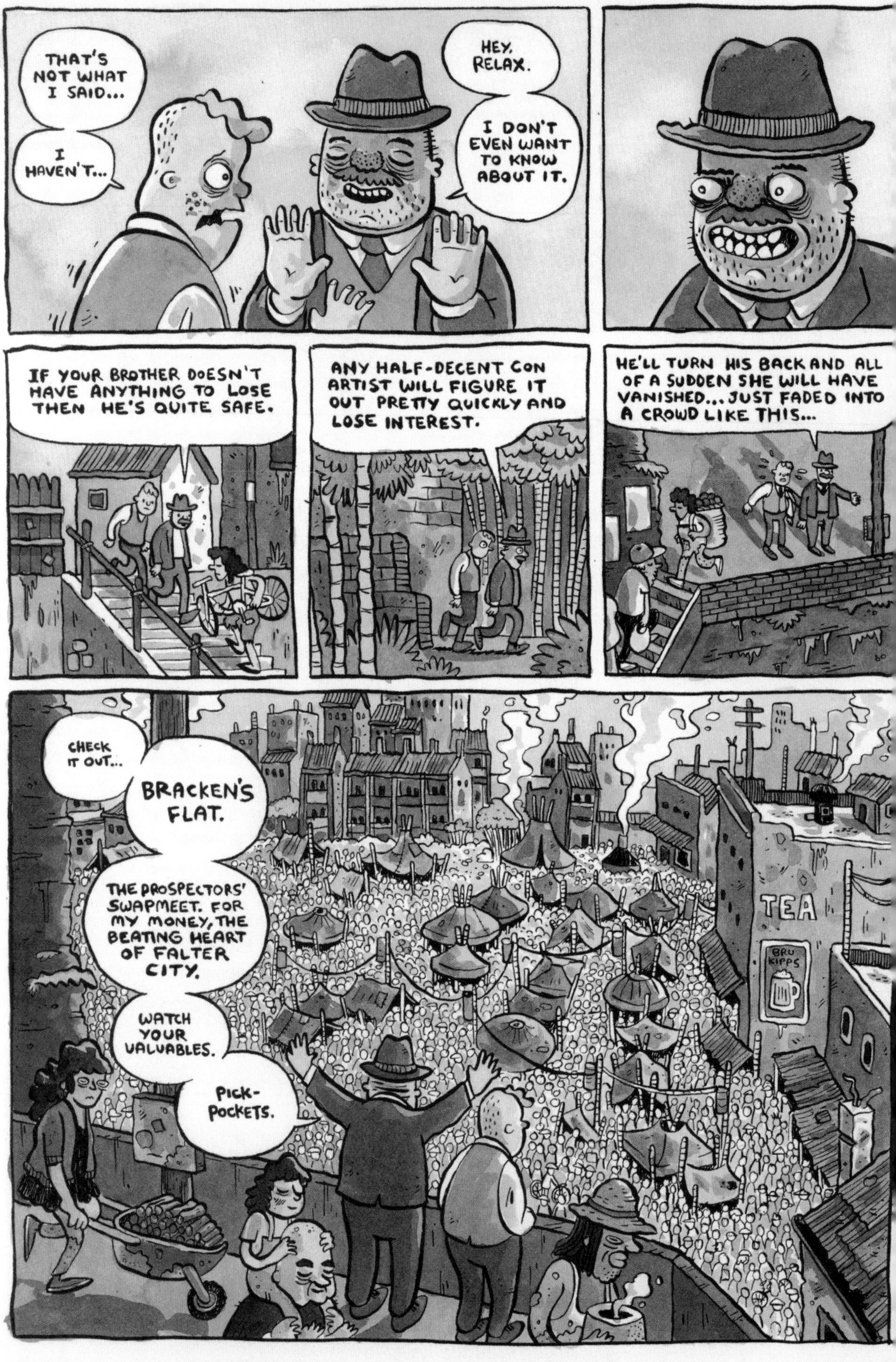
THAT'S NOT WHAT I SAID...
I HAVEN'T...
HEY, RELAX.
I DON'T EVEN WANT TO KNOW ABOUT IT.
IF YOUR BROTHER DOESN'T HAVE ANYTHING TO LOSE THEN HE'S QUITE SAFE.
ANY HALF-DECENT CON ARTIST WILL FIGURE IT OUT PRETTY QUICKLY AND LOSE INTEREST.
HE'LL TURN HIS BACK AND ALL OF A SUDDEN SHE WILL HAVE VANISHED... JUST FADED INTO A CROWD LIKE THIS...
CHECK IT OUT...
BRACKEN'S FLAT.
THE PROSPECTORS' SWAPMEET. FOR MY MONEY, THE BEATING HEART OF FALTER CITY.
WATCH YOUR VALUABLES.
PICK-POCKETS.
TEA
BRU KIPPS

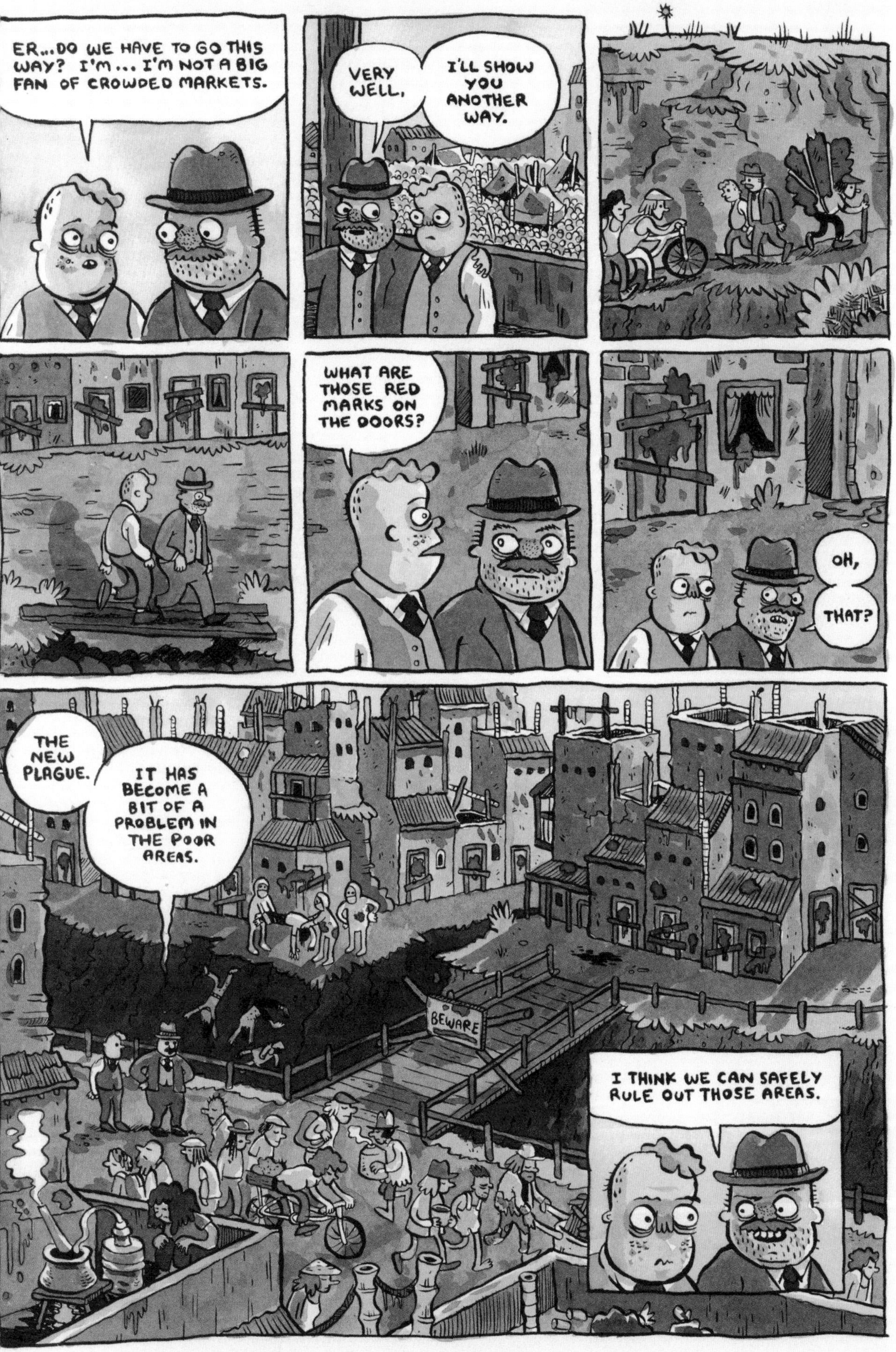
ER...DO WE HAVE TO GO THIS WAY? I'M... I'M NOT A BIG FAN OF CROWDED MARKETS.
VERY WELL,
I'LL SHOW YOU ANOTHER WAY.
WHAT ARE THOSE RED MARKS ON THE DOORS?
OH,
THAT?
THE NEW PLAGUE.
IT HAS BECOME A BIT OF A PROBLEM IN THE POOR AREAS.
BEWARE
I THINK WE CAN SAFELY RULE OUT THOSE AREAS.

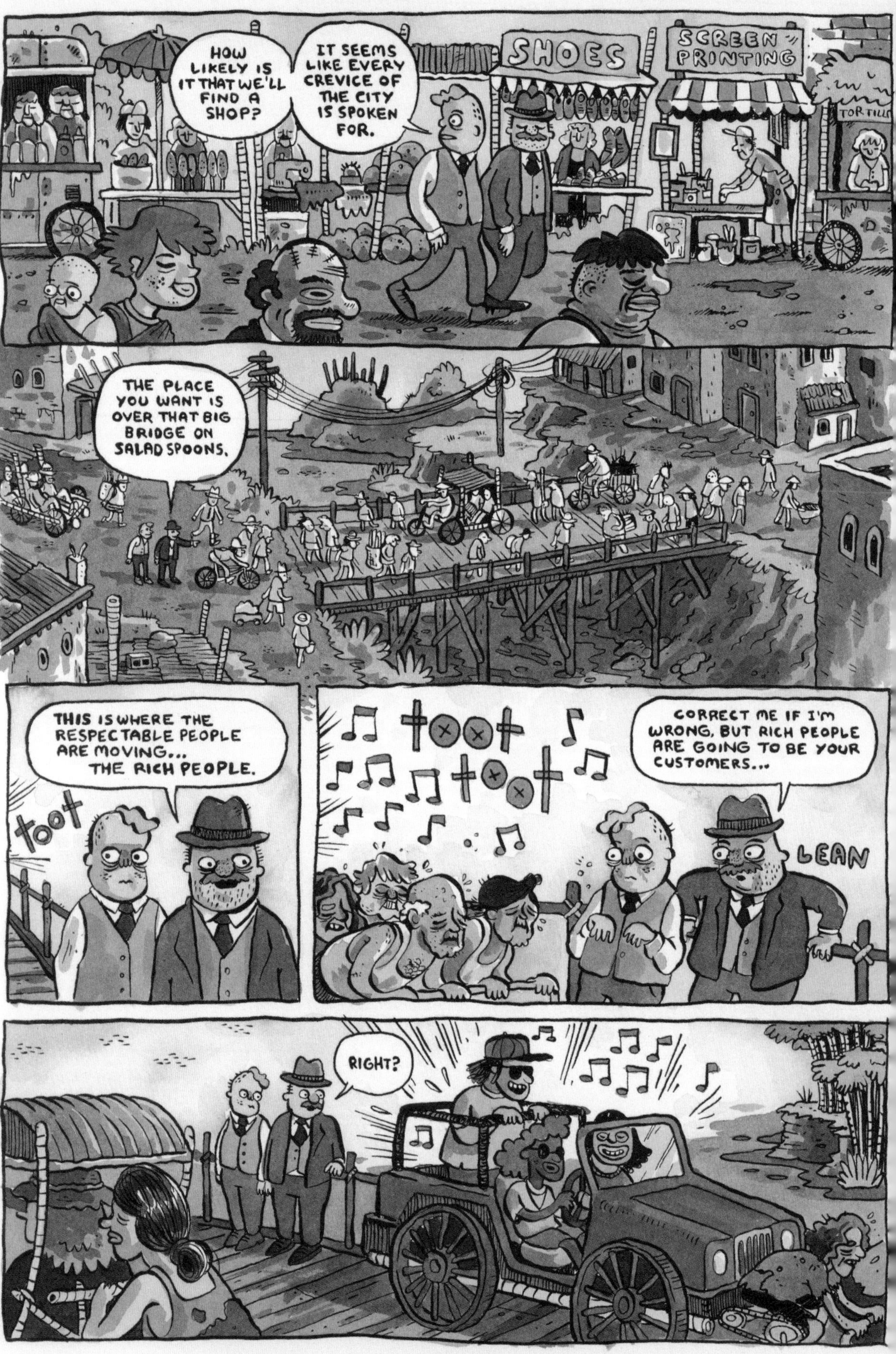
SHOES
SCREEN PRINTING
TORTILL
HOW LIKELY IS IT THAT WE'LL FIND A SHOP?
IT SEEMS LIKE EVERY CREVICE OF THE CITY IS SPOKEN FOR.
THE PLACE YOU WANT IS OVER THAT BIG BRIDGE ON SALAD SPOONS.
THIS IS WHERE THE RESPECTABLE PEOPLE ARE MOVING... THE RICH PEOPLE.
toot
toot toot
CORRECT ME IF I'M WRONG, BUT RICH PEOPLE ARE GOING TO BE YOUR CUSTOMERS...
LEAN
RIGHT?

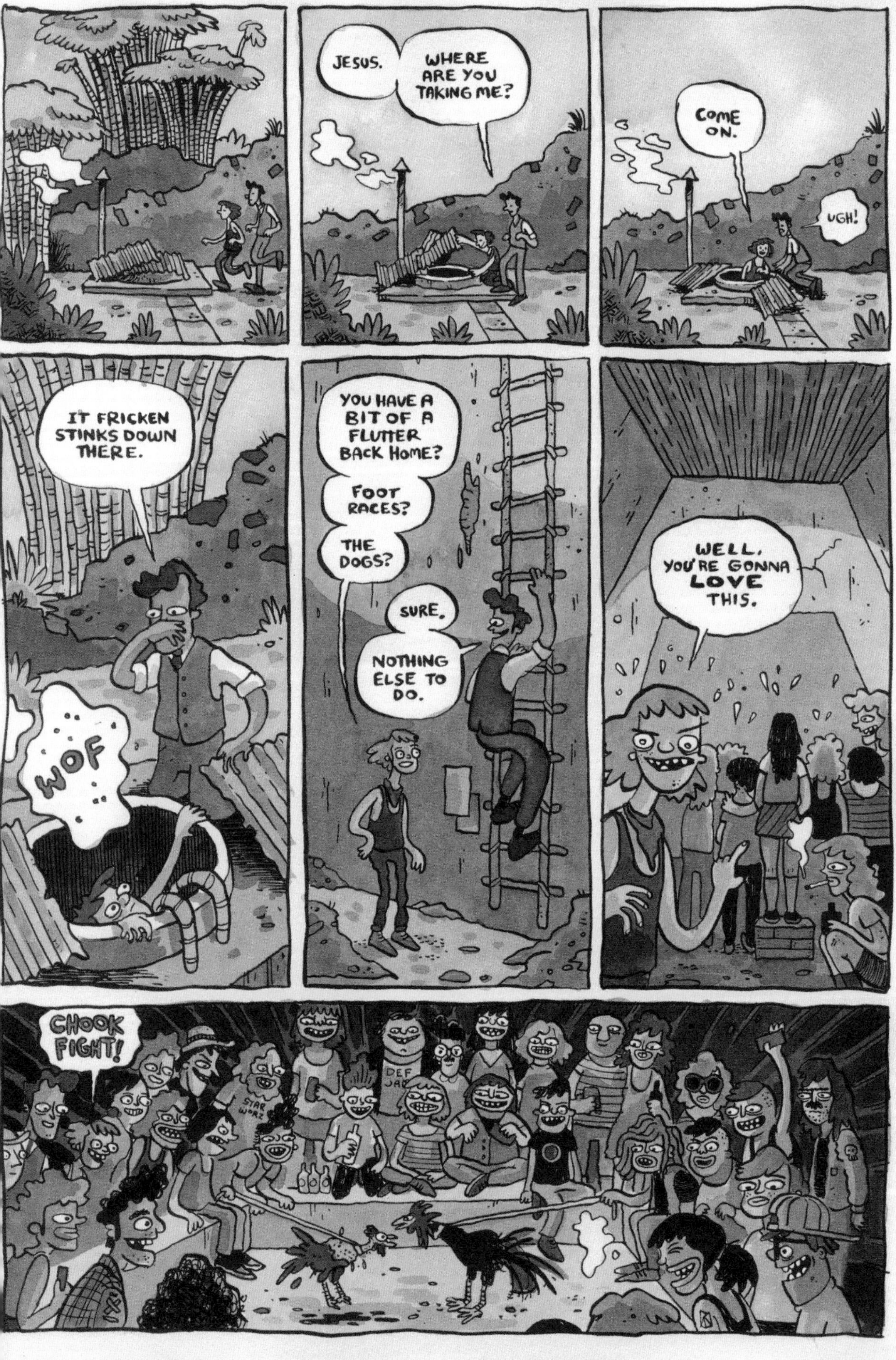
JESUS.
WHERE ARE YOU TAKING ME?
COME ON.
UGH!
IT FRICKEN STINKS DOWN THERE.
WOF
YOU HAVE A BIT OF A FLUTTER BACK HOME?
FOOT RACES?
THE DOGS?
SURE.
NOTHING ELSE TO DO.
WELL, YOU'RE GONNA LOVE THIS.
CHOOK FIGHT!
DEF JAM
STAR WORZ

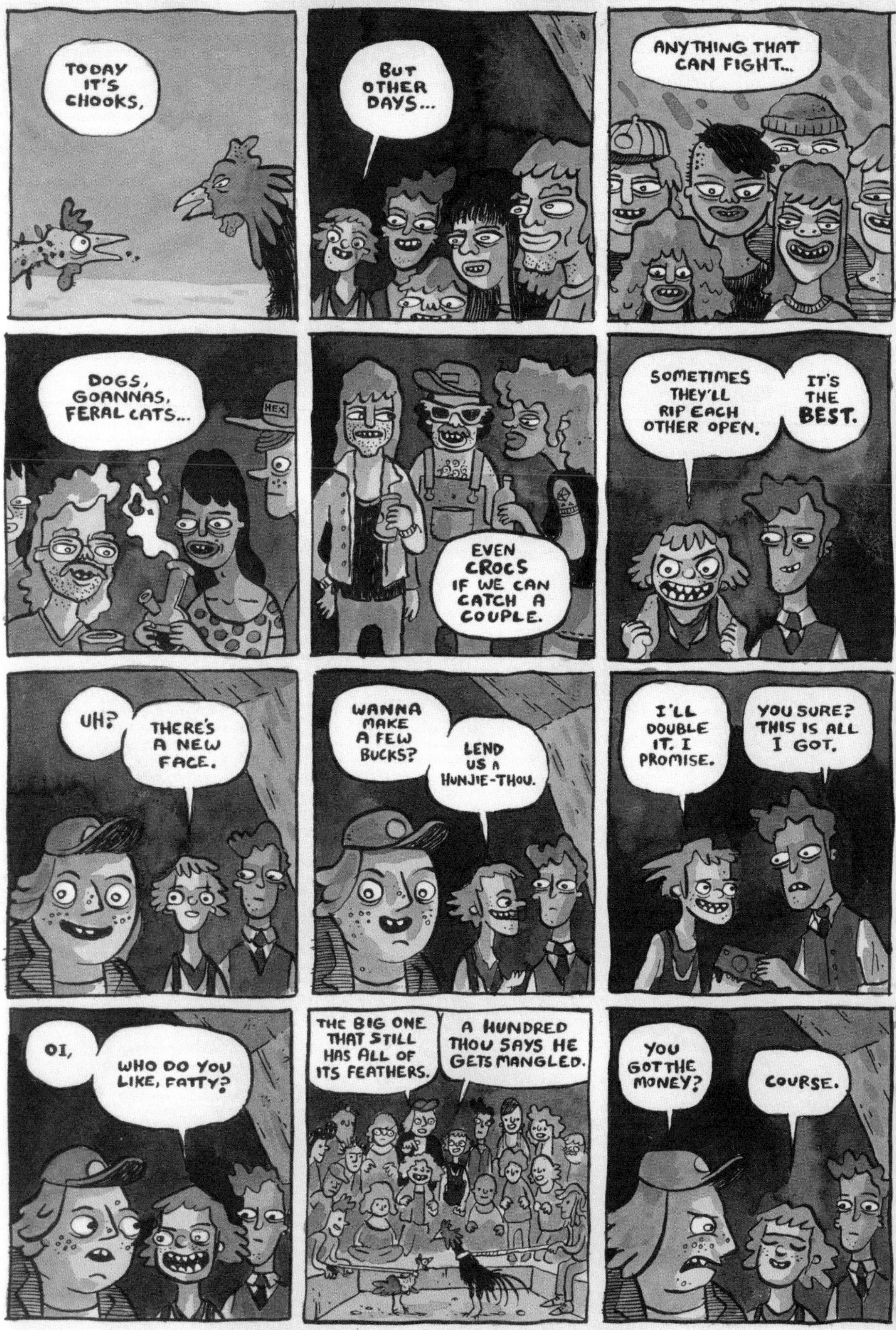
TODAY IT'S CHOOKS,
BUT OTHER DAYS...
ANYTHING THAT CAN FIGHT...
DOGS, GOANNAS, FERAL CATS...
HEX
EVEN CROCS IF WE CAN CATCH A COUPLE.
SOMETIMES THEY'LL RIP EACH OTHER OPEN.
IT'S THE BEST.
UH?
THERE'S A NEW FACE.
WANNA MAKE A FEW BUCKS?
LEND US A HUNJIE-THOU.
I'LL DOUBLE IT. I PROMISE.
YOU SURE? THIS IS ALL I GOT.
OI,
WHO DO YOU LIKE, FATTY?
THE BIG ONE THAT STILL HAS ALL OF ITS FEATHERS.
A HUNDRED THOU SAYS HE GETS MANGLED.
YOU GOT THE MONEY?
COURSE.

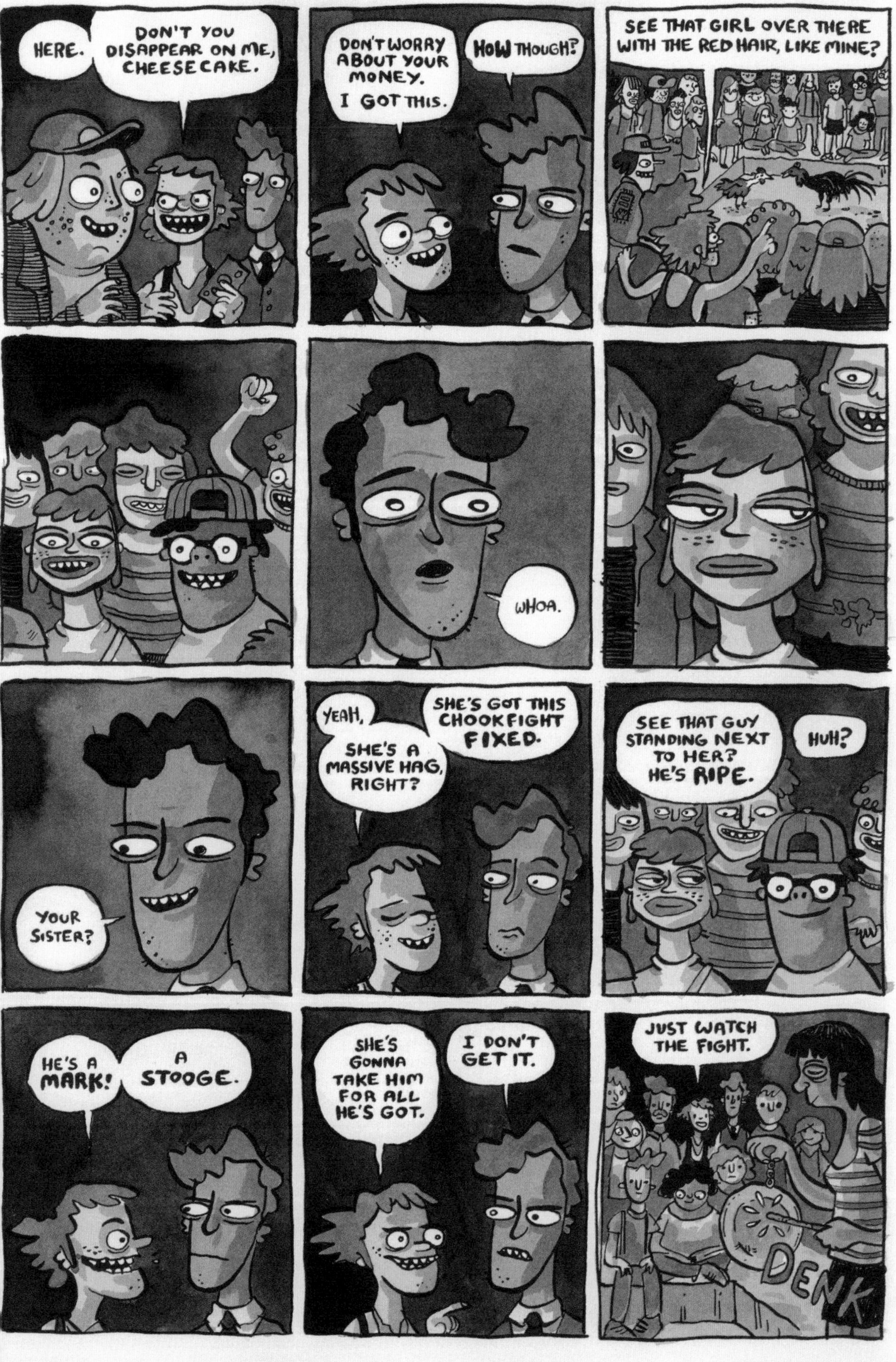
HERE.
DON'T YOU DISAPPEAR ON ME, CHEESECAKE.
DON'T WORRY ABOUT YOUR MONEY.
I GOT THIS.
HOW THOUGH?
SEE THAT GIRL OVER THERE WITH THE RED HAIR, LIKE MINE?
WHOA.
YOUR SISTER?
YEAH,
SHE'S A MASSIVE HAG, RIGHT?
SHE'S GOT THIS CHOOKFIGHT FIXED.
SEE THAT GUY STANDING NEXT TO HER? HE'S RIPE.
HUH?
HE'S A MARK!
A STOOGE.
SHE'S GONNA TAKE HIM FOR ALL HE'S GOT.
I DON'T GET IT.
JUST WATCH THE FIGHT.
DENK

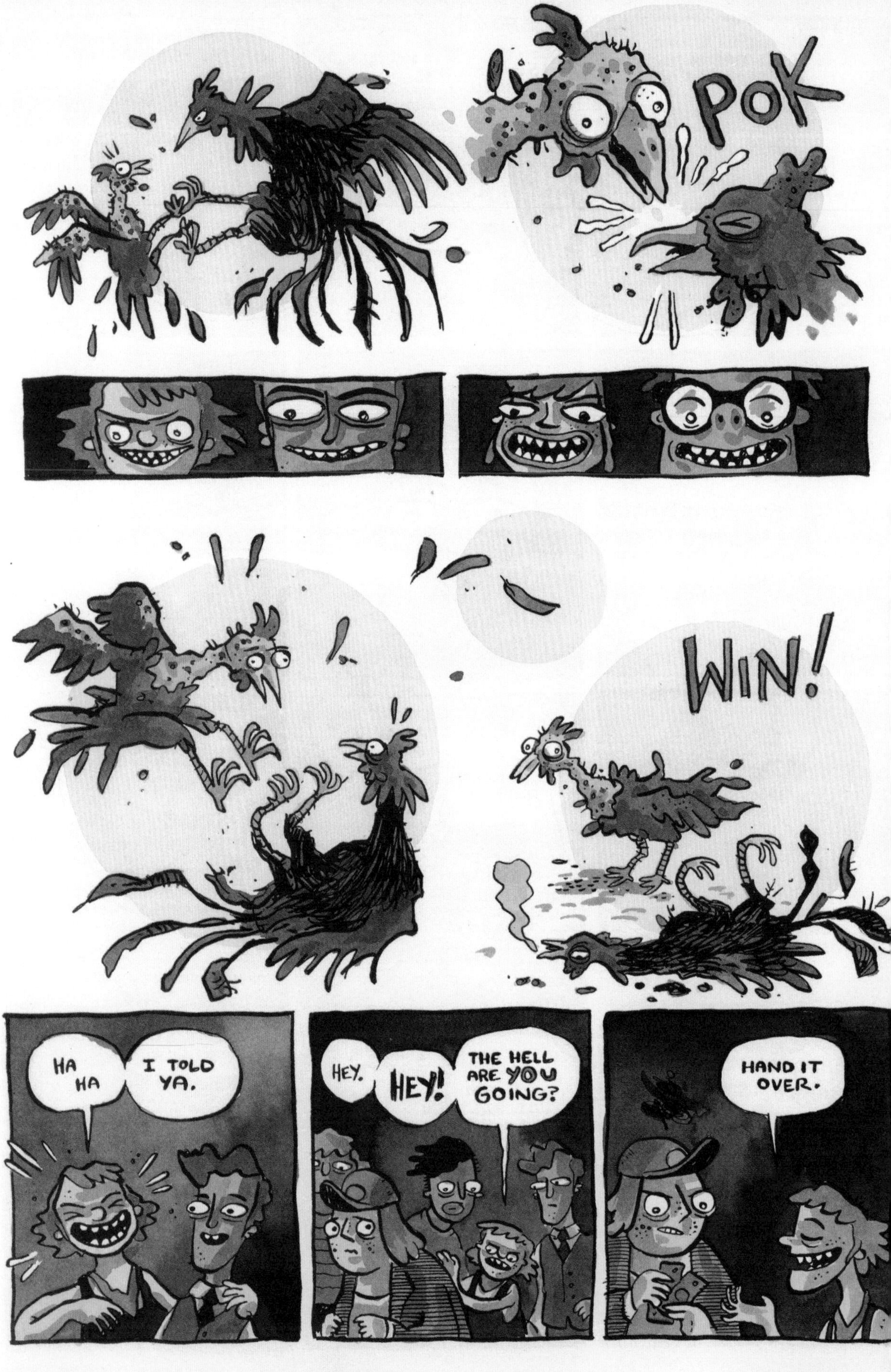
POK
WIN!
HA HA
I TOLD YA.
HEY.
HEY!
THE HELL ARE YOU GOING?
HAND IT OVER.

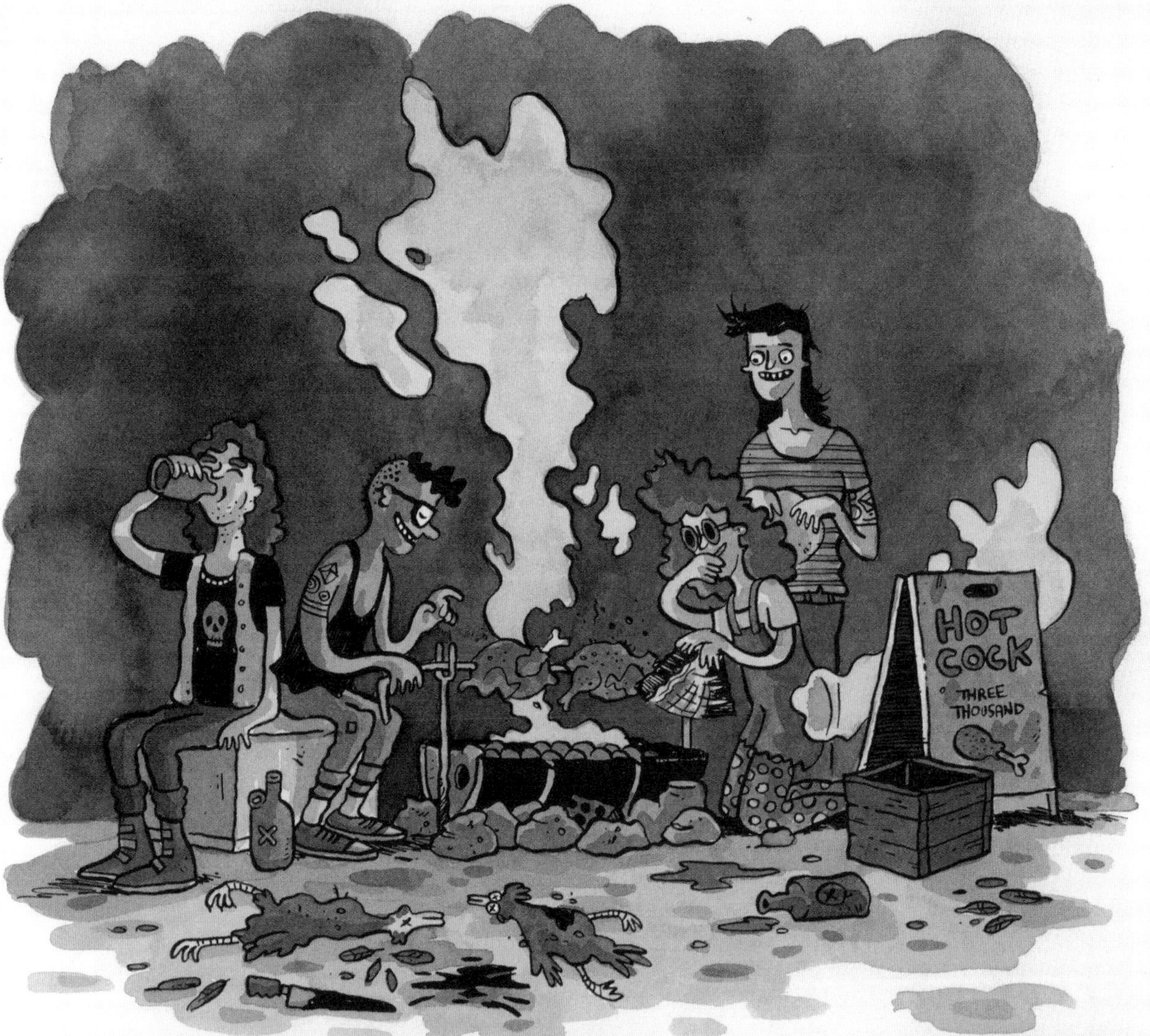
HOT COCK
THREE THOUSAND

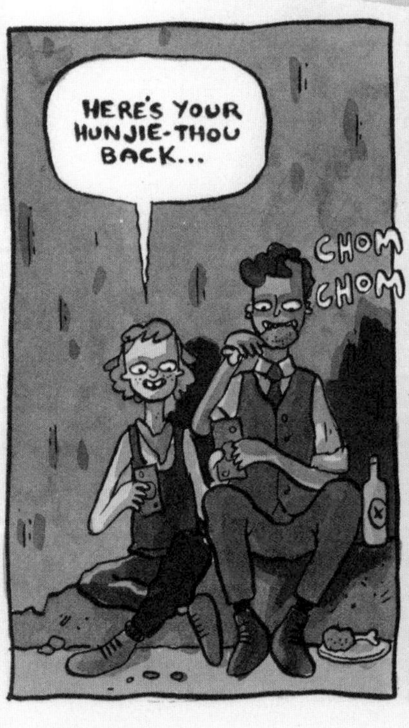
HERE'S YOUR HUNJIE-THOU BACK...
CHOM CHOM

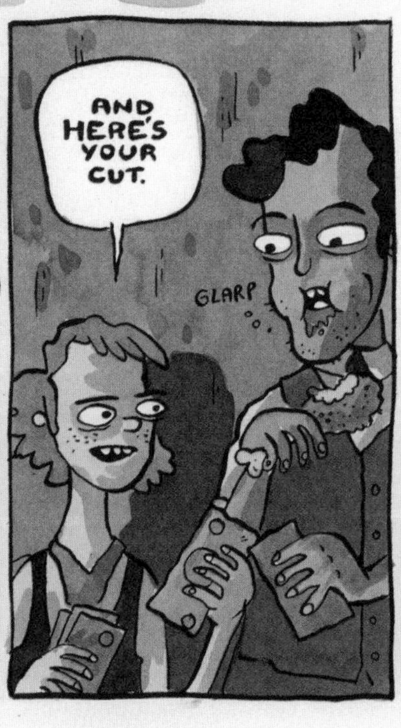
AND HERE'S YOUR CUT.
GLARP

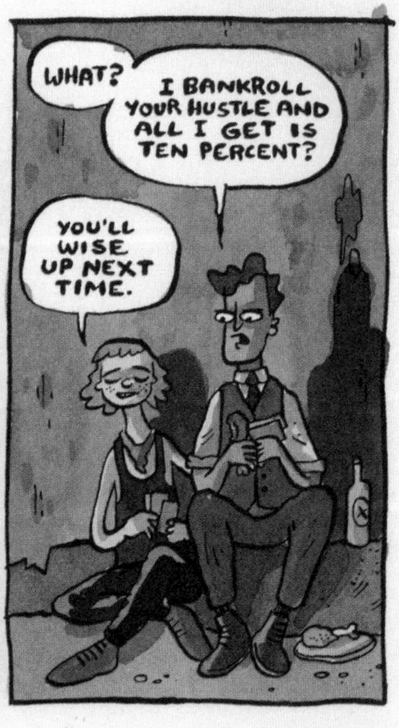
WHAT?
I BANKROLL YOUR HUSTLE AND ALL I GET IS TEN PERCENT?
YOU'LL WISE UP NEXT TIME.

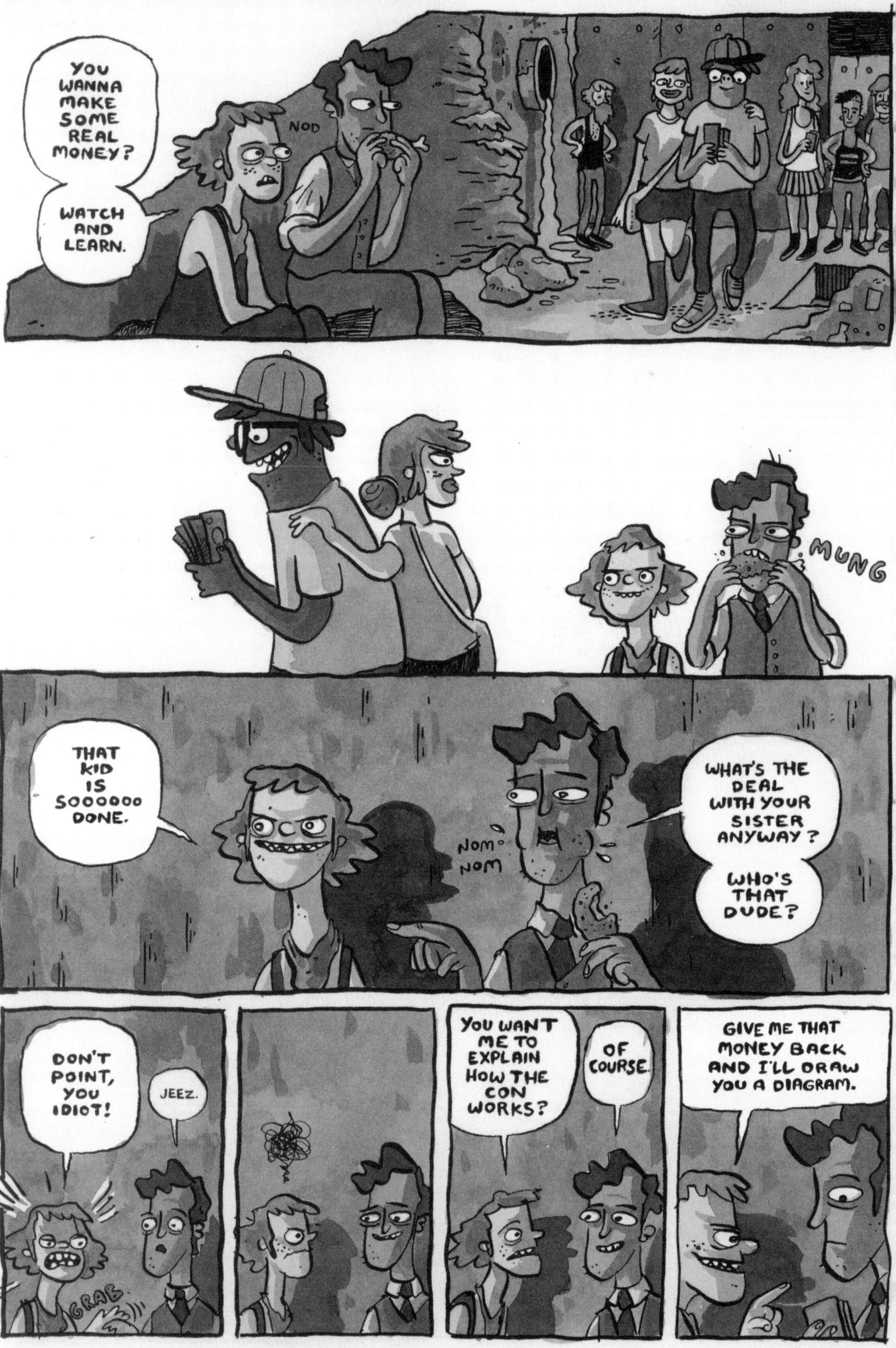
YOU WANNA MAKE SOME REAL MONEY?
WATCH AND LEARN.
NOD
MUNG
THAT KID IS SOOOOOO DONE.
NOM NOM
WHAT'S THE DEAL WITH YOUR SISTER ANYWAY?
WHO'S THAT DUDE?
DON'T POINT, YOU IDIOT!
JEEZ.
GRAB
YOU WANT ME TO EXPLAIN HOW THE CON WORKS?
OF COURSE.
GIVE ME THAT MONEY BACK AND I'LL DRAW YOU A DIAGRAM.

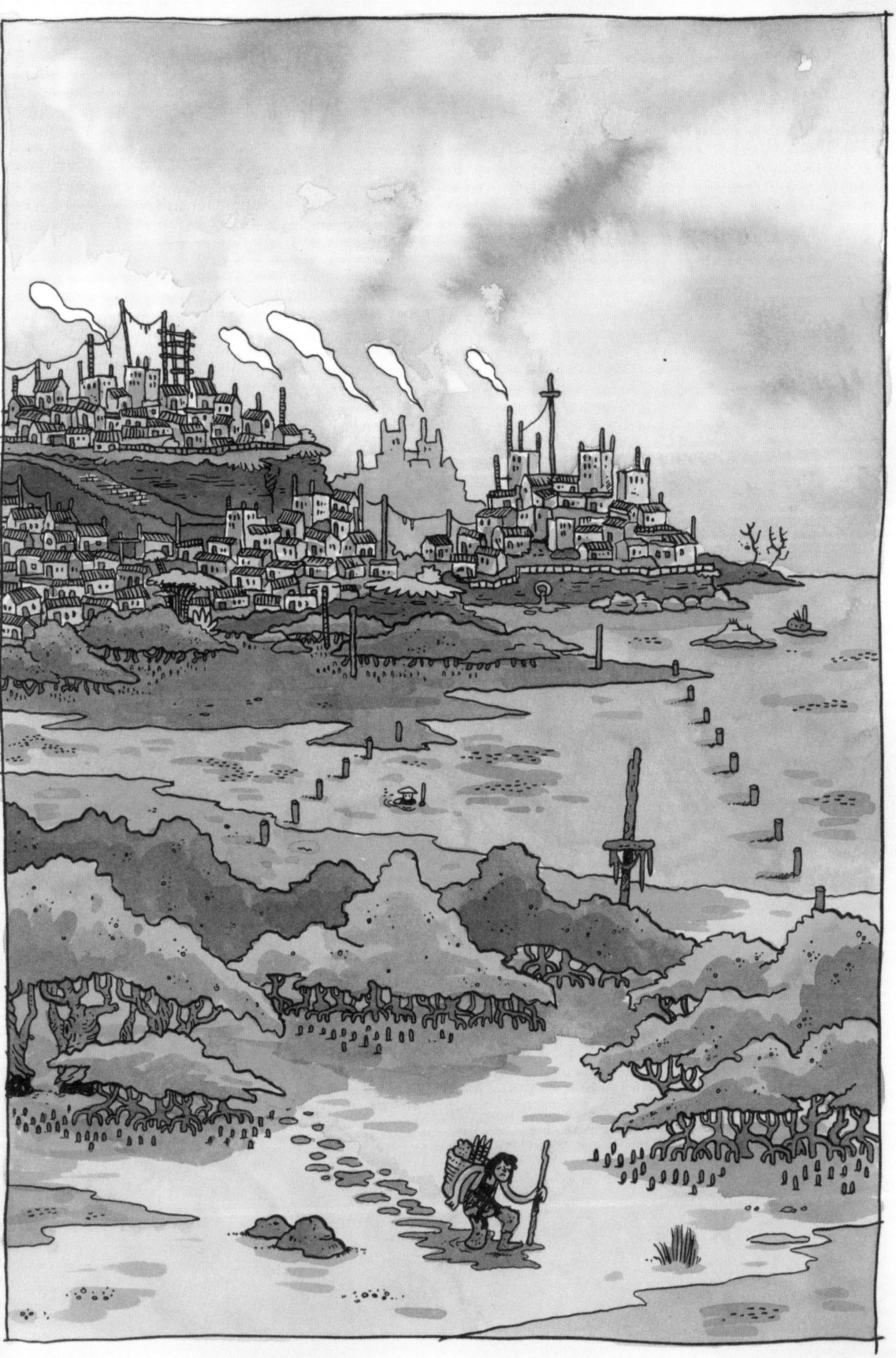

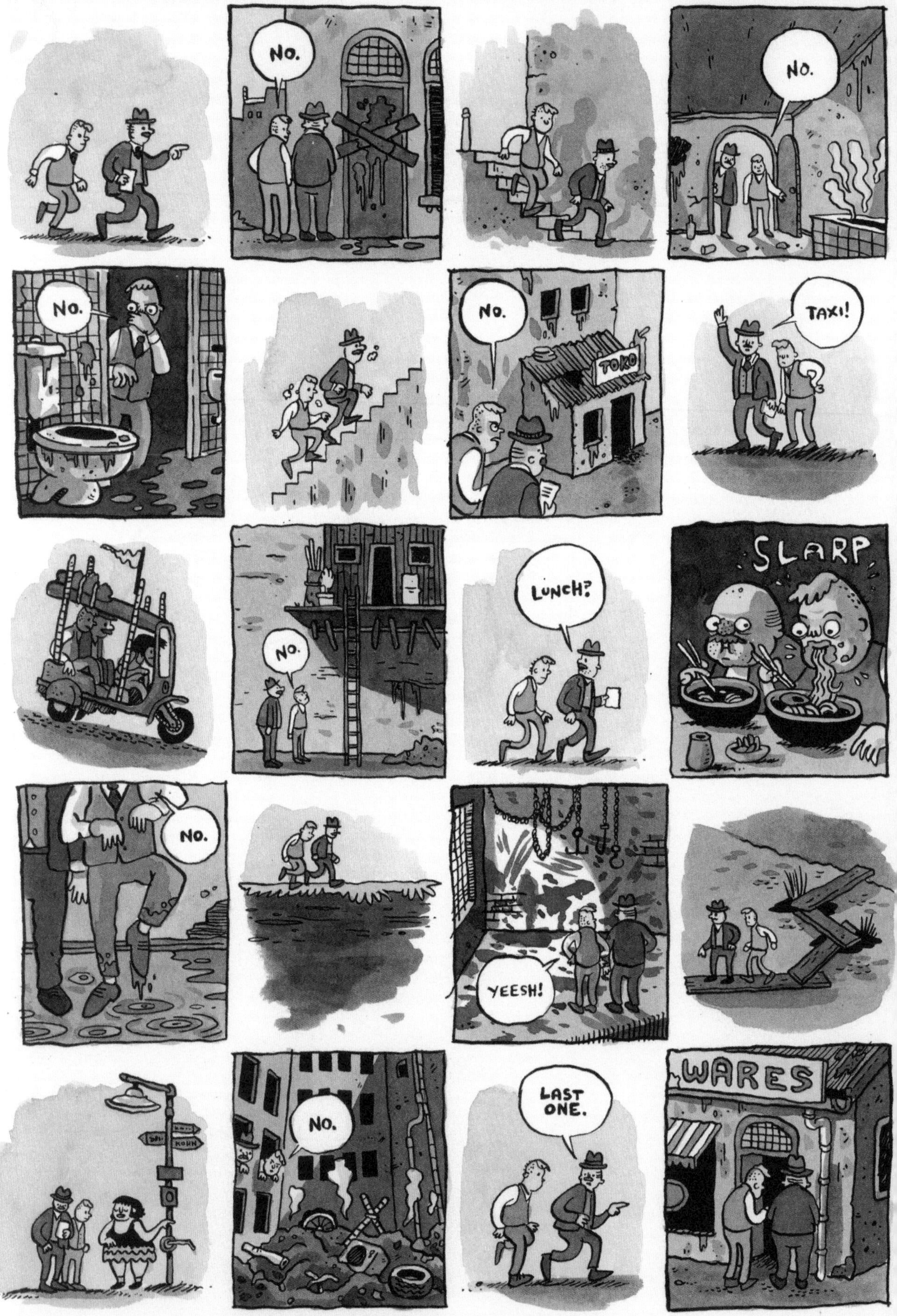
NO.
NO.
NO.
NO.
TOKO
TAXI!
NO.
LUNCH?
SLARP
NO.
YEESH!
NO.
LAST ONE.
WARES

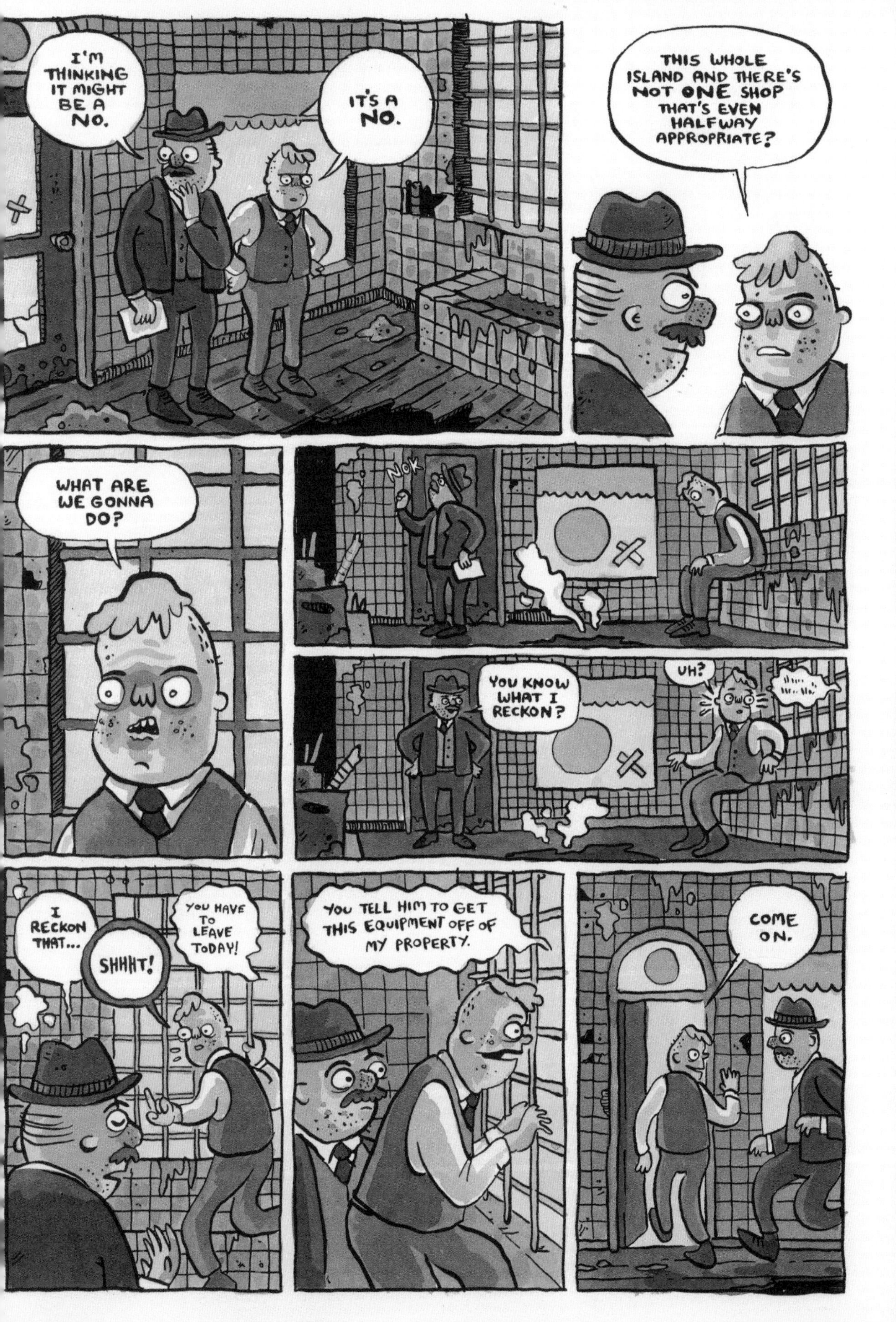
I'M THINKING IT MIGHT BE A NO.
IT'S A NO.
THIS WHOLE ISLAND AND THERE'S NOT ONE SHOP THAT'S EVEN HALFWAY APPROPRIATE?
WHAT ARE WE GONNA DO?
NOK
YOU KNOW WHAT I RECKON?
UH?
I RECKON THAT...
SHHHT!
YOU HAVE TO LEAVE TODAY!
YOU TELL HIM TO GET THIS EQUIPMENT OFF OF MY PROPERTY.
COME ON.

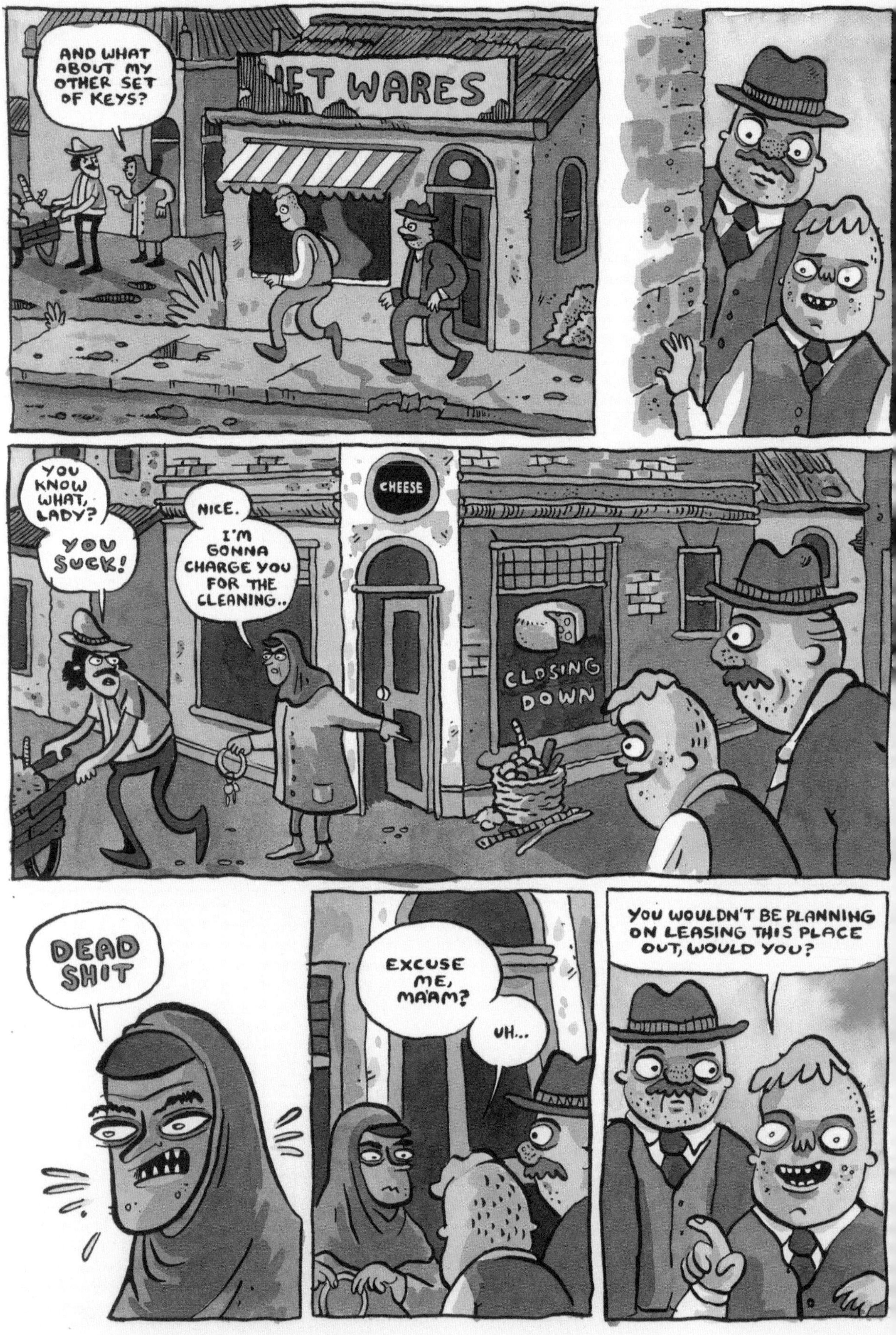
AND WHAT ABOUT MY OTHER SET OF KEYS?
FT WARES
YOU KNOW WHAT, LADY?
YOU SUCK!
NICE.
I'M GONNA CHARGE YOU FOR THE CLEANING..
CHEESE
CLOSING DOWN
DEAD SHIT
EXCUSE ME, MA'AM?
UH...
YOU WOULDN'T BE PLANNING ON LEASING THIS PLACE OUT, WOULD YOU?

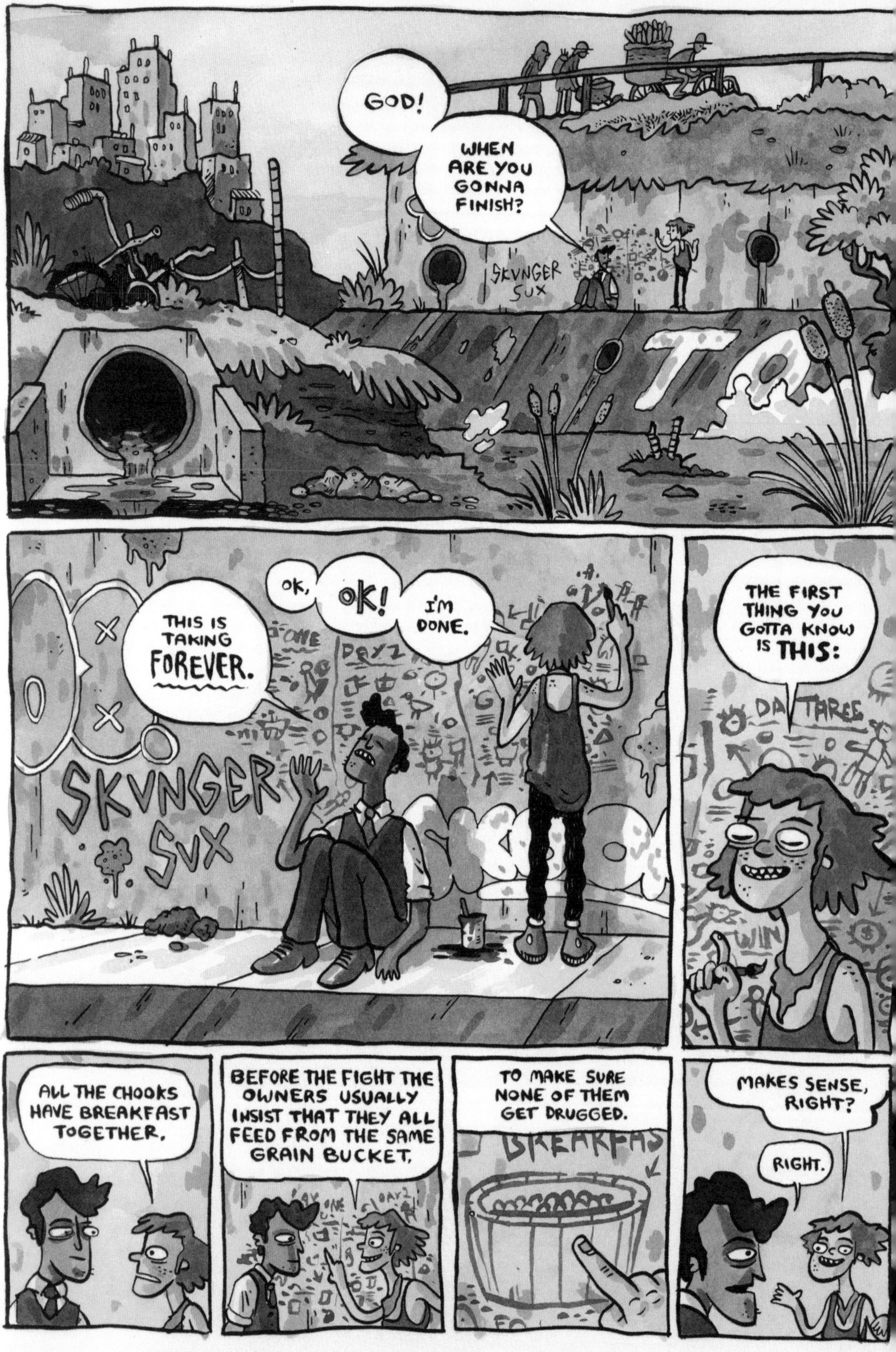
GOD!
WHEN ARE YOU GONNA FINISH?
SKVNGER SUX
THIS IS TAKING FOREVER.
OK, OK! I'M DONE.
SKVNGER SVX
THE FIRST THING YOU GOTTA KNOW IS THIS:
ALL THE CHOOKS HAVE BREAKFAST TOGETHER.
BEFORE THE FIGHT THE OWNERS USUALLY INSIST THAT THEY ALL FEED FROM THE SAME GRAIN BUCKET.
TO MAKE SURE NONE OF THEM GET DRUGGED.
MAKES SENSE, RIGHT?
RIGHT.

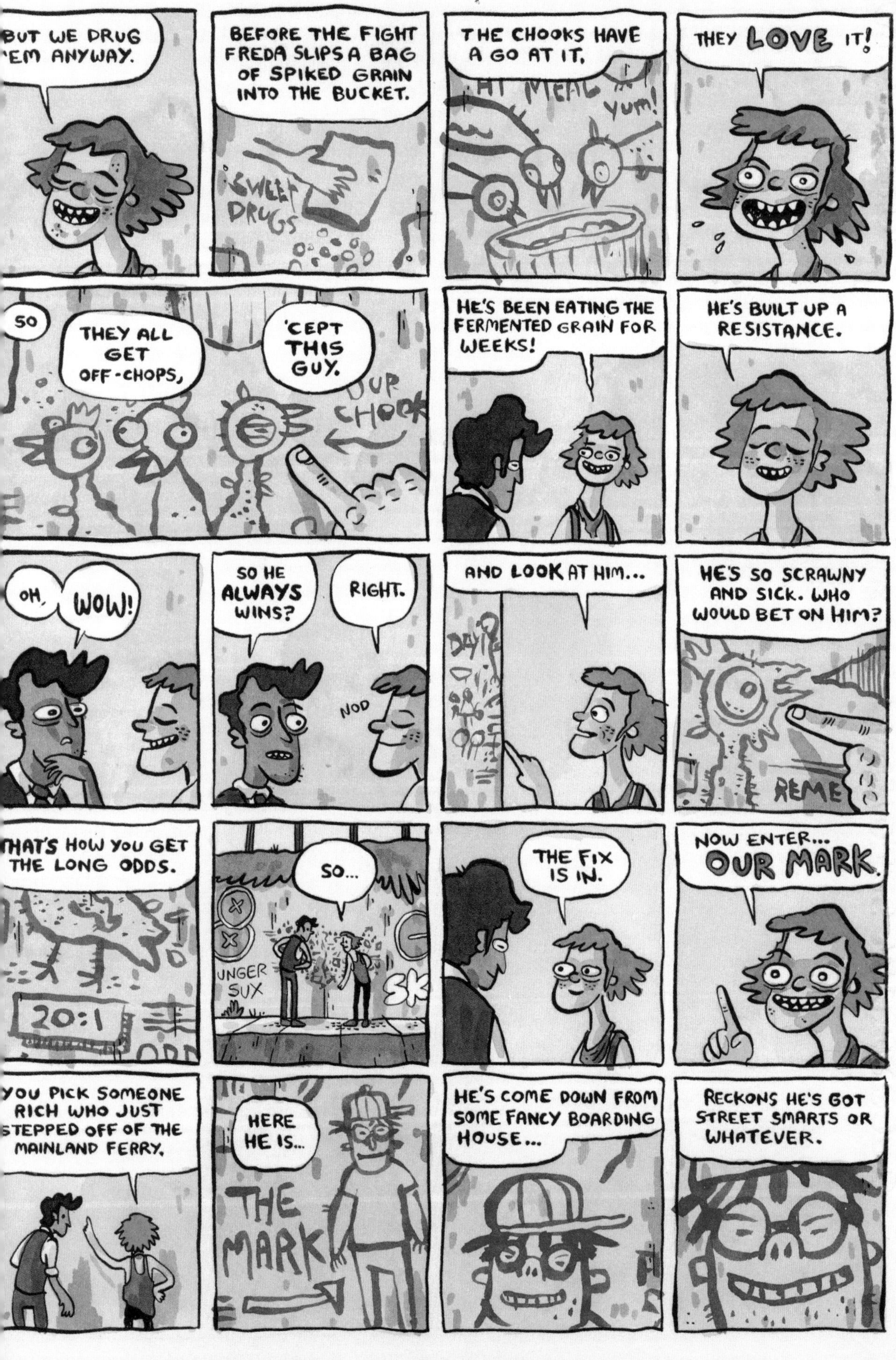
BUT WE DRUG 'EM ANYWAY.
BEFORE THE FIGHT FREDA SLIPS A BAG OF SPIKED GRAIN INTO THE BUCKET.
SWEET DRUGS
THE CHOOKS HAVE A GO AT IT.
YUM!
THEY LOVE IT!
SO
THEY ALL GET OFF-CHOPS,
'CEPT THIS GUY.
OUR CHOOK
HE'S BEEN EATING THE FERMENTED GRAIN FOR WEEKS!
HE'S BUILT UP A RESISTANCE.
OH,
WOW!
SO HE ALWAYS WINS?
RIGHT.
NOD
AND LOOK AT HIM...
HE'S SO SCRAWNY AND SICK. WHO WOULD BET ON HIM?
THAT'S HOW YOU GET THE LONG ODDS.
20:1
SO...
UNGER SUX
THE FIX IS IN.
NOW ENTER... OUR MARK.
YOU PICK SOMEONE RICH WHO JUST STEPPED OFF OF THE MAINLAND FERRY.
HERE HE IS...
THE MARK
HE'S COME DOWN FROM SOME FANCY BOARDING HOUSE...
RECKONS HE'S GOT STREET SMARTS OR WHATEVER.

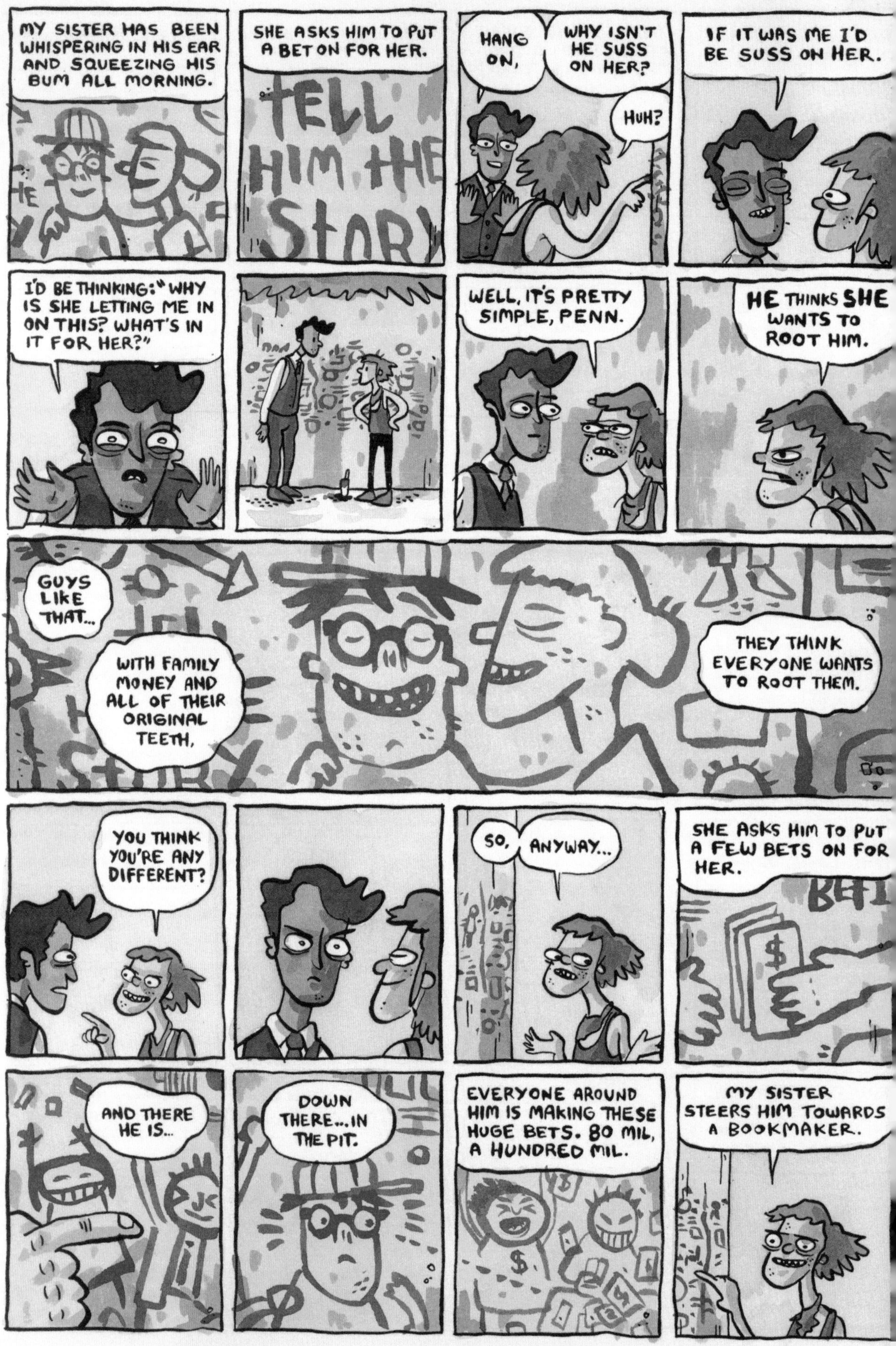
MY SISTER HAS BEEN WHISPERING IN HIS EAR AND SQUEEZING HIS BUM ALL MORNING.
SHE ASKS HIM TO PUT A BET ON FOR HER.
TELL HIM THE STORY
HANG ON,
WHY ISN'T HE SUSS ON HER?
HUH?
IF IT WAS ME I'D BE SUSS ON HER.
I'D BE THINKING: "WHY IS SHE LETTING ME IN ON THIS? WHAT'S IN IT FOR HER?"
WELL, IT'S PRETTY SIMPLE, PENN.
HE THINKS SHE WANTS TO ROOT HIM.
GUYS LIKE THAT...
WITH FAMILY MONEY AND ALL OF THEIR ORIGINAL TEETH,
THEY THINK EVERYONE WANTS TO ROOT THEM.
YOU THINK YOU'RE ANY DIFFERENT?
SO,
ANYWAY...
SHE ASKS HIM TO PUT A FEW BETS ON FOR HER.
AND THERE HE IS...
DOWN THERE...IN THE PIT.
EVERYONE AROUND HIM IS MAKING THESE HUGE BETS. 80 MIL, A HUNDRED MIL.
MY SISTER STEERS HIM TOWARDS A BOOKMAKER.

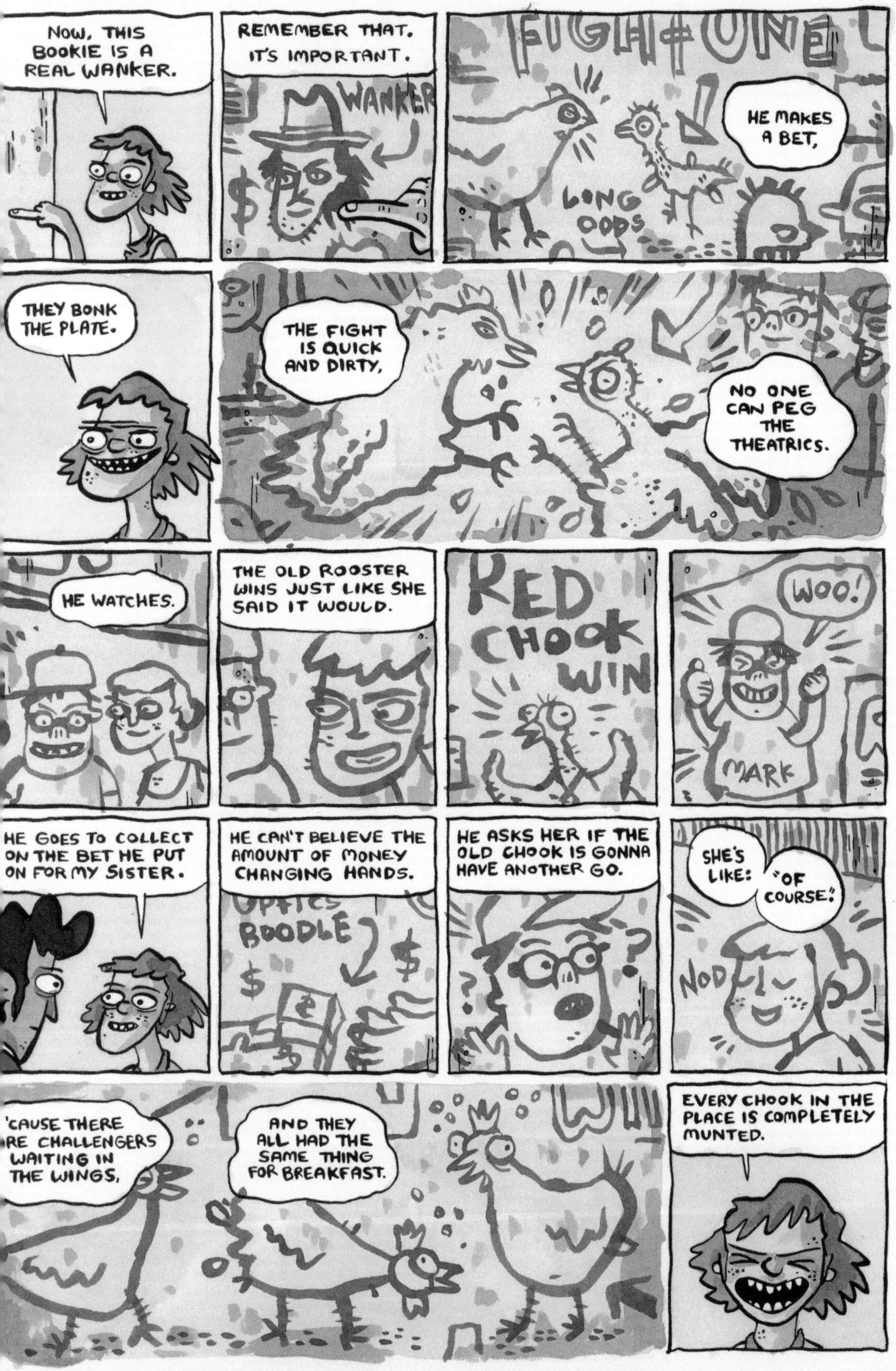
NOW, THIS BOOKIE IS A REAL WANKER.
REMEMBER THAT. IT'S IMPORTANT.
WANKER
$
FIGHT #ONE
HE MAKES A BET,
LONG ODDS
THEY BONK THE PLATE.
THE FIGHT IS QUICK AND DIRTY,
NO ONE CAN PEG THE THEATRICS.
HE WATCHES.
THE OLD ROOSTER WINS JUST LIKE SHE SAID IT WOULD.
RED CHOOK WIN
WOO!
MARK
HE GOES TO COLLECT ON THE BET HE PUT ON FOR MY SISTER.
HE CAN'T BELIEVE THE AMOUNT OF MONEY CHANGING HANDS.
BOODLE
$
$
HE ASKS HER IF THE OLD CHOOK IS GONNA HAVE ANOTHER GO.
?
?
SHE'S LIKE:
"OF COURSE."
NOD
'CAUSE THERE RE CHALLENGERS WAITING IN THE WINGS,
AND THEY ALL HAD THE SAME THING FOR BREAKFAST.
EVERY CHOOK IN THE PLACE IS COMPLETELY MUNTED.

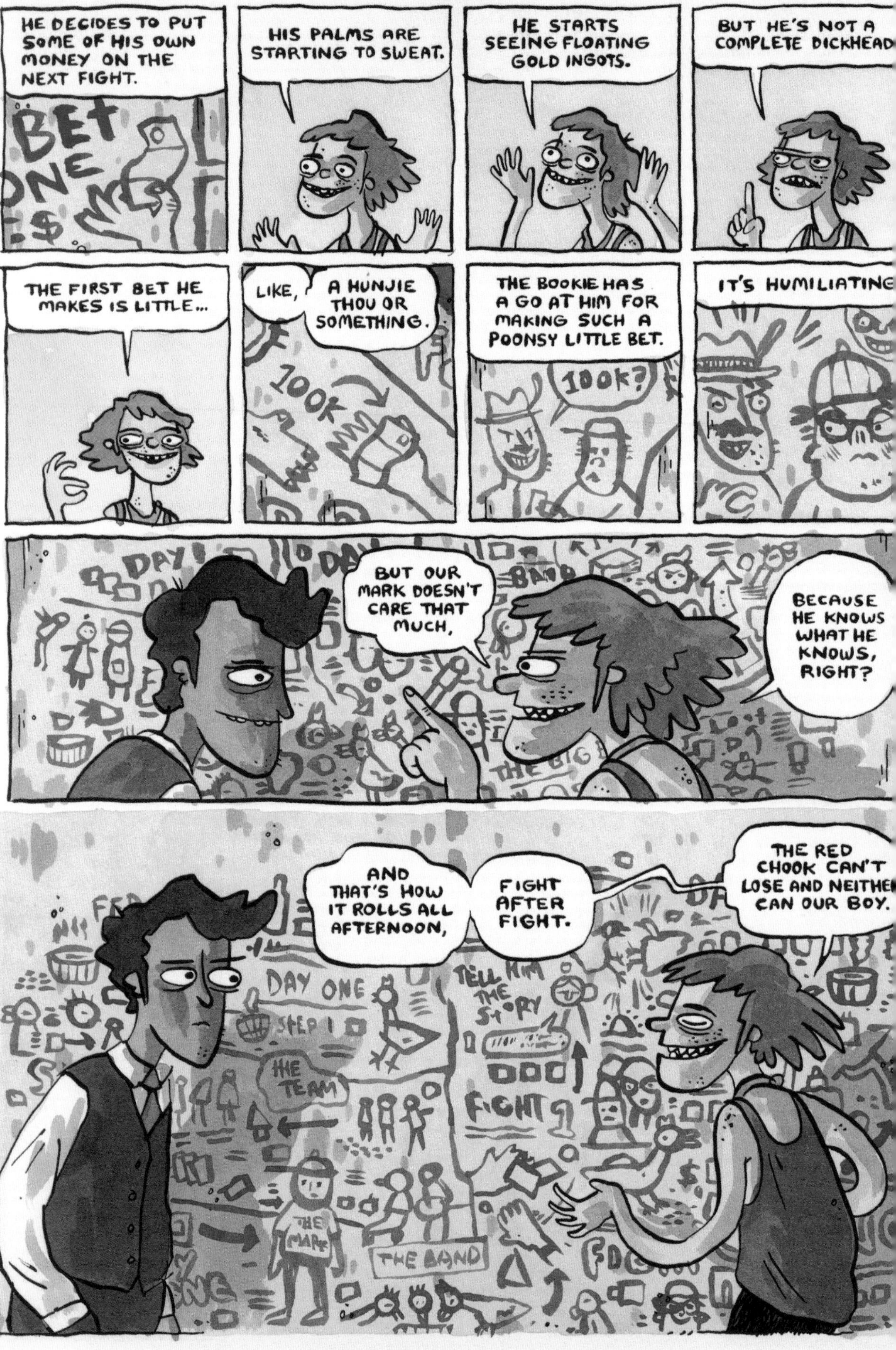
HE DECIDES TO PUT SOME OF HIS OWN MONEY ON THE NEXT FIGHT.
BET
ONE
$
HIS PALMS ARE STARTING TO SWEAT.
HE STARTS SEEING FLOATING GOLD INGOTS.
BUT HE'S NOT A COMPLETE DICKHEAD
THE FIRST BET HE MAKES IS LITTLE...
LIKE,
A HUNJIE THOU OR SOMETHING.
100K
THE BOOKIE HAS A GO AT HIM FOR MAKING SUCH A POONSY LITTLE BET.
100K?
IT'S HUMILIATING
DAY
BUT OUR MARK DOESN'T CARE THAT MUCH,
BECAUSE HE KNOWS WHAT HE KNOWS, RIGHT?
AND THAT'S HOW IT ROLLS ALL AFTERNOON,
FIGHT AFTER FIGHT.
THE RED CHOOK CAN'T LOSE AND NEITHER CAN OUR BOY.
DAY ONE
TELL HIM THE STORY
STEP 1
THE TEAM
FIGHT
THE MARK
THE BAND

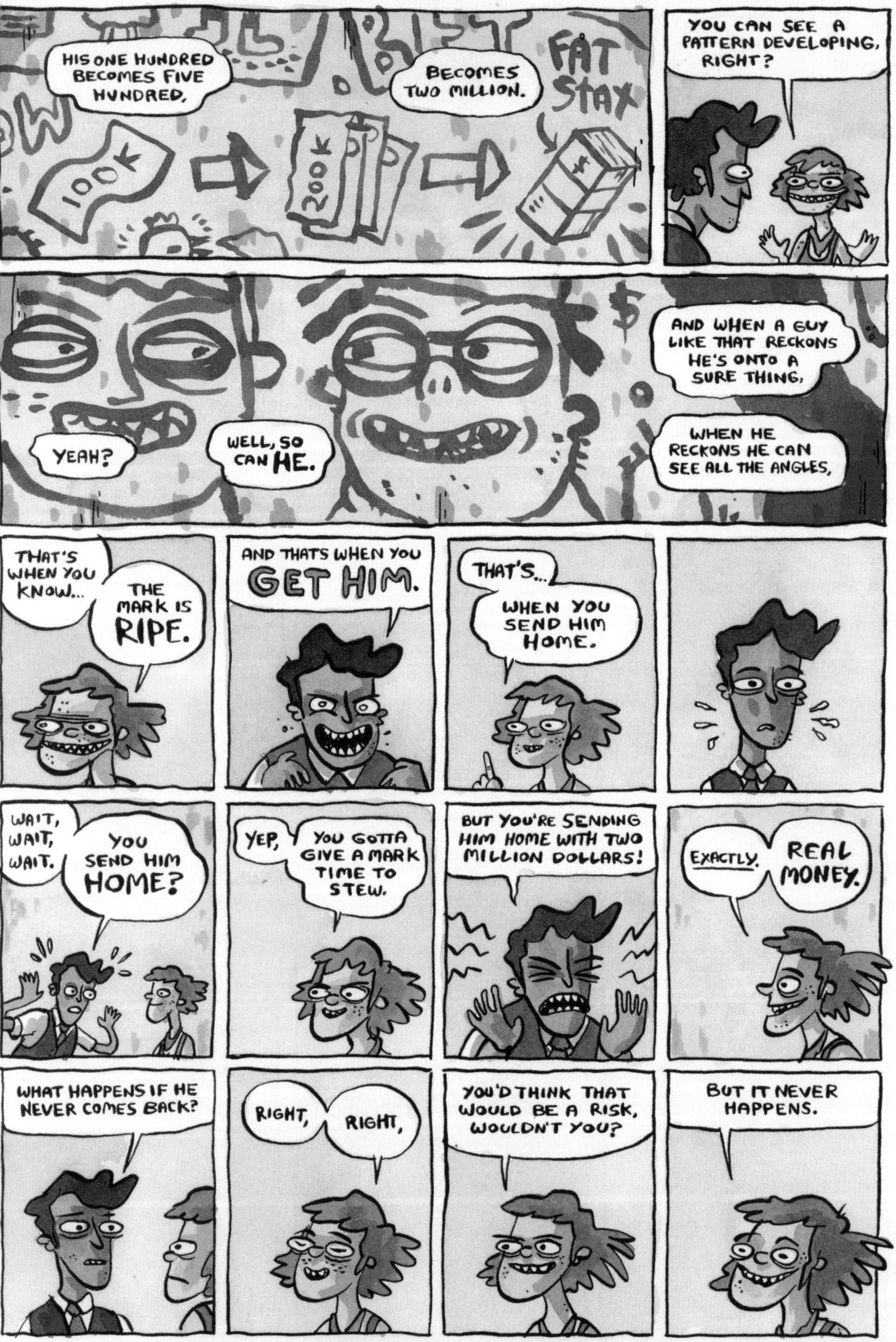
HIS ONE HUNDRED BECOMES FIVE HUNDRED,
BECOMES TWO MILLION.
FAT STAX
100K
200K
$
YOU CAN SEE A PATTERN DEVELOPING, RIGHT?
YEAH?
WELL, SO CAN HE.
$
AND WHEN A GUY LIKE THAT RECKONS HE'S ONTO A SURE THING,
WHEN HE RECKONS HE CAN SEE ALL THE ANGLES,
THAT'S WHEN YOU KNOW...
THE MARK IS RIPE.
AND THATS WHEN YOU GET HIM.
THAT'S...
WHEN YOU SEND HIM HOME.
WAIT, WAIT, WAIT.
YOU SEND HIM HOME?
YEP,
YOU GOTTA GIVE A MARK TIME TO STEW.
BUT YOU'RE SENDING HIM HOME WITH TWO MILLION DOLLARS!
EXACTLY.
REAL MONEY.
WHAT HAPPENS IF HE NEVER COMES BACK?
RIGHT,
RIGHT,
YOU'D THINK THAT WOULD BE A RISK, WOULDN'T YOU?
BUT IT NEVER HAPPENS.

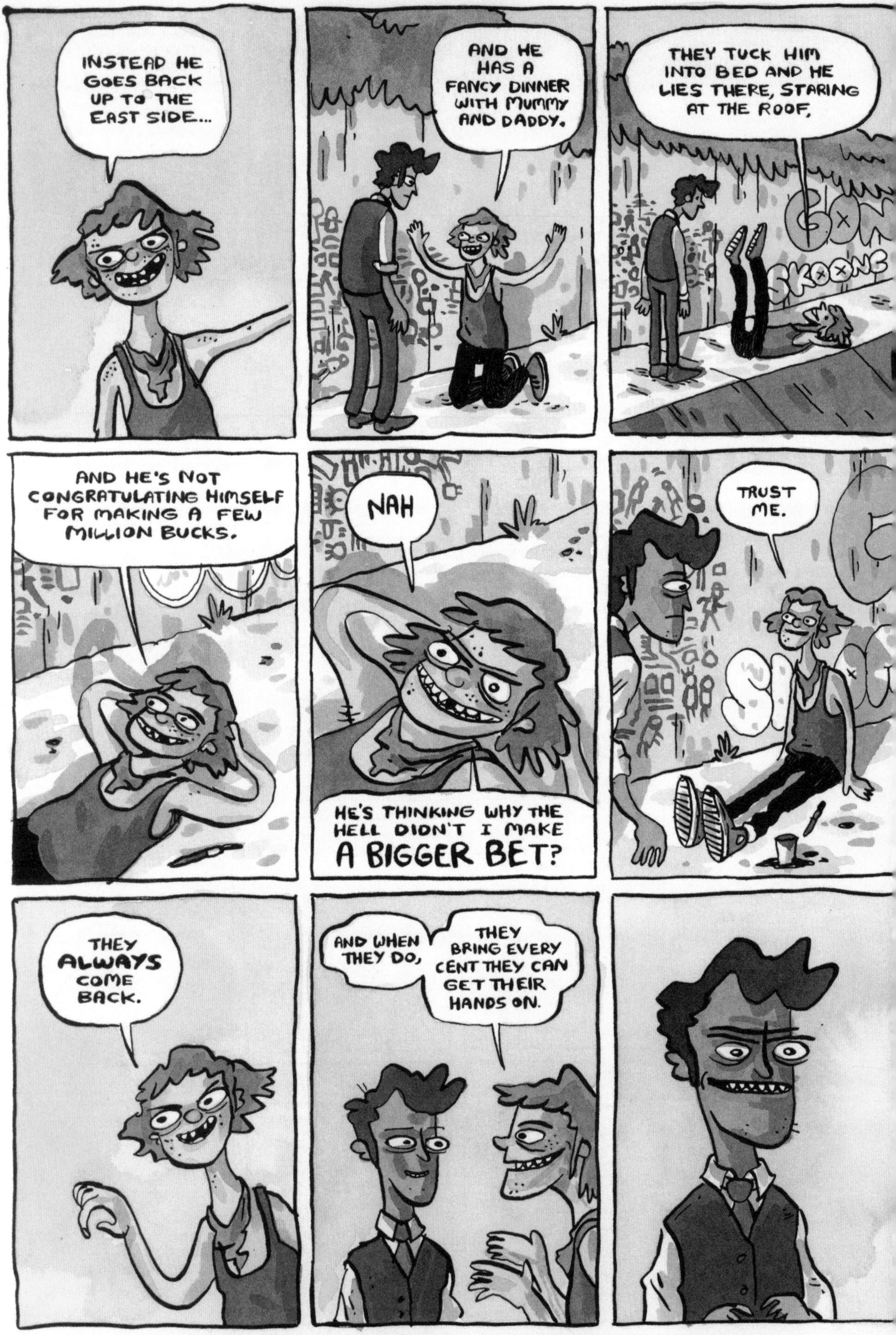
INSTEAD HE GOES BACK UP TO THE EAST SIDE...
AND HE HAS A FANCY DINNER WITH MUMMY AND DADDY.
THEY TUCK HIM INTO BED AND HE LIES THERE, STARING AT THE ROOF,
AND HE'S NOT CONGRATULATING HIMSELF FOR MAKING A FEW MILLION BUCKS.
NAH
HE'S THINKING WHY THE HELL DIDN'T I MAKE A BIGGER BET?
TRUST ME.
THEY ALWAYS COME BACK.
AND WHEN THEY DO,
THEY BRING EVERY CENT THEY CAN GET THEIR HANDS ON.

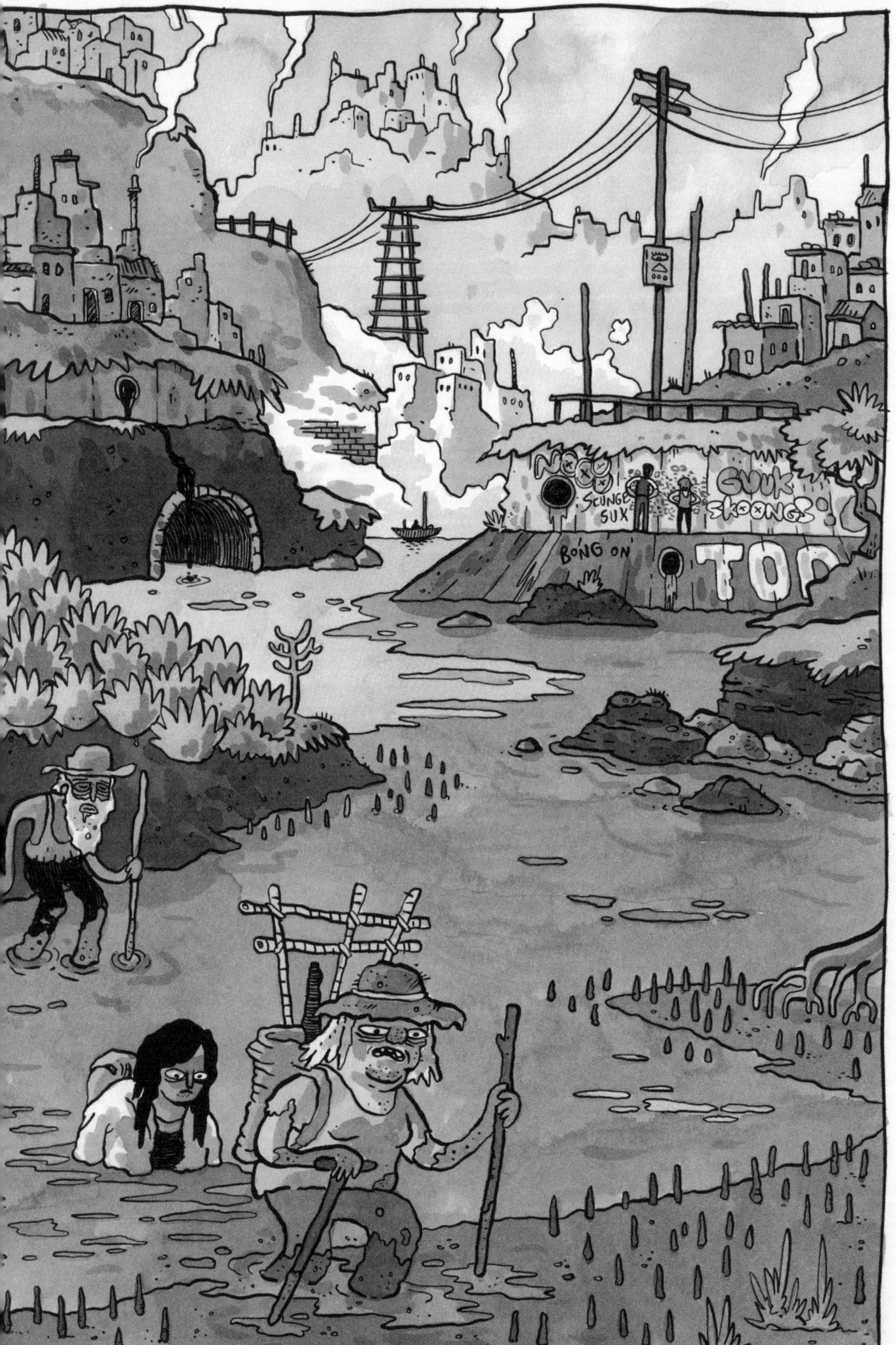
SCUNGE SUX
GUUK
SKOONGS
BONG ON
TOP

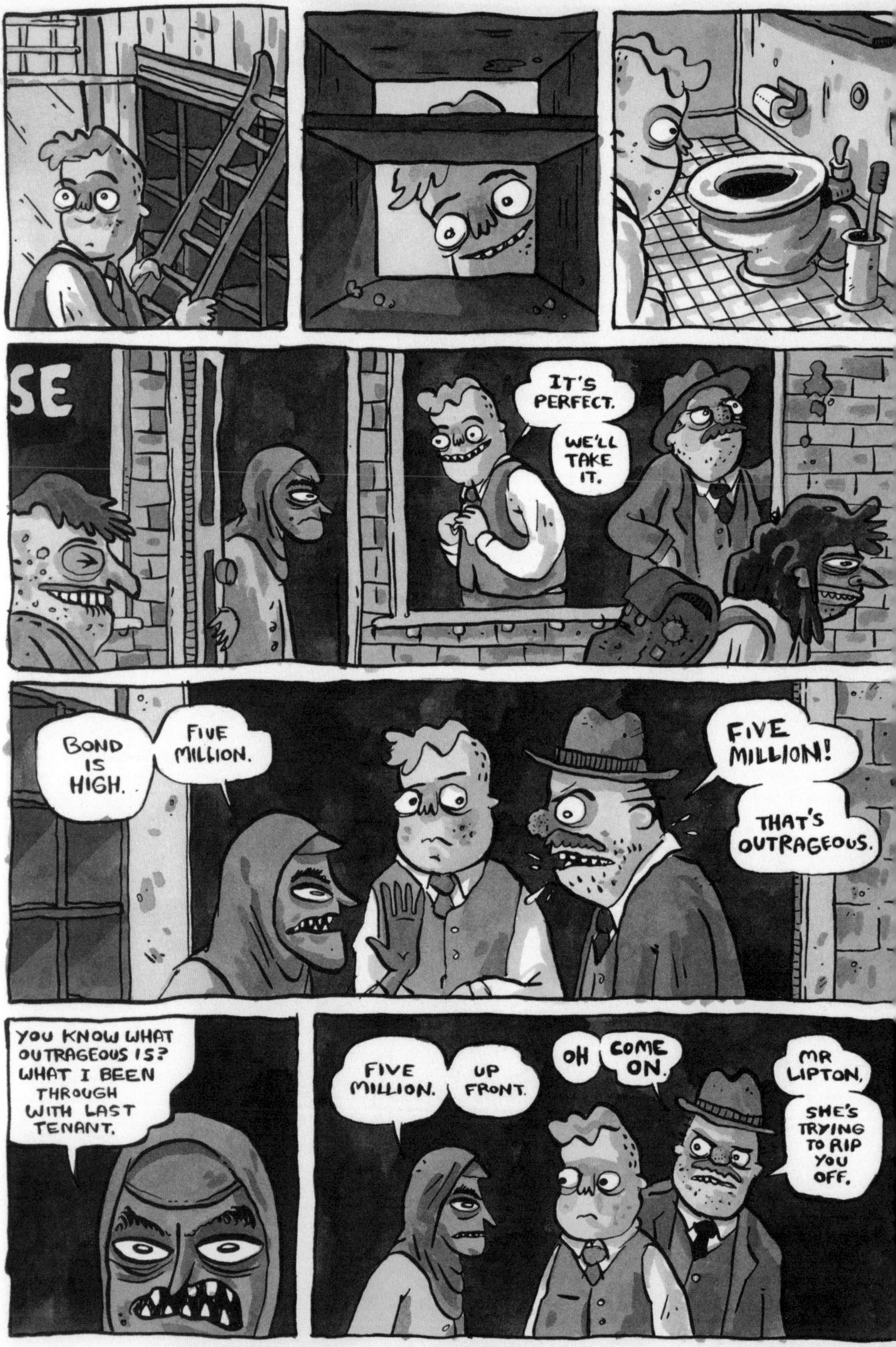
SE
IT'S PERFECT.
WE'LL TAKE IT.
BOND IS HIGH.
FIVE MILLION.
FIVE MILLION!
THAT'S OUTRAGEOUS.
YOU KNOW WHAT OUTRAGEOUS IS? WHAT I BEEN THROUGH WITH LAST TENANT.
FIVE MILLION.
UP FRONT.
OH
COME ON.
MR LIPTON,
SHE'S TRYING TO RIP YOU OFF.

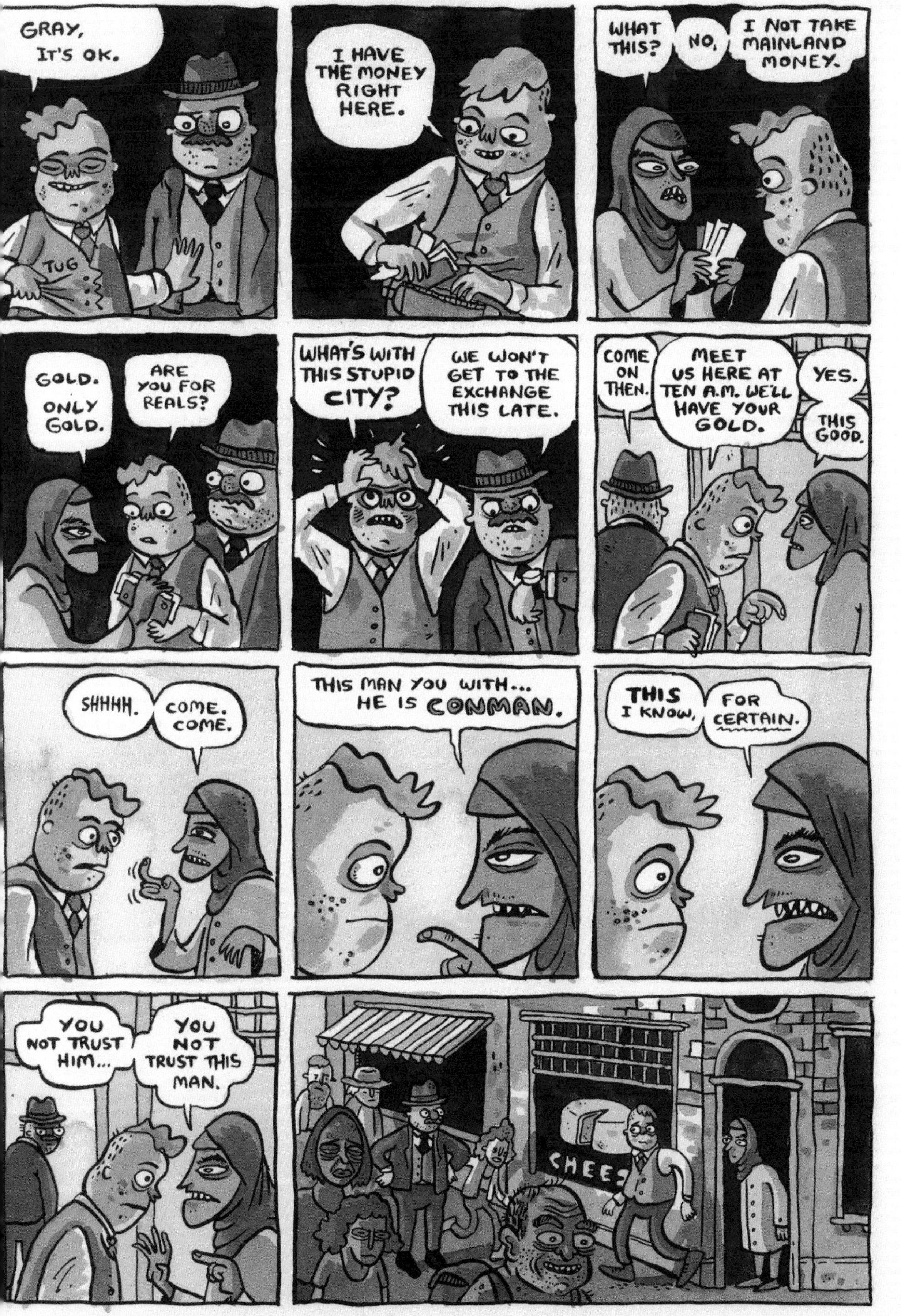
GRAY, IT'S OK.
TUG
I HAVE THE MONEY RIGHT HERE.
WHAT THIS?
NO,
I NOT TAKE MAINLAND MONEY.
GOLD. ONLY GOLD.
ARE YOU FOR REALS?
WHAT'S WITH THIS STUPID CITY?
WE WON'T GET TO THE EXCHANGE THIS LATE.
COME ON THEN.
MEET US HERE AT TEN A.M. WE'LL HAVE YOUR GOLD.
YES.
THIS GOOD.
SHHHH.
COME. COME.
THIS MAN YOU WITH... HE IS CONMAN.
THIS I KNOW,
FOR CERTAIN.
YOU NOT TRUST HIM...
YOU NOT TRUST THIS MAN.
CHEE

WHAT?

YOU HAD **FIVE MILLION** DOLLARS JUST SITTING IN THAT RIDICULOUS BELT?

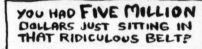

HOW MUCH MORE DO YOU HAVE?

PLEASE TELL ME THAT YOU'RE NOT HOLDING YOUR **WHOLE** BANKROLL IN THERE.

OH DEAR.

DO YOU KNOW HOW THEY SPOT **PREY** AROUND HERE?

TAKE **THIS** YOUNG MORON.

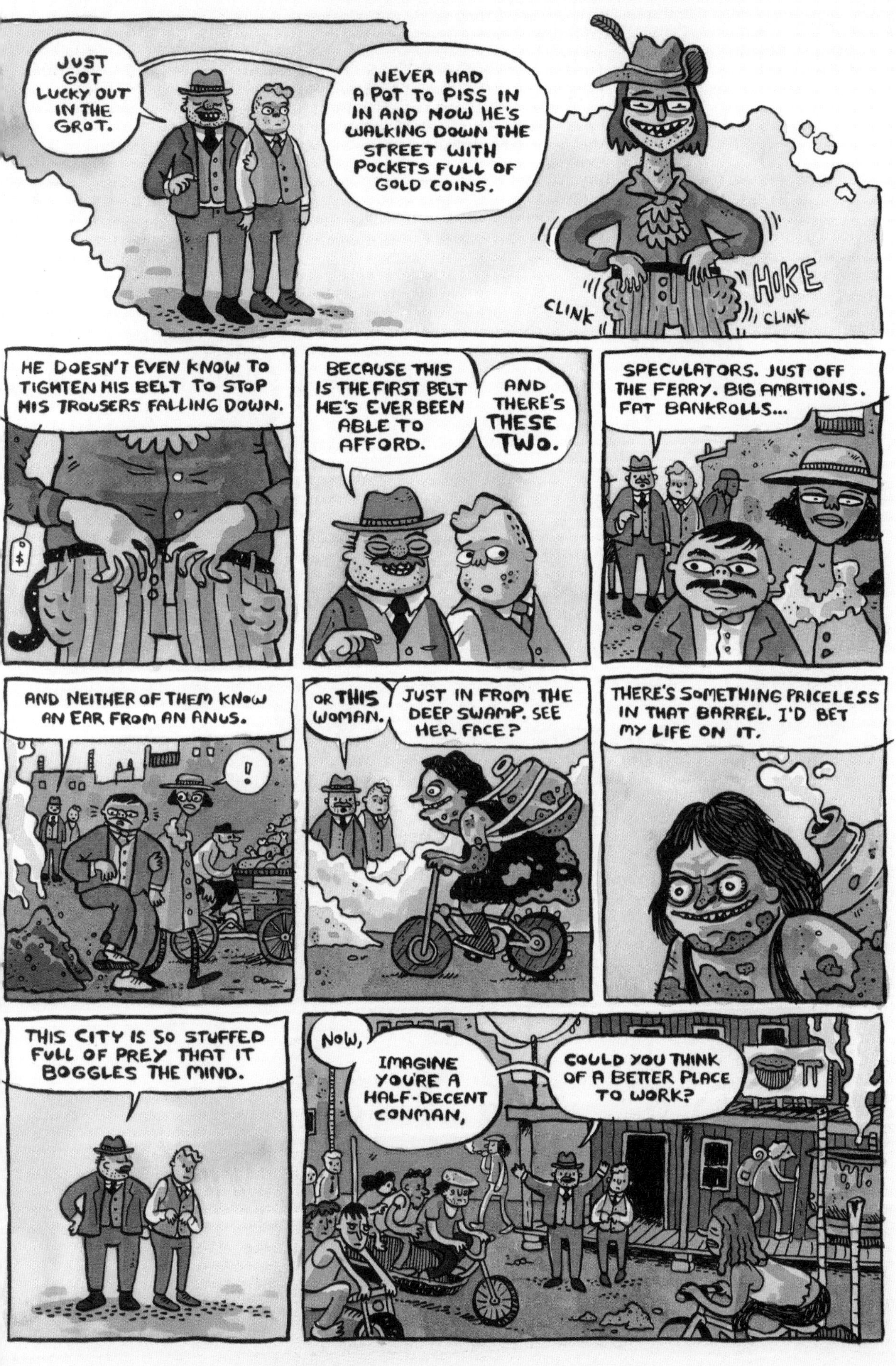
JUST GOT LUCKY OUT IN THE GROT.
NEVER HAD A POT TO PISS IN IN AND NOW HE'S WALKING DOWN THE STREET WITH POCKETS FULL OF GOLD COINS.
CLINK
HIKE
CLINK
HE DOESN'T EVEN KNOW TO TIGHTEN HIS BELT TO STOP HIS TROUSERS FALLING DOWN.
$
BECAUSE THIS IS THE FIRST BELT HE'S EVER BEEN ABLE TO AFFORD.
AND THERE'S THESE TWO.
SPECULATORS. JUST OFF THE FERRY. BIG AMBITIONS. FAT BANKROLLS...
AND NEITHER OF THEM KNOW AN EAR FROM AN ANUS.
!
OR THIS WOMAN.
JUST IN FROM THE DEEP SWAMP. SEE HER FACE?
THERE'S SOMETHING PRICELESS IN THAT BARREL. I'D BET MY LIFE ON IT.
THIS CITY IS SO STUFFED FULL OF PREY THAT IT BOGGLES THE MIND.
NOW,
IMAGINE YOU'RE A HALF-DECENT CONMAN,
COULD YOU THINK OF A BETTER PLACE TO WORK?

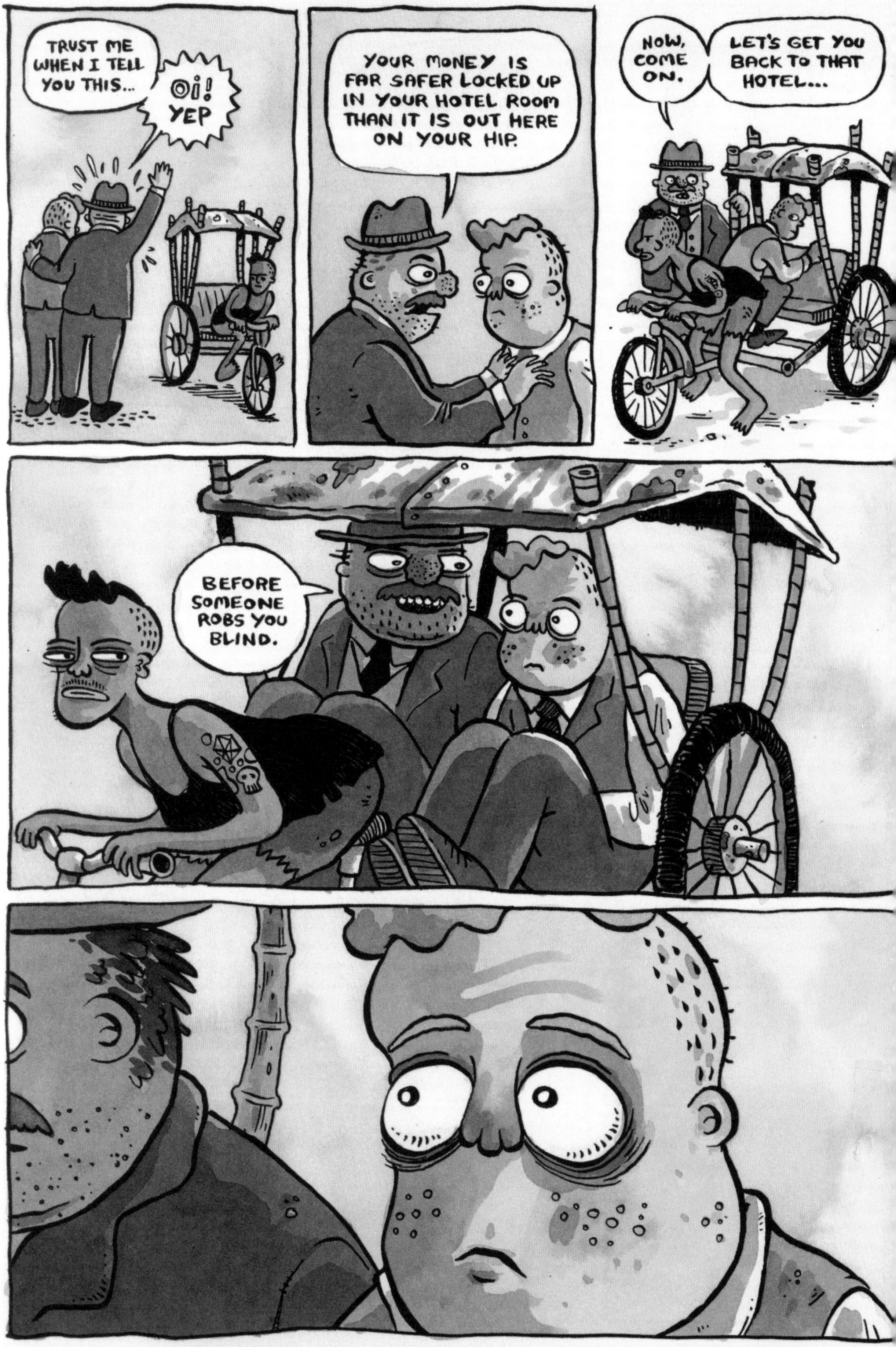
TRUST ME WHEN I TELL YOU THIS...
Oi! YEP
YOUR MONEY IS FAR SAFER LOCKED UP IN YOUR HOTEL ROOM THAN IT IS OUT HERE ON YOUR HIP.
NOW, COME ON.
LET'S GET YOU BACK TO THAT HOTEL...
BEFORE SOMEONE ROBS YOU BLIND.

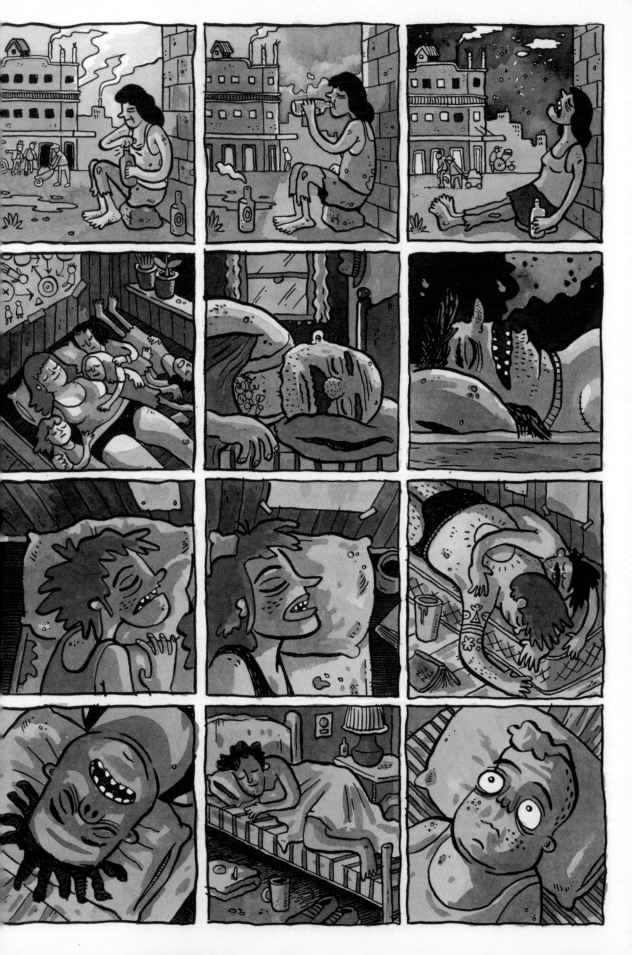

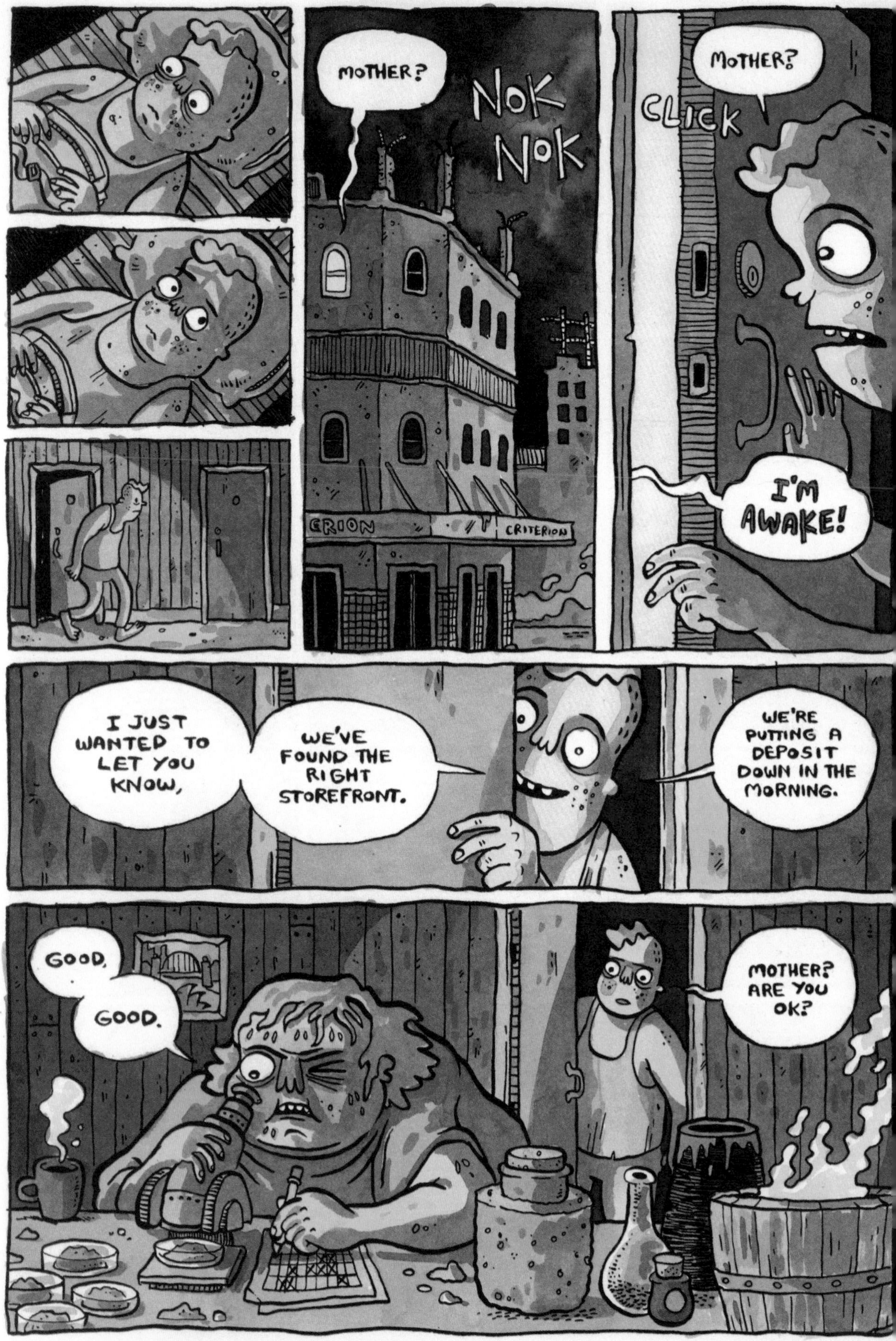
MOTHER?
NOK NOK
CRION
CRITERION
MOTHER?
CLICK
I'M AWAKE!
I JUST WANTED TO LET YOU KNOW,
WE'VE FOUND THE RIGHT STOREFRONT.
WE'RE PUTTING A DEPOSIT DOWN IN THE MORNING.
GOOD,
GOOD.
MOTHER? ARE YOU OK?

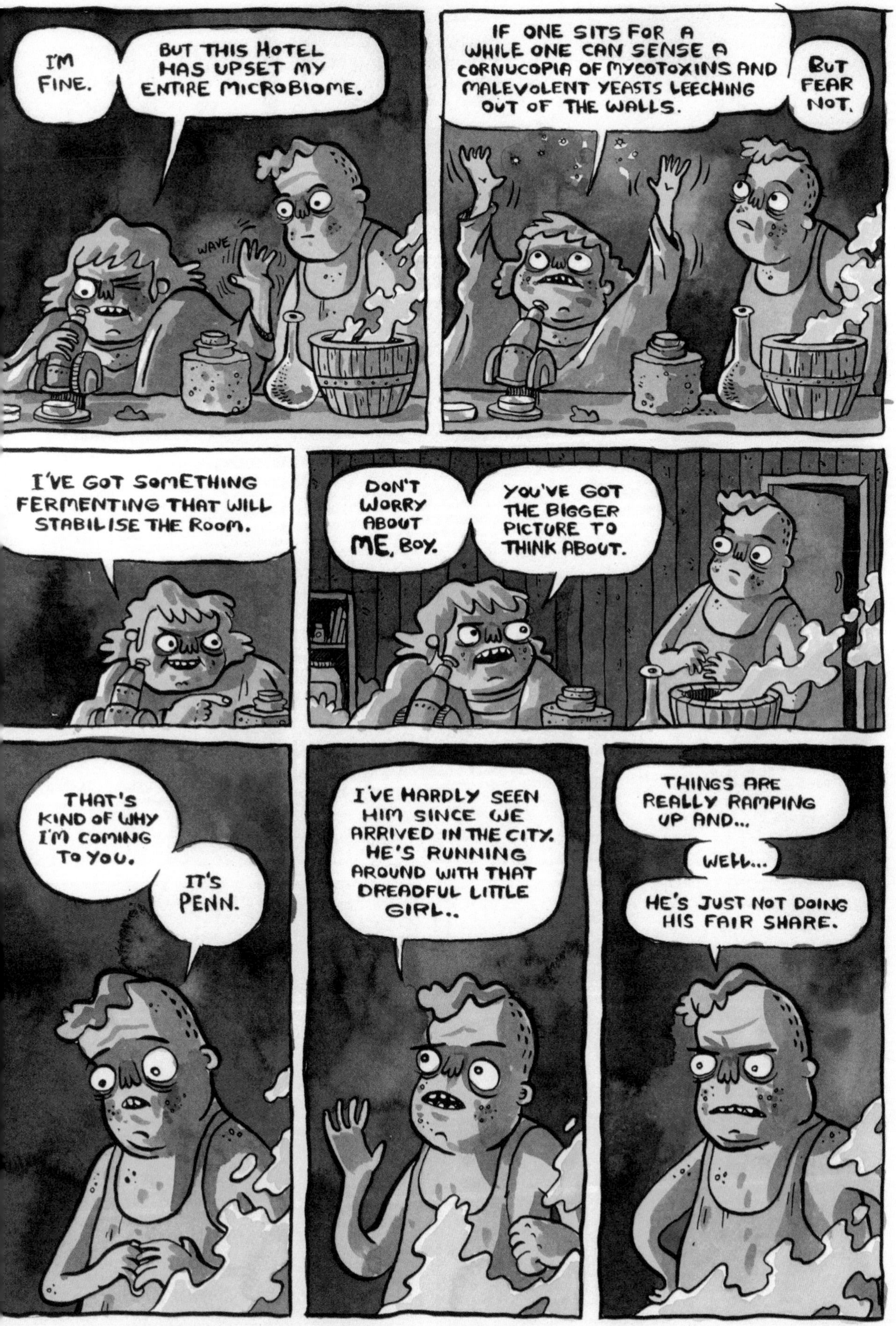
I'M FINE.
BUT THIS HOTEL HAS UPSET MY ENTIRE MICROBIOME.
WAVE
IF ONE SITS FOR A WHILE ONE CAN SENSE A CORNUCOPIA OF MYCOTOXINS AND MALEVOLENT YEASTS LEECHING OUT OF THE WALLS.
BUT FEAR NOT.
I'VE GOT SOMETHING FERMENTING THAT WILL STABILISE THE ROOM.
DON'T WORRY ABOUT ME, BOY.
YOU'VE GOT THE BIGGER PICTURE TO THINK ABOUT.
THAT'S KIND OF WHY I'M COMING TO YOU.
IT'S PENN.
I'VE HARDLY SEEN HIM SINCE WE ARRIVED IN THE CITY. HE'S RUNNING AROUND WITH THAT DREADFUL LITTLE GIRL..
THINGS ARE REALLY RAMPING UP AND...
WELL...
HE'S JUST NOT DOING HIS FAIR SHARE.

NOSE BREATHES

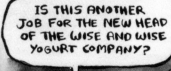
IS THIS ANOTHER JOB FOR THE NEW HEAD OF THE WISE AND WISE YOGURT COMPANY?

BUT HE WON'T LISTEN TO ME.

I SUPPOSE YOU'LL HAVE TO MAKE HIM.

IT'S MORE THAN THAT, MOTHER.

THE CITY IS CRAWLING WITH MISANTHROPES AND SCUMBAGS,

AND, HAS IT EVER OCCURRED TO YOU THAT...

THAT...

PENN MIGHT...

FIT IN HERE.

FOR PETE'S SAKE, LIPPY, HE'S YOUR BROTHER!

YOU'RE SAYING YOU CAN'T TRUST YOUR BROTHER?

UM, YEAH.

MORE NOSE BREATHES

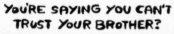

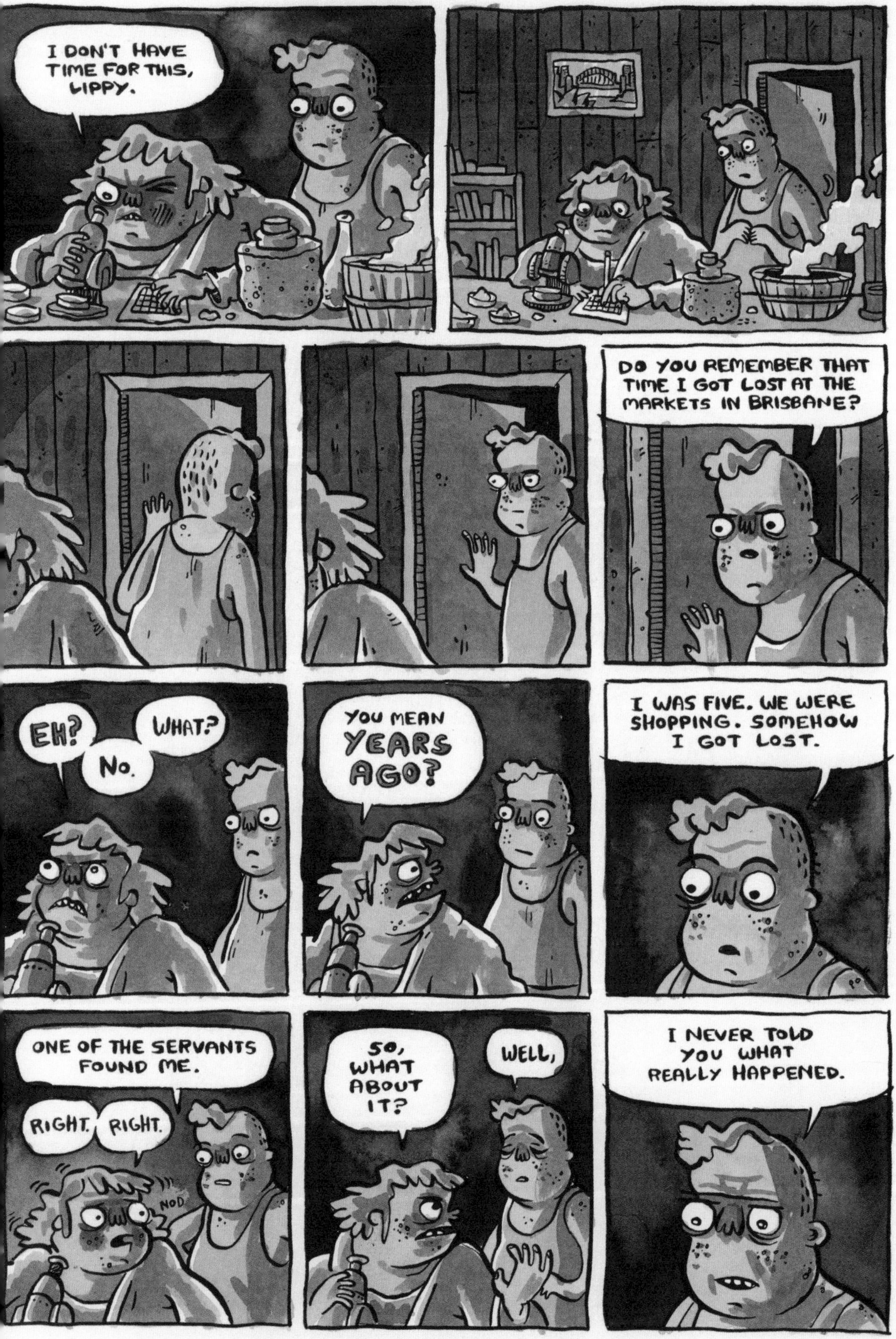
I DON'T HAVE TIME FOR THIS, LIPPY.
DO YOU REMEMBER THAT TIME I GOT LOST AT THE MARKETS IN BRISBANE?
EH?
NO.
WHAT?
YOU MEAN YEARS AGO?
I WAS FIVE. WE WERE SHOPPING. SOMEHOW I GOT LOST.
ONE OF THE SERVANTS FOUND ME.
RIGHT.
RIGHT.
NOD
SO, WHAT ABOUT IT?
WELL,
I NEVER TOLD YOU WHAT REALLY HAPPENED.

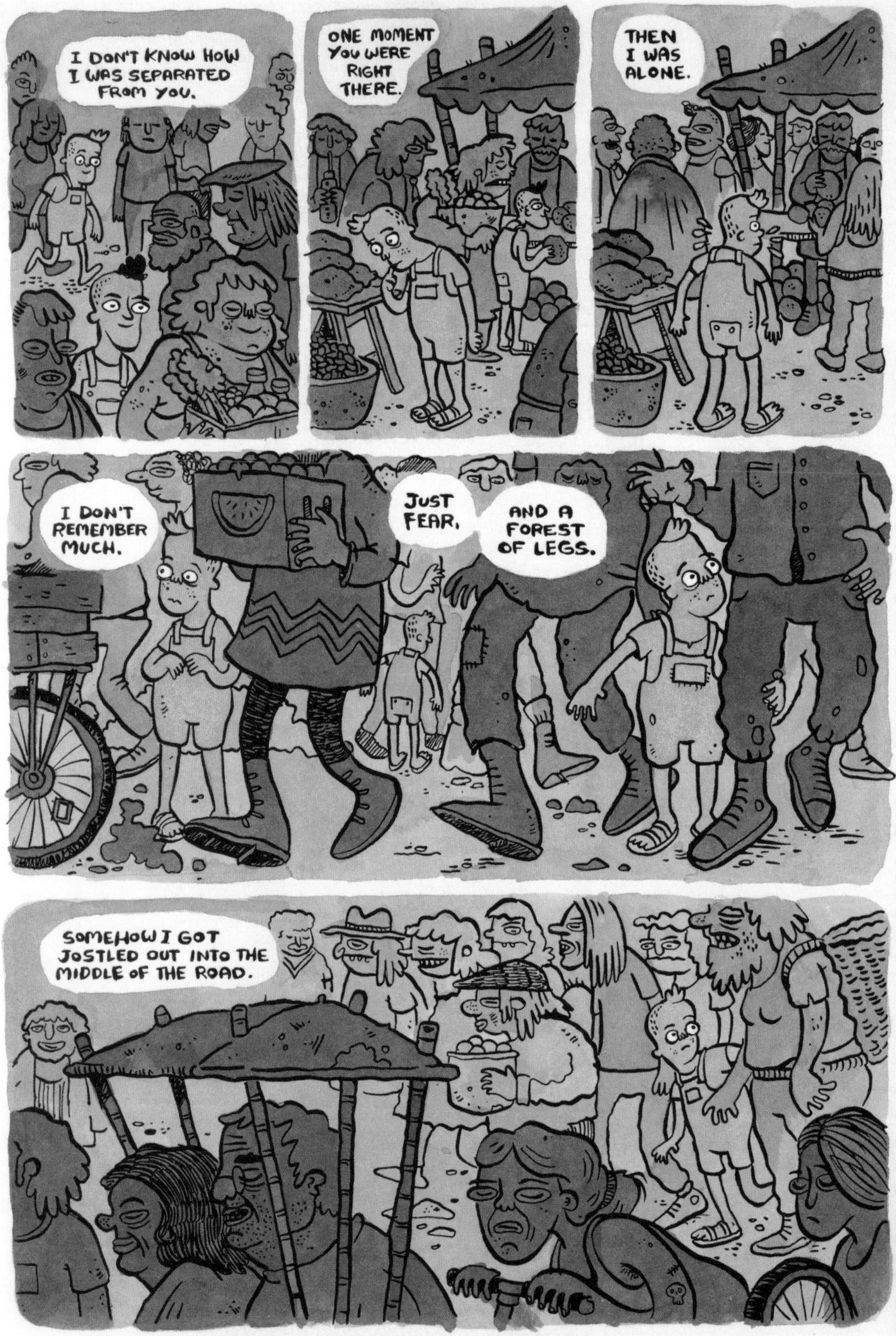
I DON'T KNOW HOW I WAS SEPARATED FROM YOU.
ONE MOMENT YOU WERE RIGHT THERE.
THEN I WAS ALONE.
I DON'T REMEMBER MUCH.
JUST FEAR,
AND A FOREST OF LEGS.
SOMEHOW I GOT JOSTLED OUT INTO THE MIDDLE OF THE ROAD.

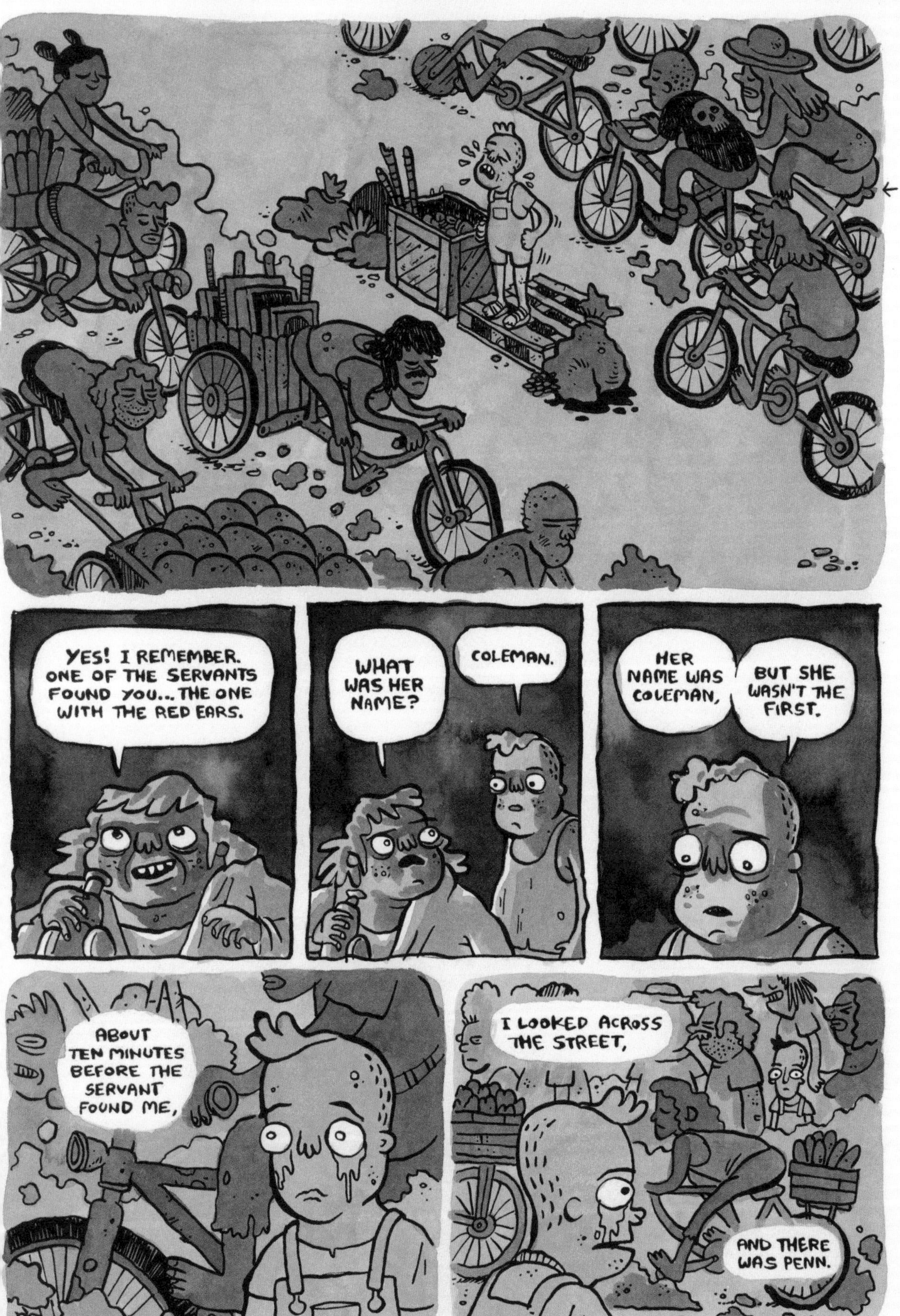
YES! I REMEMBER. ONE OF THE SERVANTS FOUND YOU... THE ONE WITH THE RED EARS.
WHAT WAS HER NAME?
COLEMAN.
HER NAME WAS COLEMAN,
BUT SHE WASN'T THE FIRST.
ABOUT TEN MINUTES BEFORE THE SERVANT FOUND ME,
I LOOKED ACROSS THE STREET,
AND THERE WAS PENN.

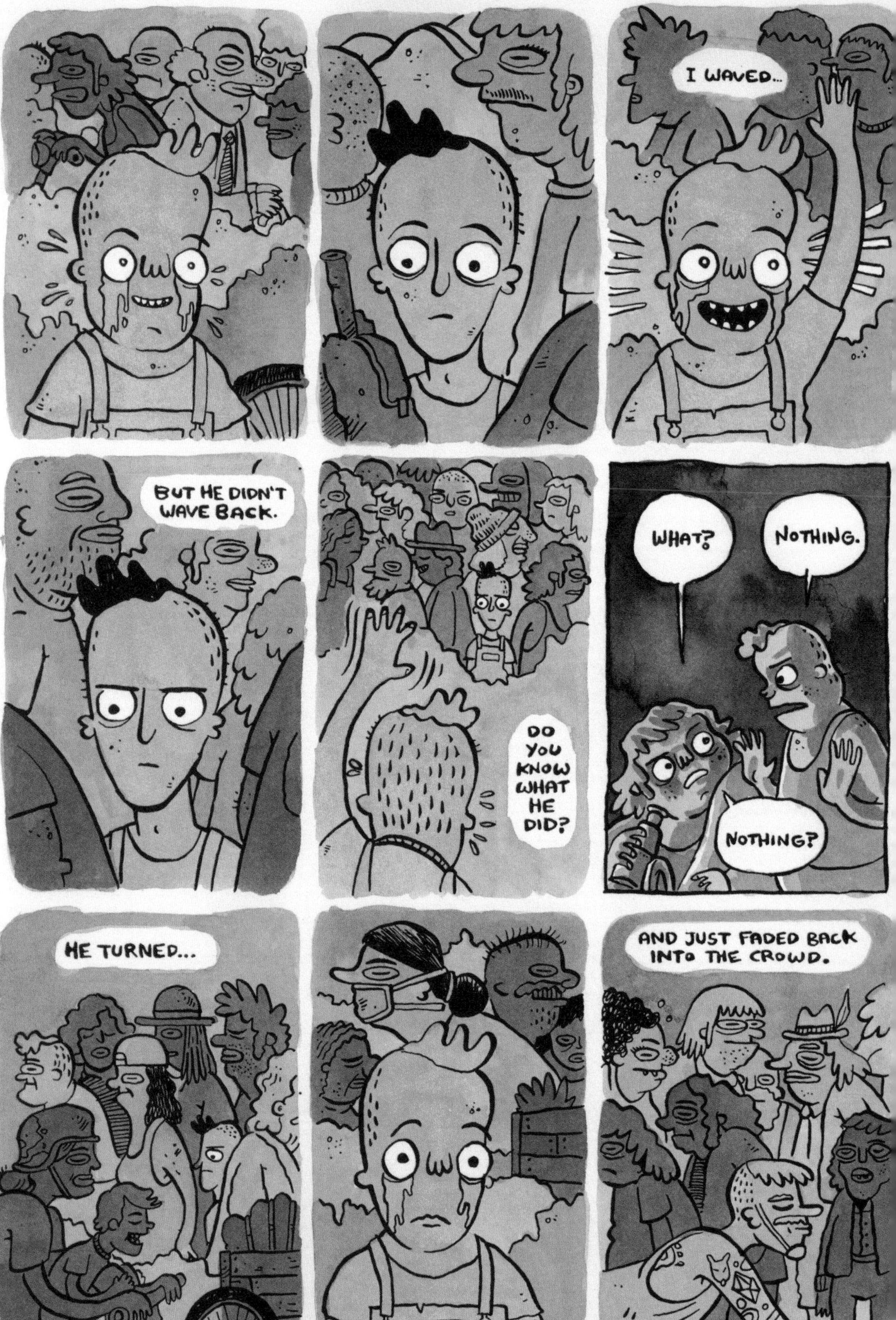
I WAVED...
BUT HE DIDN'T WAVE BACK.
DO YOU KNOW WHAT HE DID?
WHAT?
NOTHING.
NOTHING?
HE TURNED...
AND JUST FADED BACK INTO THE CROWD.

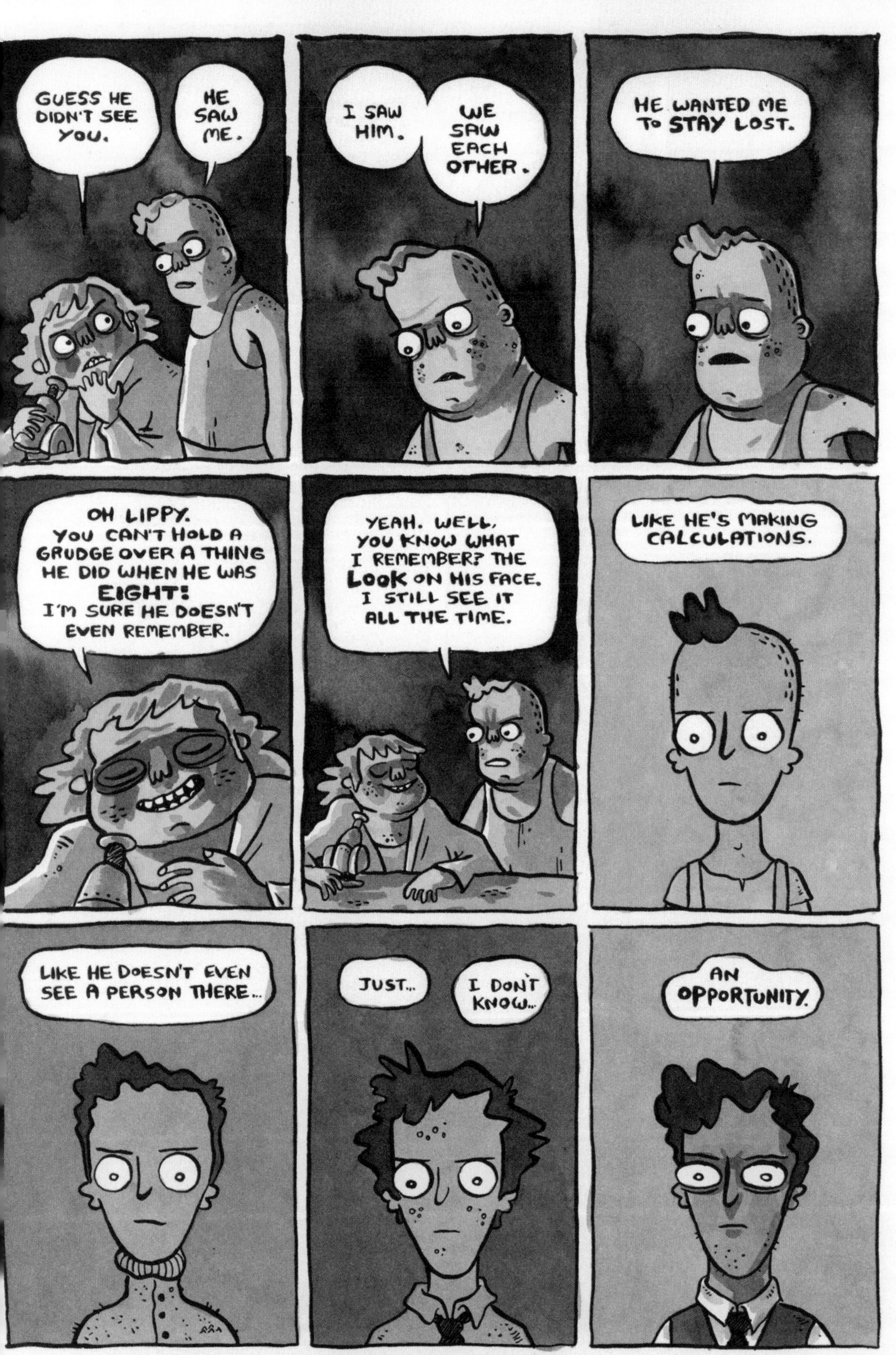
GUESS HE DIDN'T SEE YOU.
HE SAW ME.
I SAW HIM.
WE SAW EACH OTHER.
HE WANTED ME TO STAY LOST.
OH LIPPY. YOU CAN'T HOLD A GRUDGE OVER A THING HE DID WHEN HE WAS EIGHT! I'M SURE HE DOESN'T EVEN REMEMBER.
YEAH. WELL, YOU KNOW WHAT I REMEMBER? THE LOOK ON HIS FACE. I STILL SEE IT ALL THE TIME.
LIKE HE'S MAKING CALCULATIONS.
LIKE HE DOESN'T EVEN SEE A PERSON THERE...
JUST...
I DON'T KNOW...
AN OPPORTUNITY.

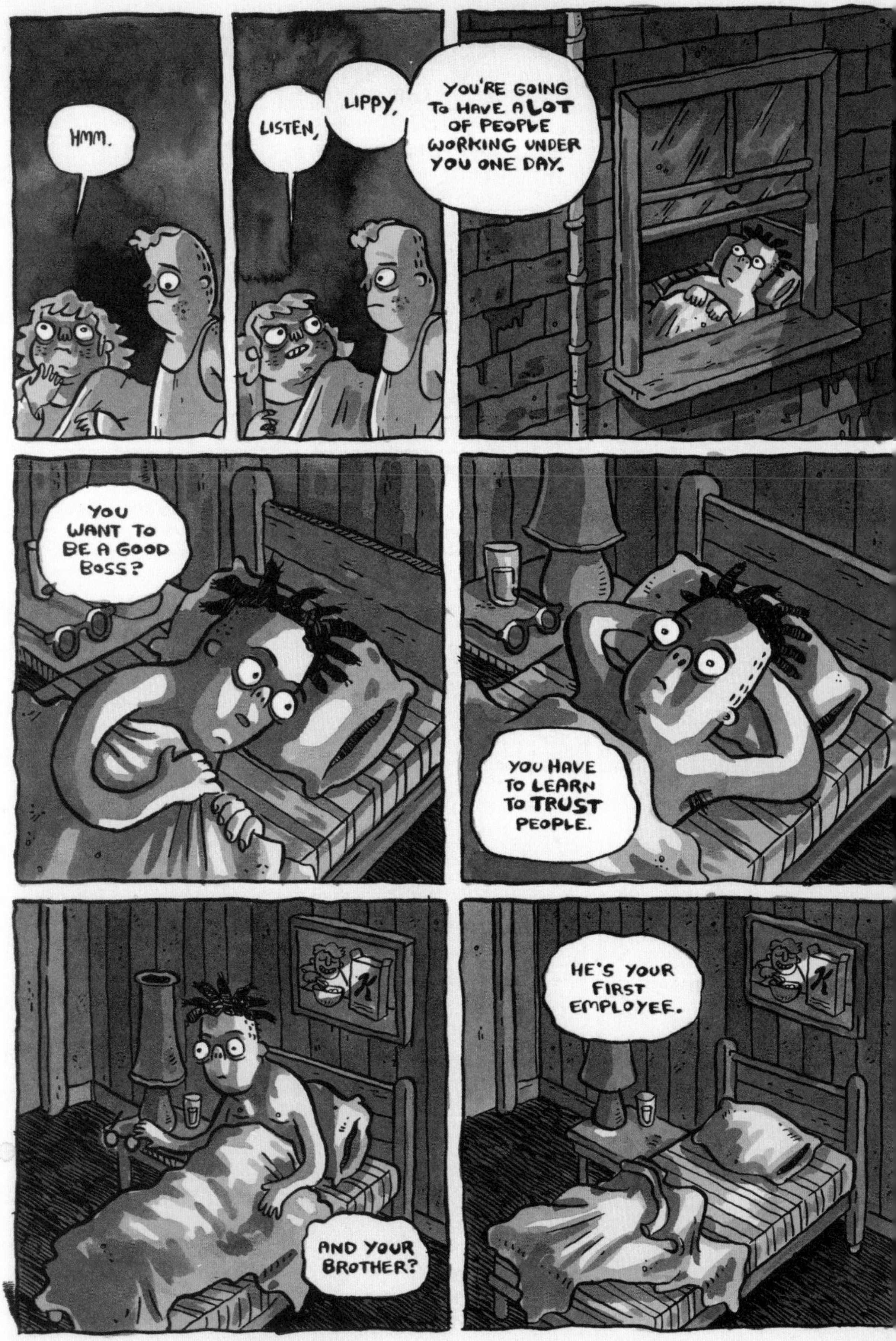

HMM.
LISTEN,
LIPPY,
YOU'RE GOING TO HAVE A LOT OF PEOPLE WORKING UNDER YOU ONE DAY.
YOU WANT TO BE A GOOD BOSS?
YOU HAVE TO LEARN TO TRUST PEOPLE.
AND YOUR BROTHER?
HE'S YOUR FIRST EMPLOYEE.

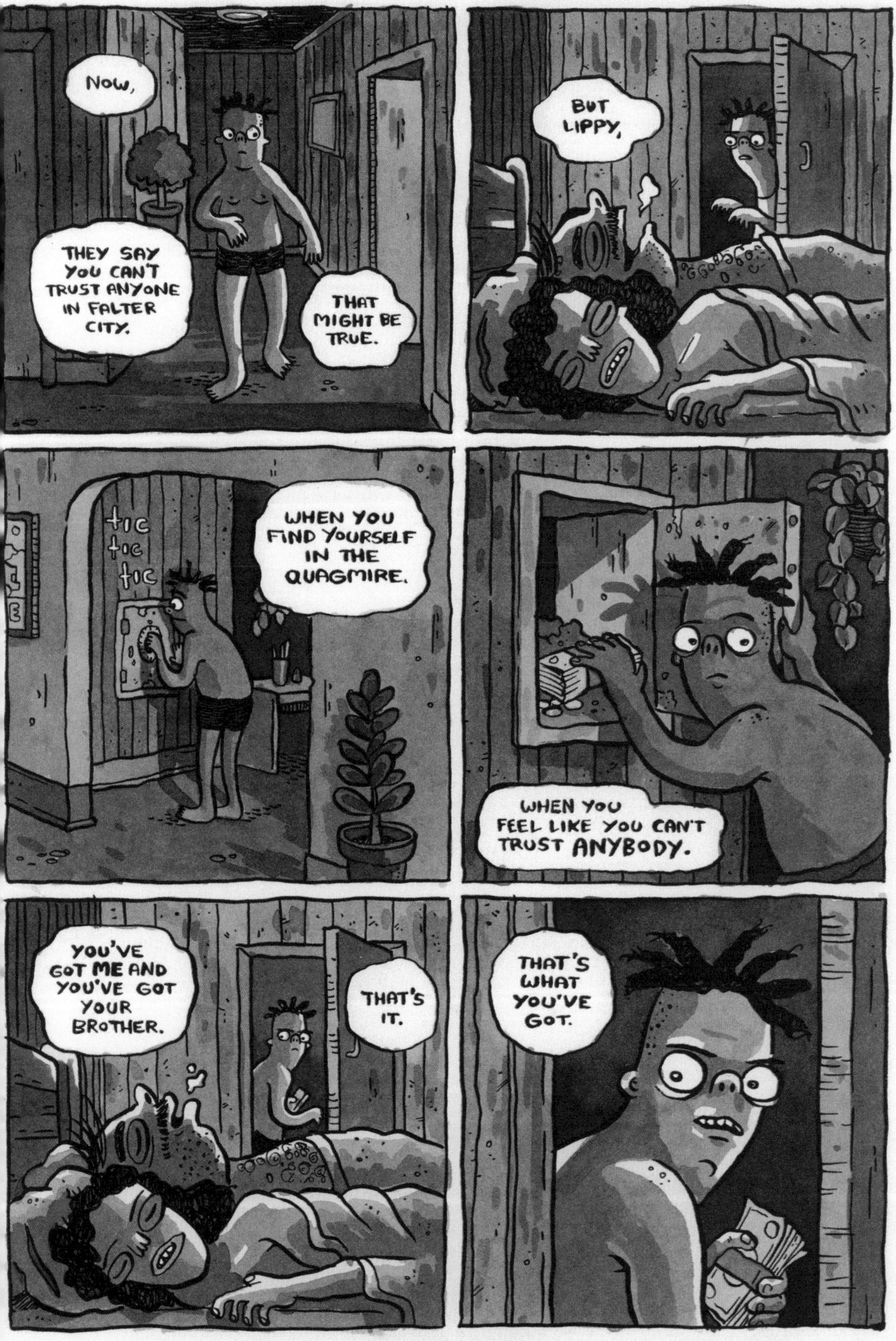
NOW,
THEY SAY YOU CAN'T TRUST ANYONE IN FALTER CITY.
THAT MIGHT BE TRUE.
BUT LIPPY,
tic tic tic
WHEN YOU FIND YOURSELF IN THE QUAGMIRE.
WHEN YOU FEEL LIKE YOU CAN'T TRUST ANYBODY.
YOU'VE GOT ME AND YOU'VE GOT YOUR BROTHER.
THAT'S IT.
THAT'S WHAT YOU'VE GOT.

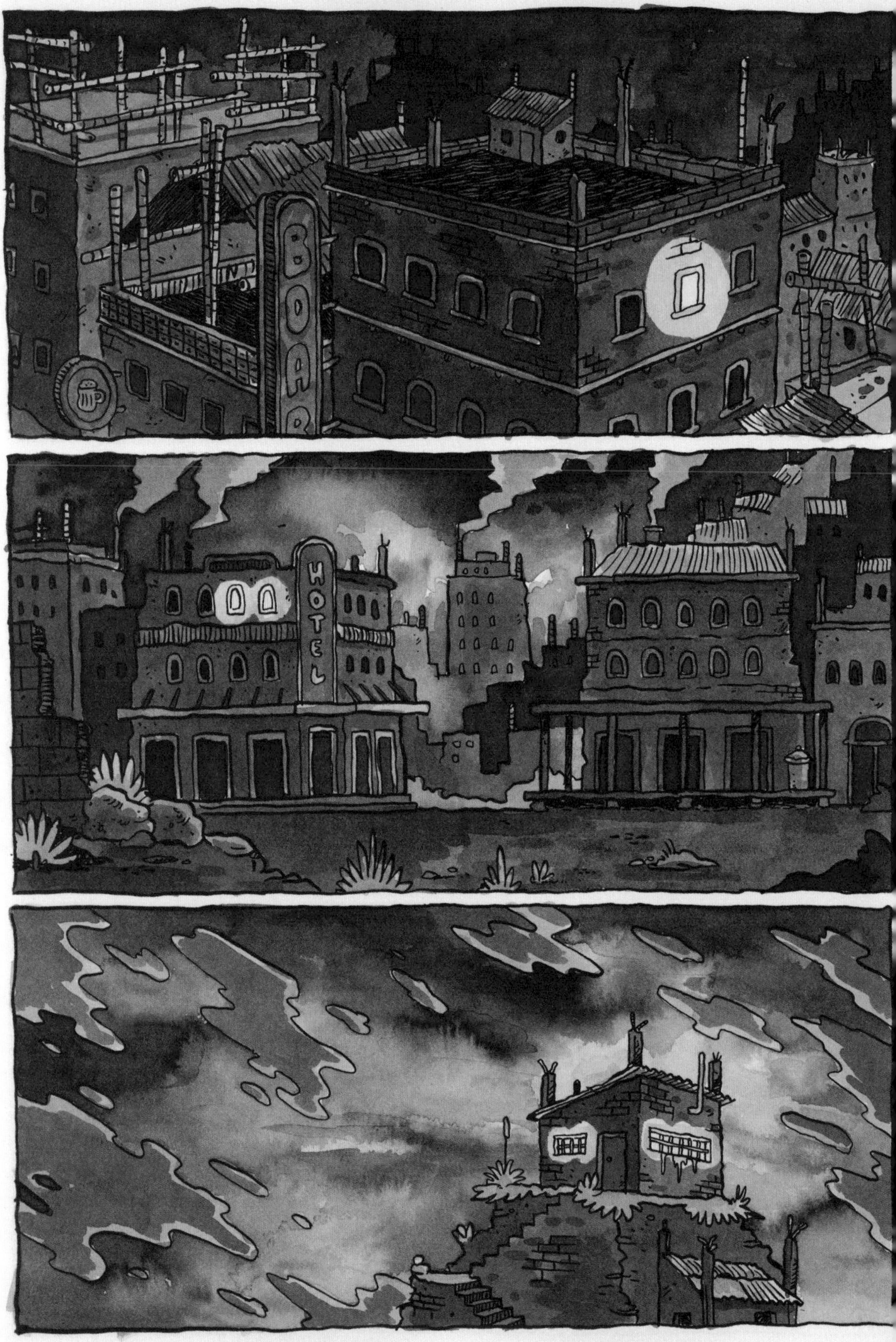
HOTEL

PART THREE

THE STANG

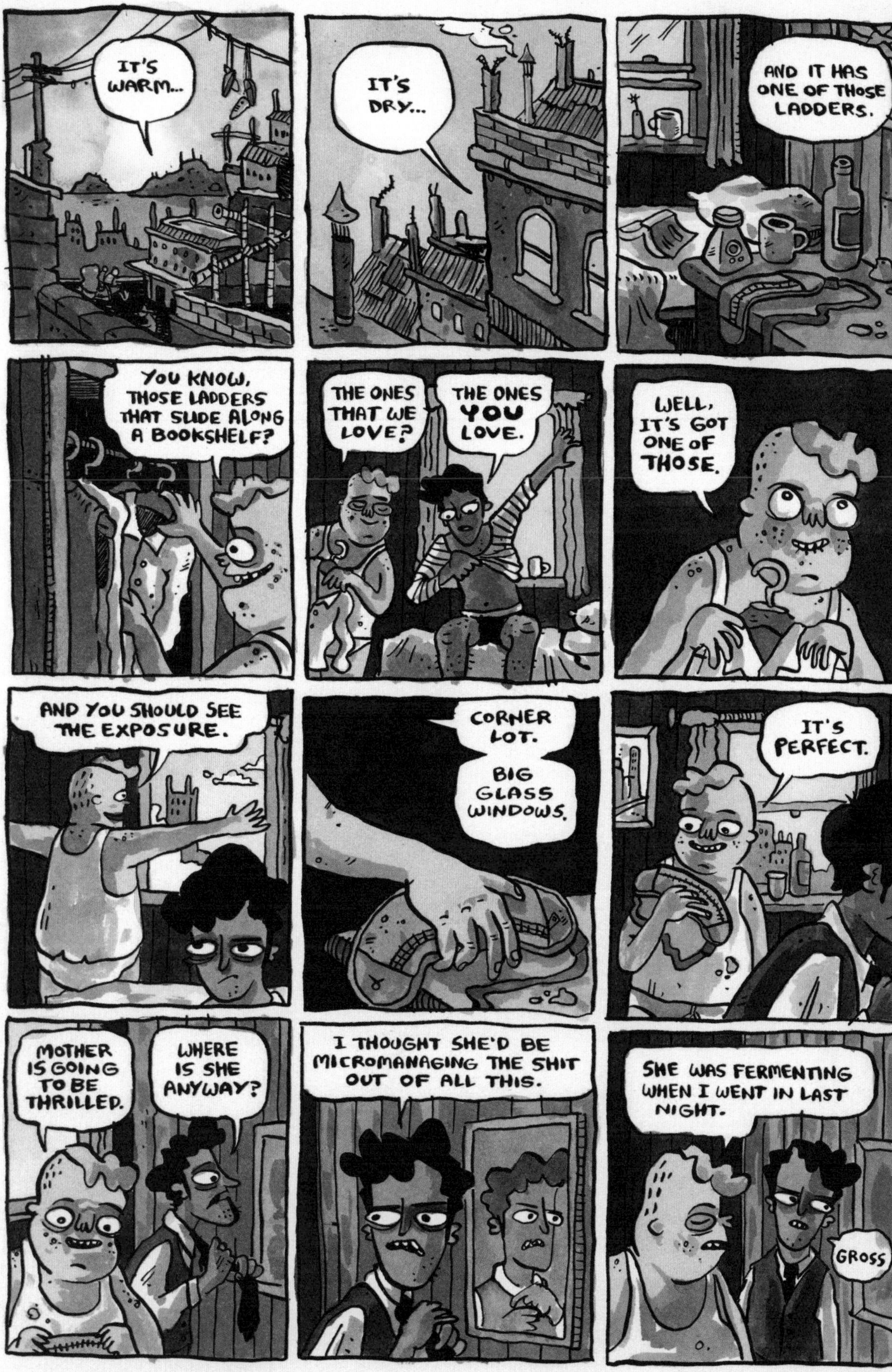
IT'S WARM...
IT'S DRY...
AND IT HAS ONE OF THOSE LADDERS.
YOU KNOW, THOSE LADDERS THAT SLIDE ALONG A BOOKSHELF?
THE ONES THAT WE LOVE?
THE ONES YOU LOVE.
WELL, IT'S GOT ONE OF THOSE.
AND YOU SHOULD SEE THE EXPOSURE.
CORNER LOT.
BIG GLASS WINDOWS.
IT'S PERFECT.
MOTHER IS GOING TO BE THRILLED.
WHERE IS SHE ANYWAY?
I THOUGHT SHE'D BE MICROMANAGING THE SHIT OUT OF ALL THIS.
SHE WAS FERMENTING WHEN I WENT IN LAST NIGHT.
GROSS

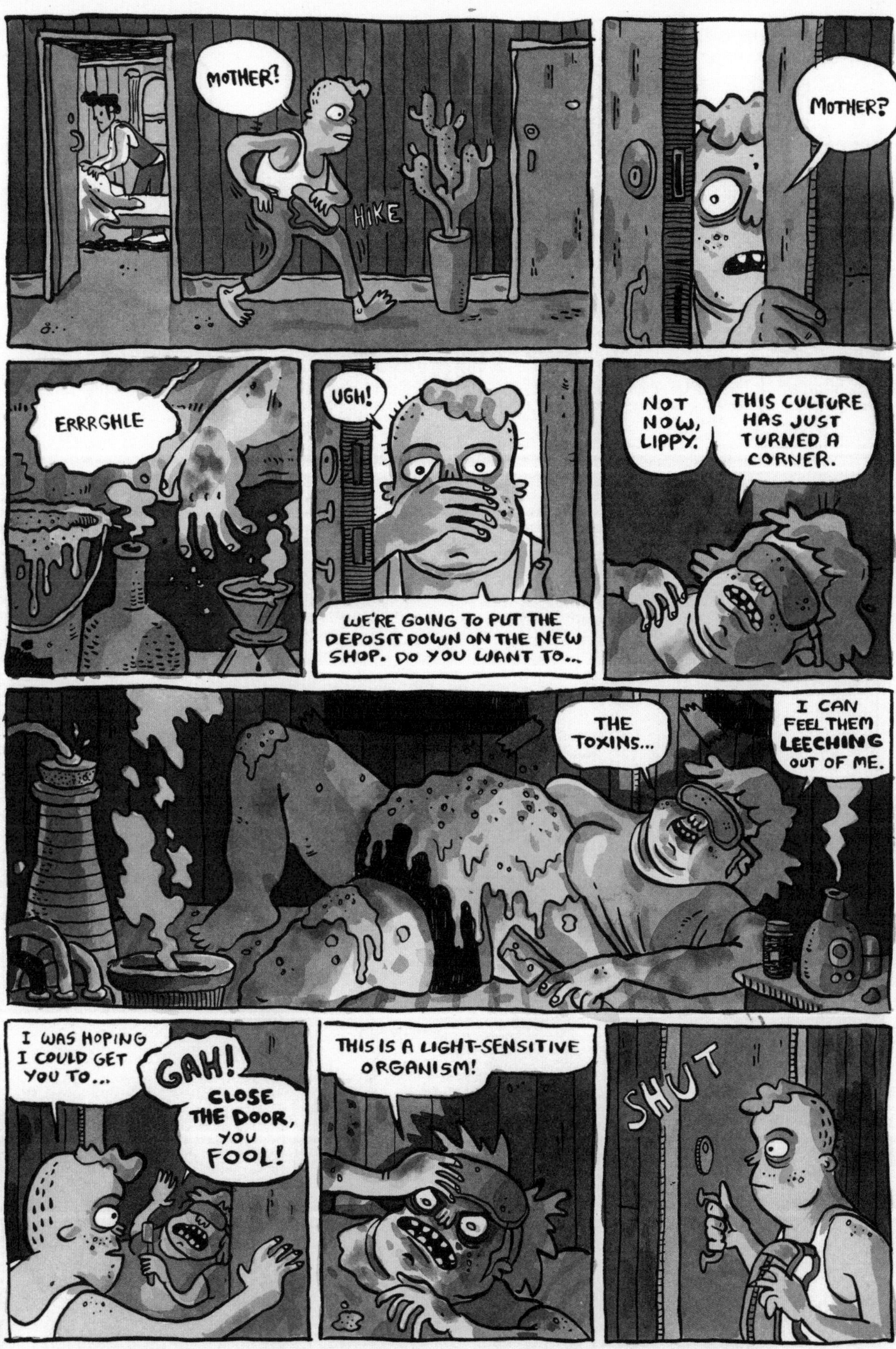
MOTHER?
HIKE
MOTHER?
ERRRGHLE
UGH!
WE'RE GOING TO PUT THE DEPOSIT DOWN ON THE NEW SHOP. DO YOU WANT TO...
NOT NOW, LIPPY.
THIS CULTURE HAS JUST TURNED A CORNER.
THE TOXINS...
I CAN FEEL THEM LEECHING OUT OF ME.
I WAS HOPING I COULD GET YOU TO...
GAH!
CLOSE THE DOOR, YOU FOOL!
THIS IS A LIGHT-SENSITIVE ORGANISM!
SHUT

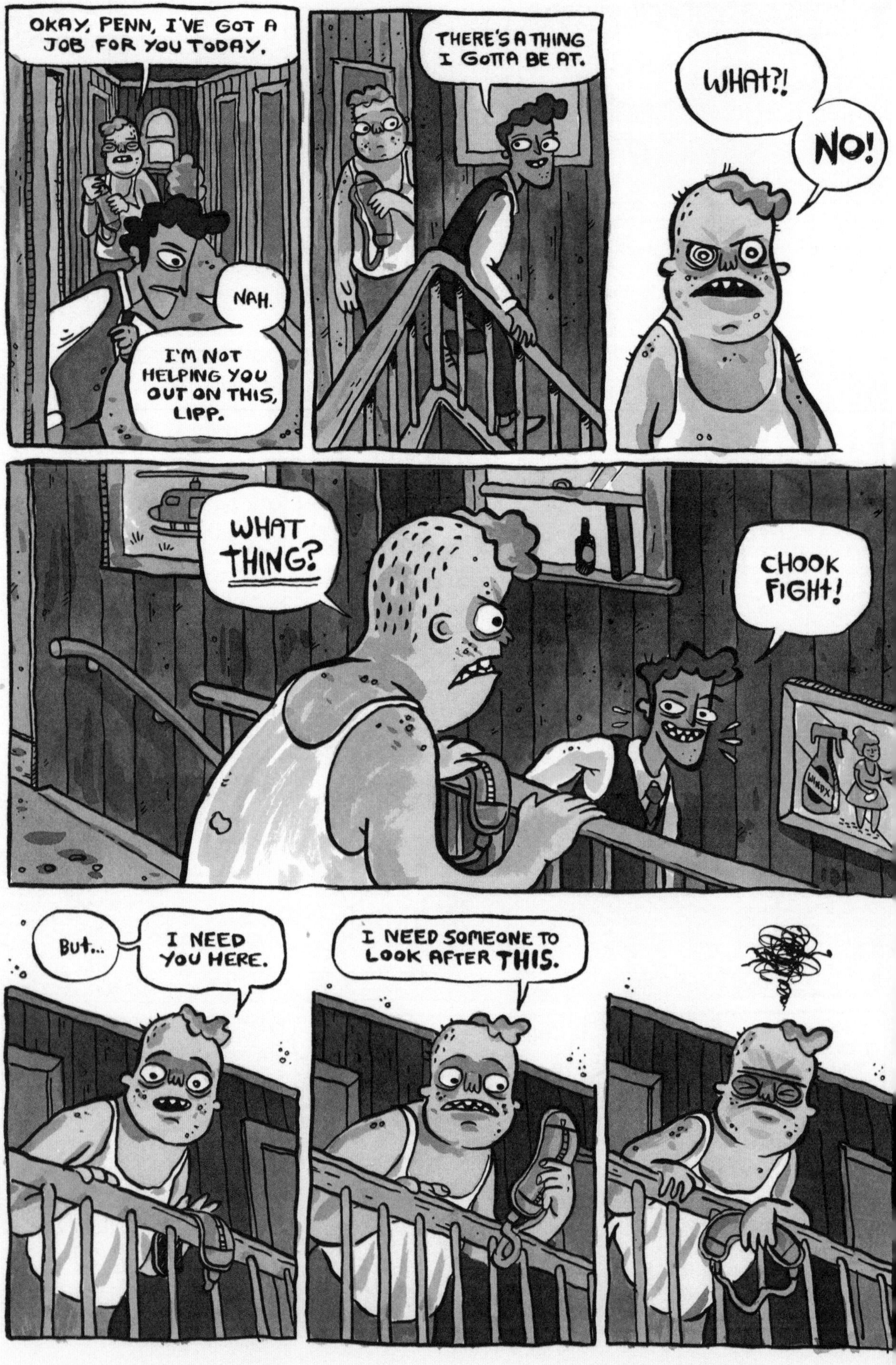
OKAY, PENN, I'VE GOT A JOB FOR YOU TODAY.
NAH.
I'M NOT HELPING YOU OUT ON THIS, LIPP.
THERE'S A THING I GOTTA BE AT.
WHAT?!
NO!
WHAT THING?
CHOOK FIGHT!
WINDX
BUT...
I NEED YOU HERE.
I NEED SOMEONE TO LOOK AFTER THIS.

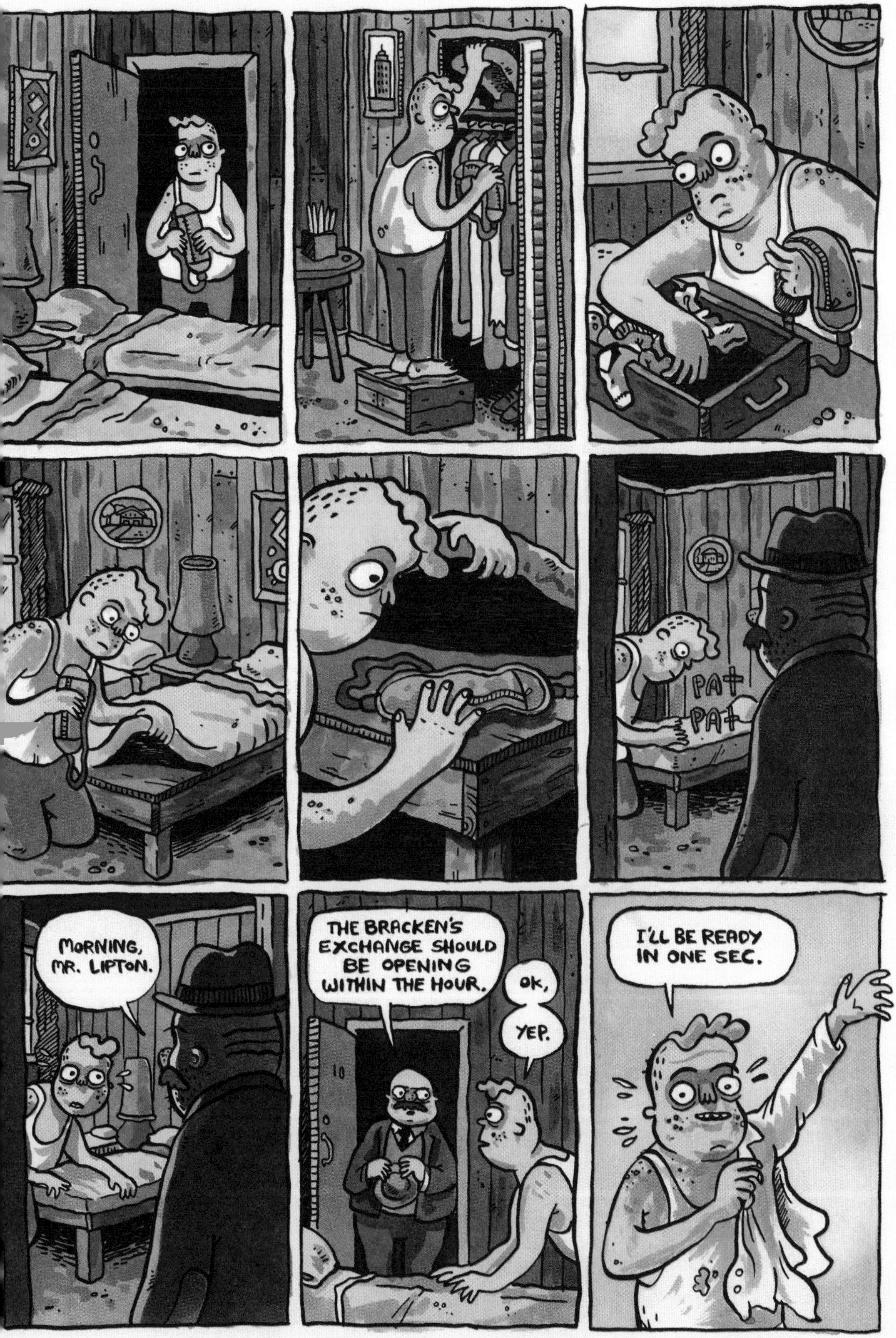
PAT
PAT
MORNING, MR. LIPTON.
THE BRACKEN'S EXCHANGE SHOULD BE OPENING WITHIN THE HOUR.
OK,
YEP.
I'LL BE READY IN ONE SEC.

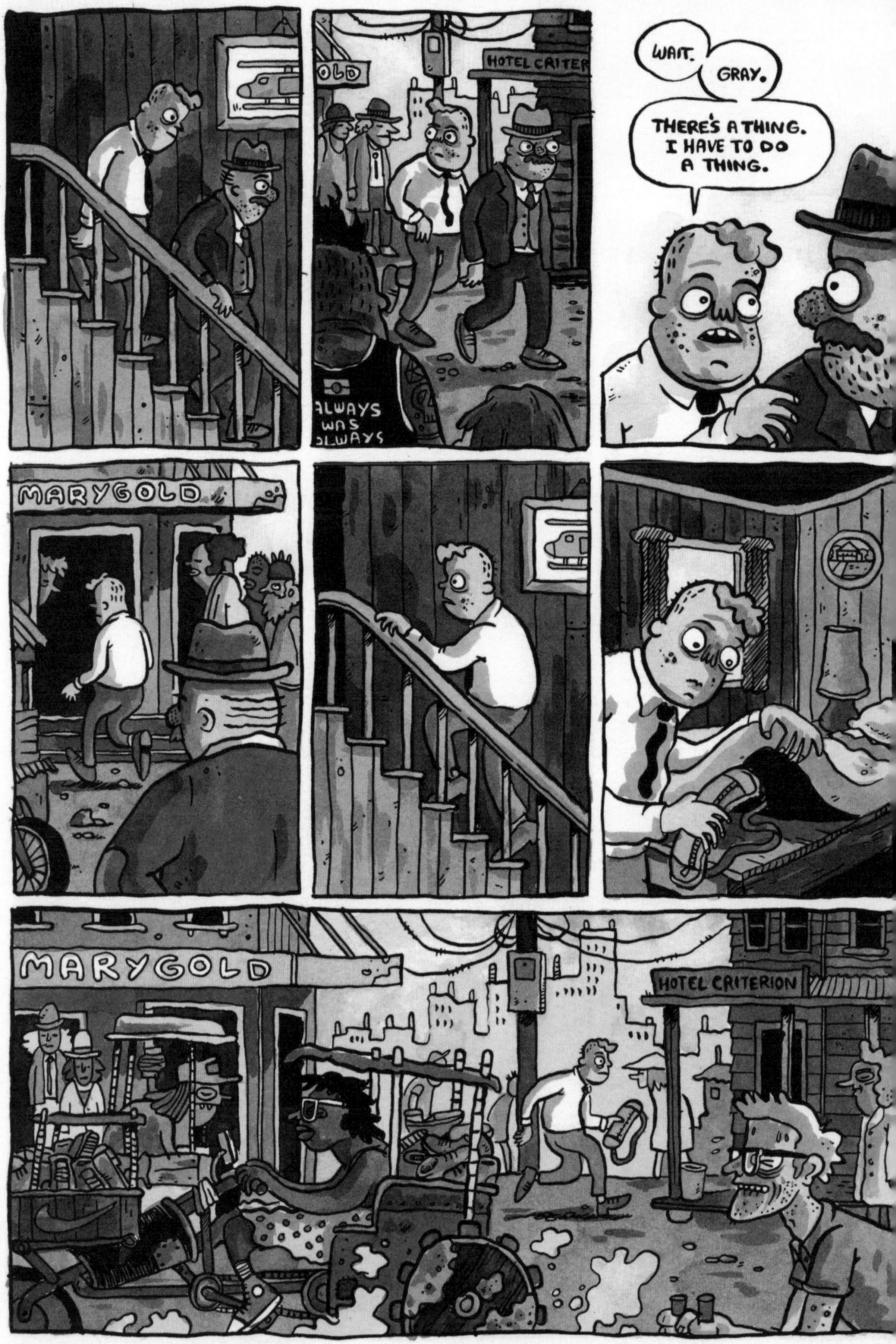
OLD
HOTEL CRITER
ALWAYS
WAS
ALWAYS
WAIT.
GRAY.
THERE'S A THING. I HAVE TO DO A THING.
MARYGOLD
MARYGOLD
HOTEL CRITERION

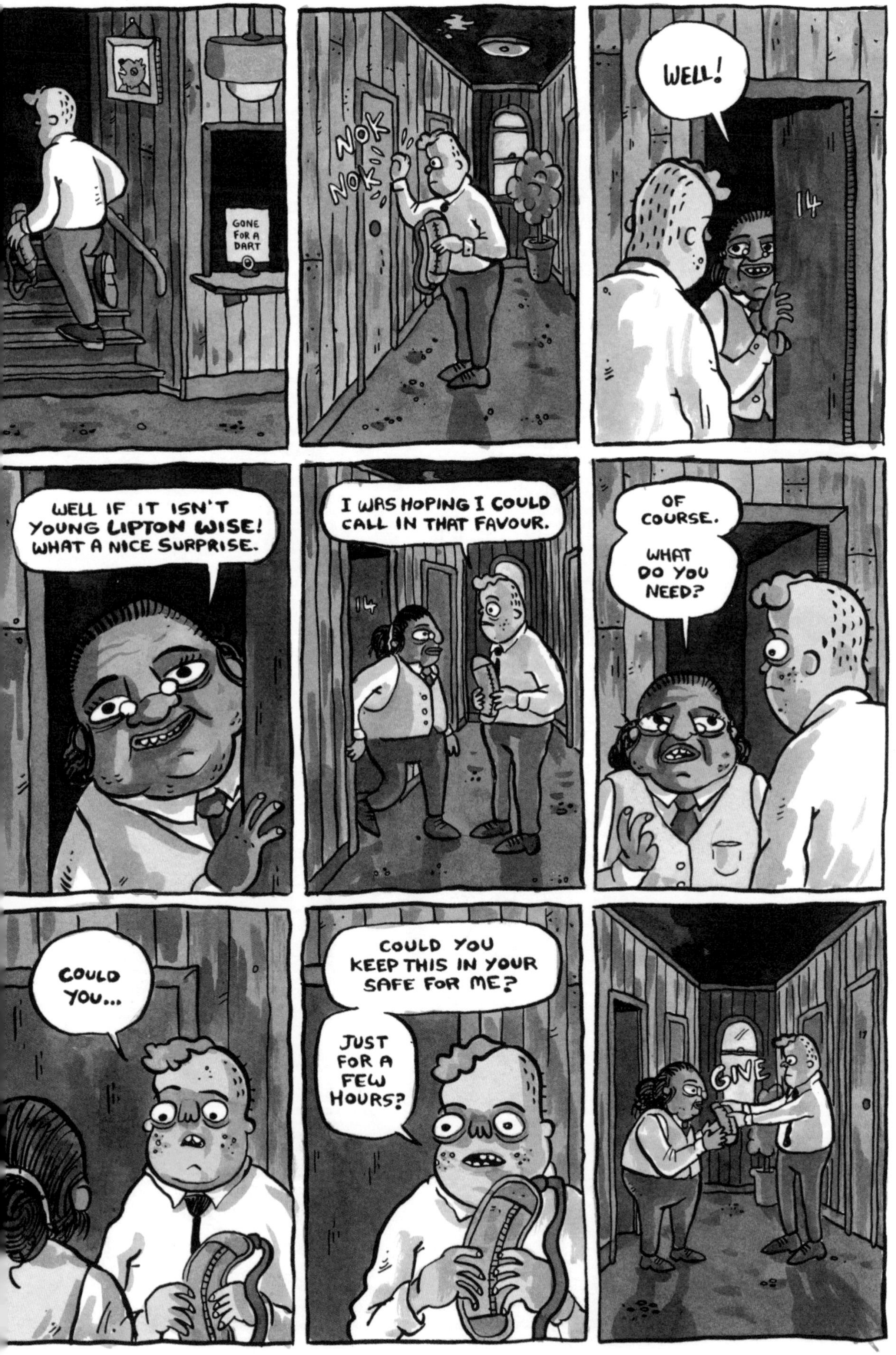
GONE FOR A DART
NOK NOK
WELL!
14
WELL IF IT ISN'T YOUNG LIPTON WISE! WHAT A NICE SURPRISE.
I WAS HOPING I COULD CALL IN THAT FAVOUR.
14
OF COURSE.
WHAT DO YOU NEED?
COULD YOU...
COULD YOU KEEP THIS IN YOUR SAFE FOR ME?
JUST FOR A FEW HOURS?
GIVE

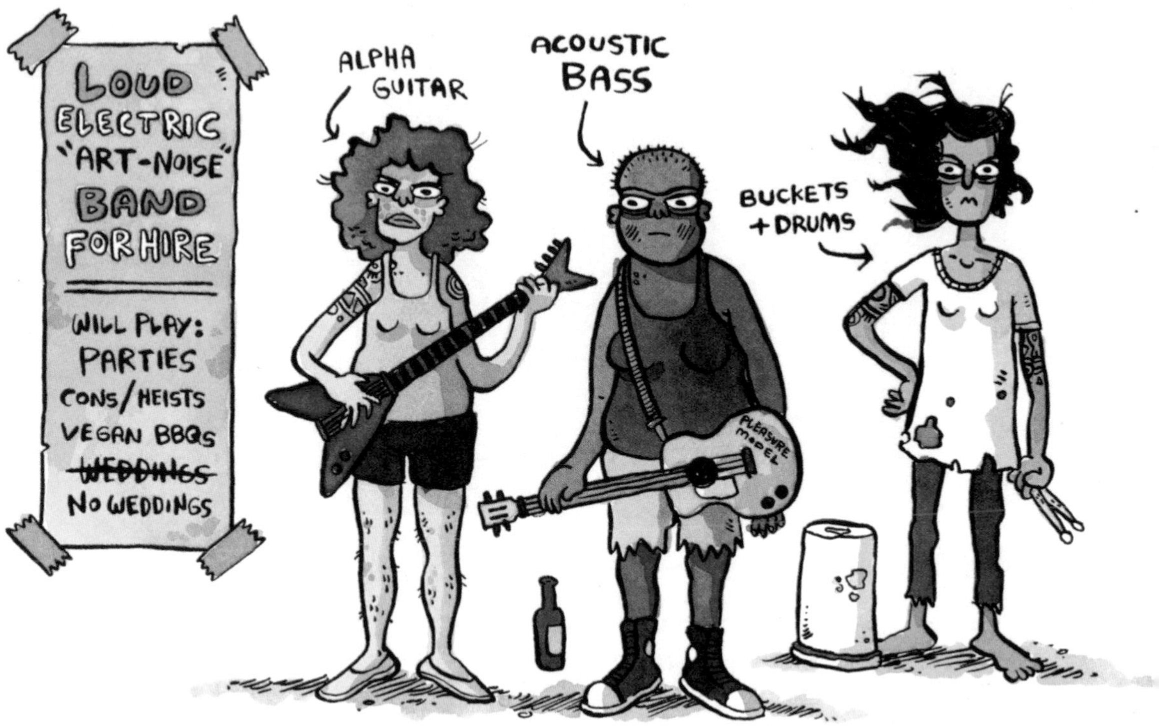
LOUD ELECTRIC "ART-NOISE" BAND FOR HIRE
WILL PLAY:
PARTIES
CONS/HEISTS
VEGAN BBQS
WEDDINGS
NO WEDDINGS
ALPHA GUITAR
ACOUSTIC BASS
PLEASURE MODEL
BUCKETS + DRUMS

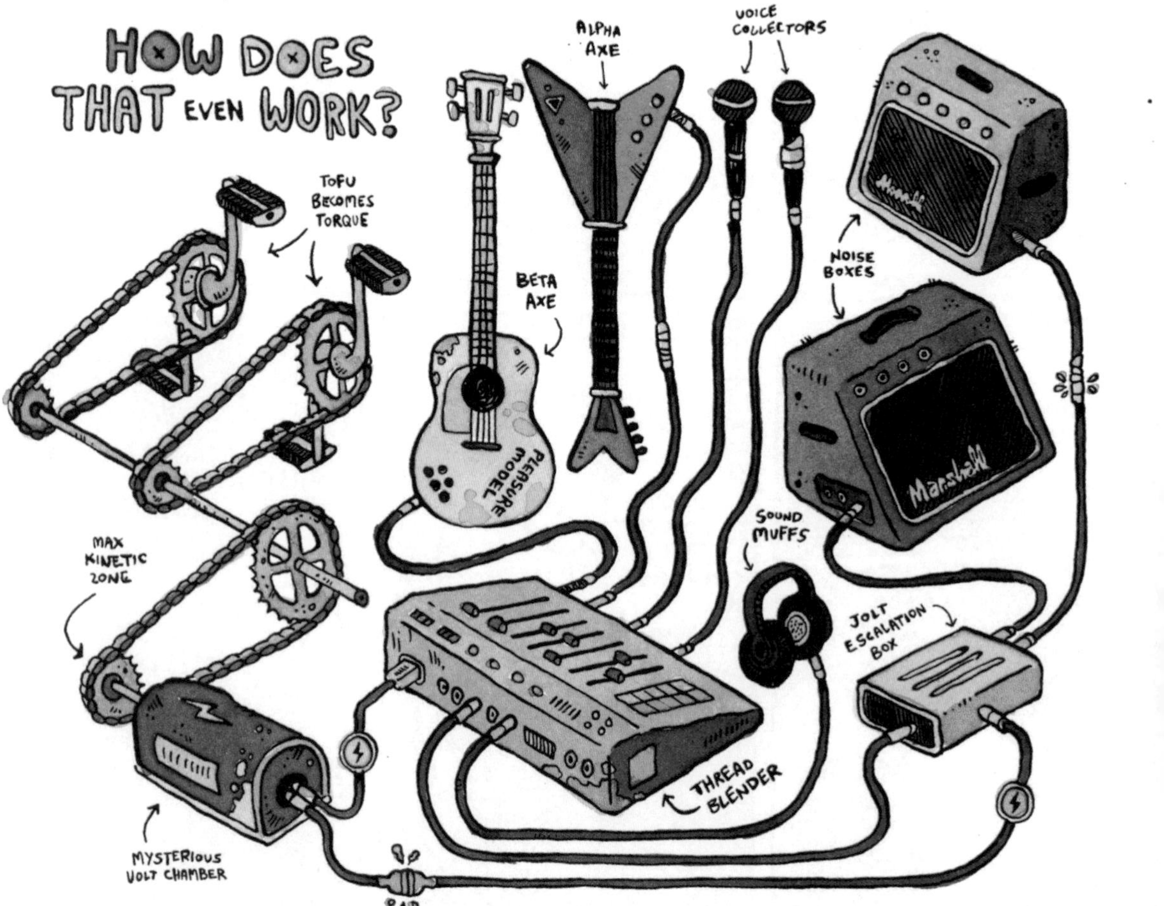
HOW DOES THAT EVEN WORK?
TOFU BECOMES TORQUE
ALPHA AXE
VOICE COLLECTORS
BETA AXE
PLEASURE MODEL
NOISE BOXES
Marshall
MAX KINETIC ZONE
SOUND MUFFS
JOLT ESCALATION BOX
THREAD BLENDER
MYSTERIOUS VOLT CHAMBER

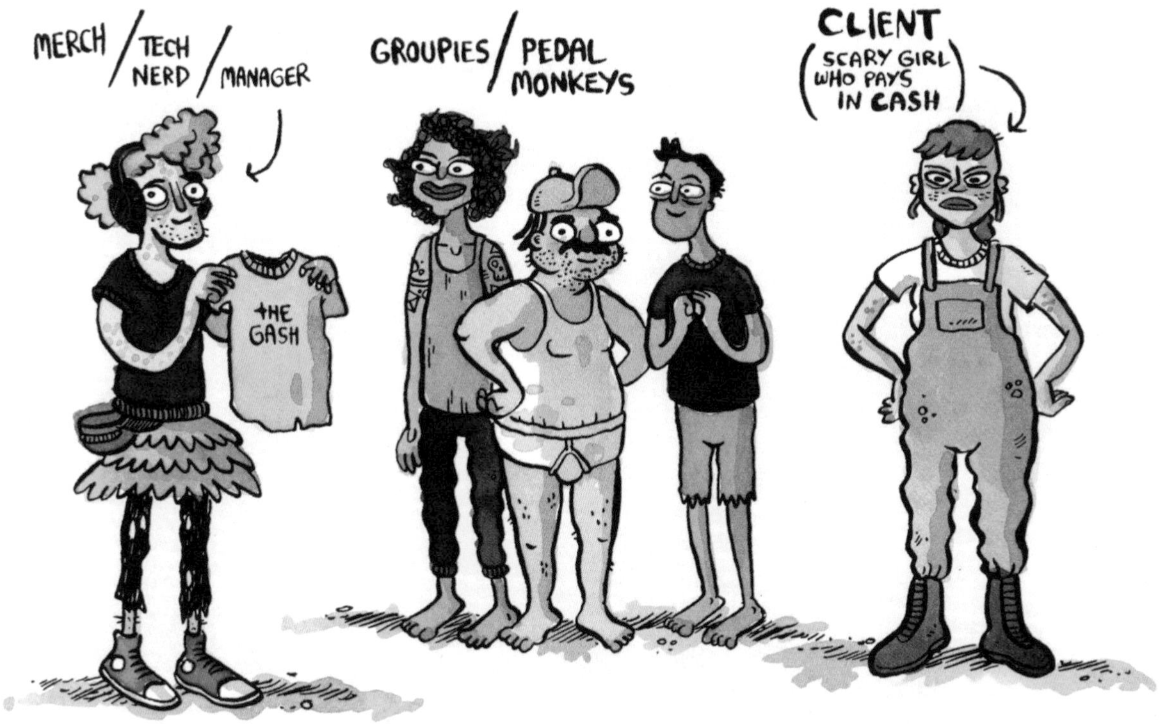
MERCH / TECH NERD / MANAGER
THE GASH
GROUPIES / PEDAL MONKEYS
CLIENT
(SCARY GIRL WHO PAYS IN CASH)

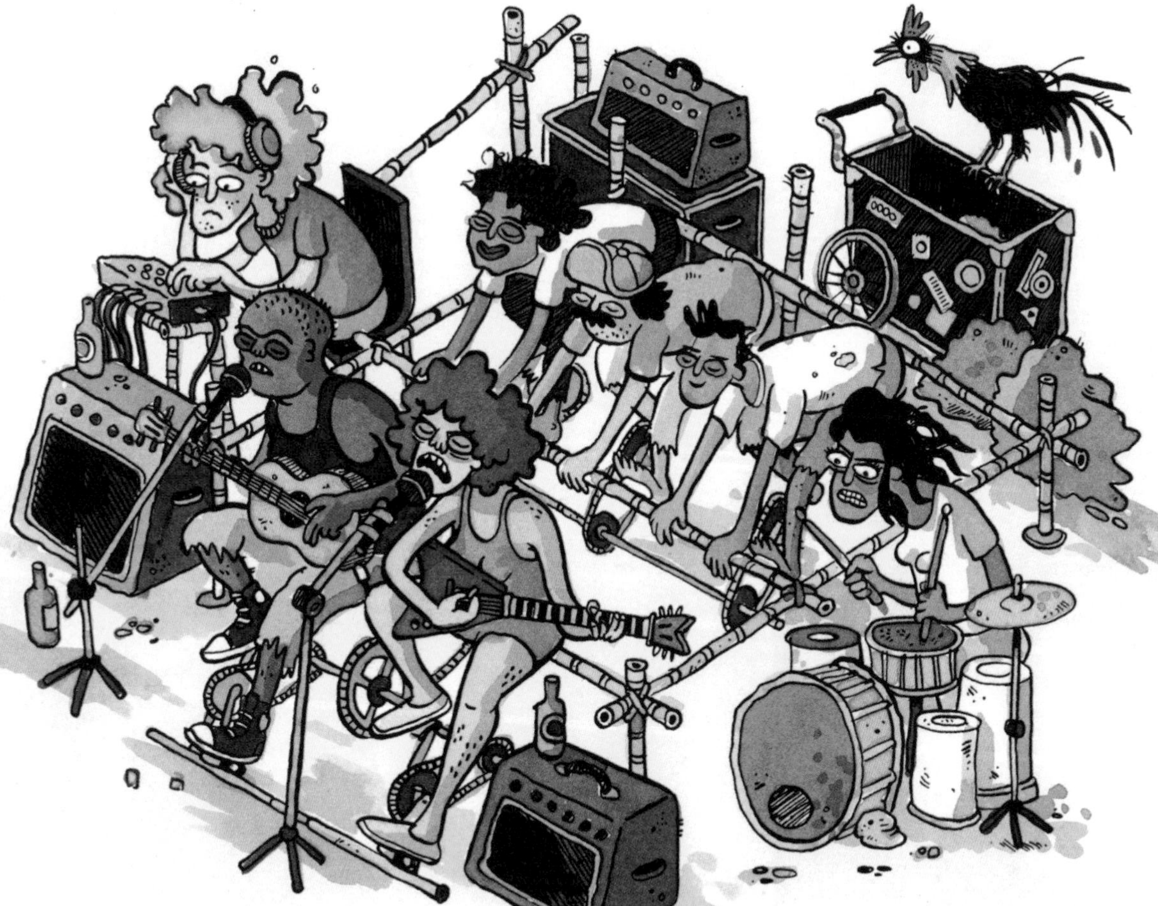

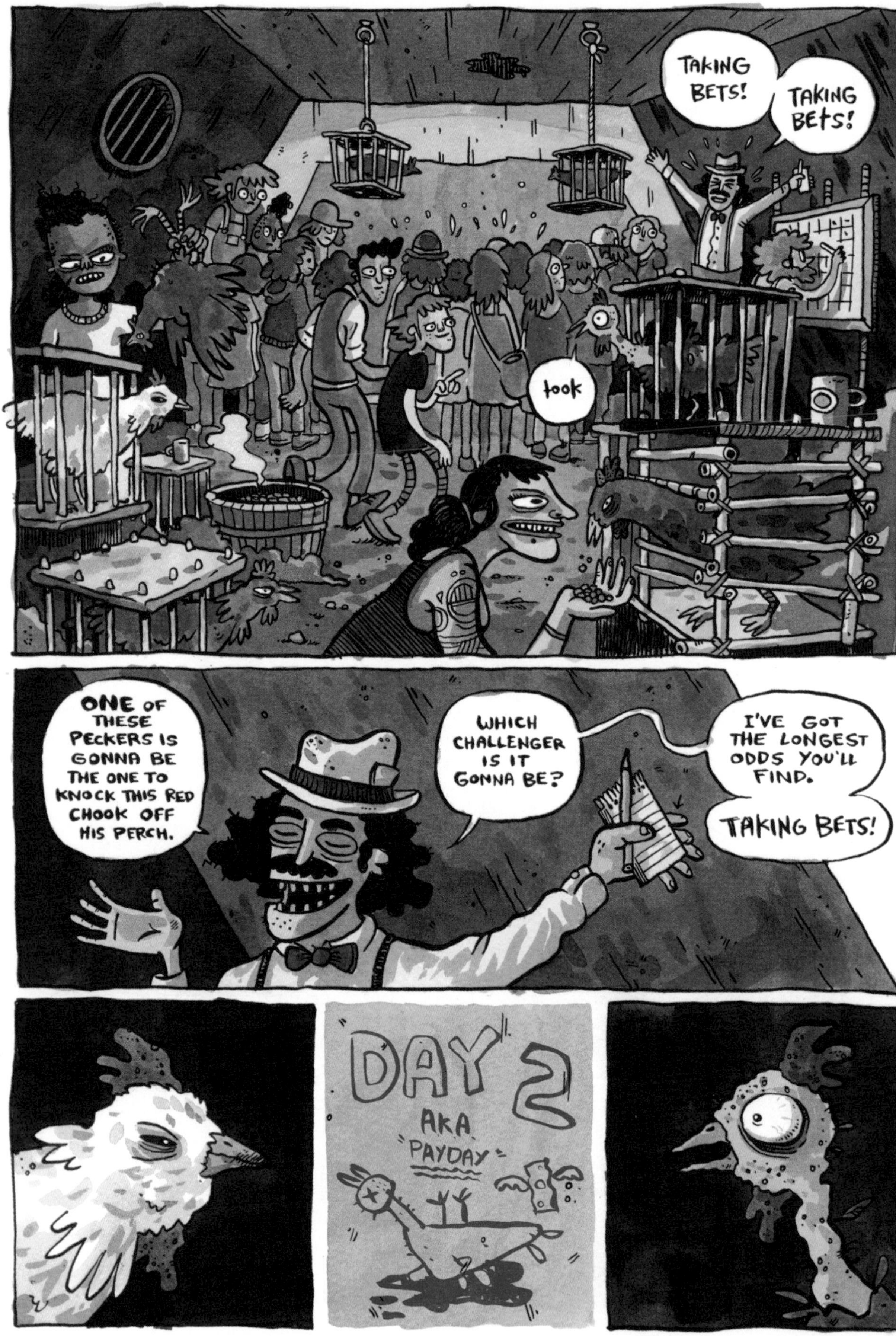
TAKING BETS!
TAKING BETS!
took
ONE OF THESE PECKERS IS GONNA BE THE ONE TO KNOCK THIS RED CHOOK OFF HIS PERCH.
WHICH CHALLENGER IS IT GONNA BE?
I'VE GOT THE LONGEST ODDS YOU'LL FIND.
TAKING BETS!
DAY 2
AKA
PAYDAY

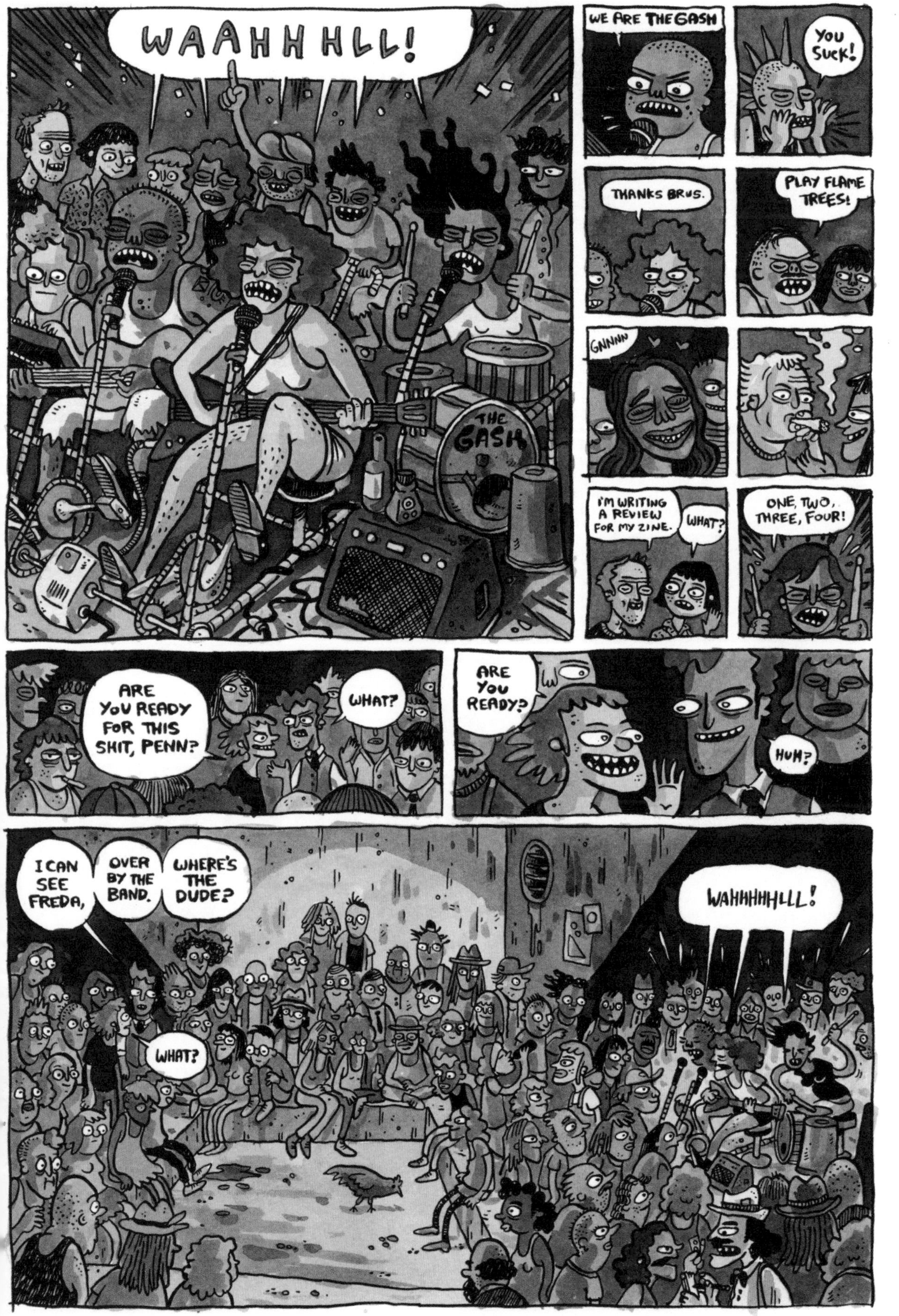
WAAHHHLL!
WE ARE THE GASH
YOU SUCK!
THANKS BRUS.
PLAY FLAME TREES!
GNNNN
I'M WRITING A REVIEW FOR MY ZINE.
WHAT?
ONE, TWO, THREE, FOUR!
THE GASH
ARE YOU READY FOR THIS SHIT, PENN?
WHAT?
ARE YOU READY?
HUH?
I CAN SEE FREDA,
OVER BY THE BAND.
WHERE'S THE DUDE?
WHAT?
WAHHHHHLLL!

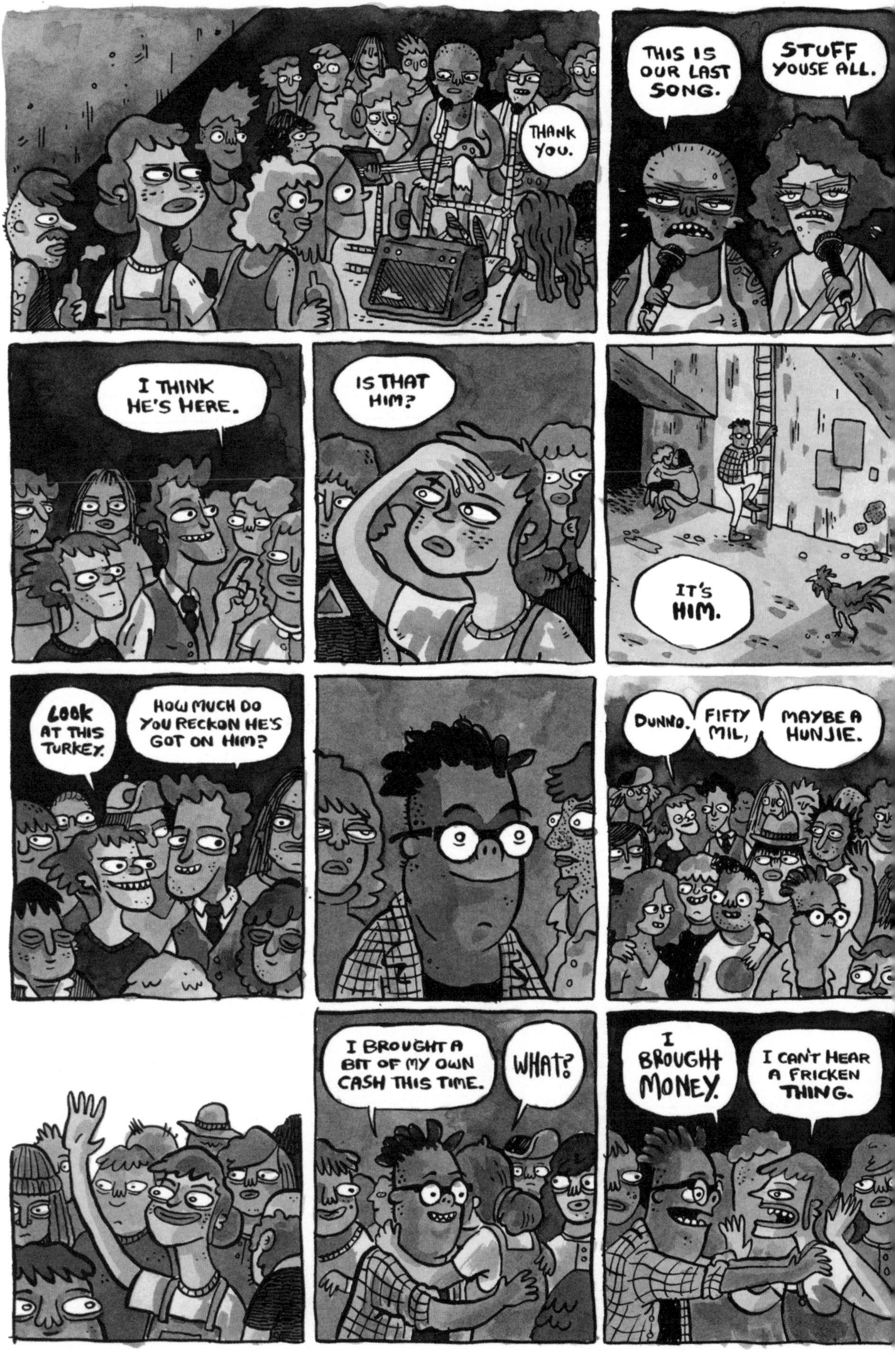
THANK YOU.
THIS IS OUR LAST SONG.
STUFF YOUSE ALL.
I THINK HE'S HERE.
IS THAT HIM?
IT'S HIM.
LOOK AT THIS TURKEY.
HOW MUCH DO YOU RECKON HE'S GOT ON HIM?
DUNNO.
FIFTY MIL,
MAYBE A HUNJIE.
I BROUGHT A BIT OF MY OWN CASH THIS TIME.
WHAT?
I BROUGHT MONEY.
I CAN'T HEAR A FRICKEN THING.

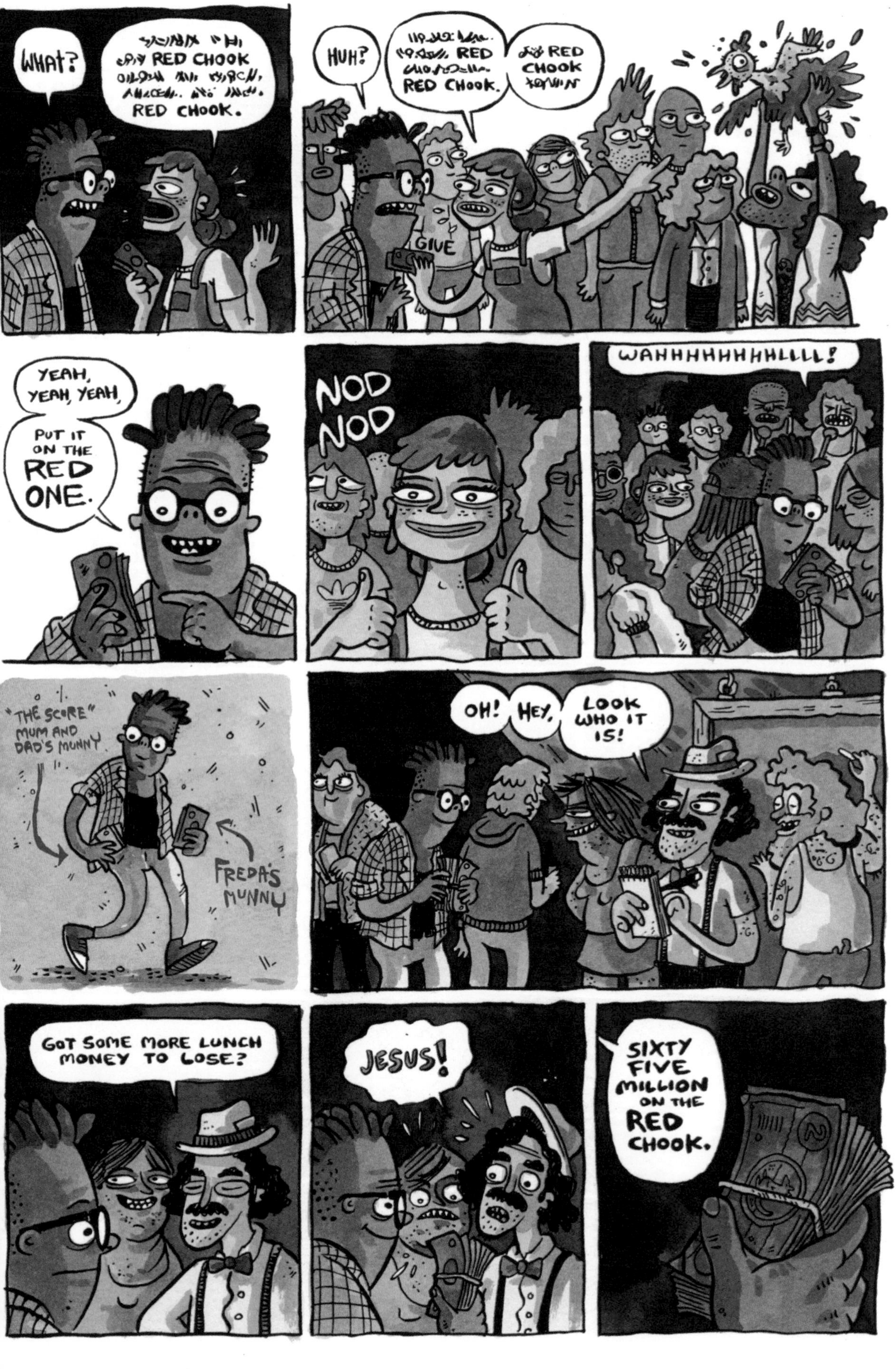
WHAT?
RED CHOOK
RED CHOOK.
HUH?
RED
RED CHOOK.
RED CHOOK
GIVE
YEAH, YEAH, YEAH,
PUT IT ON THE RED ONE.
NOD NOD
WAHHHHHHHHLLLLL!
"THE SCORE" MUM AND DAD'S MUNNY
FREDA'S MUNNY
OH!
HEY,
LOOK WHO IT IS!
GOT SOME MORE LUNCH MONEY TO LOSE?
JESUS!
SIXTY FIVE MILLION ON THE RED CHOOK.

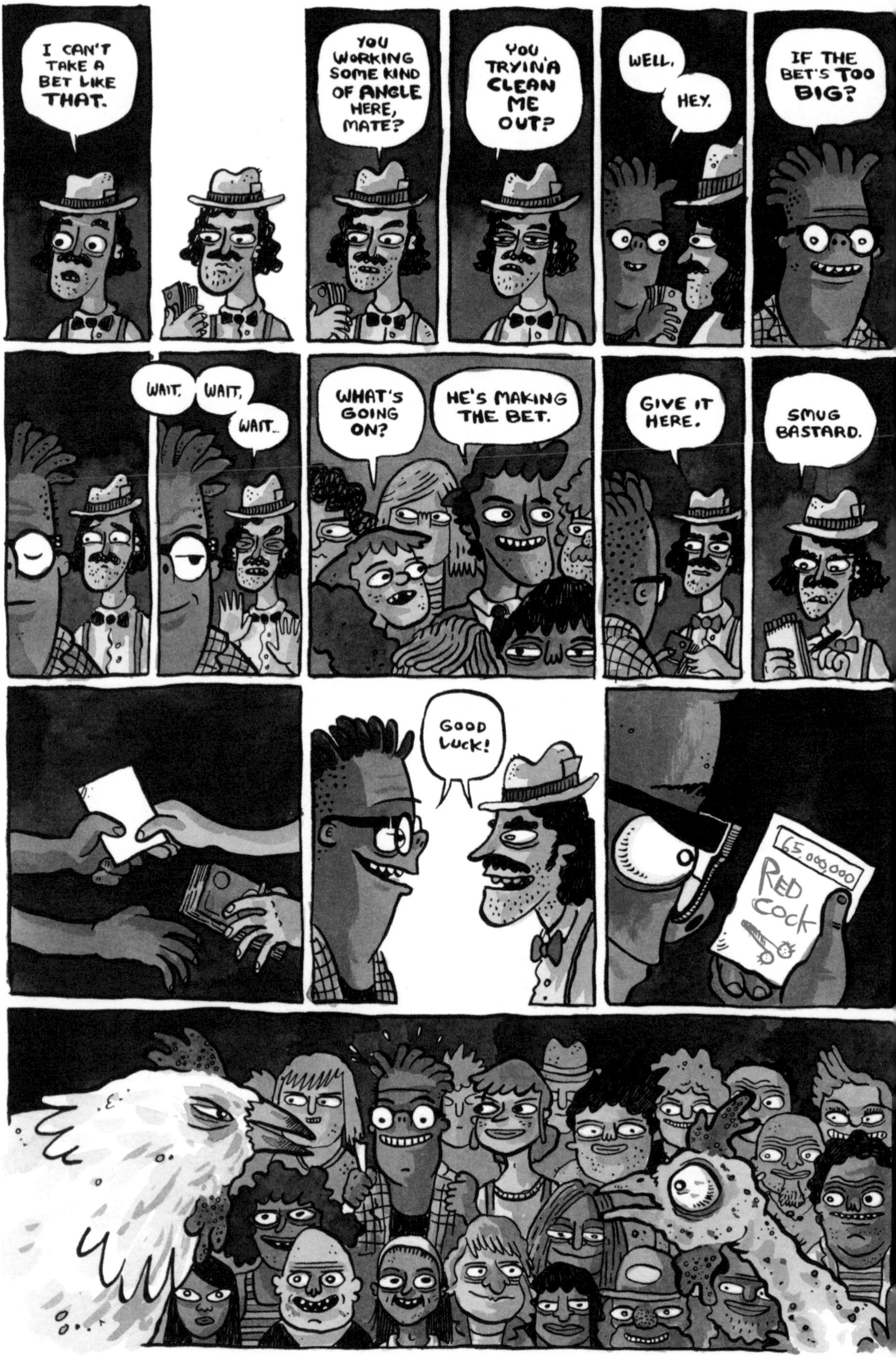
I CAN'T TAKE A BET LIKE THAT.
YOU WORKING SOME KIND OF ANGLE HERE, MATE?
YOU TRYIN'A CLEAN ME OUT?
WELL,
HEY.
IF THE BET'S TOO BIG?
WAIT.
WAIT,
WAIT...
WHAT'S GOING ON?
HE'S MAKING THE BET.
GIVE IT HERE.
SMUG BASTARD.
GOOD LUCK!
65,000,000
RED COCK

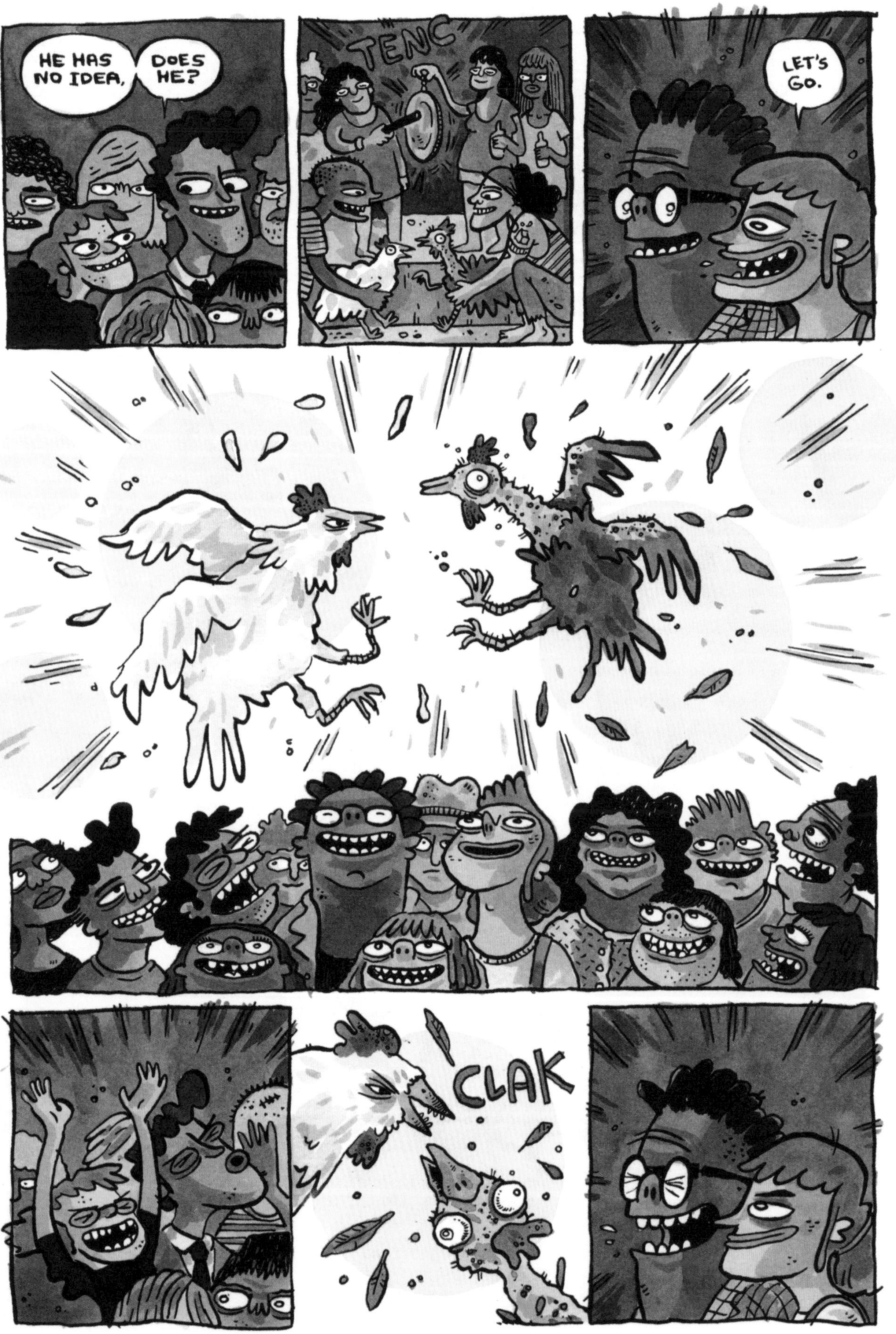
HE HAS NO IDEA,
DOES HE?
TENC
LET'S GO.
CLAK

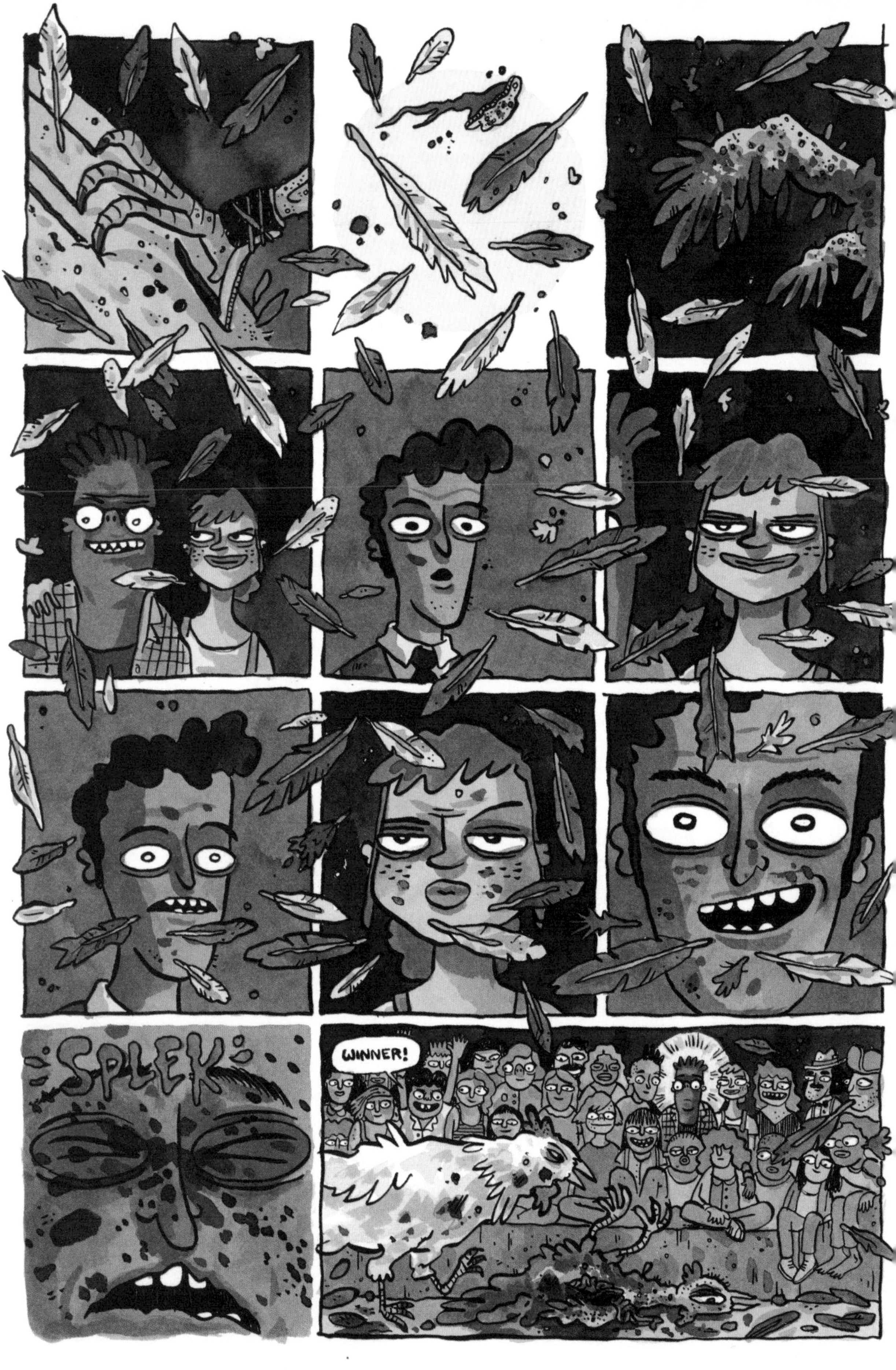
SPLEK
WINNER!

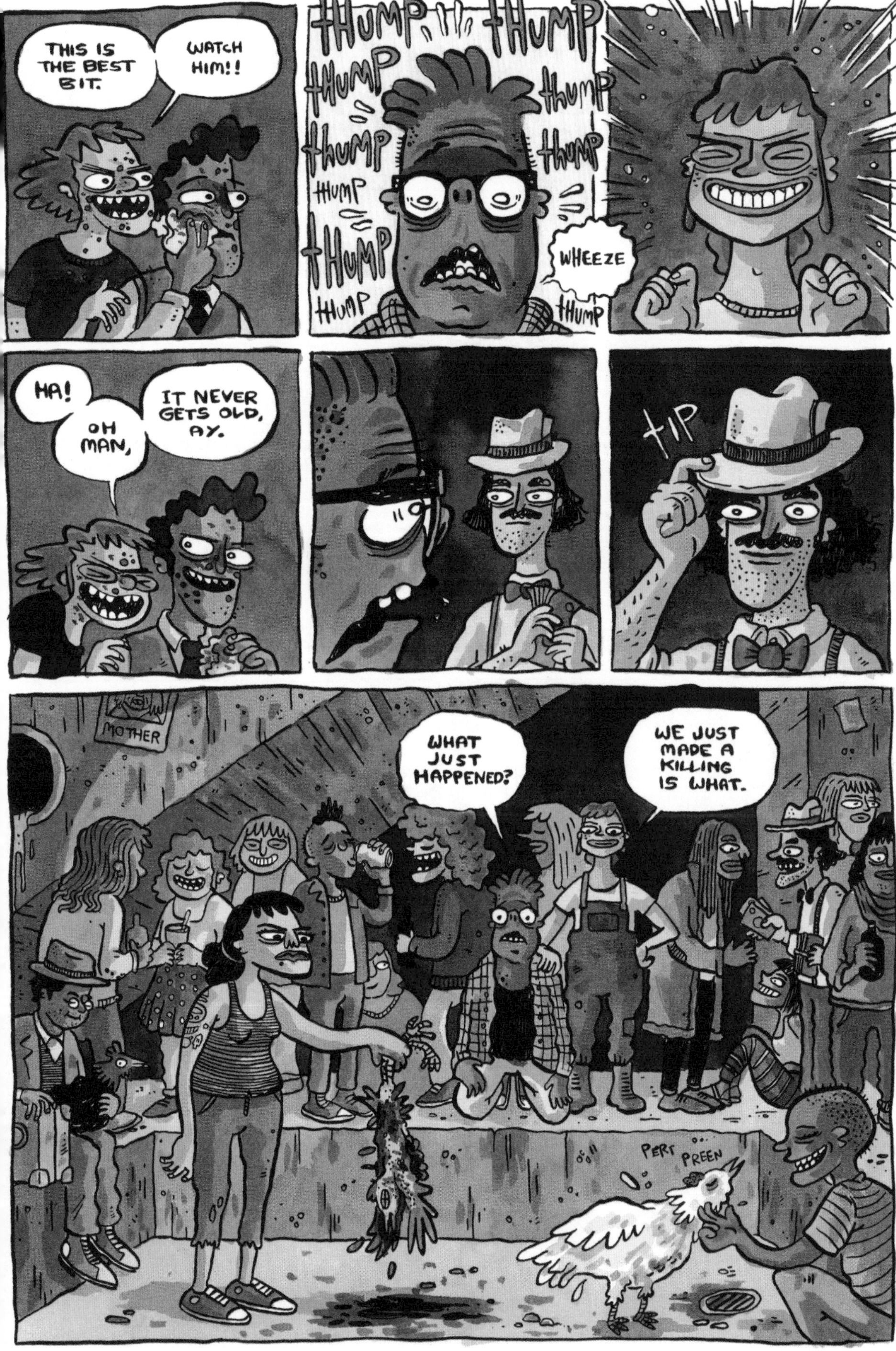
THIS IS THE BEST BIT.
WATCH HIM!!
THUMP THUMP THUMP THUMP THUMP THUMP THUMP THUMP THUMP THUMP
WHEEZE
HA!
OH MAN,
IT NEVER GETS OLD, AY.
TIP
MOTHER
WHAT JUST HAPPENED?
WE JUST MADE A KILLING IS WHAT.
PERT
PREEN

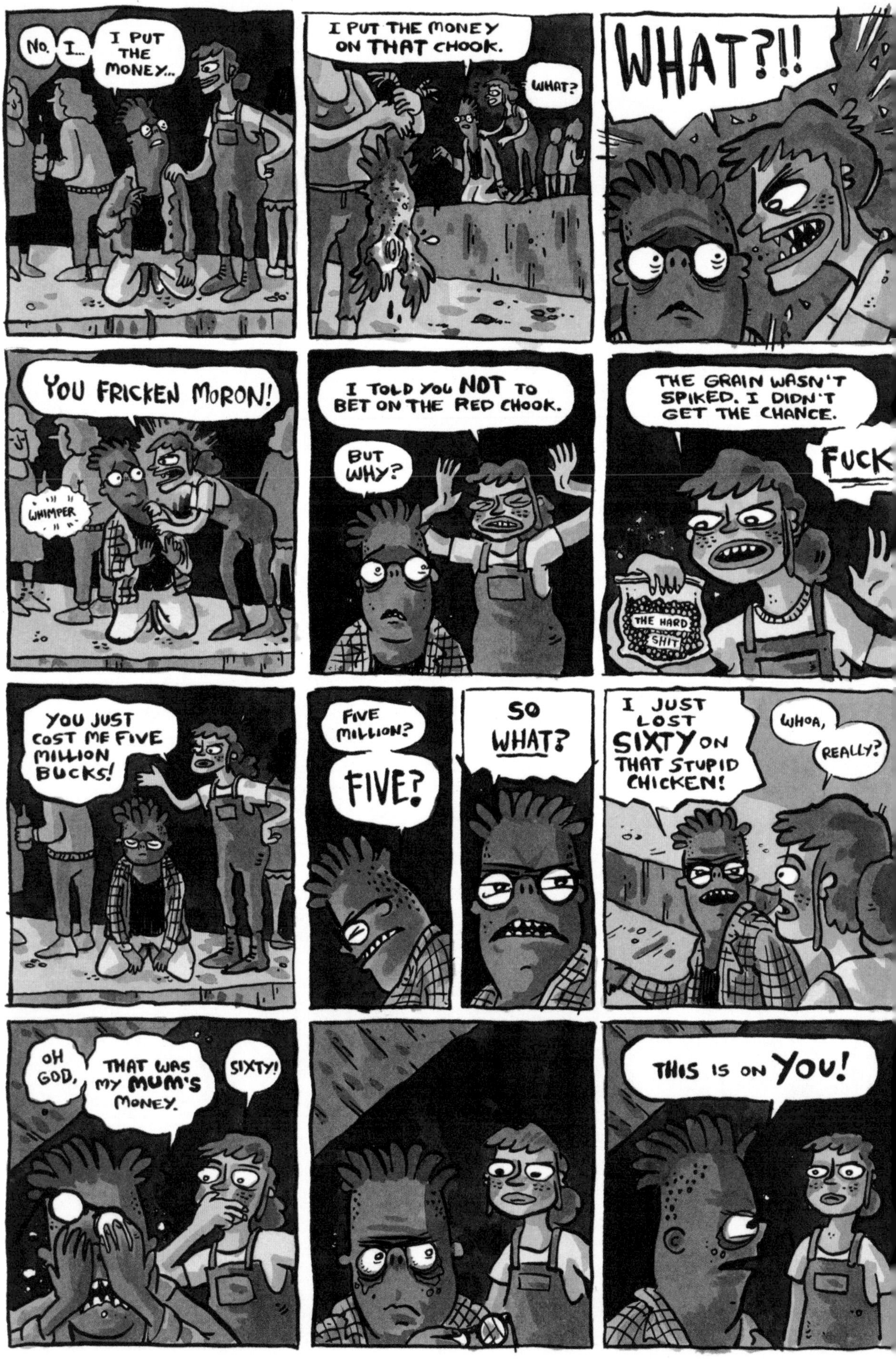
No.
I...
I PUT THE MONEY...
I PUT THE MONEY ON THAT CHOOK.
WHAT?
WHAT?!!
YOU FRICKEN MORON!
WHIMPER
I TOLD YOU NOT TO BET ON THE RED CHOOK.
BUT WHY?
THE GRAIN WASN'T SPIKED. I DIDN'T GET THE CHANCE.
FUCK
THE HARD SHIT
YOU JUST COST ME FIVE MILLION BUCKS!
FIVE MILLION?
FIVE?
SO WHAT?
I JUST LOST SIXTY ON THAT STUPID CHICKEN!
WHOA,
REALLY?
OH GOD,
THAT WAS MY MUM'S MONEY.
SIXTY!
THIS IS ON YOU!

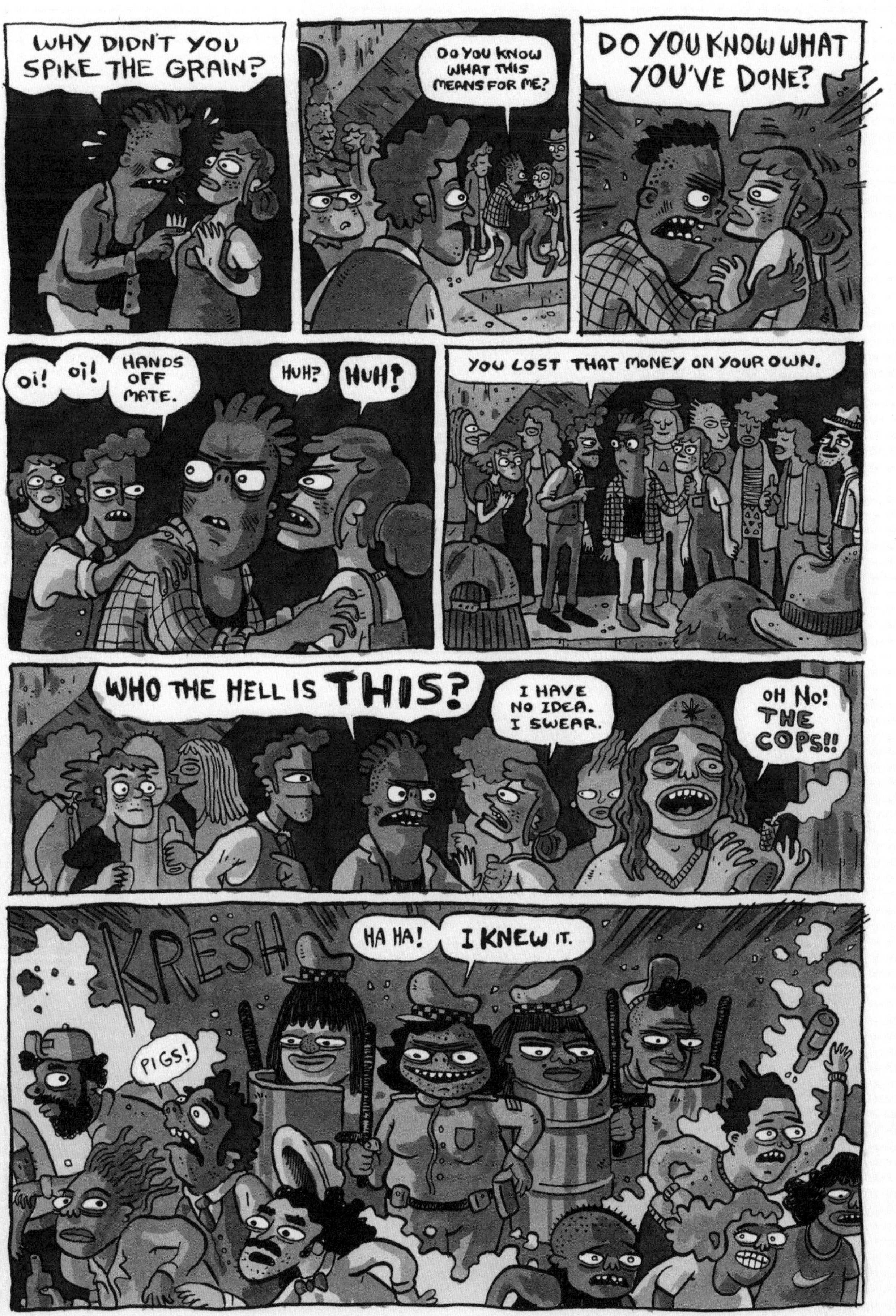
WHY DIDN'T YOU SPIKE THE GRAIN?
DO YOU KNOW WHAT THIS MEANS FOR ME?
DO YOU KNOW WHAT YOU'VE DONE?
oi!
oi!
HANDS OFF MATE.
HUH?
HUH?
YOU LOST THAT MONEY ON YOUR OWN.
WHO THE HELL IS THIS?
I HAVE NO IDEA. I SWEAR.
OH NO! THE COPS!!
KRESH
HA HA!
I KNEW IT.
PIGS!

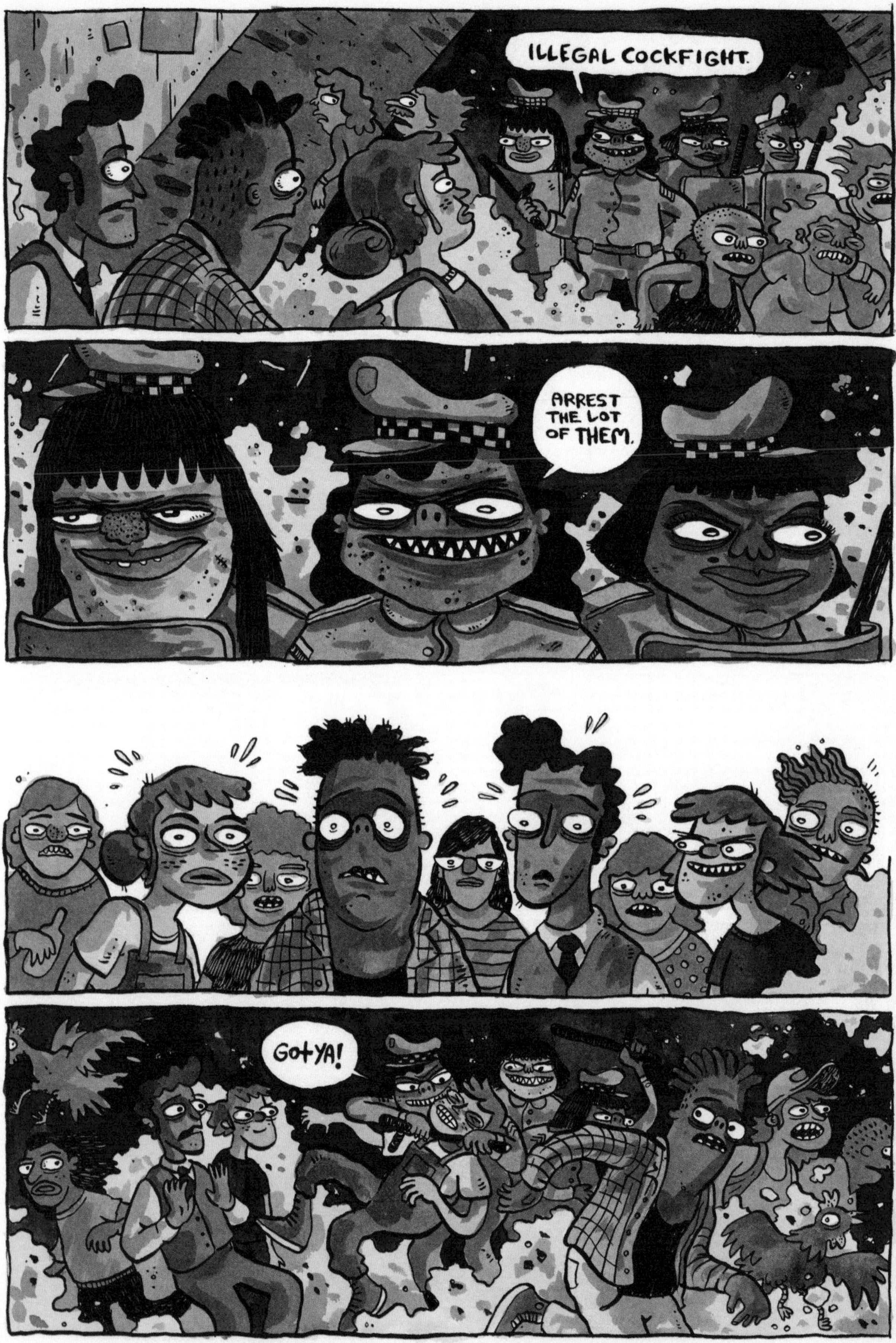
ILLEGAL COCKFIGHT.
ARREST THE LOT OF THEM.
GotYA!

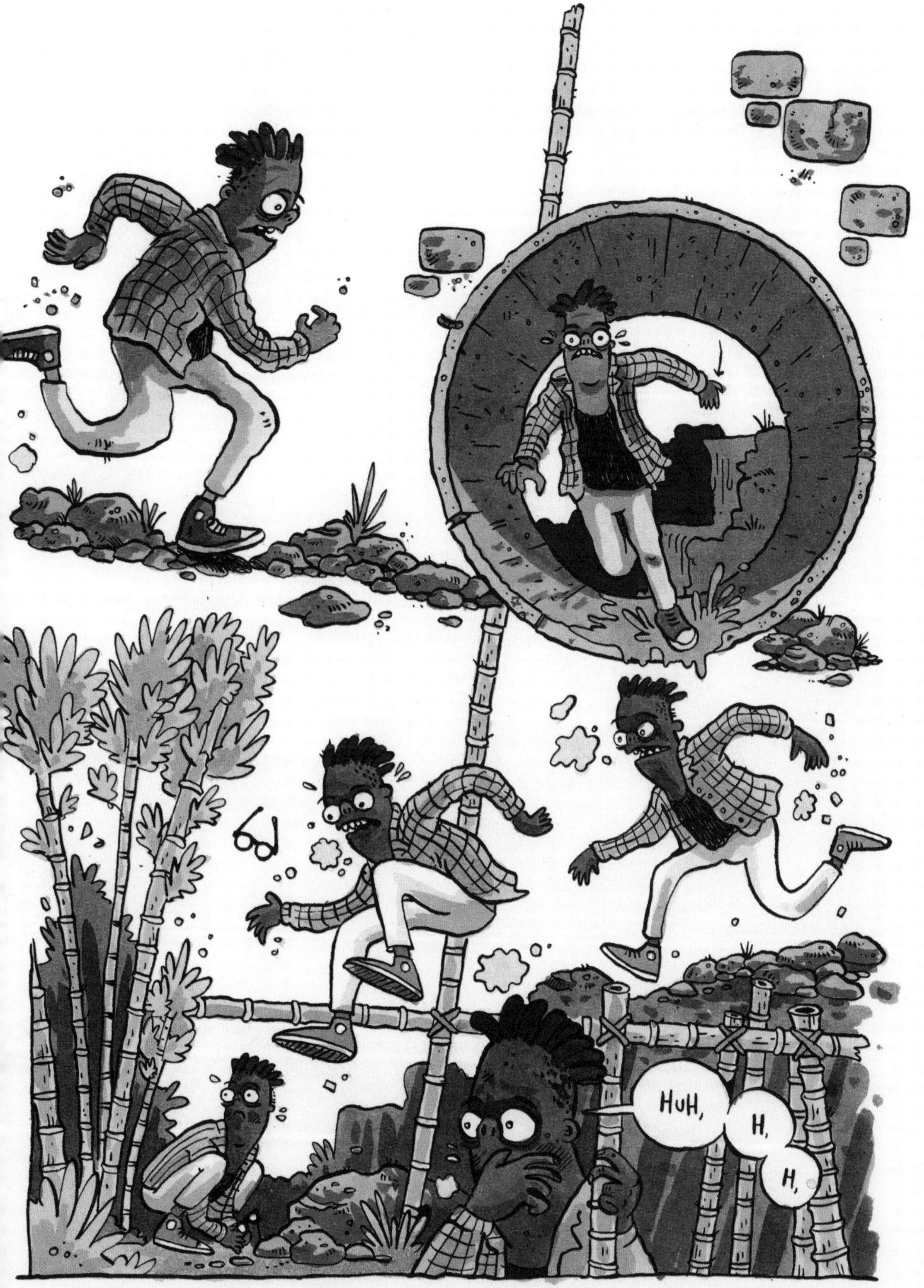
HUH,
H,
H,

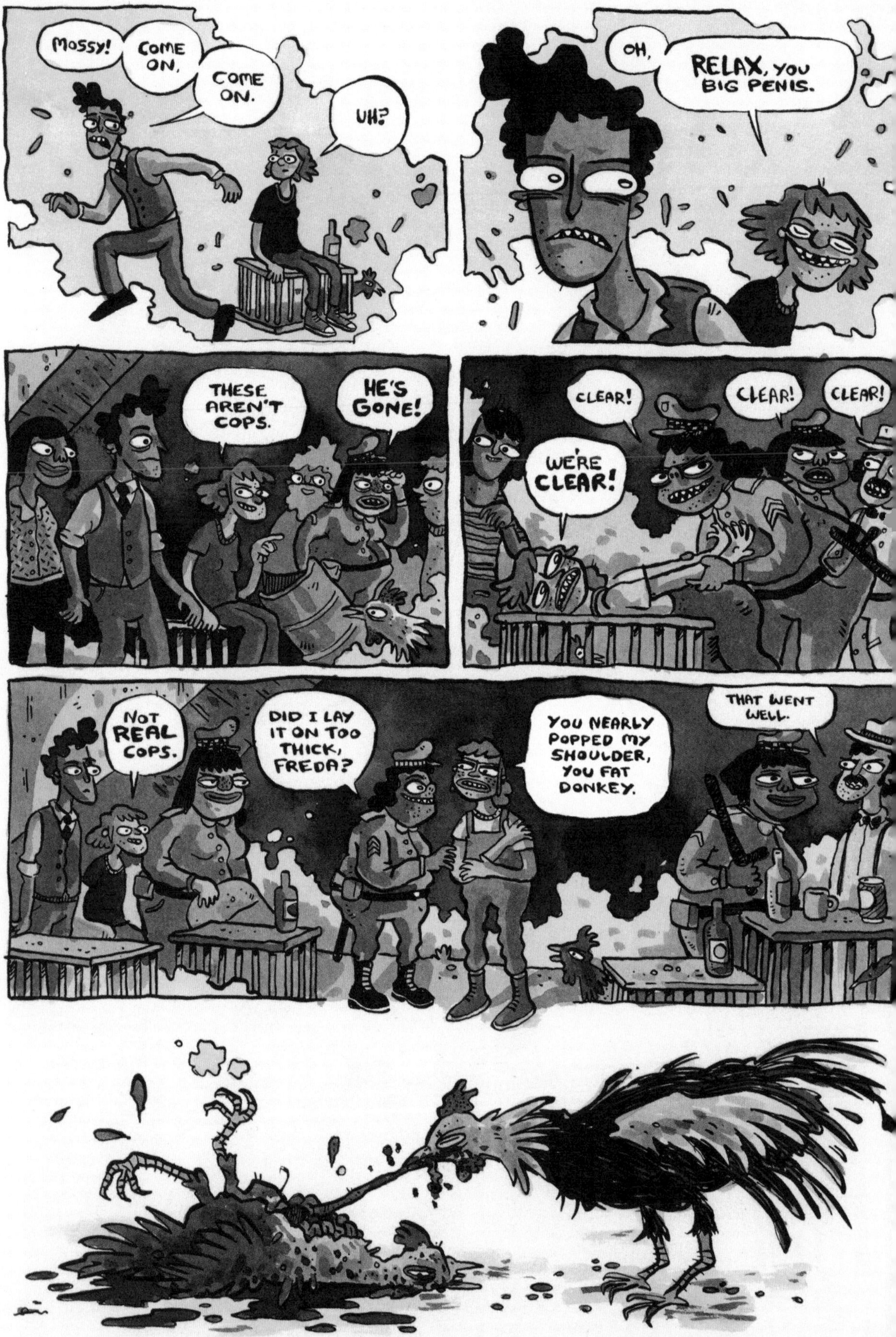
MOSSY!
COME ON,
COME ON.
UH?
OH,
RELAX, YOU BIG PENIS.
THESE AREN'T COPS.
HE'S GONE!
CLEAR!
CLEAR!
CLEAR!
WE'RE CLEAR!
NOT REAL COPS.
DID I LAY IT ON TOO THICK, FREDA?
YOU NEARLY POPPED MY SHOULDER, YOU FAT DONKEY.
THAT WENT WELL.

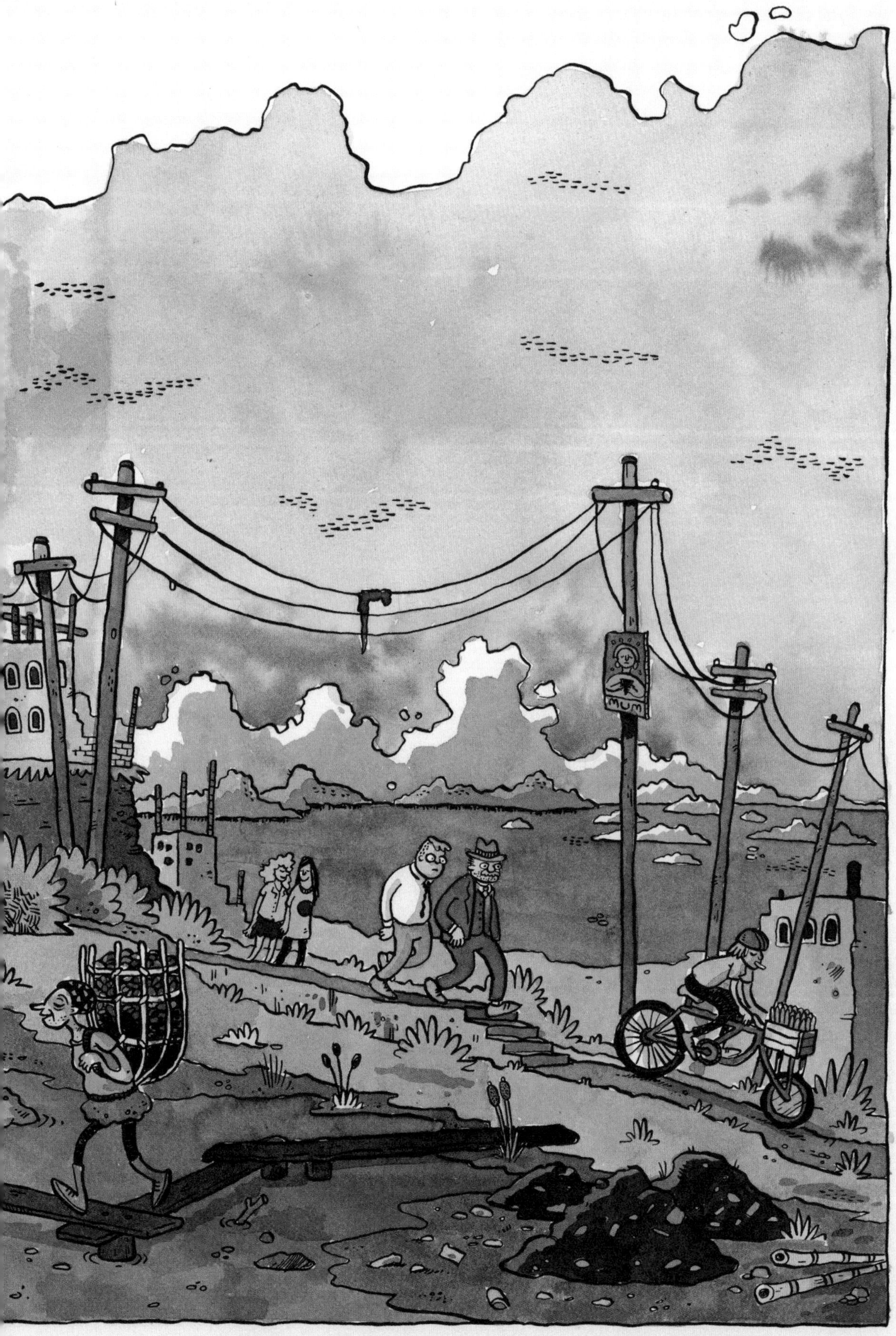
MUM

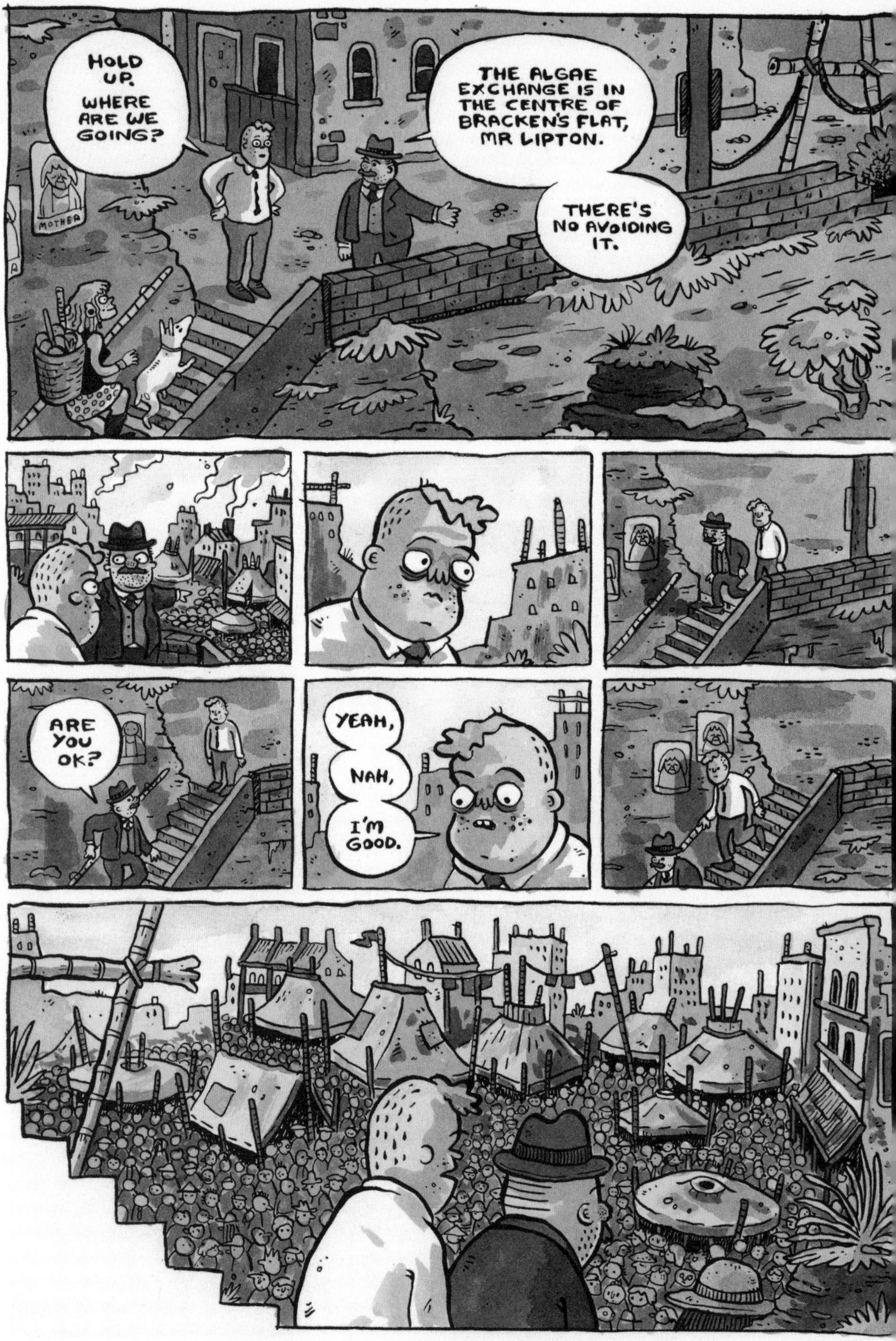
HOLD UP. WHERE ARE WE GOING?
MOTHER
THE ALGAE EXCHANGE IS IN THE CENTRE OF BRACKEN'S FLAT, MR LIPTON.
THERE'S NO AVOIDING IT.
ARE YOU OK?
YEAH,
NAH,
I'M GOOD.

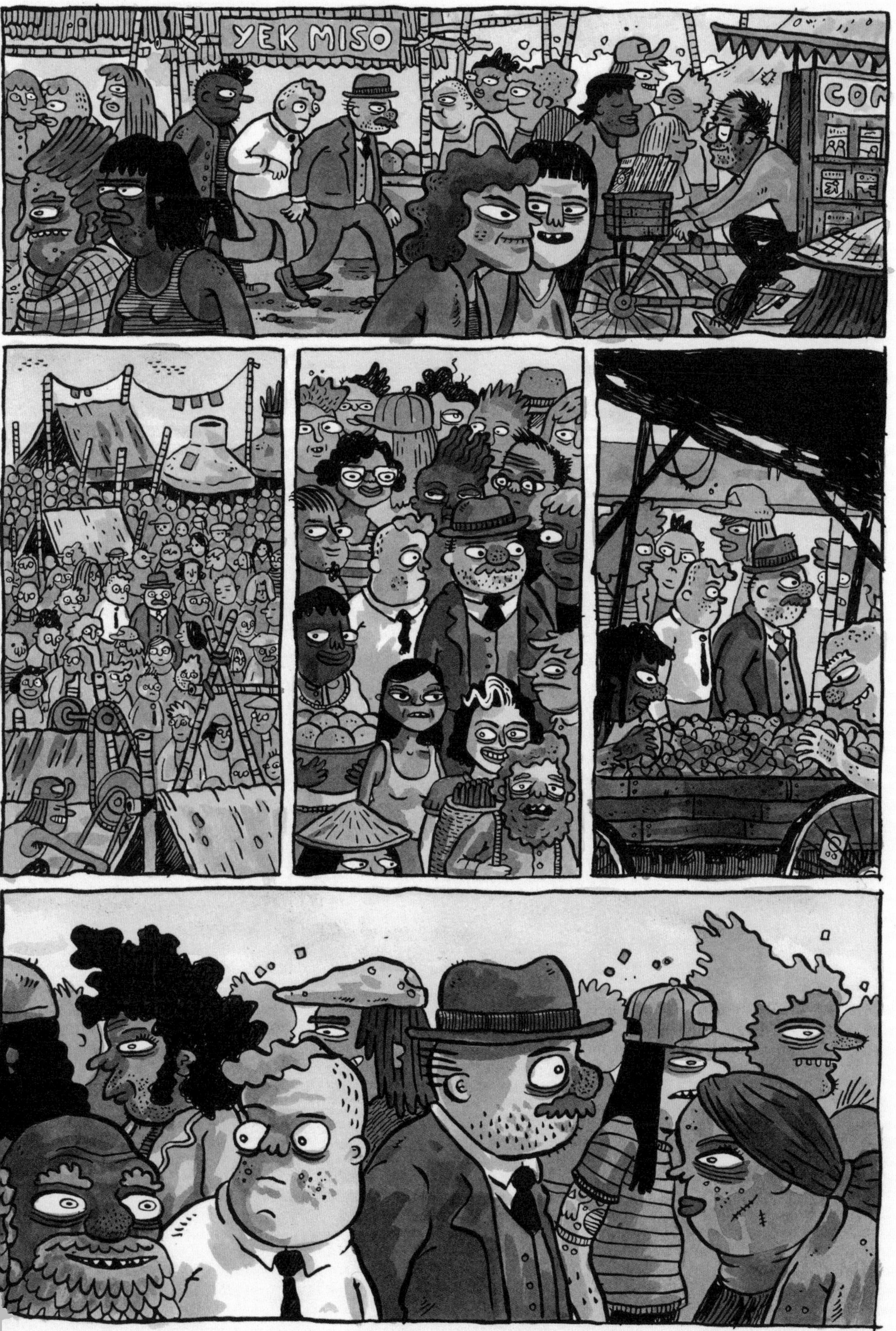
YEK MISO

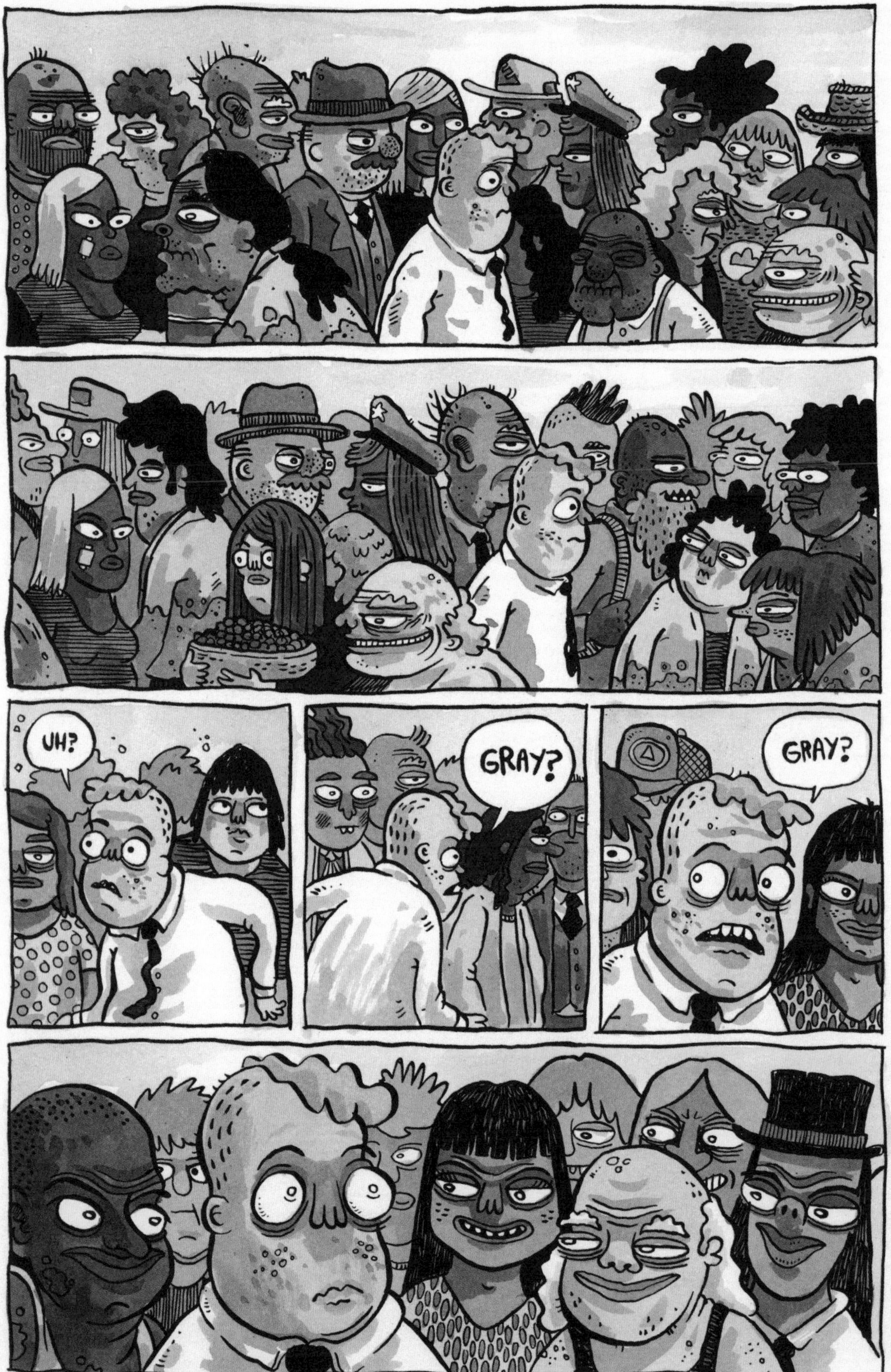
UH?
GRAY?
GRAY?

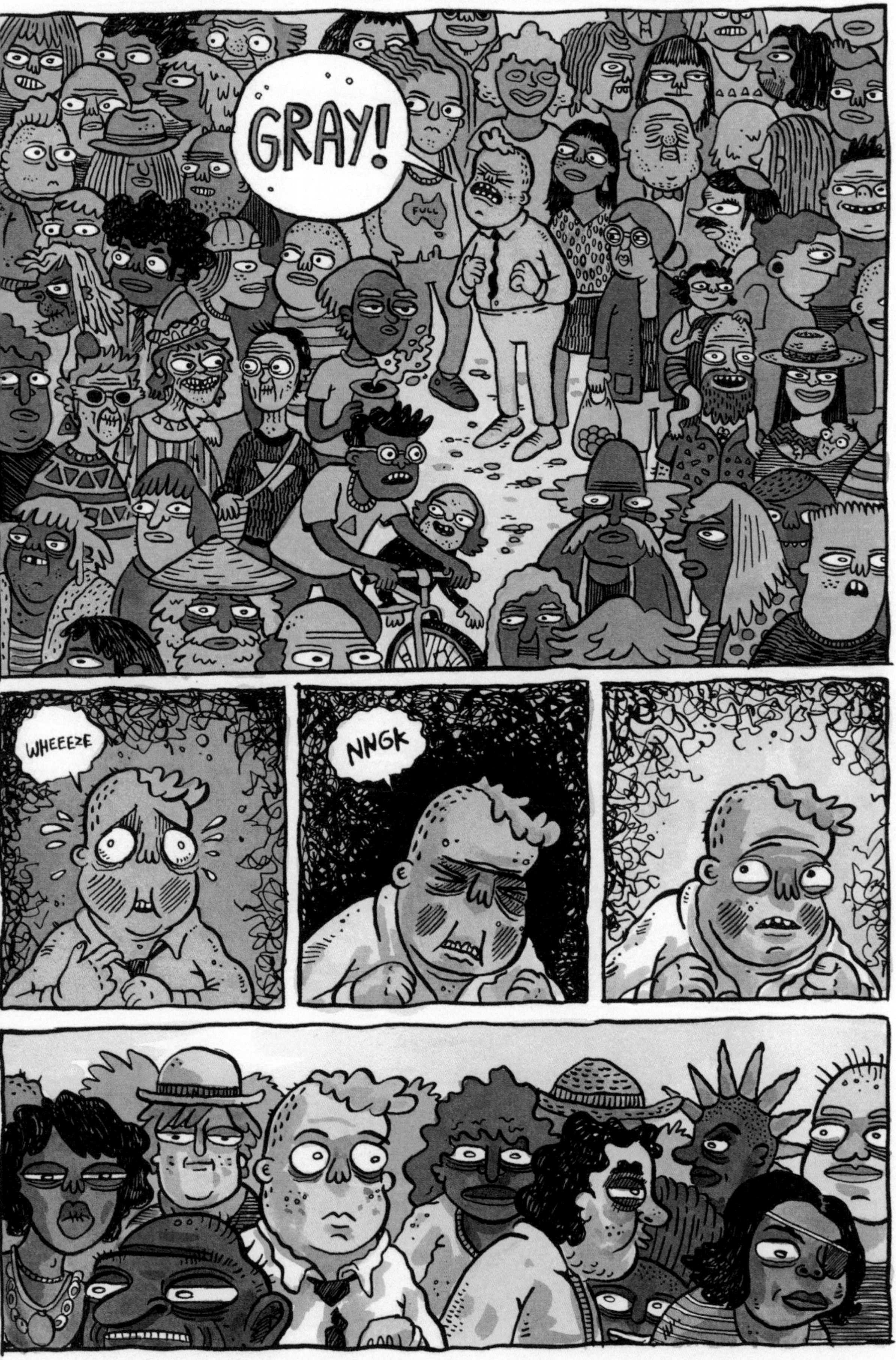
GRAY!
FULL
WHEEEZE
NNGK

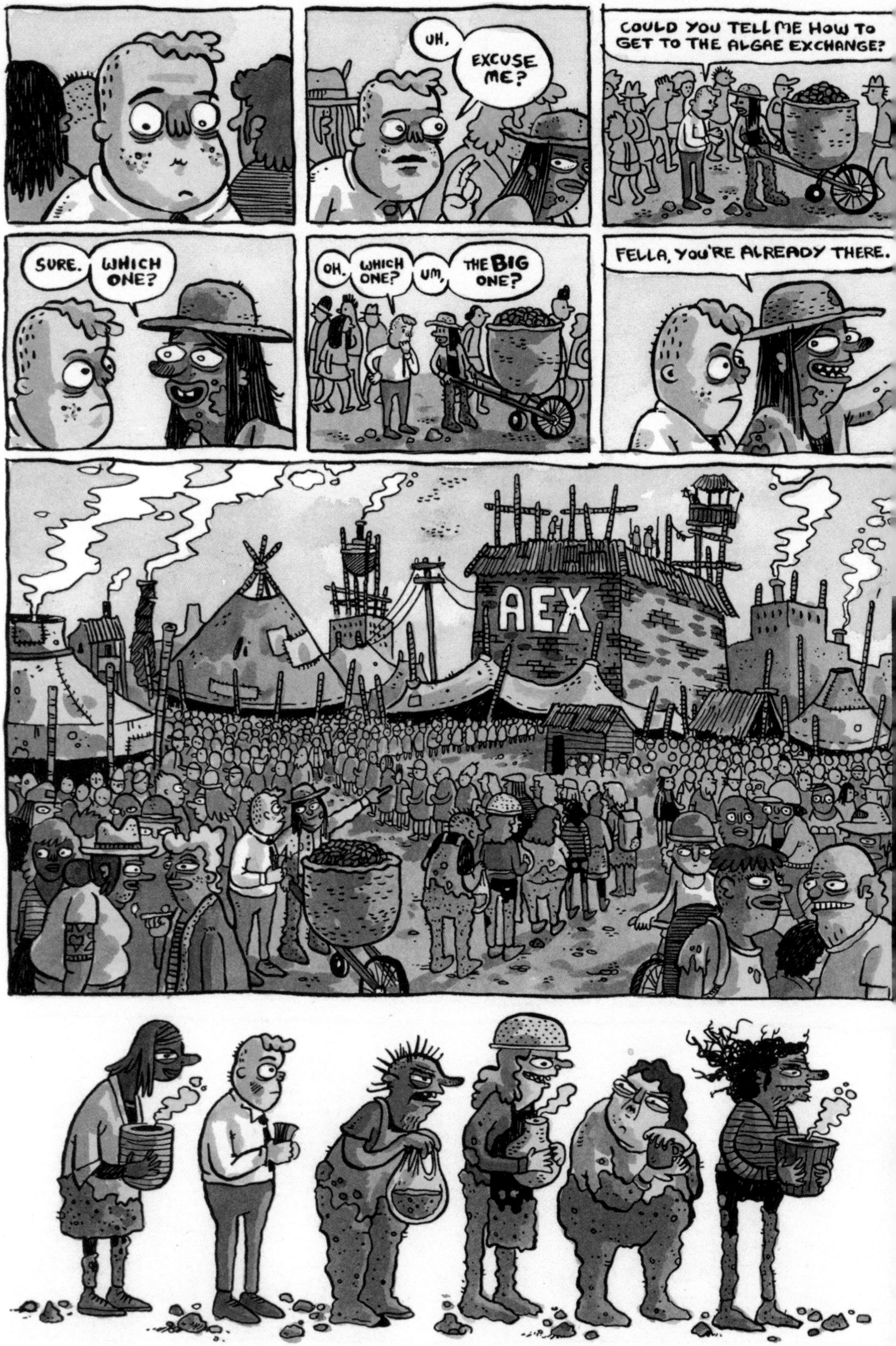
UH,
EXCUSE ME?
COULD YOU TELL ME HOW TO GET TO THE ALGAE EXCHANGE?
SURE.
WHICH ONE?
OH,
WHICH ONE?
UM,
THE BIG ONE?
FELLA, YOU'RE ALREADY THERE.
AEX

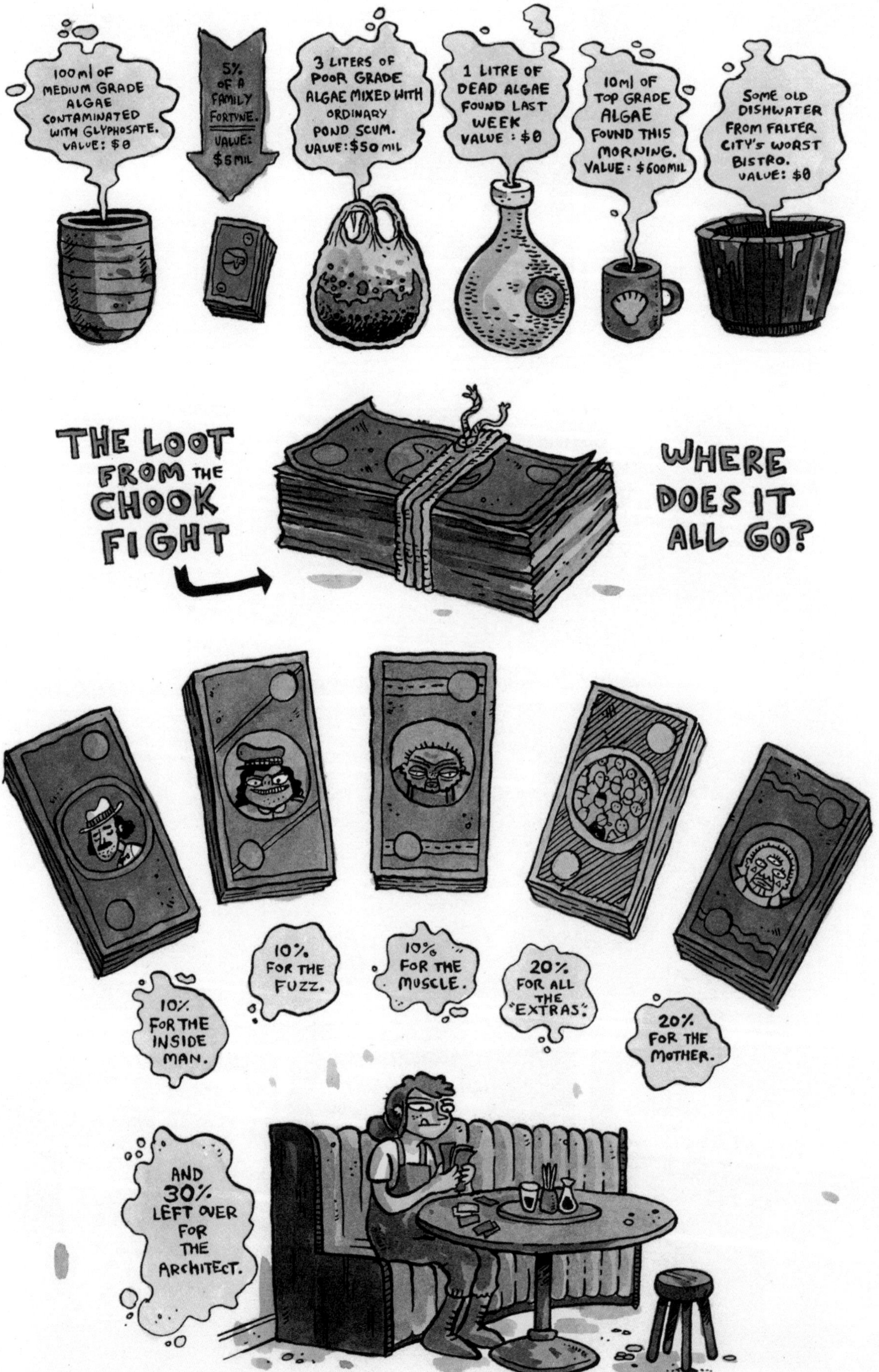
100ml OF MEDIUM GRADE ALGAE CONTAMINATED WITH GLYPHOSATE. VALUE: $0
5% OF A FAMILY FORTUNE. VALUE: $5MIL
3 LITERS OF POOR GRADE ALGAE MIXED WITH ORDINARY POND SCUM. VALUE: $50 MIL
1 LITRE OF DEAD ALGAE FOUND LAST WEEK VALUE : $0
10ml OF TOP GRADE ALGAE FOUND THIS MORNING. VALUE: $600MIL
SOME OLD DISHWATER FROM FALTER CITY'S WORST BISTRO. VALUE: $0
THE LOOT FROM THE CHOOK FIGHT
WHERE DOES IT ALL GO?
10% FOR THE INSIDE MAN.
10% FOR THE FUZZ.
10% FOR THE MUSCLE.
20% FOR ALL THE "EXTRAS".
20% FOR THE MOTHER.
AND 30% LEFT OVER FOR THE ARCHITECT.

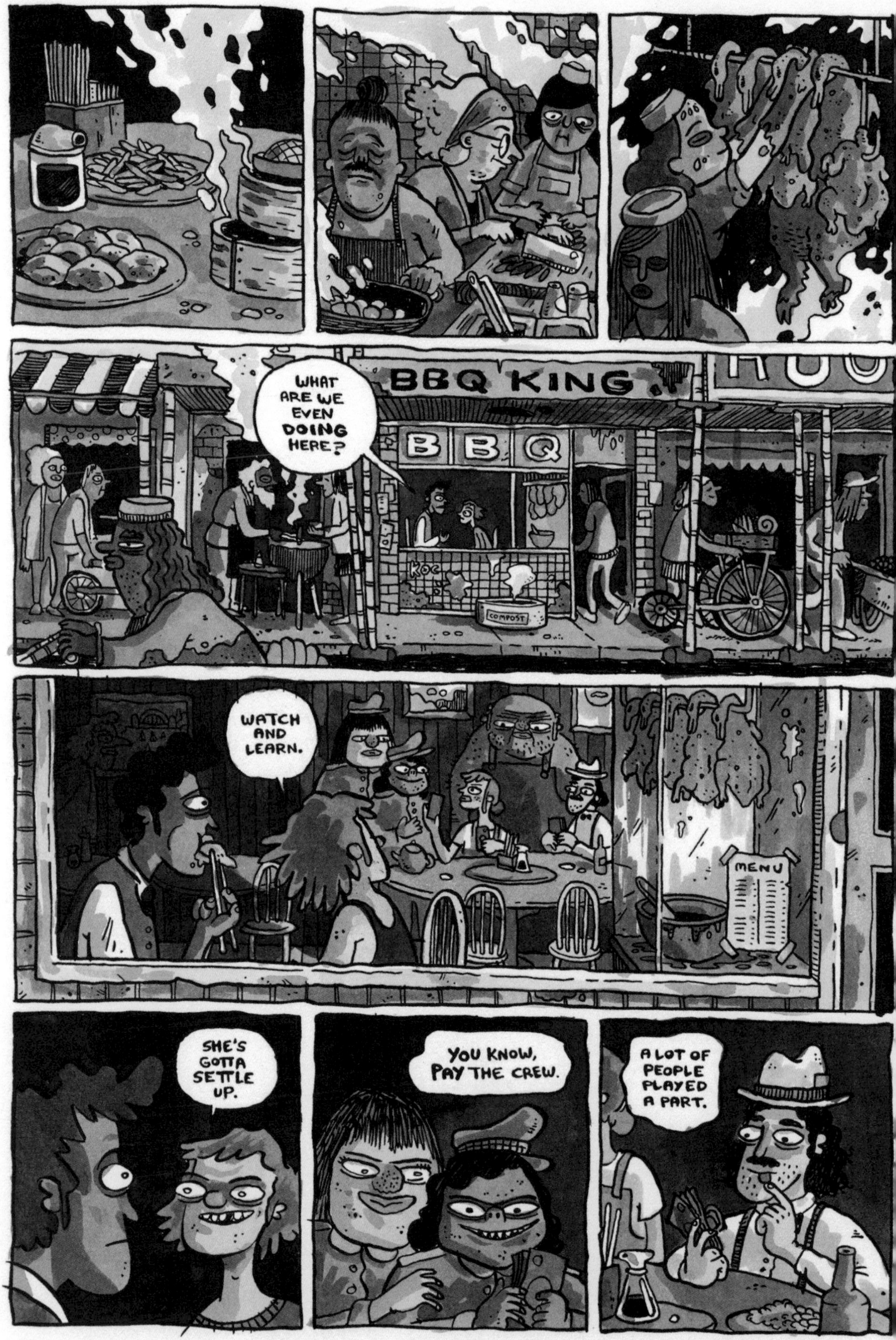

BBQ KING
WHAT ARE WE EVEN DOING HERE?
BBQ
COMPOST
WATCH AND LEARN.
MENU
SHE'S GOTTA SETTLE UP.
YOU KNOW, PAY THE CREW.
A LOT OF PEOPLE PLAYED A PART.

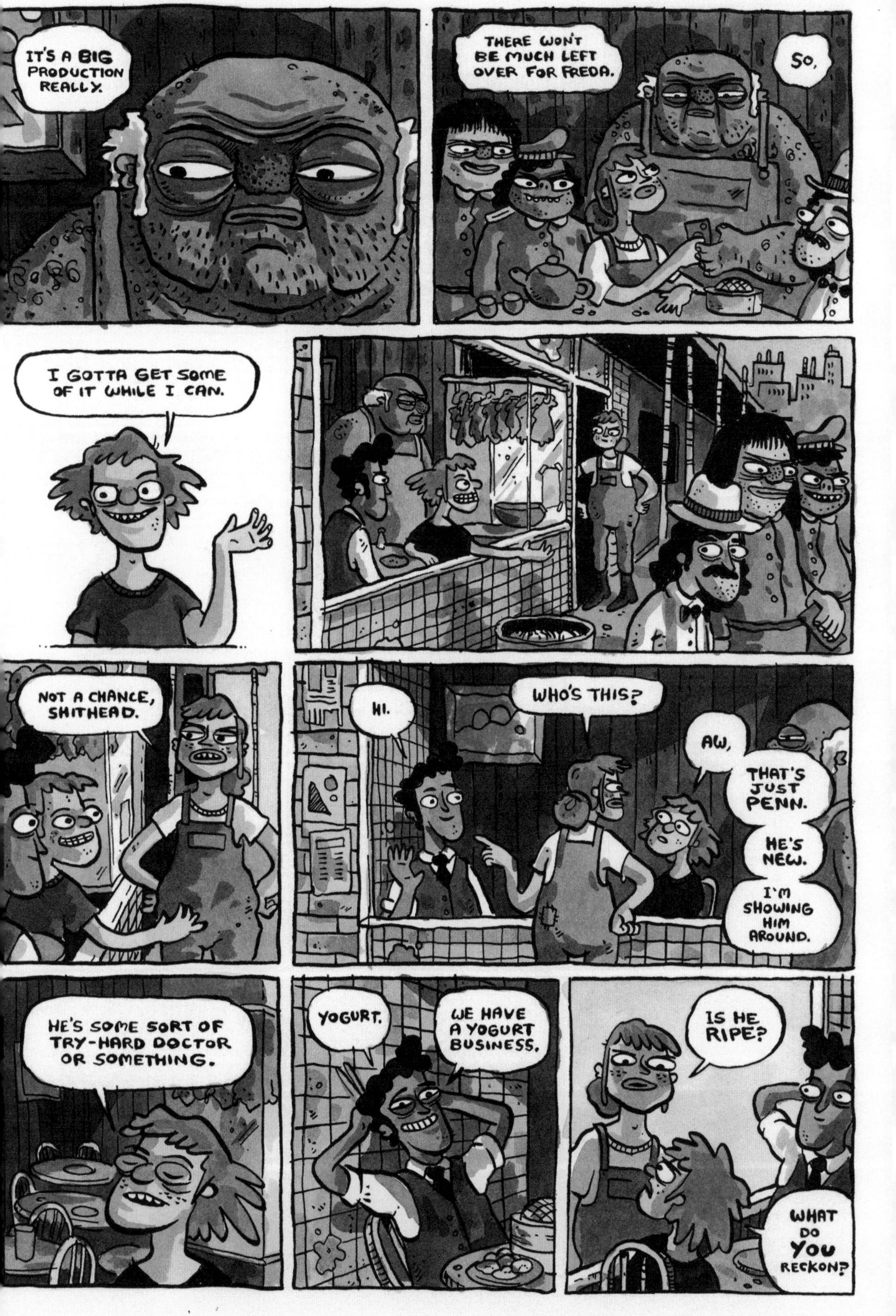
IT'S A BIG PRODUCTION REALLY.
THERE WON'T BE MUCH LEFT OVER FOR FREDA.
SO,
I GOTTA GET SOME OF IT WHILE I CAN.
NOT A CHANCE, SHITHEAD.
HI.
WHO'S THIS?
AW,
THAT'S JUST PENN.
HE'S NEW.
I'M SHOWING HIM AROUND.
HE'S SOME SORT OF TRY-HARD DOCTOR OR SOMETHING.
YOGURT.
WE HAVE A YOGURT BUSINESS.
IS HE RIPE?
WHAT DO YOU RECKON?

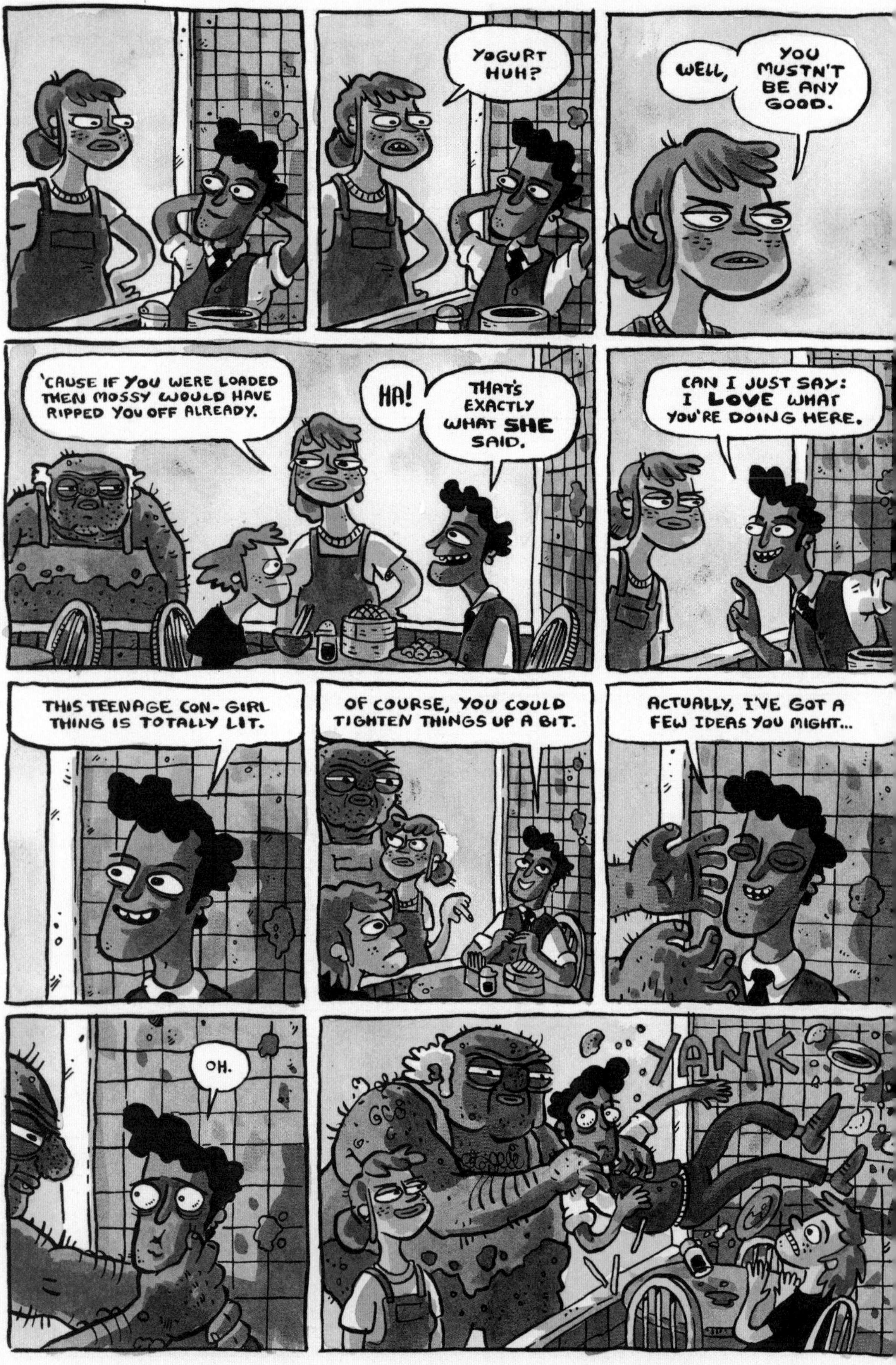
YOGURT HUH?
WELL,
YOU MUSTN'T BE ANY GOOD.
'CAUSE IF YOU WERE LOADED THEN MOSSY WOULD HAVE RIPPED YOU OFF ALREADY.
HA!
THAT'S EXACTLY WHAT SHE SAID.
CAN I JUST SAY: I LOVE WHAT YOU'RE DOING HERE.
THIS TEENAGE CON-GIRL THING IS TOTALLY LIT.
OF COURSE, YOU COULD TIGHTEN THINGS UP A BIT.
ACTUALLY, I'VE GOT A FEW IDEAS YOU MIGHT...
OH.
YANK

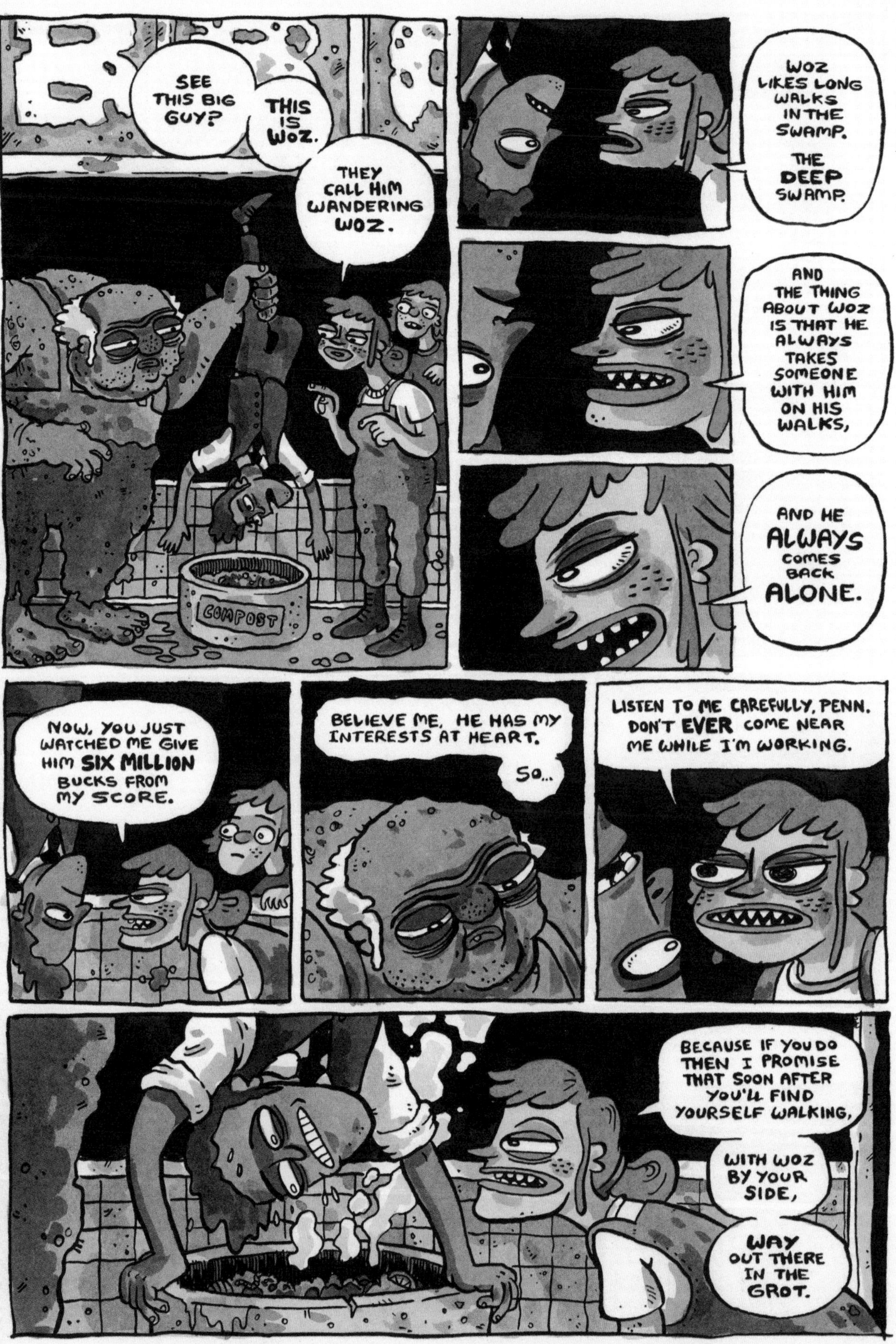
SEE THIS BIG GUY?
THIS IS WOZ.
THEY CALL HIM WANDERING WOZ.
COMPOST
WOZ LIKES LONG WALKS IN THE SWAMP.
THE DEEP SWAMP.
AND THE THING ABOUT WOZ IS THAT HE ALWAYS TAKES SOMEONE WITH HIM ON HIS WALKS,
AND HE ALWAYS COMES BACK ALONE.
NOW, YOU JUST WATCHED ME GIVE HIM SIX MILLION BUCKS FROM MY SCORE.
BELIEVE ME, HE HAS MY INTERESTS AT HEART.
SO...
LISTEN TO ME CAREFULLY, PENN. DON'T EVER COME NEAR ME WHILE I'M WORKING.
BECAUSE IF YOU DO THEN I PROMISE THAT SOON AFTER YOU'LL FIND YOURSELF WALKING,
WITH WOZ BY YOUR SIDE,
WAY OUT THERE IN THE GROT.

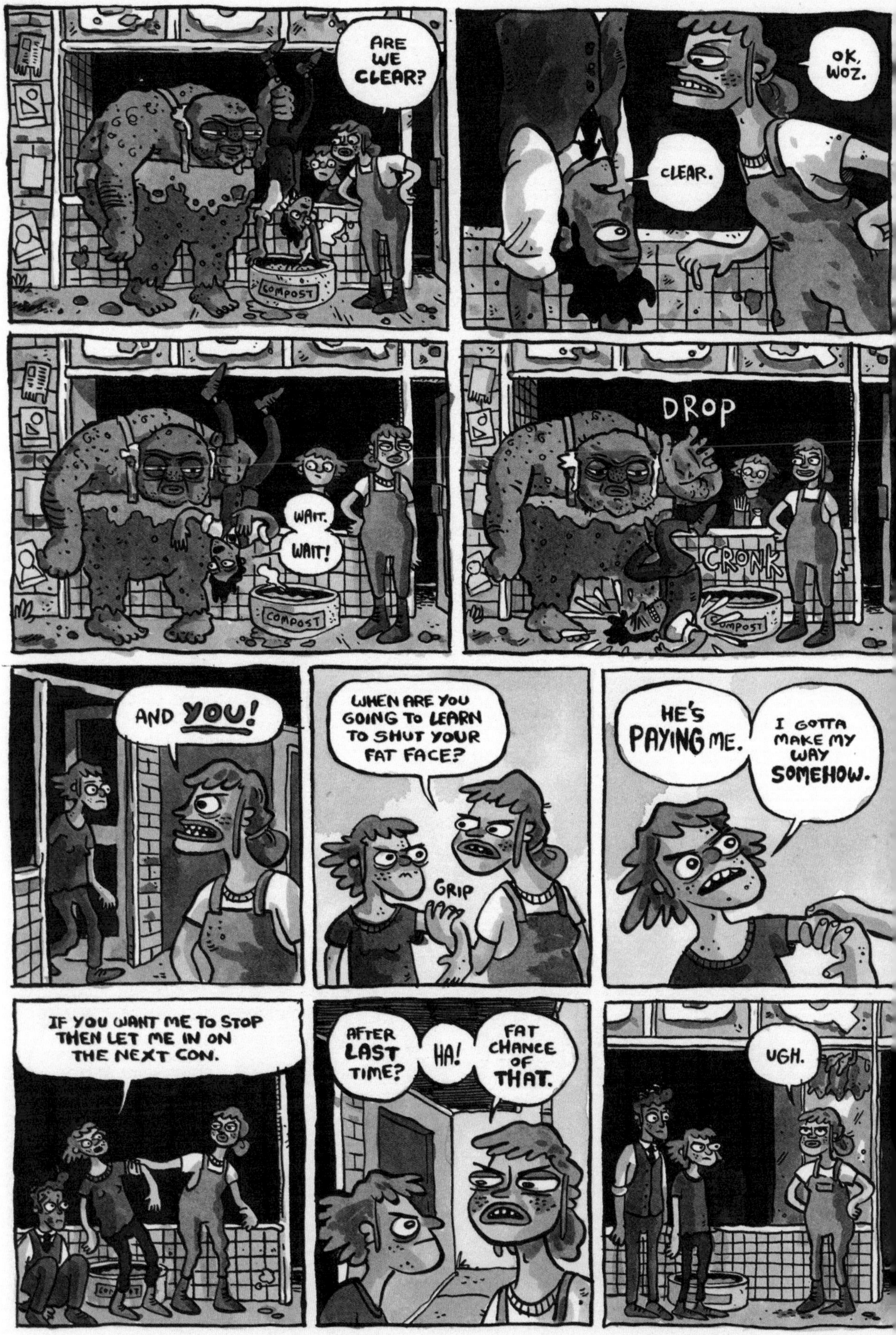
ARE WE CLEAR?
COMPOST
OK, WOZ.
CLEAR.
WAIT.
WAIT!
COMPOST
DROP
CRONK
COMPOST
AND YOU!
WHEN ARE YOU GOING TO LEARN TO SHUT YOUR FAT FACE?
GRIP
HE'S PAYING ME.
I GOTTA MAKE MY WAY SOMEHOW.
IF YOU WANT ME TO STOP THEN LET ME IN ON THE NEXT CON.
AFTER LAST TIME?
HA!
FAT CHANCE OF THAT.
UGH.

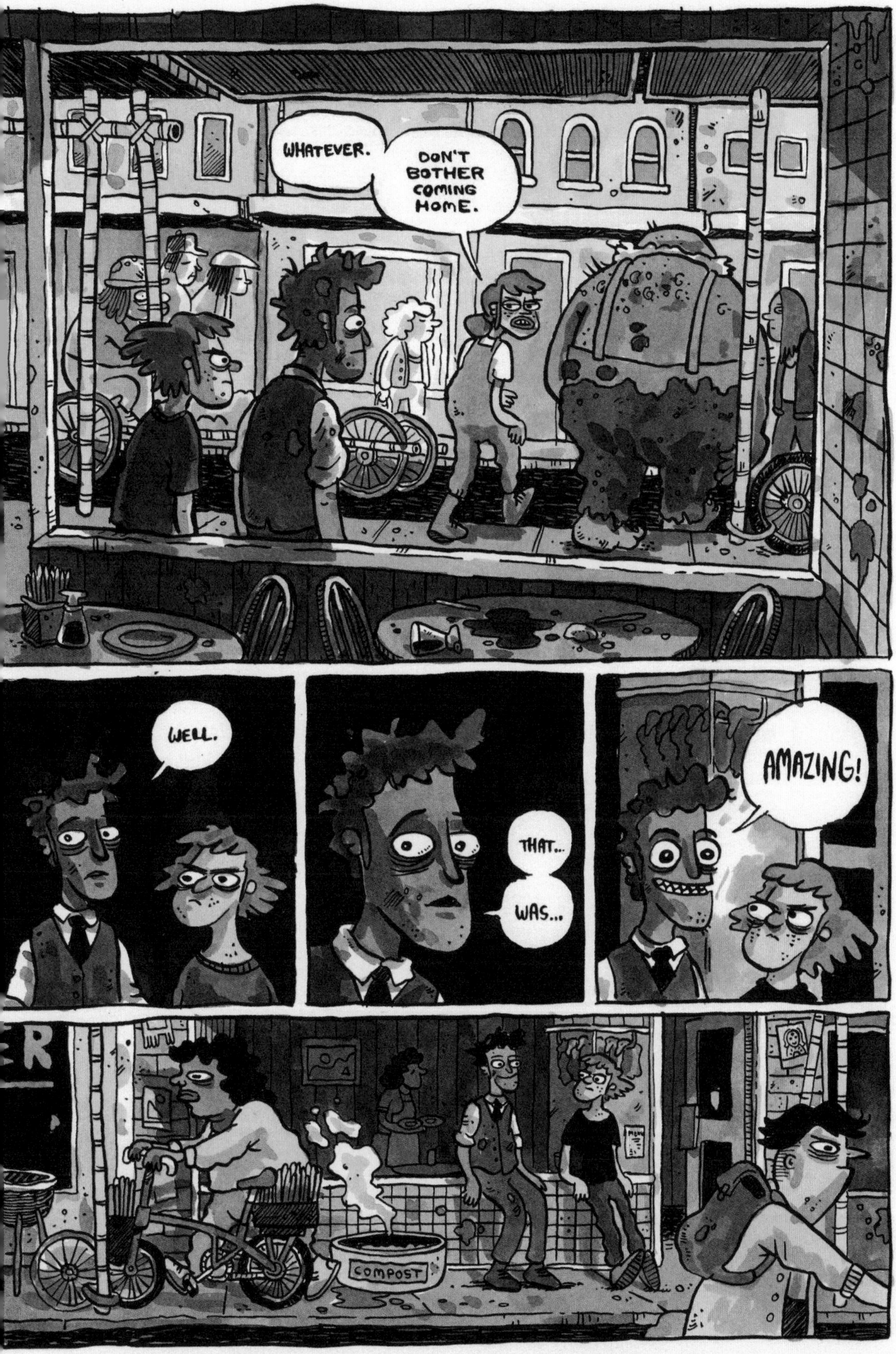
WHATEVER.
DON'T BOTHER COMING HOME.
WELL.
THAT...
WAS...
AMAZING!
R
COMPOST

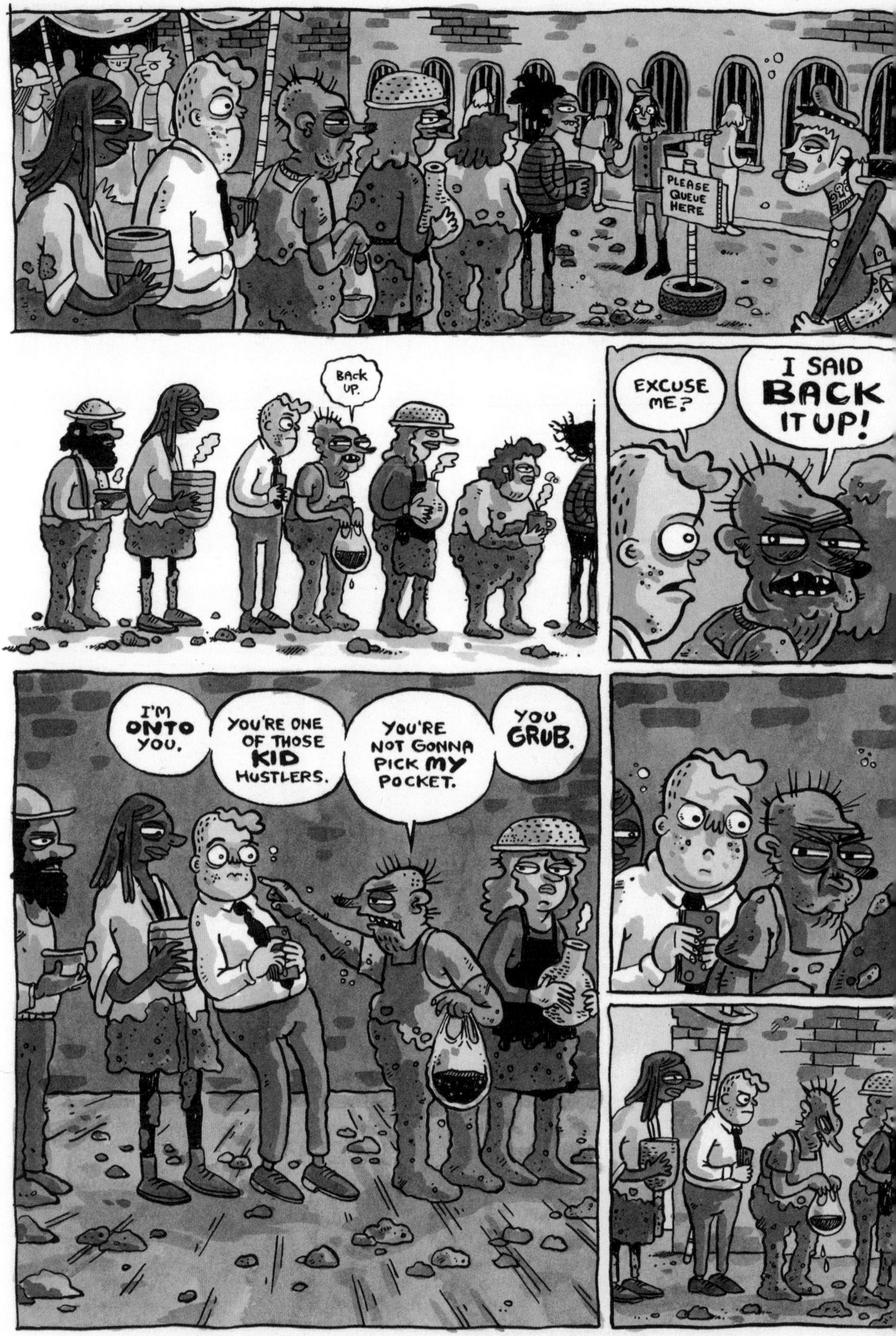
PLEASE QUEUE HERE
BACK UP.
EXCUSE ME?
I SAID BACK IT UP!
I'M ONTO YOU.
YOU'RE ONE OF THOSE KID HUSTLERS.
YOU'RE NOT GONNA PICK MY POCKET.
YOU GRUB.

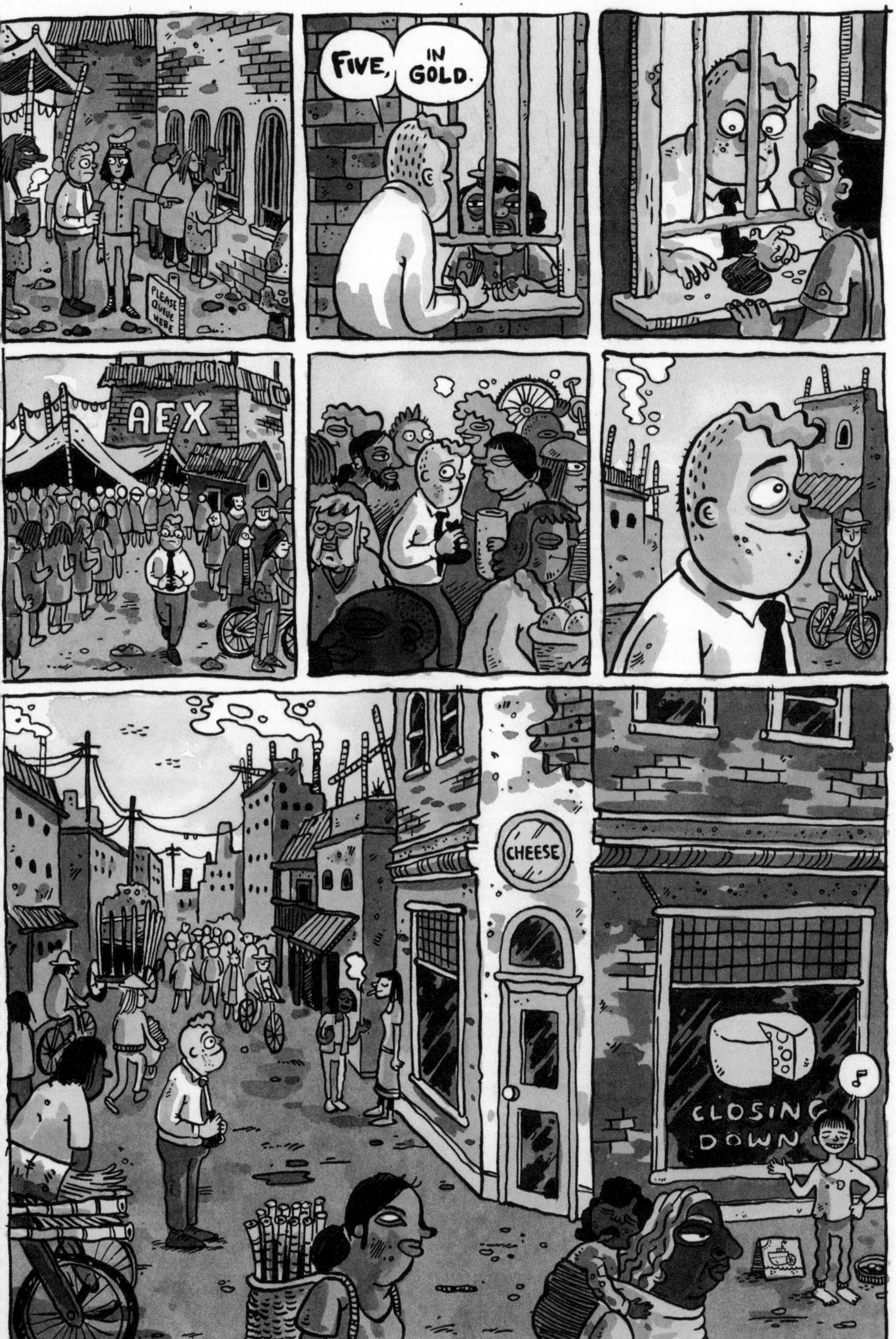
PLEASE QUEUE HERE
FIVE,
IN GOLD.
AEX
CHEESE
CLOSING DOWN
♪

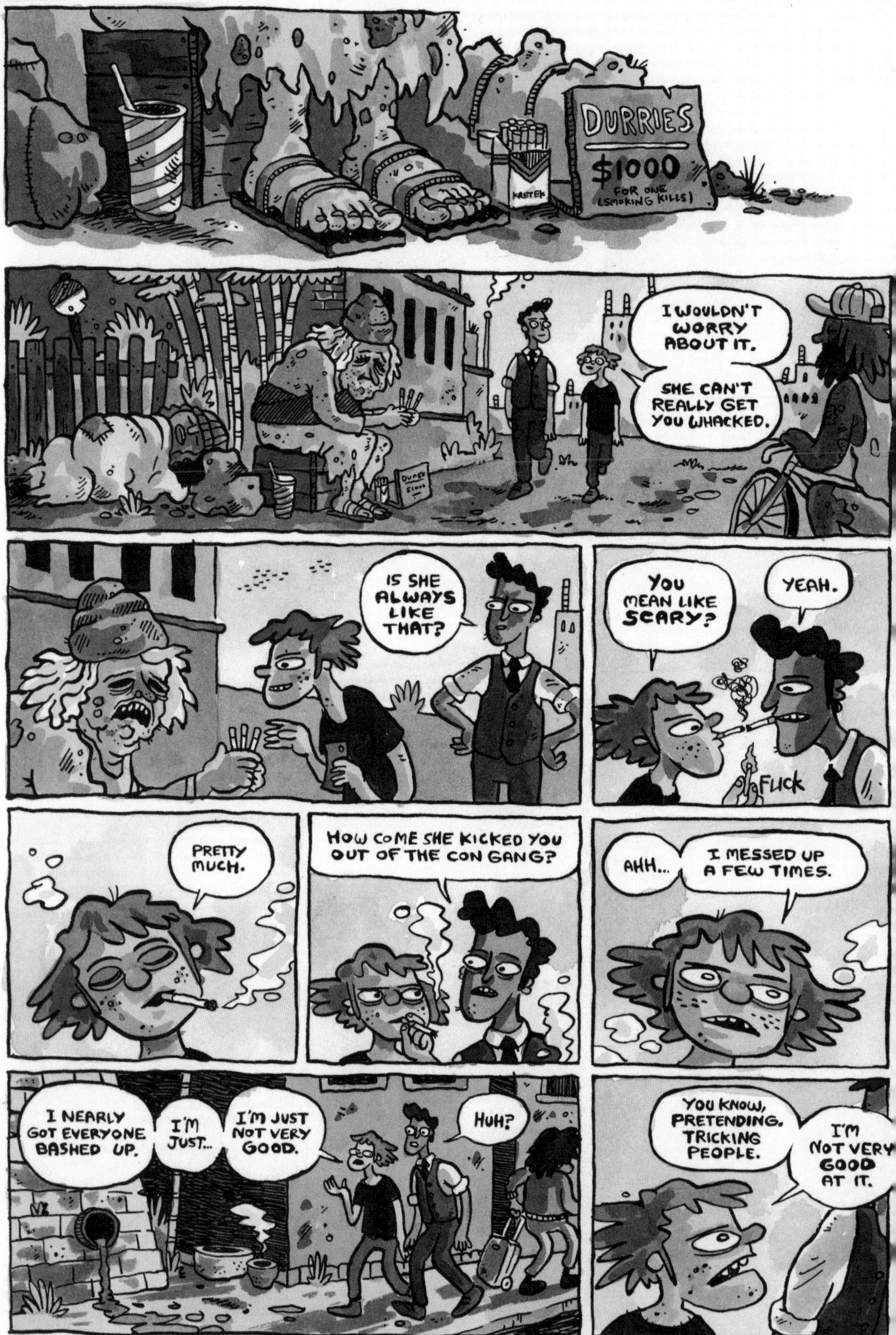
DURRIES
$1000
FOR ONE (SMOKING KILLS)
KRETEK
I WOULDN'T WORRY ABOUT IT.
SHE CAN'T REALLY GET YOU WHACKED.
IS SHE ALWAYS LIKE THAT?
YOU MEAN LIKE SCARY?
YEAH.
FLICK
PRETTY MUCH.
HOW COME SHE KICKED YOU OUT OF THE CON GANG?
AHH...
I MESSED UP A FEW TIMES.
I NEARLY GOT EVERYONE BASHED UP.
I'M JUST...
I'M JUST NOT VERY GOOD.
HUH?
YOU KNOW, PRETENDING. TRICKING PEOPLE.
I'M NOT VERY GOOD AT IT.

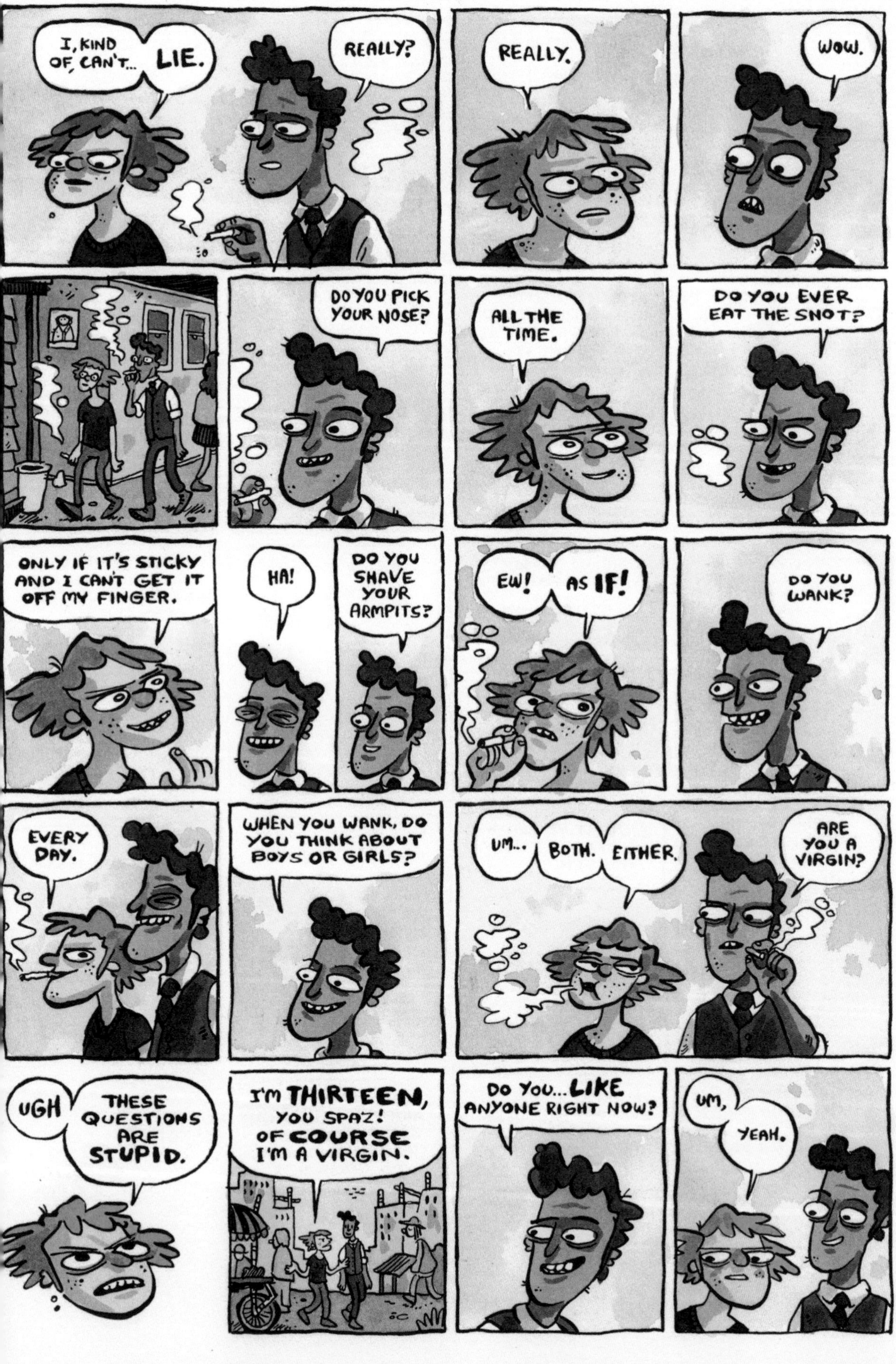
I, KIND OF, CAN'T... LIE.
REALLY?
REALLY.
WOW.
DO YOU PICK YOUR NOSE?
ALL THE TIME.
DO YOU EVER EAT THE SNOT?
ONLY IF IT'S STICKY AND I CAN'T GET IT OFF MY FINGER.
HA!
DO YOU SHAVE YOUR ARMPITS?
EW!
AS IF!
DO YOU WANK?
EVERY DAY.
WHEN YOU WANK, DO YOU THINK ABOUT BOYS OR GIRLS?
UM...
BOTH.
EITHER.
ARE YOU A VIRGIN?
UGH
THESE QUESTIONS ARE STUPID.
I'M THIRTEEN, YOU SPAZ! OF COURSE I'M A VIRGIN.
DO YOU... LIKE ANYONE RIGHT NOW?
UM,
YEAH.

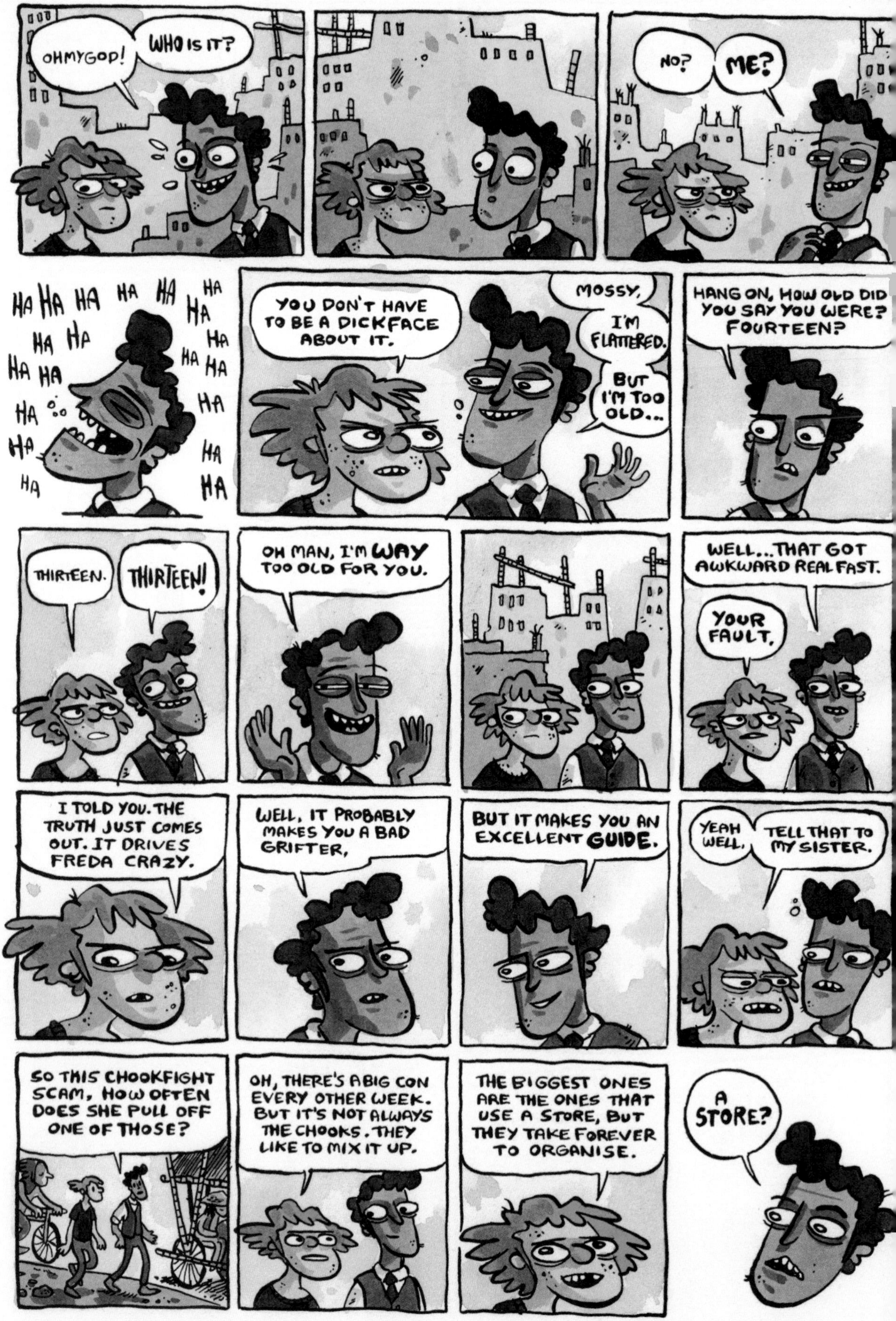
OHMYGOD!
WHO IS IT?
NO?
ME?
HA HA HA HA HA HA HA HA HA HA HA HA HA HA HA HA HA HA HA HA HA
YOU DON'T HAVE TO BE A DICKFACE ABOUT IT.
MOSSY,
I'M FLATTERED.
BUT I'M TOO OLD...
HANG ON, HOW OLD DID YOU SAY YOU WERE? FOURTEEN?
THIRTEEN.
THIRTEEN!
OH MAN, I'M WAY TOO OLD FOR YOU.
WELL... THAT GOT AWKWARD REAL FAST.
YOUR FAULT.
I TOLD YOU. THE TRUTH JUST COMES OUT. IT DRIVES FREDA CRAZY.
WELL, IT PROBABLY MAKES YOU A BAD GRIFTER,
BUT IT MAKES YOU AN EXCELLENT GUIDE.
YEAH WELL,
TELL THAT TO MY SISTER.
SO THIS CHOOKFIGHT SCAM, HOW OFTEN DOES SHE PULL OFF ONE OF THOSE?
OH, THERE'S A BIG CON EVERY OTHER WEEK. BUT IT'S NOT ALWAYS THE CHOOKS. THEY LIKE TO MIX IT UP.
THE BIGGEST ONES ARE THE ONES THAT USE A STORE, BUT THEY TAKE FOREVER TO ORGANISE.
A STORE?

 IT'S JUST LIKE IT SOUNDS... A **STORE**.

 A FAKE SHOPFRONT THAT THEY SET UP TO TRICK SOME GOONER INTO HANDING YOU HIS BANKROLL.

 THERE'S ONE ON THIS BLOCK. I'LL SHOW YOU. SOMETIMES IT'S, LIKE, A FAKE ALGAE EXCHANGE OR A FAKE POKER ROOM.

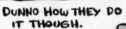 THEY GOTTA ORGANISE FURNITURE AND STUFF, YOU KNOW, "DRESS THE SET."

 IT'S A BIT OF A SHIT FIGHT.

 BUT I'VE HEARD ABOUT THIS CREW OF GRIFTERS THAT HAVE BEEN WORKING A BIG STORE CON OUT OF AN EMPTY SHOP.

 DUNNO HOW THEY DO IT THOUGH.

 AN EMPTY **SHOP**!!

 YEAH, THAT'S IT RIGHT THERE.

 OH CRAP.

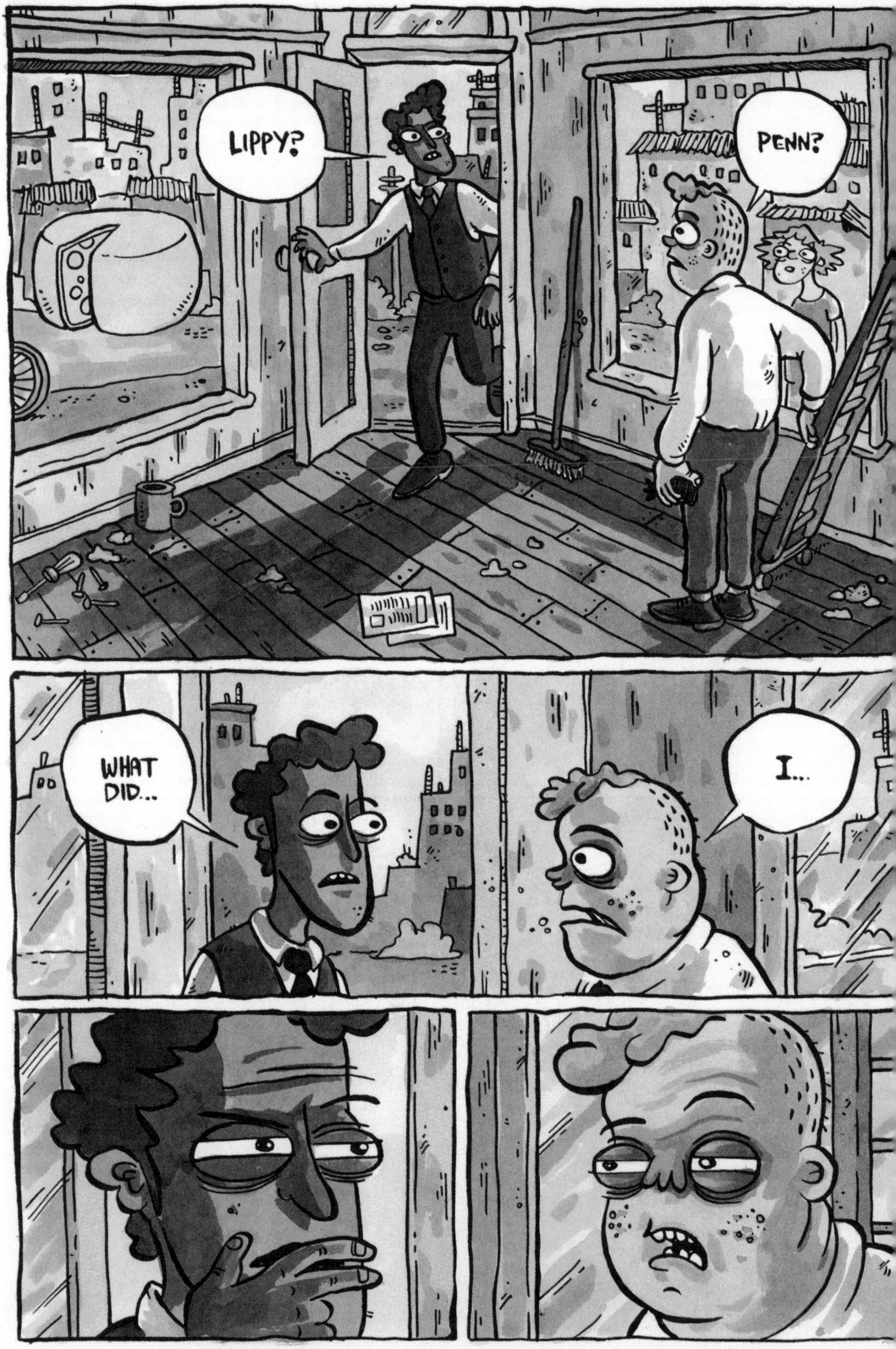
LIPPY?
PENN?
WHAT DID...
I...

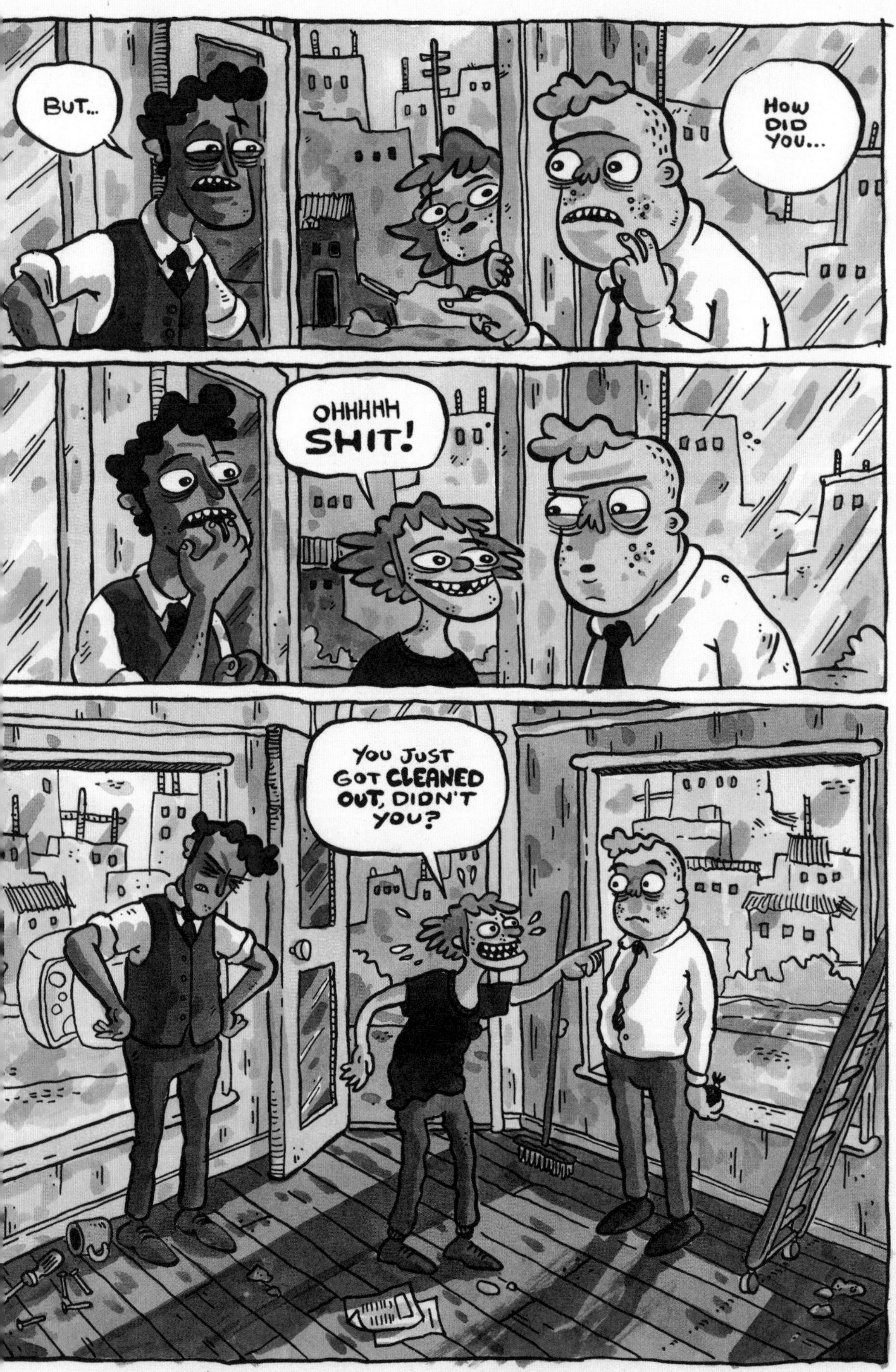
BUT...
HOW DID YOU...
OHHHHH SHIT!
YOU JUST GOT CLEANED OUT, DIDN'T YOU?

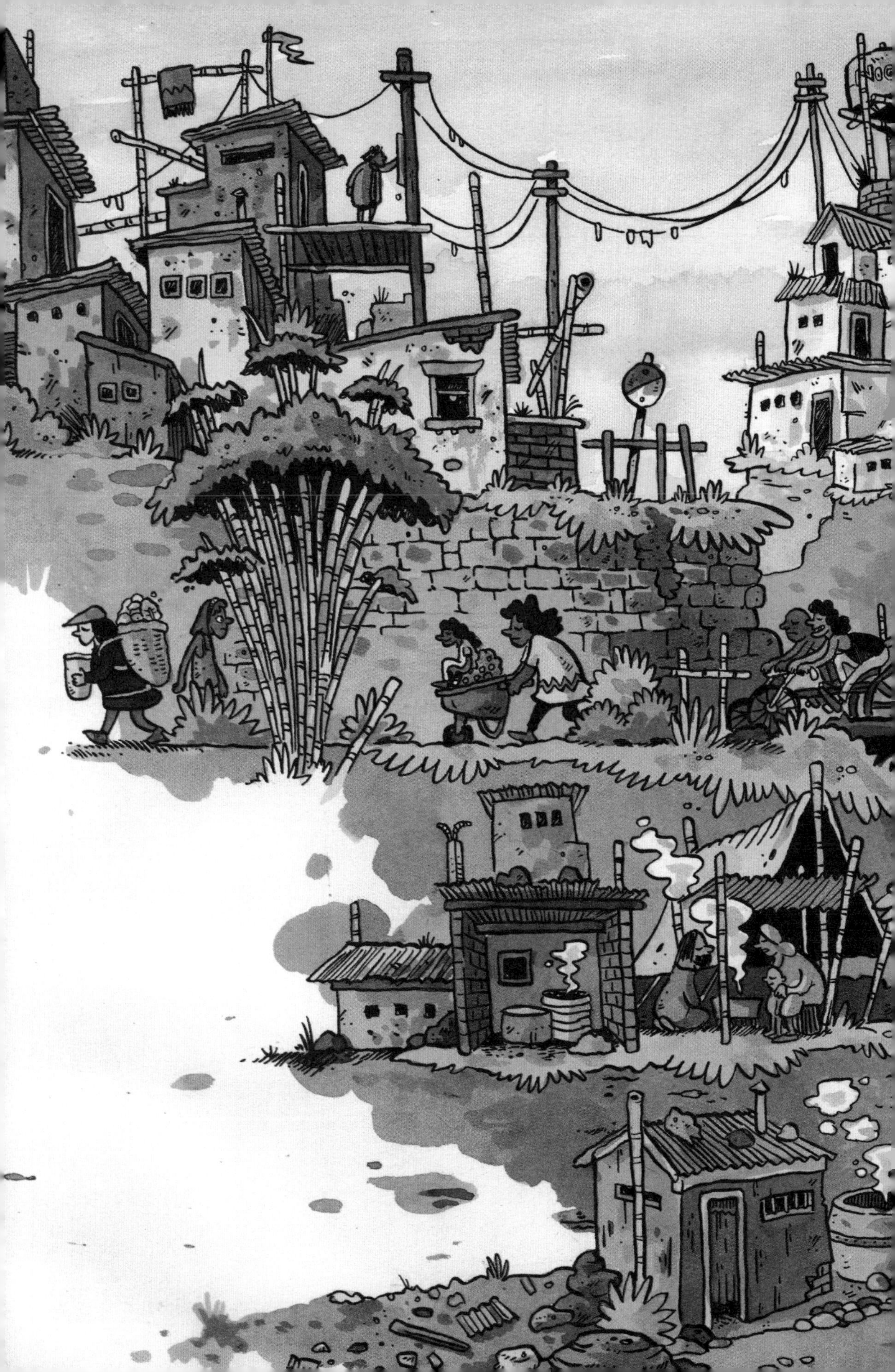

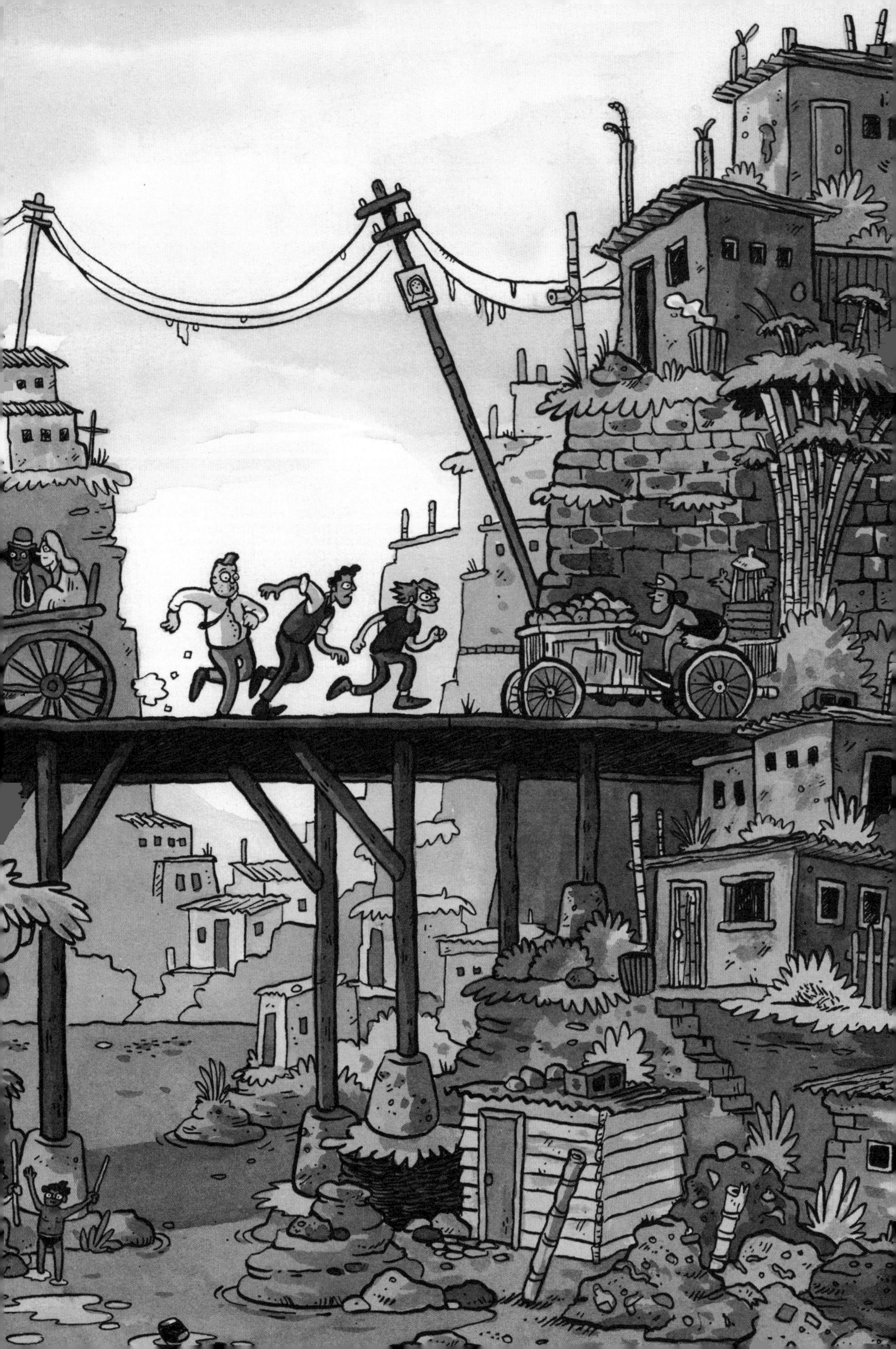

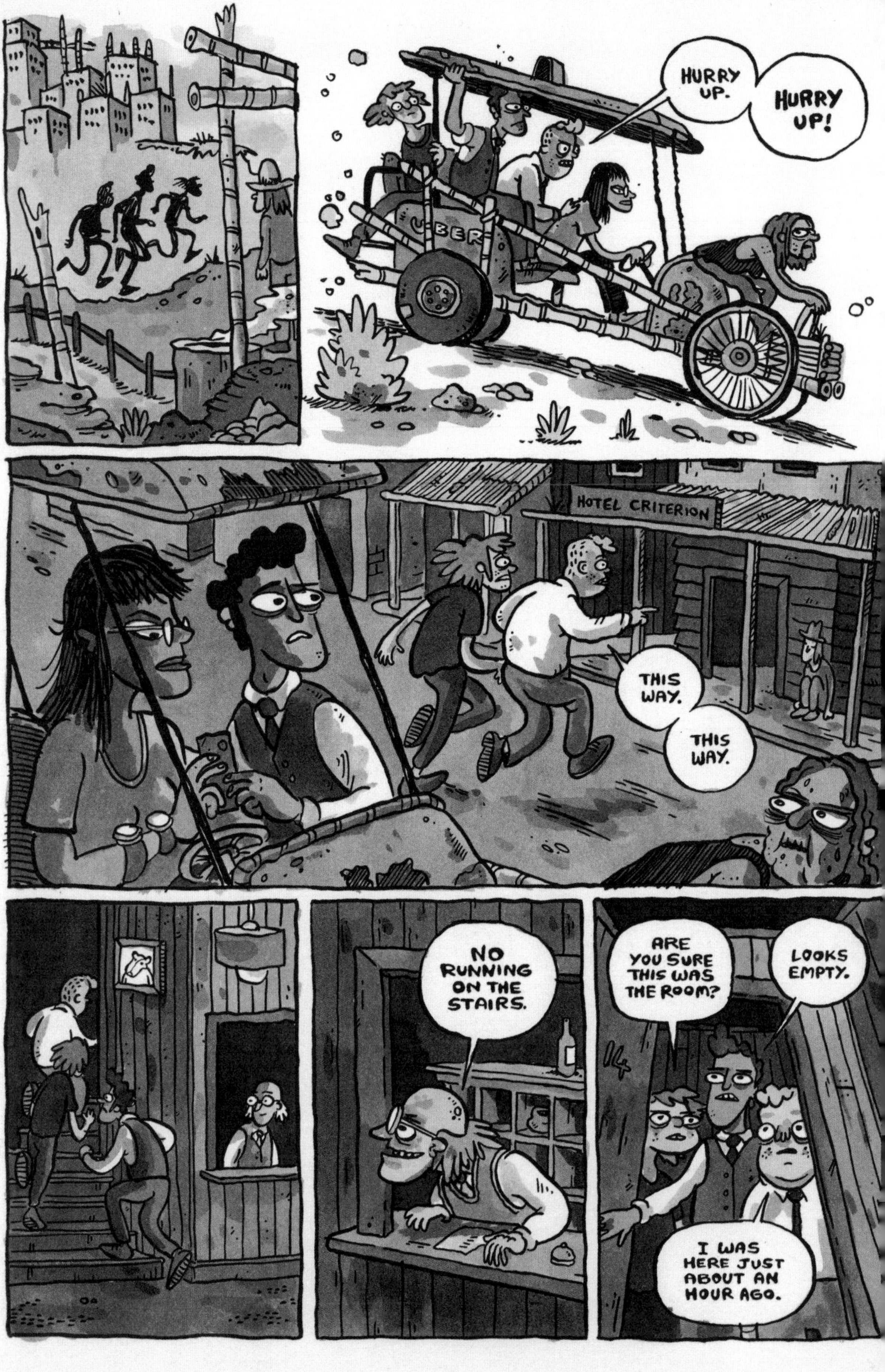
HURRY UP.
HURRY UP!
UBER
HOTEL CRITERION
THIS WAY.
THIS WAY.
NO RUNNING ON THE STAIRS.
14
ARE YOU SURE THIS WAS THE ROOM?
LOOKS EMPTY.
I WAS HERE JUST ABOUT AN HOUR AGO.

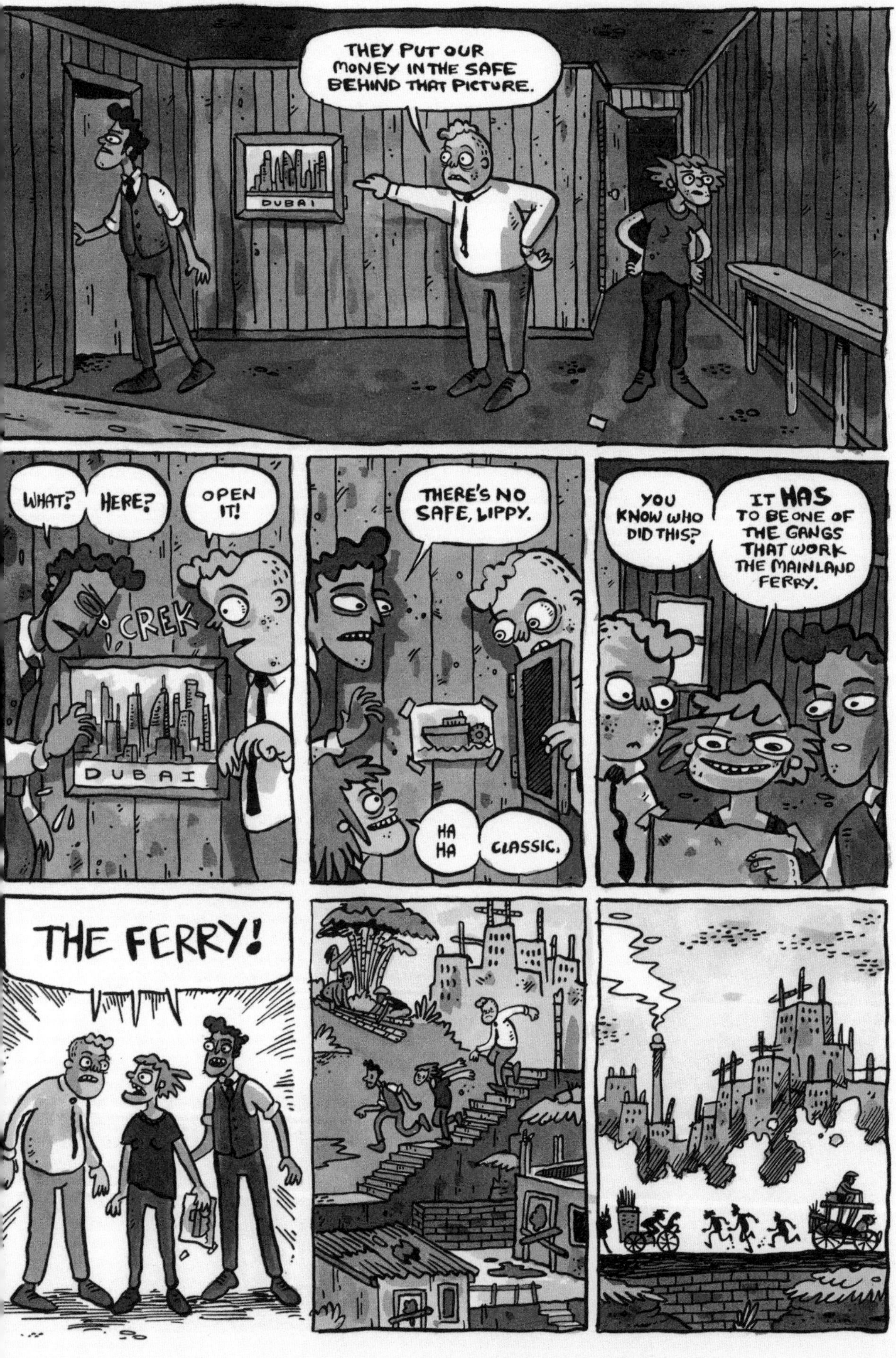
THEY PUT OUR MONEY IN THE SAFE BEHIND THAT PICTURE.
DUBAI
WHAT?
HERE?
OPEN IT!
CREK
DUBAI
THERE'S NO SAFE, LIPPY.
HA HA
CLASSIC.
YOU KNOW WHO DID THIS?
IT HAS TO BE ONE OF THE GANGS THAT WORK THE MAINLAND FERRY.
THE FERRY!

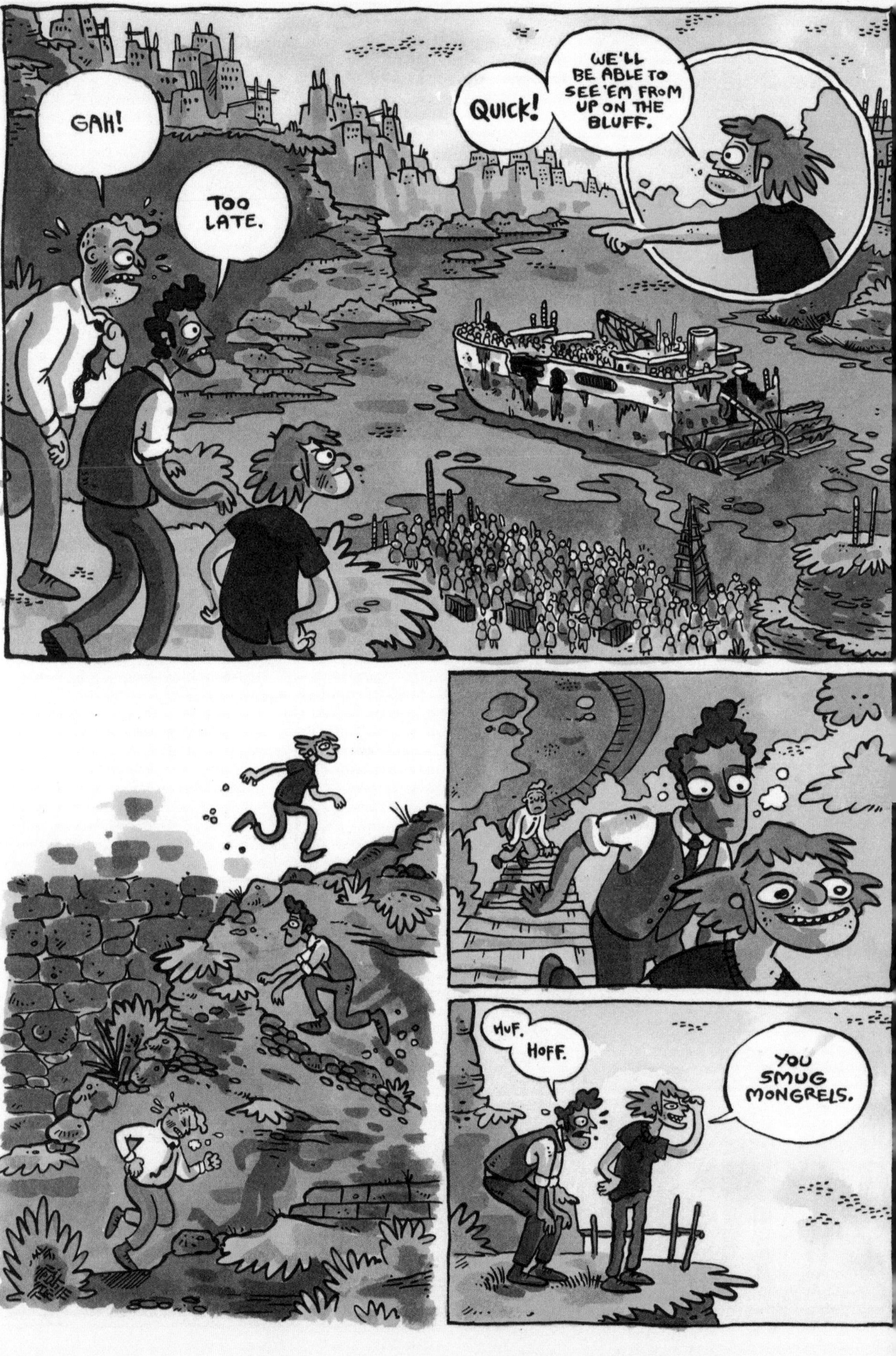
GAH!
TOO LATE.
QUICK!
WE'LL BE ABLE TO SEE 'EM FROM UP ON THE BLUFF.
HUF.
HOFF.
YOU SMUG MONGRELS.

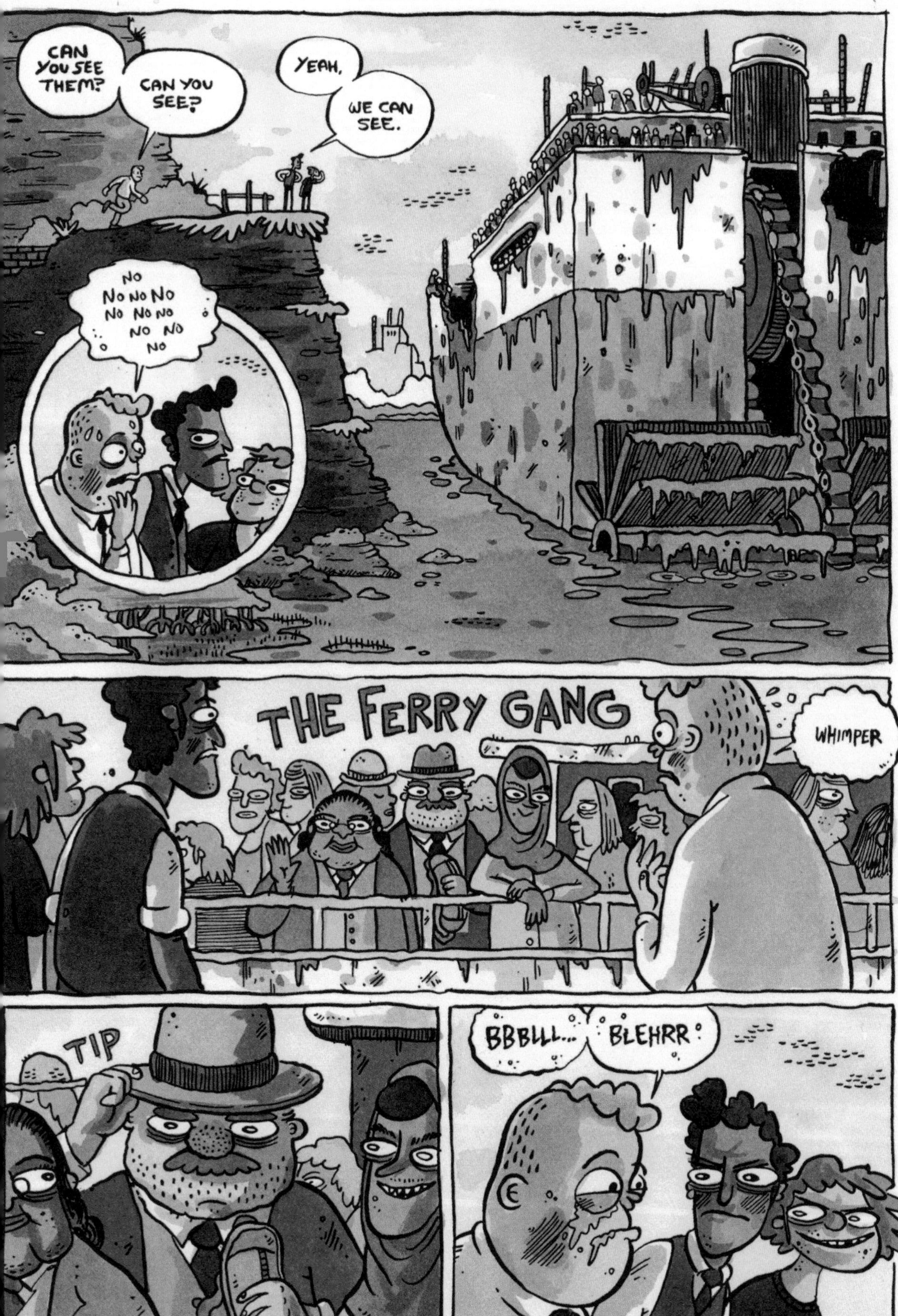
CAN YOU SEE THEM?
CAN YOU SEE?
YEAH,
WE CAN SEE.
NO NO NO NO NO NO NO NO NO NO NO
THE FERRY GANG
WHIMPER
TIP
BBBLLL...
BLEHRR

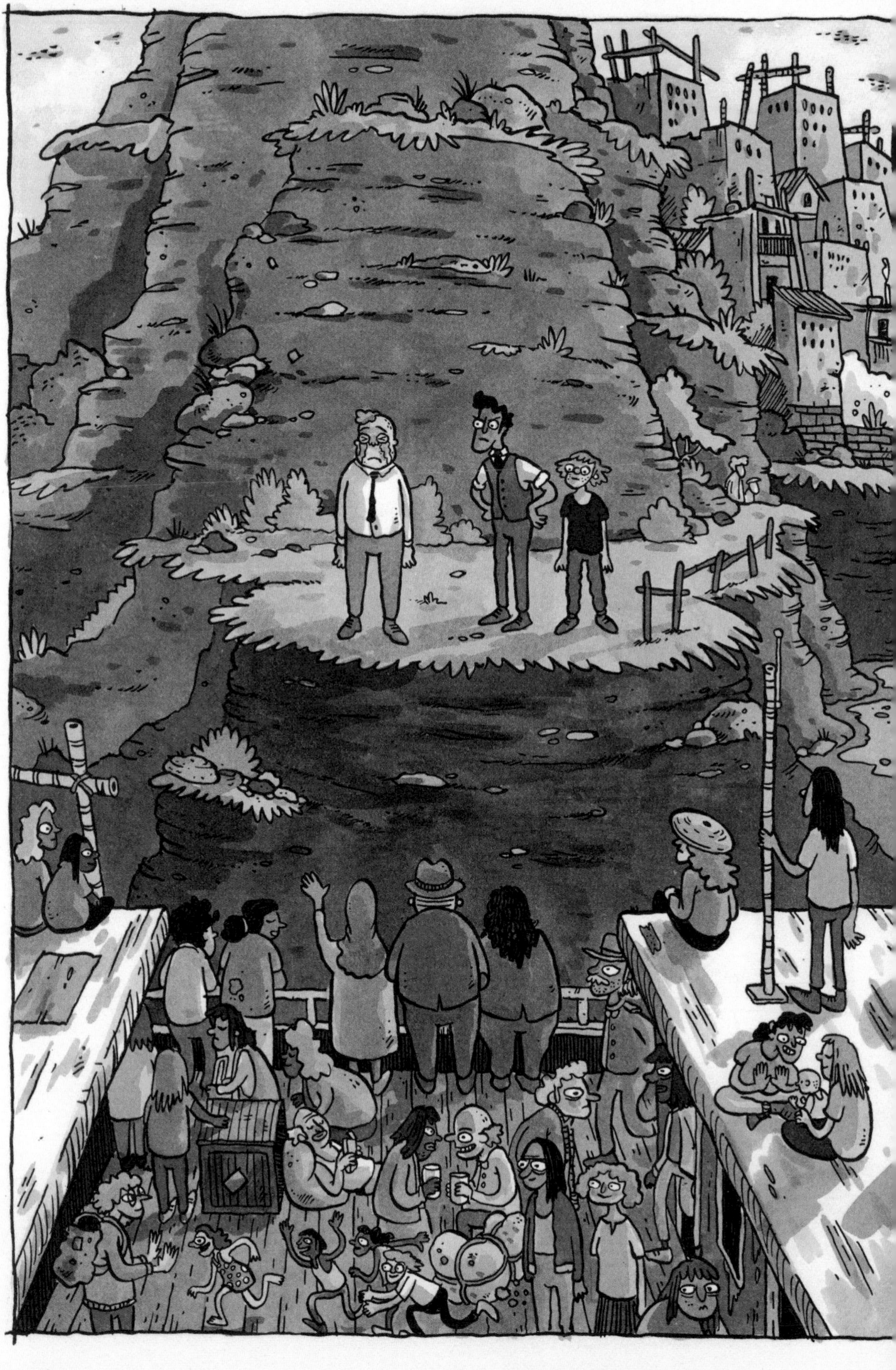

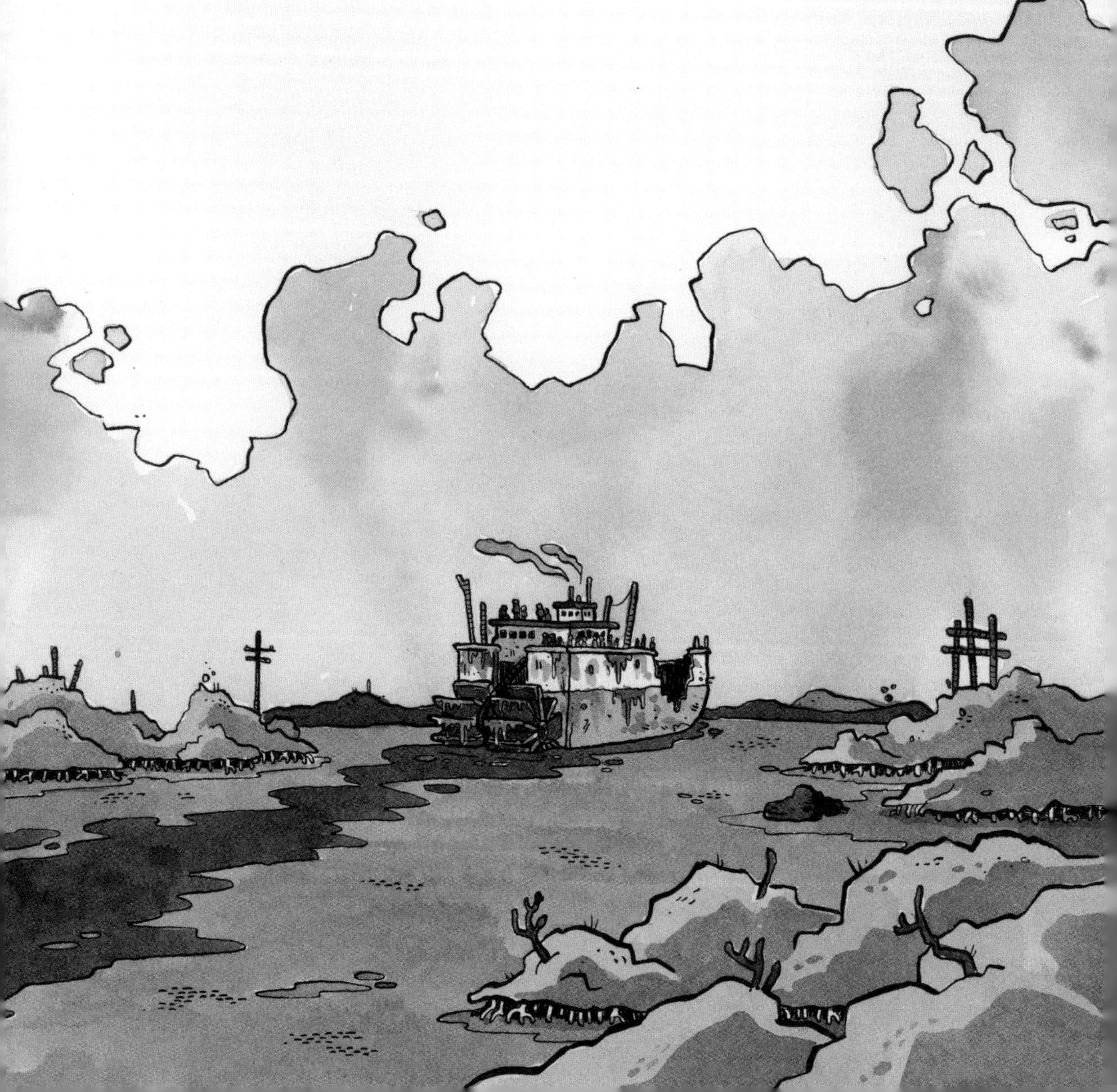

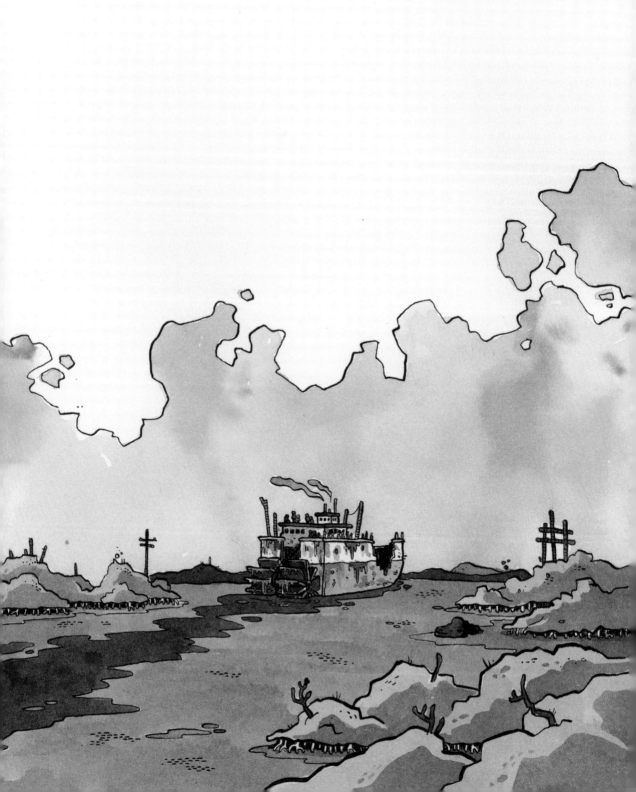

EPILOGUE

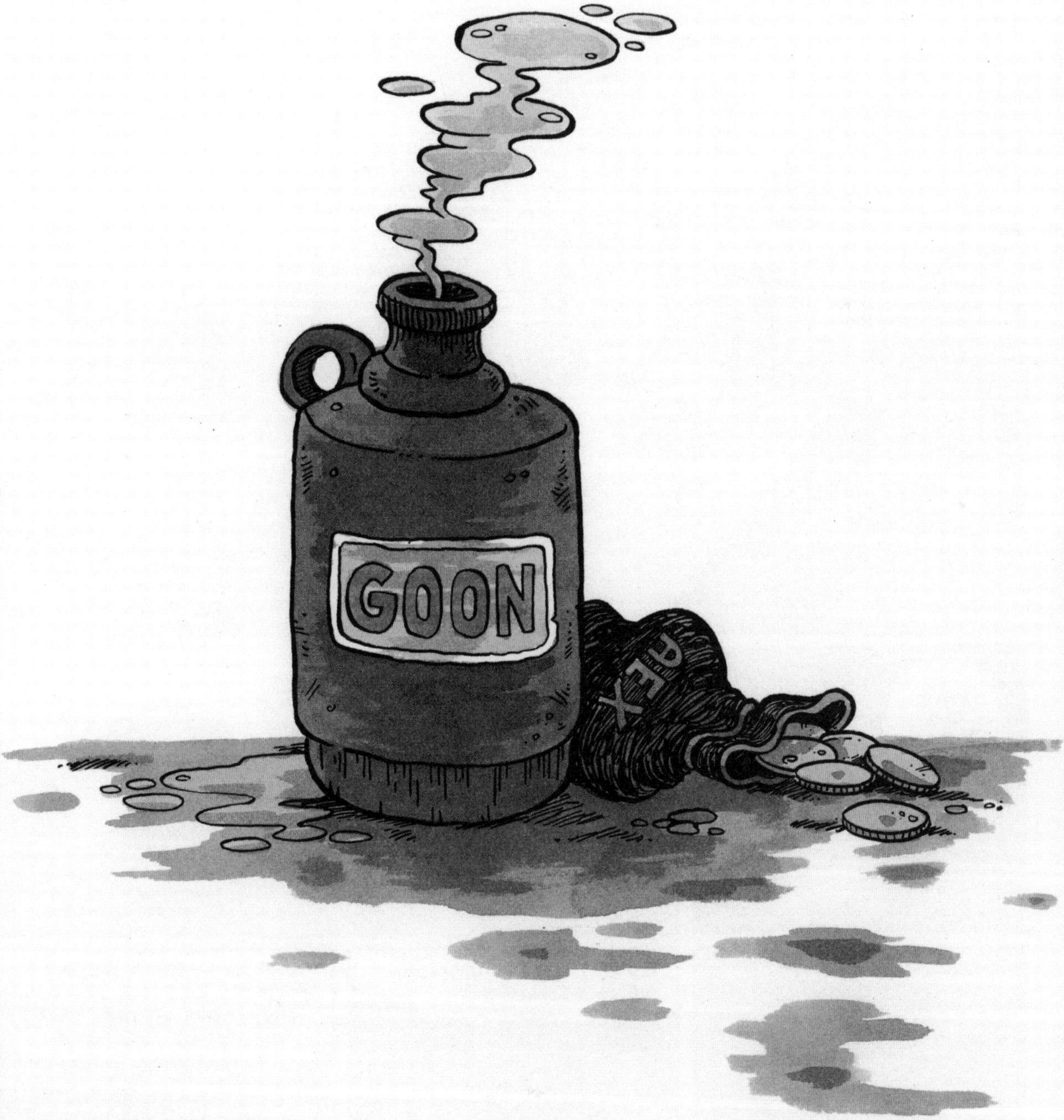
GOON
REX

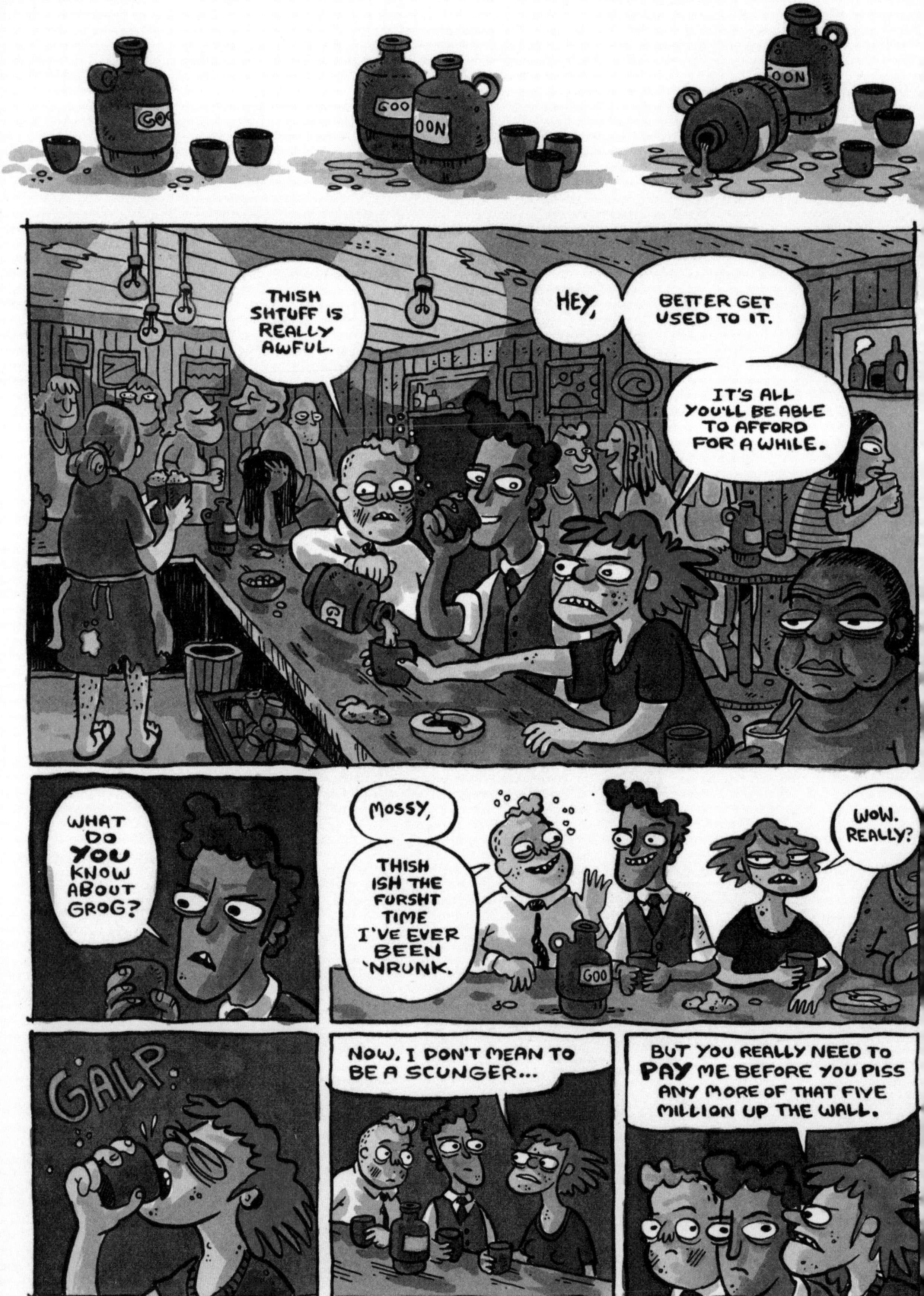
GOO
GOO
OON
OON
THISH SHTUFF IS REALLY AWFUL.
HEY,
BETTER GET USED TO IT.
IT'S ALL YOU'LL BE ABLE TO AFFORD FOR A WHILE.
GOO
WHAT DO YOU KNOW ABOUT GROG?
MOSSY,
THISH ISH THE FURSHT TIME I'VE EVER BEEN 'NRUNK.
WOW. REALLY?
GOO
GALP
NOW, I DON'T MEAN TO BE A SCUNGER...
BUT YOU REALLY NEED TO PAY ME BEFORE YOU PISS ANY MORE OF THAT FIVE MILLION UP THE WALL.

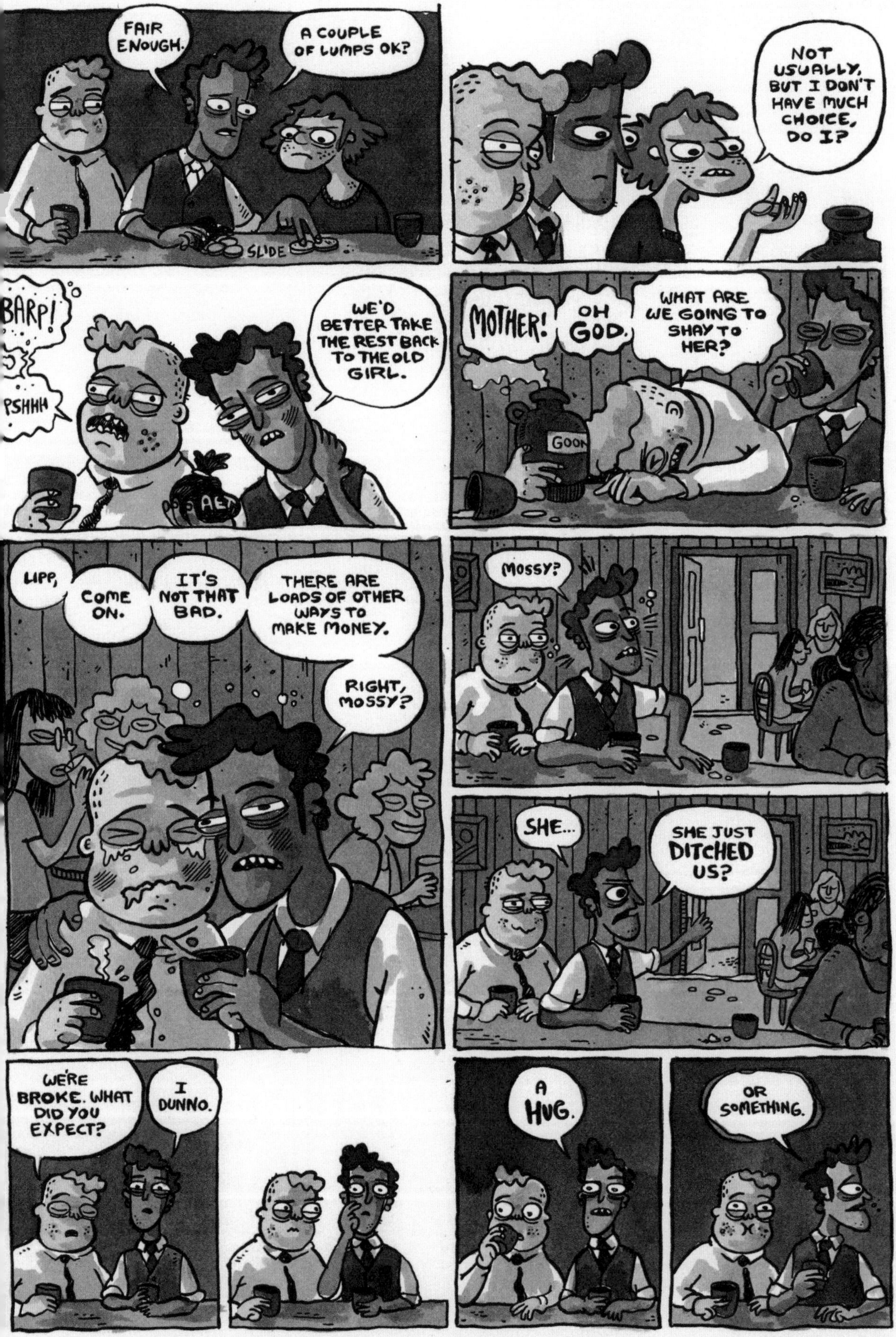

FAIR ENOUGH.
A COUPLE OF LUMPS OK?
SLIDE
NOT USUALLY, BUT I DON'T HAVE MUCH CHOICE, DO I?
BARP!
PSHHH
WE'D BETTER TAKE THE REST BACK TO THE OLD GIRL.
MOTHER!
OH GOD.
WHAT ARE WE GOING TO SHAY TO HER?
GOON
LIPP,
COME ON.
IT'S NOT THAT BAD.
THERE ARE LOADS OF OTHER WAYS TO MAKE MONEY.
RIGHT, MOSSY?
MOSSY?
SHE...
SHE JUST DITCHED US?
WE'RE BROKE. WHAT DID YOU EXPECT?
I DUNNO.
A HUG.
OR SOMETHING.

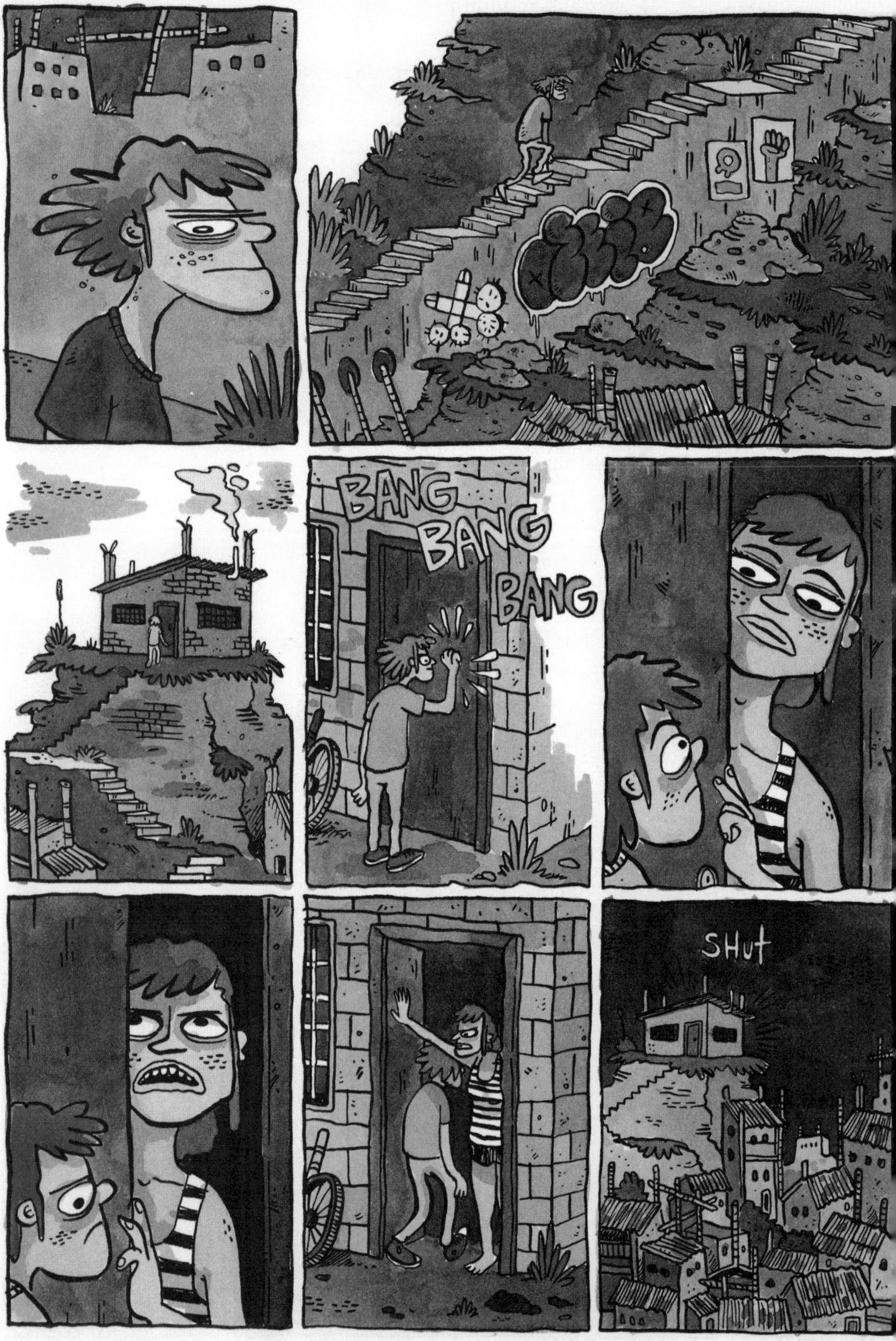
BANG
BANG
BANG
SHUT

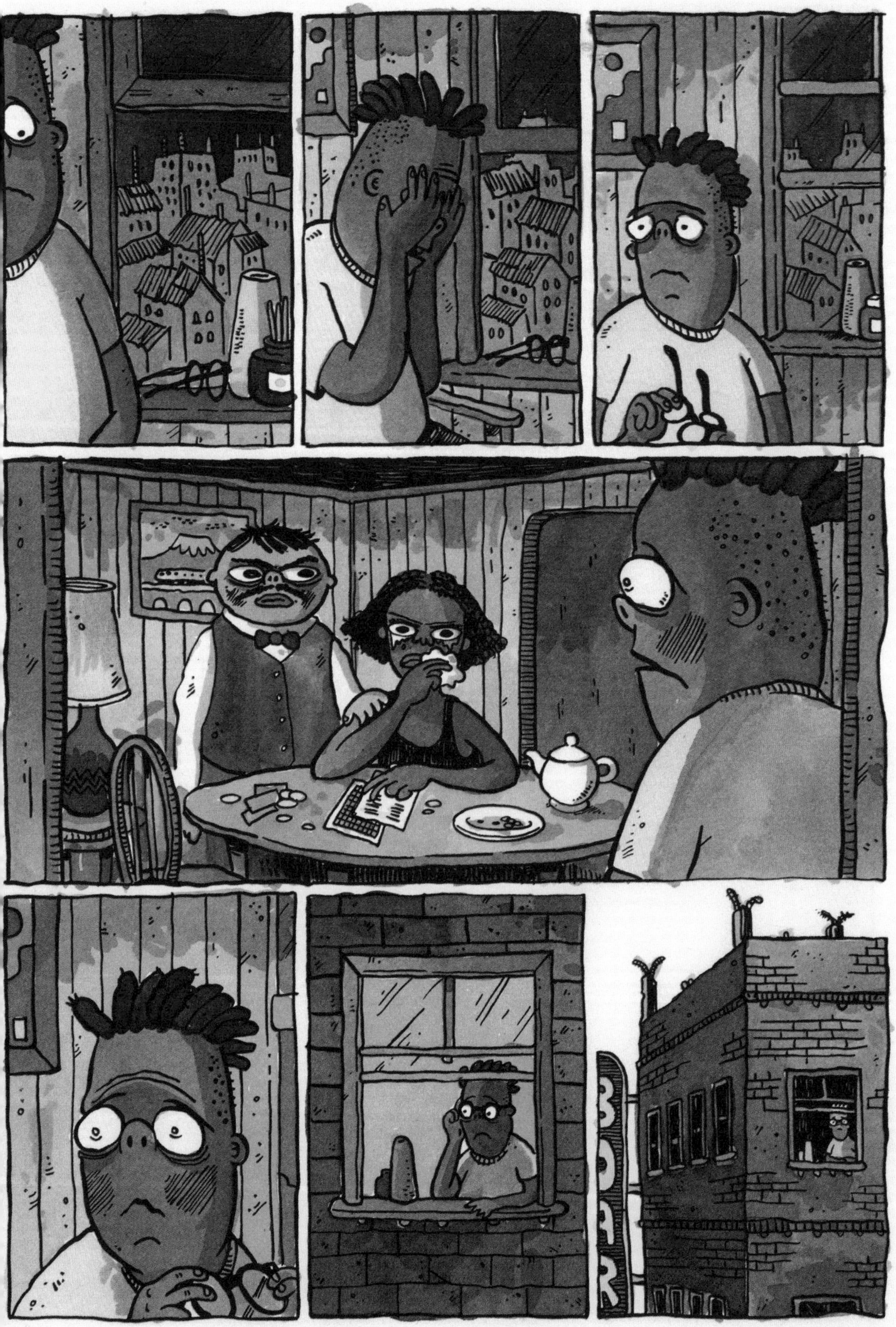

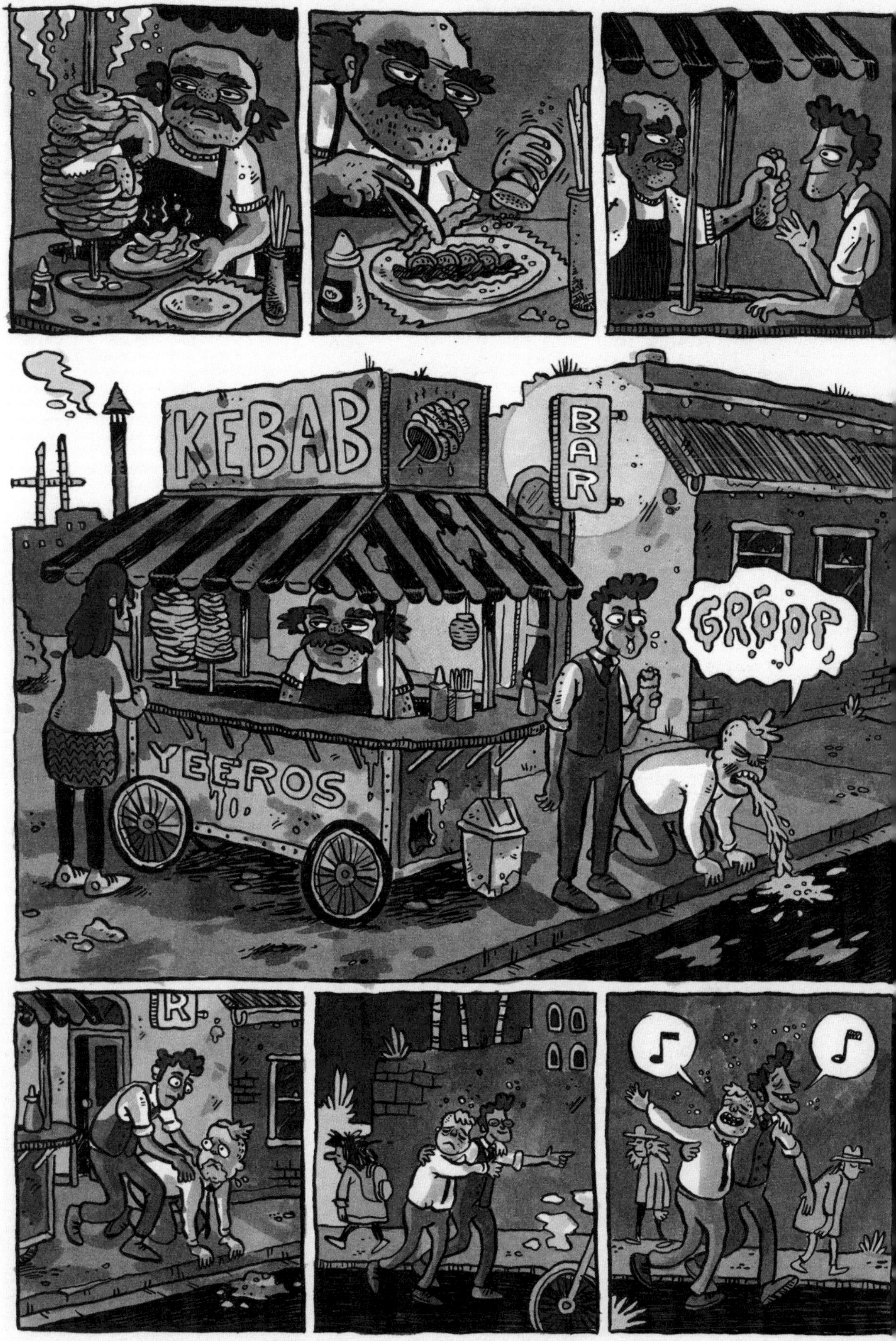
KEBAB
BAR
YEEROS
GROOP
R
♪
♪

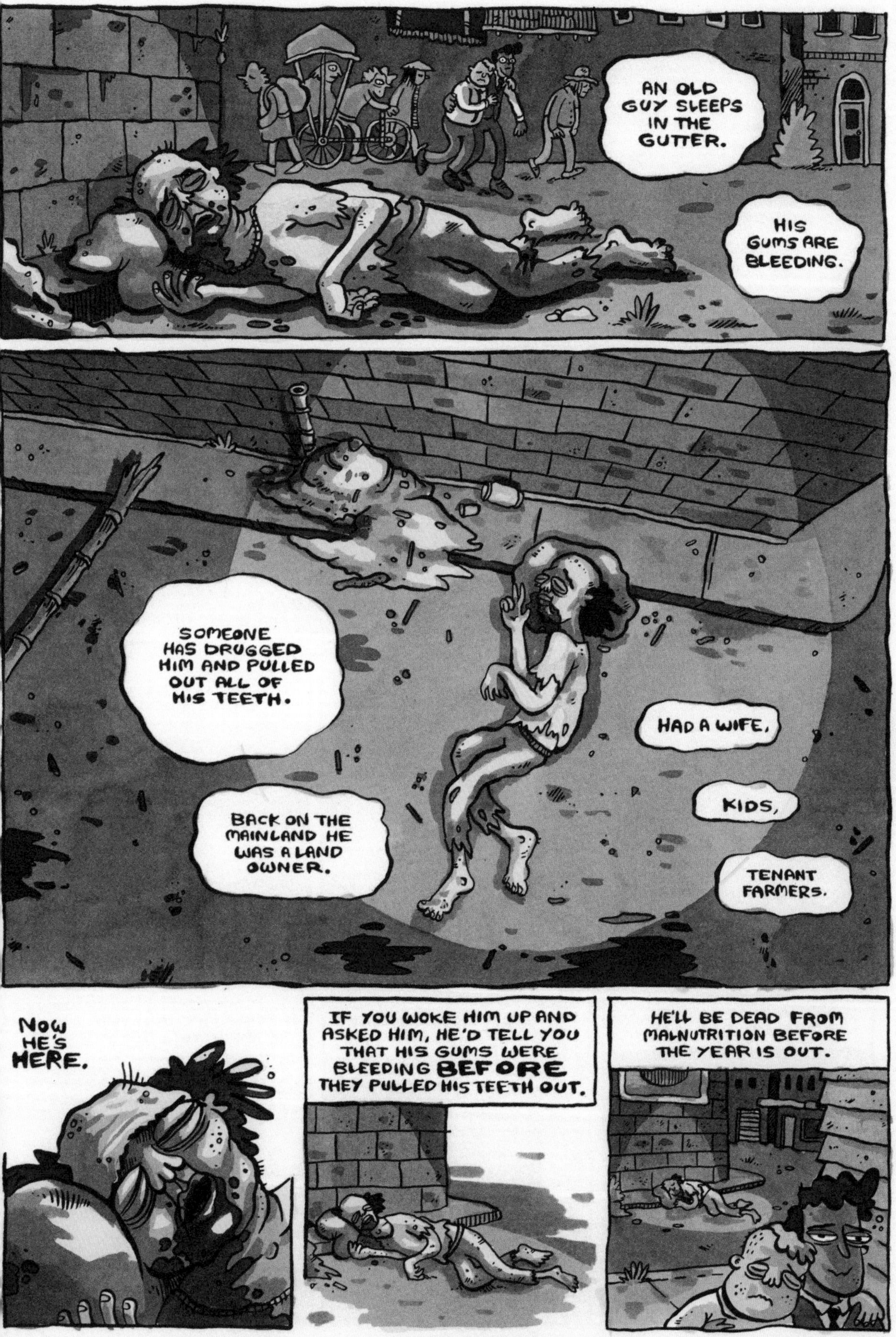
AN OLD GUY SLEEPS IN THE GUTTER.
HIS GUMS ARE BLEEDING.
SOMEONE HAS DRUGGED HIM AND PULLED OUT ALL OF HIS TEETH.
BACK ON THE MAINLAND HE WAS A LAND OWNER.
HAD A WIFE,
KIDS,
TENANT FARMERS.
NOW HE'S HERE.
IF YOU WOKE HIM UP AND ASKED HIM, HE'D TELL YOU THAT HIS GUMS WERE BLEEDING BEFORE THEY PULLED HIS TEETH OUT.
HE'LL BE DEAD FROM MALNUTRITION BEFORE THE YEAR IS OUT.

A YOUNG WOMAN WITH A LITTLE KID STRAPPED TO HER BACK WINCES AS SHE WALKS HOME.

SHE'S GOT WHAT THEY CALL THE **FALTER SWAMP STAGGERS.**

TRENCH FOOT.

SHE CAME TO THE CITY WITH A SMALL INHERITANCE BUT LOST IT WITHIN A FEW WEEKS.

SHE'LL GET UP EARLY TOMORROW,

PUT ON HER WET SANDALS, STRAP HER BABY ON,

AND SHE'LL HEAD BACK OUT THERE, INTO THE SWAMP.

A MONTH FROM NOW THEY WILL BE AMPUTATING HER FEET.

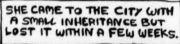

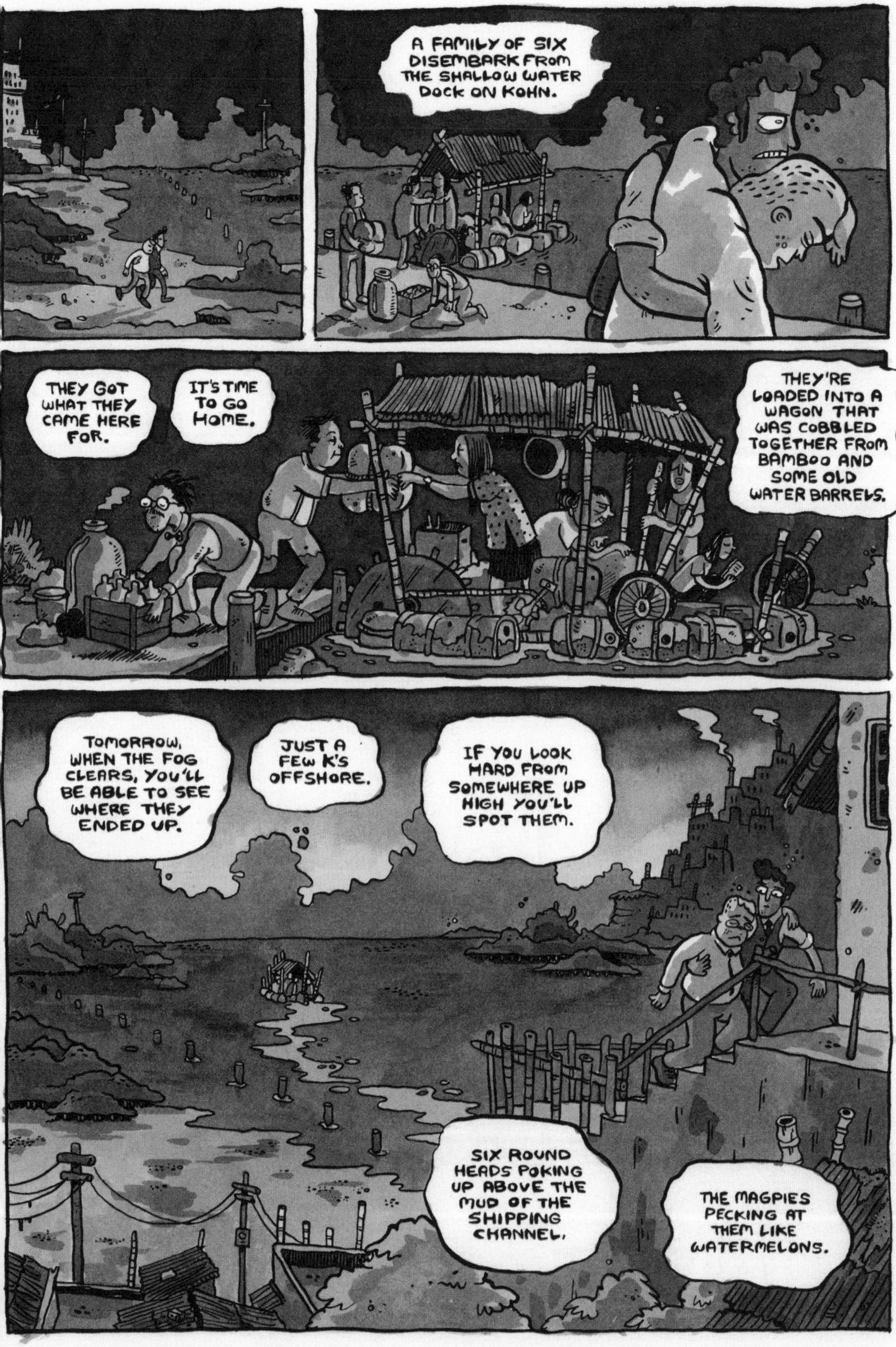
A FAMILY OF SIX DISEMBARK FROM THE SHALLOW WATER DOCK ON KOHN.
THEY GOT WHAT THEY CAME HERE FOR.
IT'S TIME TO GO HOME.
THEY'RE LOADED INTO A WAGON THAT WAS COBBLED TOGETHER FROM BAMBOO AND SOME OLD WATER BARRELS.
TOMORROW, WHEN THE FOG CLEARS, YOU'LL BE ABLE TO SEE WHERE THEY ENDED UP.
JUST A FEW K'S OFFSHORE.
IF YOU LOOK HARD FROM SOMEWHERE UP HIGH YOU'LL SPOT THEM.
SIX ROUND HEADS POKING UP ABOVE THE MUD OF THE SHIPPING CHANNEL.
THE MAGPIES PECKING AT THEM LIKE WATERMELONS.

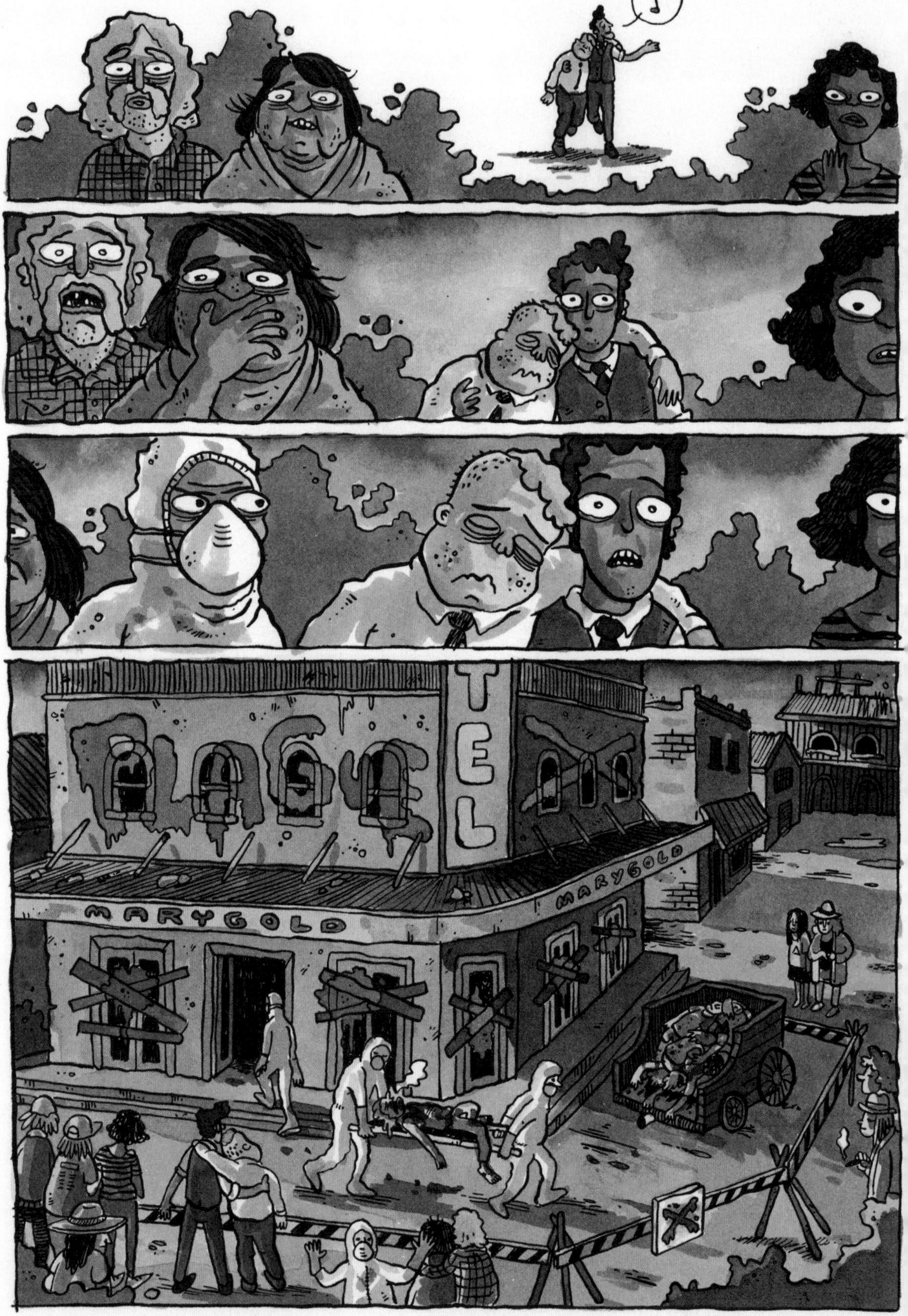
PLAGUE
TEL
MARYGOLD
MARYGOLD

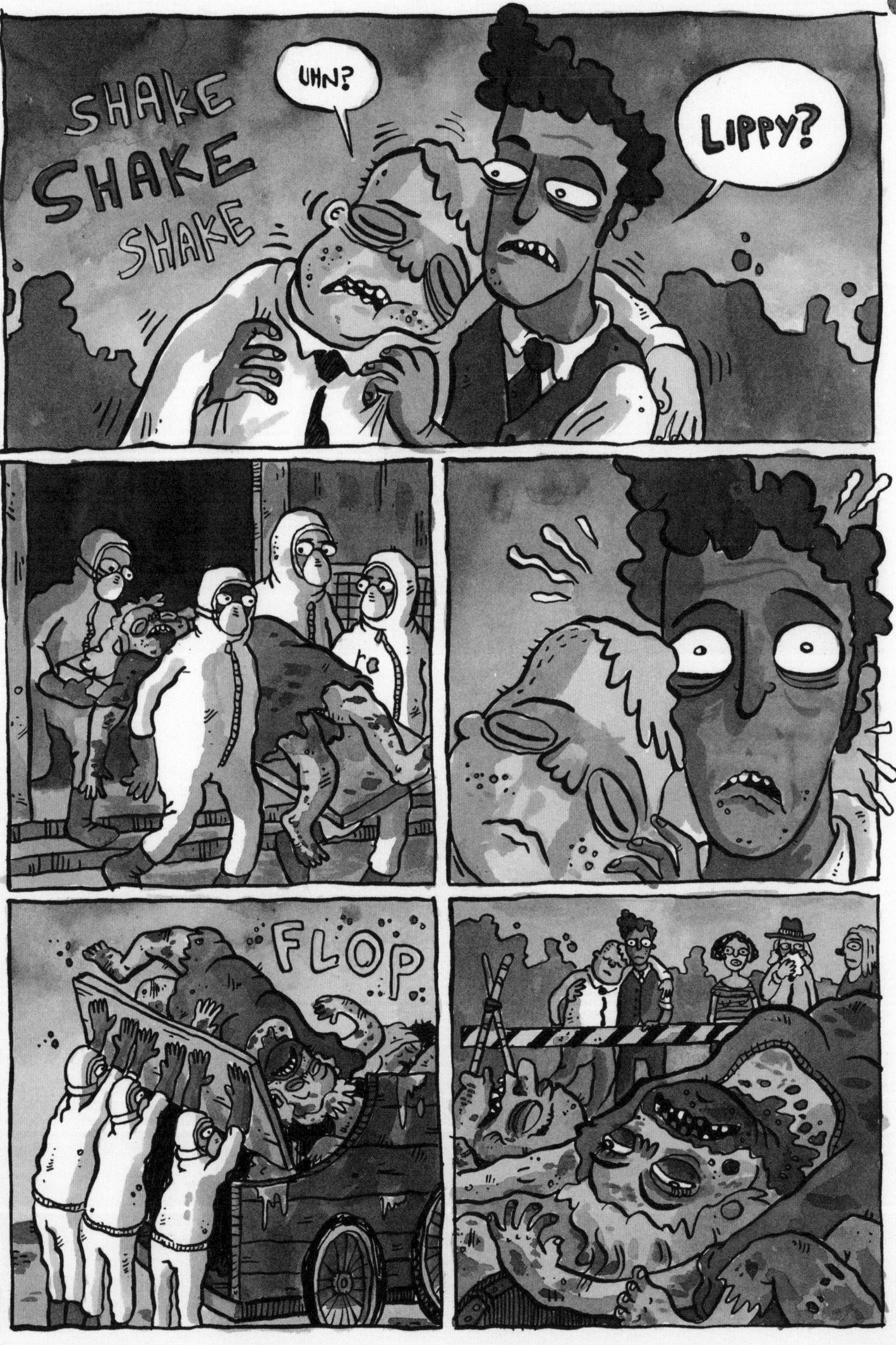
SHAKE
SHAKE
SHAKE
UHN?
LIPPY?
FLOP

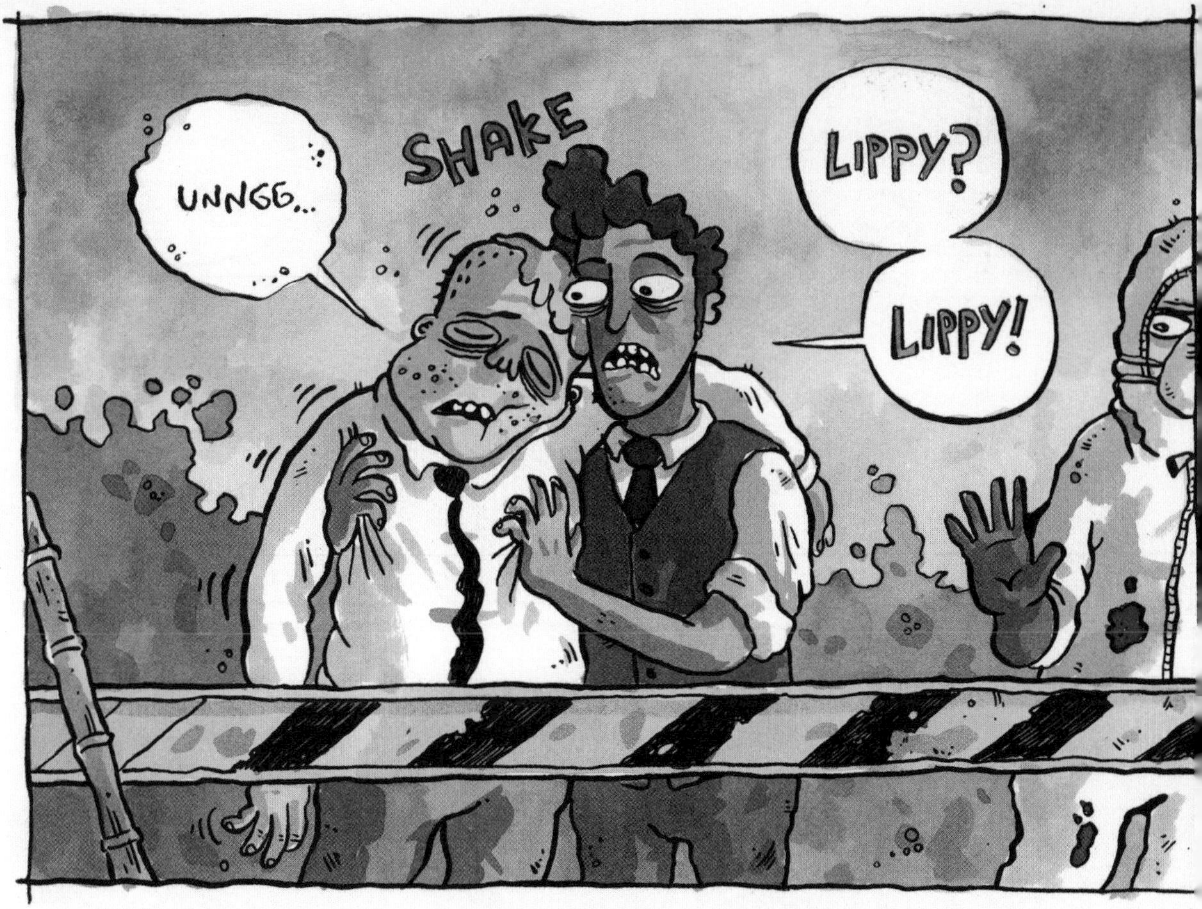
UNNGG...
SHAKE
LIPPY?
LIPPY!

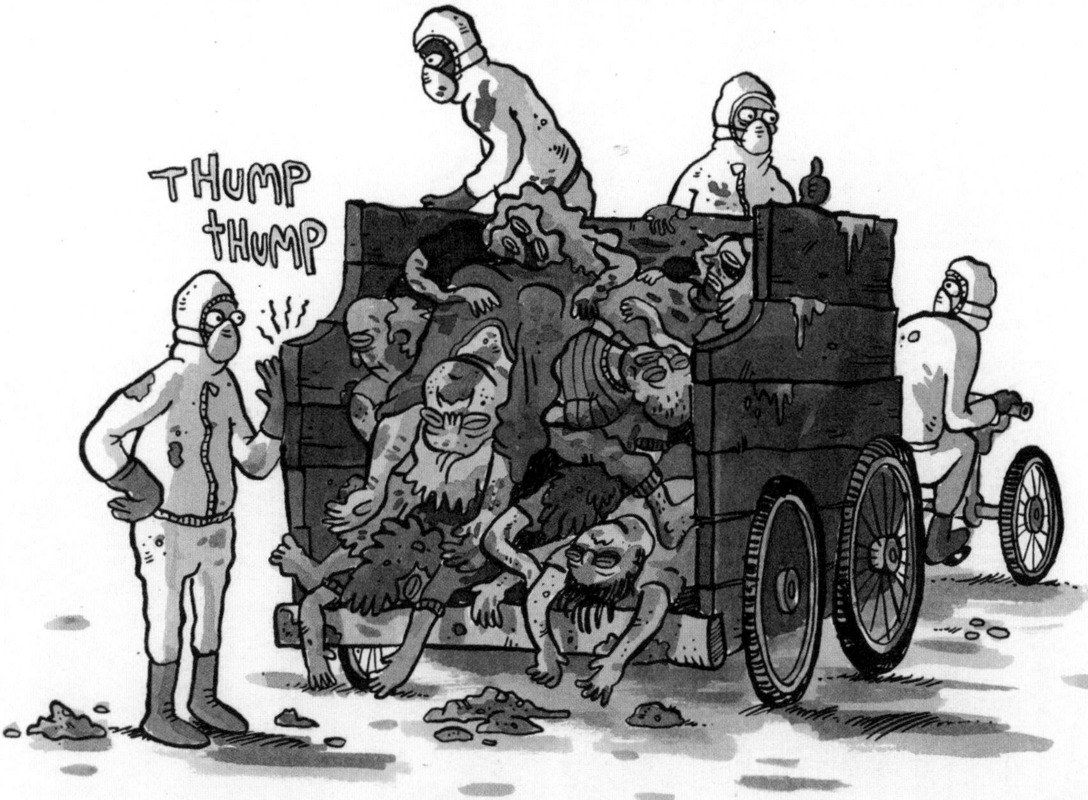
THUMP
THUMP

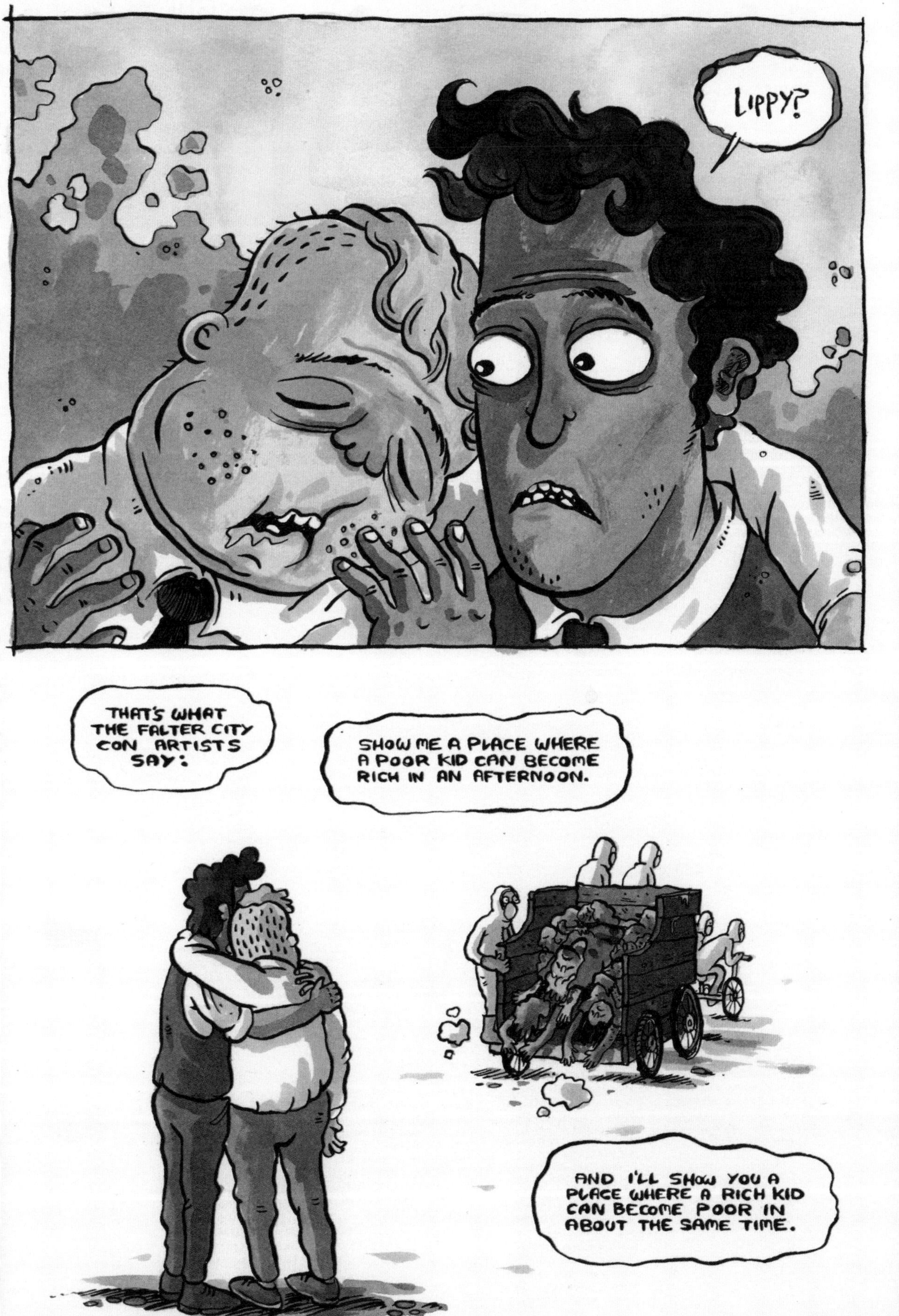
LIPPY?
THAT'S WHAT THE FALTER CITY CON ARTISTS SAY:
SHOW ME A PLACE WHERE A POOR KID CAN BECOME RICH IN AN AFTERNOON.
AND I'LL SHOW YOU A PLACE WHERE A RICH KID CAN BECOME POOR IN ABOUT THE SAME TIME.

THE GROT IS AN ONGOING SERIES. LOOK OUT FOR MORE STORIES ABOUT PENN, LIPPY AND THE TEEN CON-ARTISTS OF FALTER CITY.

GO FIND MY OTHER BOOK "BLUE" ALSO THROUGH TOP SHELF.

PAT GRANT LIVES IN AUSTINMER, NSW WITH HIS SWEETHEART AND TWO DREADFUL LITTLE BOYS WHO LIKE TO BE DANGLED UPSIDE DOWN OVER THE COMPOST BIN. HE HAS MADE YOGURT MANY TIMES BEFORE BUT NEVER ON PURPOSE.

FIONN McCABE IS AN ARTIST AND PRINTMAKER FRO MASSACHUSETTS. HE NOW LIV IN THE INNER-WEST OF SYDNE WITH HIS BEAUTIFUL WIFE AND THEIR TWO HANDSOME, INTELLIG WELL BEHAVED CHILDREN. HE I TALL AND GOOD-LOOKING AND KIND, LIKE A CROSS BETWEE NICK NOLTE AND MOTHER THERESA. HE BUYS HIS YOGUR AT THE SHOP.

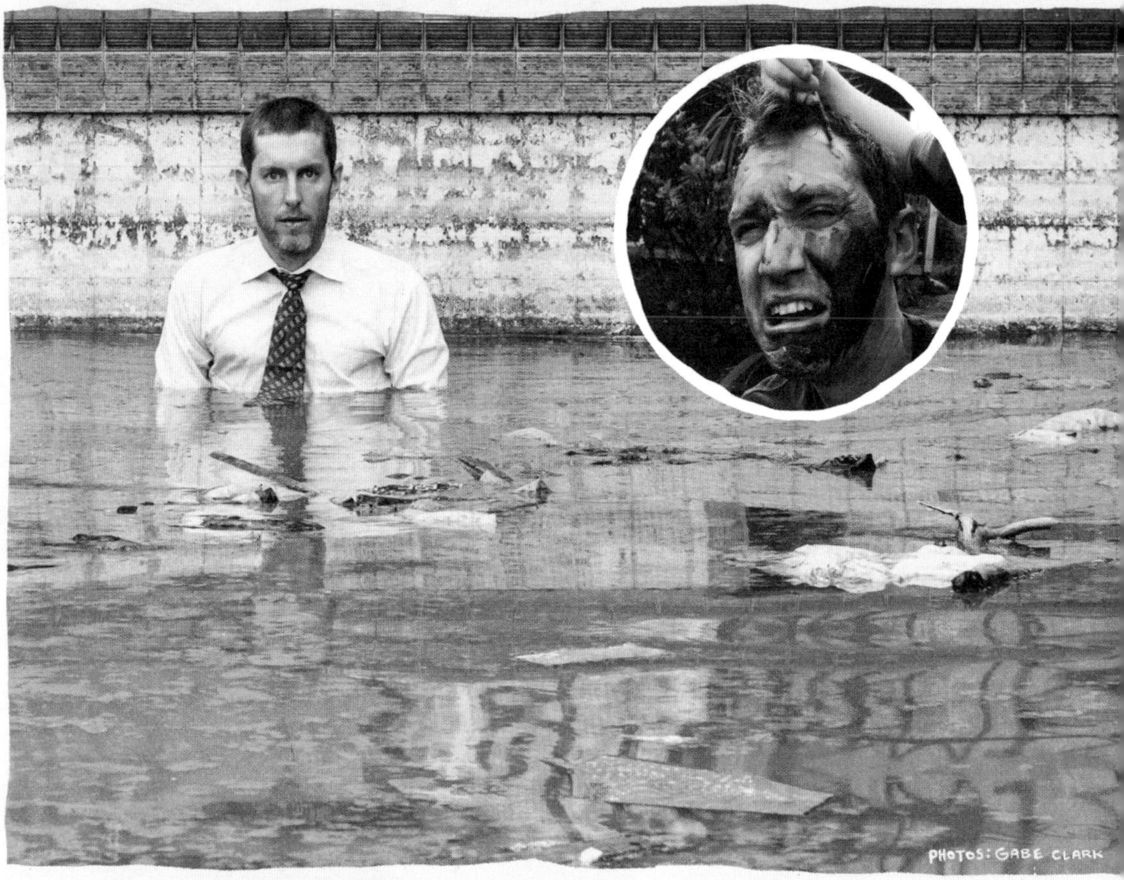
PHOTOS: GABE CLARK

I STARTED WRITING THIS BOOK IN 2012 ON A FANCY DRAWING TABLE AT CRAIG THOMPSON'S PLACE.

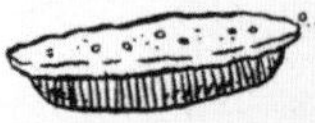

I MADE HIM A PIE TO SAY THANKS BUT OVER THESE SEVEN LONG YEARS SO MANY OTHER WRITERS, DRAWERS AND THINKERS HAVE HELPED ME OUT WITH TWINKLY-EYED FEEDBACK, ADVICE AND CONVERSATION. I HAVE GIFTS FOR ALL!

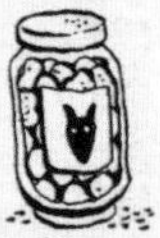

I WOULD LIKE TO PRESENT A JAR OF FERMENTED WALLABY KNUCKLES TO BRIOHNY DOYLE, ADEN ROLFE, DOUG HOLGATE, IVOR INDYK, SHAUN TAN, SAM COONEY, KATE ROSSMANITH, PETER DOYLE, JEN MILLS, NICK KEYS, TOM LEE, TOM DOIG, SAM TWYFORD-MOORE, JAKE WYATT, SAM ALDEN, JED McGOWAN, MEG O'SHEA, BAILEY SHARP, BEN JUERS, CAN YALCINKAYA, SAFDAR AHMED, CLAUDIA CHINYERE AKOLE, TOM McLACH, JEN MALEY, DAVID BLUMENSTEIN, THE TIMBER MILL GOONERS, TREE-HOUSE DAVE, LUCAS IHLIEN, ANDREI BUTERS, RONNIE SCOTT, SIMON HANSELMANN, MICHAEL FIKARIS, LOUIE JOYCE AND GLENNO.

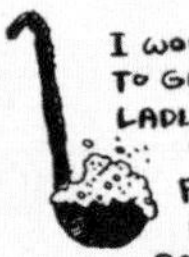

I WOULD LIKE TO GIVE A LADLE OF HOT FROTH FROM AN ILLEGAL BANYA NUT BEER TO EACH OF THE WORKSHOP CREW WHO CAME ALONG ON CRAZY ADVENTURES: TOM, LEELA, SANCHIA, MAX, MINUS, WALLMAN, OWEN, ELERI, GOOCH, SARAH, MIRRANDA, GINA, LEIGH, ALISHA, GREG, LEONIE, AND TALA. WHEN I THINK OF YOU GUYS MY CHEST GETS WARM LIKE THE BUNKER AT KRACK OR THE MARIA ISLAND COMPOST BIN.

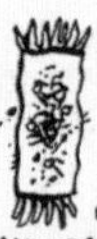

THIS MOULD SPORE TAPESTRY GOES TO SARA HIRNER FOR AMAZING PRODUCTION ASSISTANCE AND HILARIOUS IMPRESSIONS.

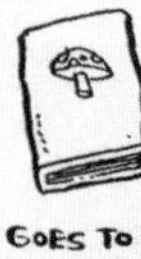

THIS RARE MYCOLOGY TEXTBOOK PRINTED ON FUNGAL FILAMENT MESH GOES TO MY PEOPLE IN PUBLISHING: NICOLAS GRIVEL, BERENGERE ORIEUX, MICHELE FOSCHINI, CHRIS STAROS, GILBERTO LAZCANO, AND LEIGH WALTON.

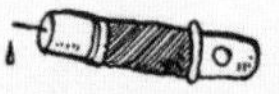

ONE OF THESE "MYSTER EPIPENS GO TO EACH O MY ROLE MODELS IN ART AND LIFE: JOSH SANTO SPIRITO, THI BUI, CAMPBELL WHYTE AN LIZ MacFARLANE.

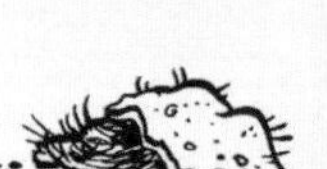

AND LASTLY, THESE PICKLED C.E.O. SCALP WITH MYSTERIOUS HEALING PROPERTIES GO TO MY SISTERWIV GABRIEL CLARK AND FIONN McCABE WHO ARE ALWAYS THE BES PART OF A WORK DAY.

XXX PAT